"I don't need directions to small-town rodeo arenas; dually pickups pulling horse trailers show the way," Mark Harris writes. *"In summertime I share rural highways with these shiny six-wheeled pickups hauling long, white horse trailers topped with air conditioners and bales of hay."*

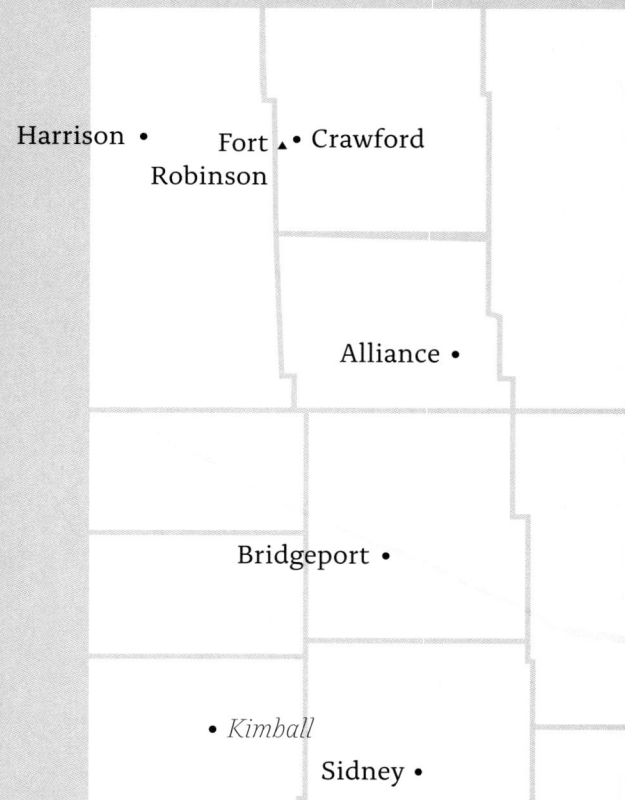

THIS MAP SHOWS THE TOWNS AND RANCHES HARRIS VISITED IN HIS EIGHT-YEAR QUEST—A PROJECT THAT LED HIM TO EIGHTY-TWO EVENTS IN SIXTY-TWO LOCATIONS. EXCEPT FOR PLACE NAMES SHOWN IN *italics*, ALL LOCATIONS ARE PICTURED IN THE BOOK.

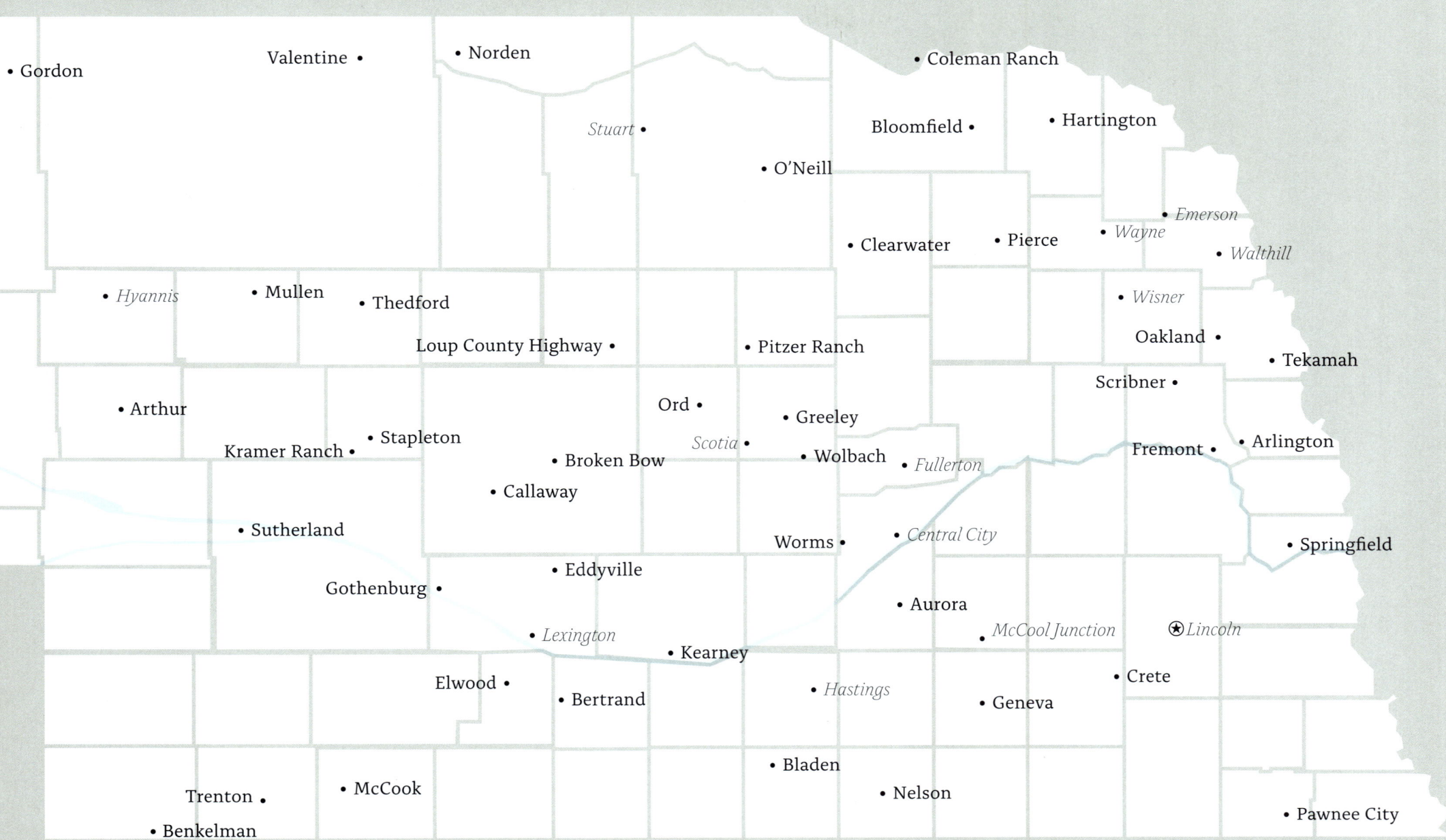

• Gordon

Valentine •   • Norden   • Coleman Ranch

Stuart •   Bloomfield •   • Hartington

• O'Neill

Emerson

Clearwater •   • Pierce   • *Wayne*   • *Walthill*

Hyannis   • Mullen

• Thedford   • *Wisner*

Oakland •

Loup County Highway •   • Pitzer Ranch

Scribner •   • Tekamah

• Arthur   Ord •   • Greeley

• Stapleton   *Scotia* •   • Wolbach   Fremont •   • Arlington

Kramer Ranch •   • Broken Bow   • *Fullerton*

• Callaway

• Sutherland   Worms •   *Central City*   • Springfield

• Eddyville

Gothenburg •   • Aurora

• *Lexington*   • *McCool Junction*   ⊛*Lincoln*

• Kearney

Elwood •   *Hastings* •   • Crete

• Bertrand   • Geneva

• Bladen

Trenton •   • McCook   • Nelson

• Benkelman   • Pawnee City

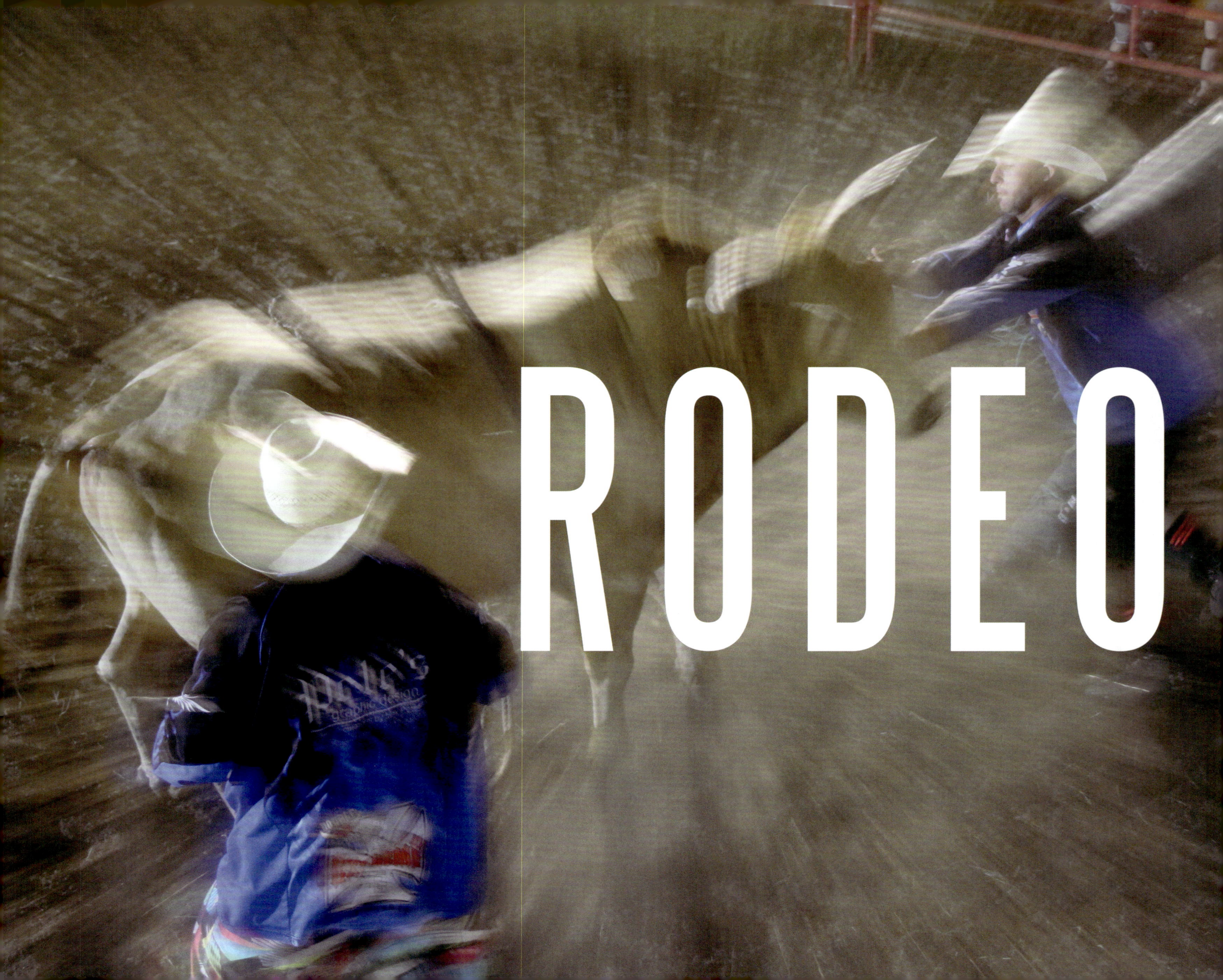

RODEO

By Mark Harris

Foreword by Candy Moulton

NEBRASKA

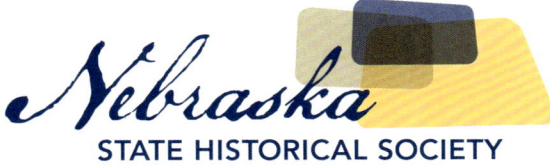

Nebraska State Historical Society Books | Lincoln

ISBN 978-0-933307-36-0
The paper in this book meets the guidelines for
permanence and durability of the Committee
on Production Guidelines for Book Longevity of
the Council on Library Resources, Inc. ∞

Library of Congress Control Number:
2015935340
Printed in Canada

Frontispiece photo: Pierce, Nebraska
Book design by N. Putens

To Colton

CONTENTS

Foreword, "Chasing Rodeo: Nebraska's Long
Connection to America's Sport," *by Candy Moulton*   **xi**

For the Love of It   **1**

Capturing Chaos and Culture   **7**

Tuck Your Chin and Brace for Hell: Bronc Riding   **15**

Innocent Eyes   **29**

The Frantic and the Focused:
Pickup Men and Bronc Contractors   **39**

"I'll be ropin' 'til I can't get on a horse no more":
Men's Timed Events   **51**

The Cowgirls: Women's Timed Events   **65**

Sandhills Speedsters: Speed-Event Horses   **75**

Lonely Roads and Where They Lead   **89**

Hooves, Horns, Wrecks and Fury: Bull Riding   **99**

Adrenaline!   **115**

Bull Fighters   **119**

Hard Knocks: Rodeo and Injury   **129**

Animal Welfare   **141**

Weird Wild West: Unsanctioned Events   **151**

Making Monsters: Bull Contractors   **161**

Get on Young and Ride 'em Hard: Kids' Events   **171**

Age and Experience: Seniors   **189**

Small Towns and Summer Nights   **197**

Rodeo's Future   **215**

Acknowledgements   **219**

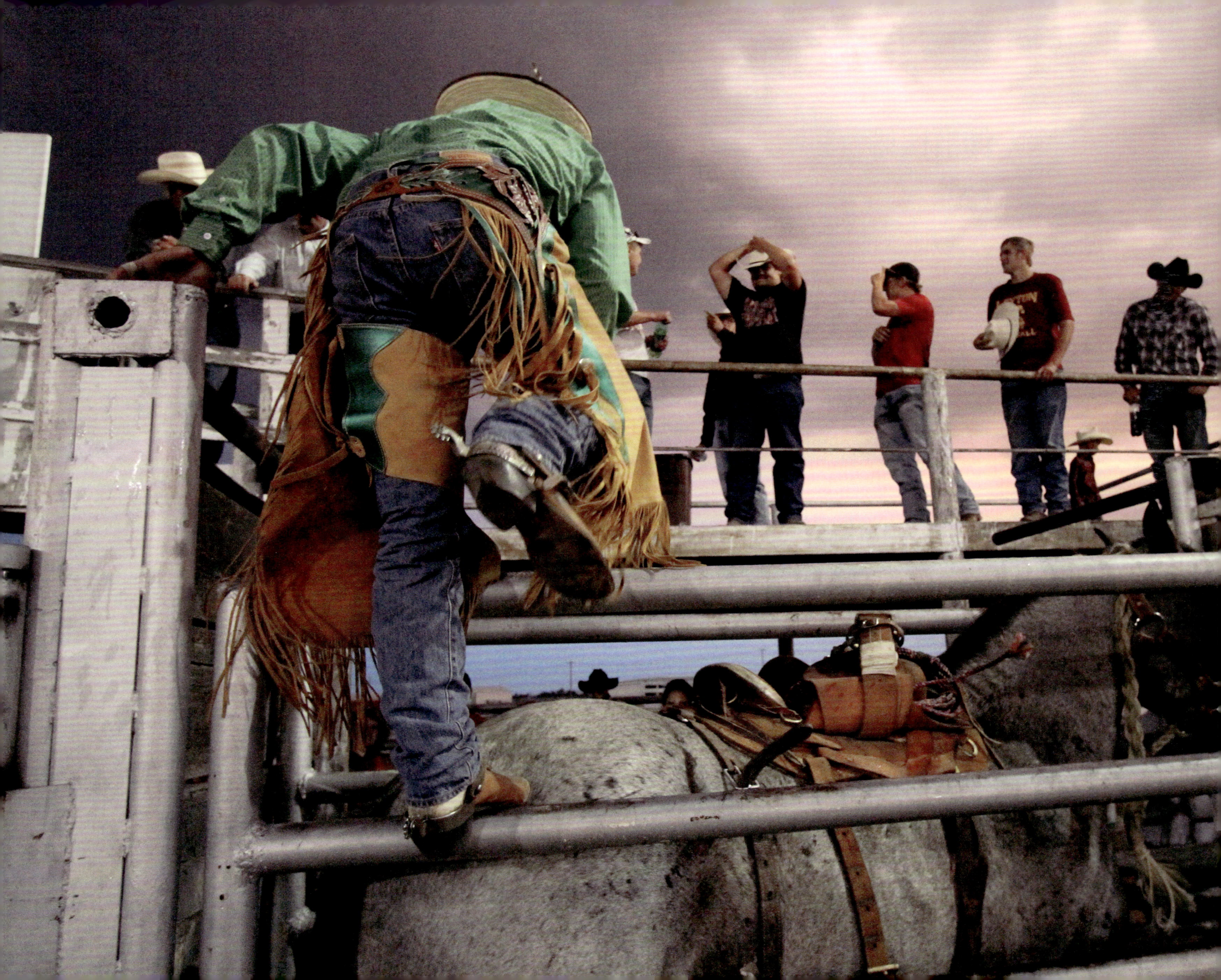

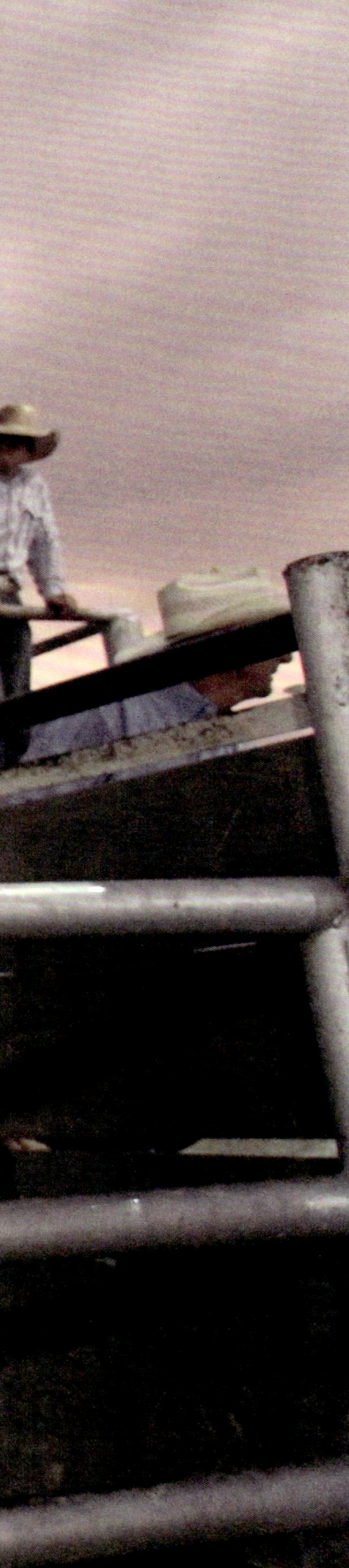

A saddle-bronc rider prepares his horse. BRIDGEPORT

FOREWORD

Chasing Rodeo

NEBRASKA'S LONG CONNECTION
TO AMERICA'S SPORT

By Candy Moulton

Rural communities thrive on their annual celebrations where folks come from down the road or a wider geographic area to socialize, be entertained, and sometimes to compete. In the nineteenth century the most common yearly event was the Fourth of July, with patriotic speeches, picnics, and a dance to the strains of the best fiddle player in the region—though in some places the main attractions were the county fair or a regional festival.

These gatherings served (and continue to serve) multiple purposes, not the least of which is an opportunity for families in the neighborhood to set aside work for a day or two, and get together to enjoy each other's company. In Nebraska, O'Neill hangs its hat on St. Patrick's Day; Hastings holds Kool-Aid Days in honor of the local invention of the classic kids' drink. In Wayne they celebrate chickens, in Grand Island it is farming at Husker Harvest Days, and Nebraska City recognizes trees at the annual Arbor Day celebration.

William F. Cody, the Pony Express rider, frontier military scout, and dime novel hero who wore a beaded and fringed leather jacket, and who earned the nickname "Buffalo Bill" by killing thousands of head of buffalo for the railroad, gave the West one of its enduring symbols when he organized Indians and cowboys, former frontiersmen, sharpshooters, and others into an extravaganza for North Platte in 1882.

The Old Glory Blowout was both a festival and—with action events like cowboys riding bucking broncos—precursor to a sport: Rodeo.

Cody combined two things he knew well, cowboys and theatrical performance. He had taken to the stage when he starred in the melodramatic story of his own life in *Scouts of the Prairie*, first presented in Chicago in 1872. He toured as a theatrical group with James Butler "Wild Bill" Hickok and John Burwell "Texas Jack" Omohundro. For a decade the Buffalo Bill Combination, with a varying cast of performers, visited cities across America during the winter, but Cody returned to the West to spend summers scouting for the Army and guiding hunters on the Plains. He had a home in North Platte, Nebraska, so when the community wanted a Fourth of July celebration, Buffalo Bill Cody was the natural choice to organize it. He wanted something that would entertain, that people would talk about for days or weeks—or, as it turned out, for well over a century.

Steeped in the traditions of American Independence, the Blowout was a preview of Cody's next big adventure—organizing and touring Buffalo Bill's Wild West, a show that went on the road across America, and to England and Europe.

Following the Civil War, cowboys gathered wild and domestic longhorn cattle in Texas, then trailed them north to railheads in Kansas, and to Ogallala, Nebraska, the end of the Texas Trail. Around 400,000 head of cattle reached Ogallala in 1884. "Now bear in mind that to drive and handle these cattle required a force of about 2,500 to 3,000 men and fully 20,000 horses," Lincoln's *Nebraska State Journal* reported in September 1884.

While the majority of the cattle were shipped to markets in such places as Omaha or Chicago, other stock was sold to Nebraska ranchers and then moved onto the high plains grasslands that had once nurtured hundreds of thousands of head of buffalo.

Cody's connections with cowboys who would ride in his Old Glory Blowout and perform in his Wild West came from his own endeavors along the Dismal River, where he operated the North and Cody Ranch with Frank and Luther North, men whom he had known from their years of involvement in the frontier Indian wars. In 1877 Cody and

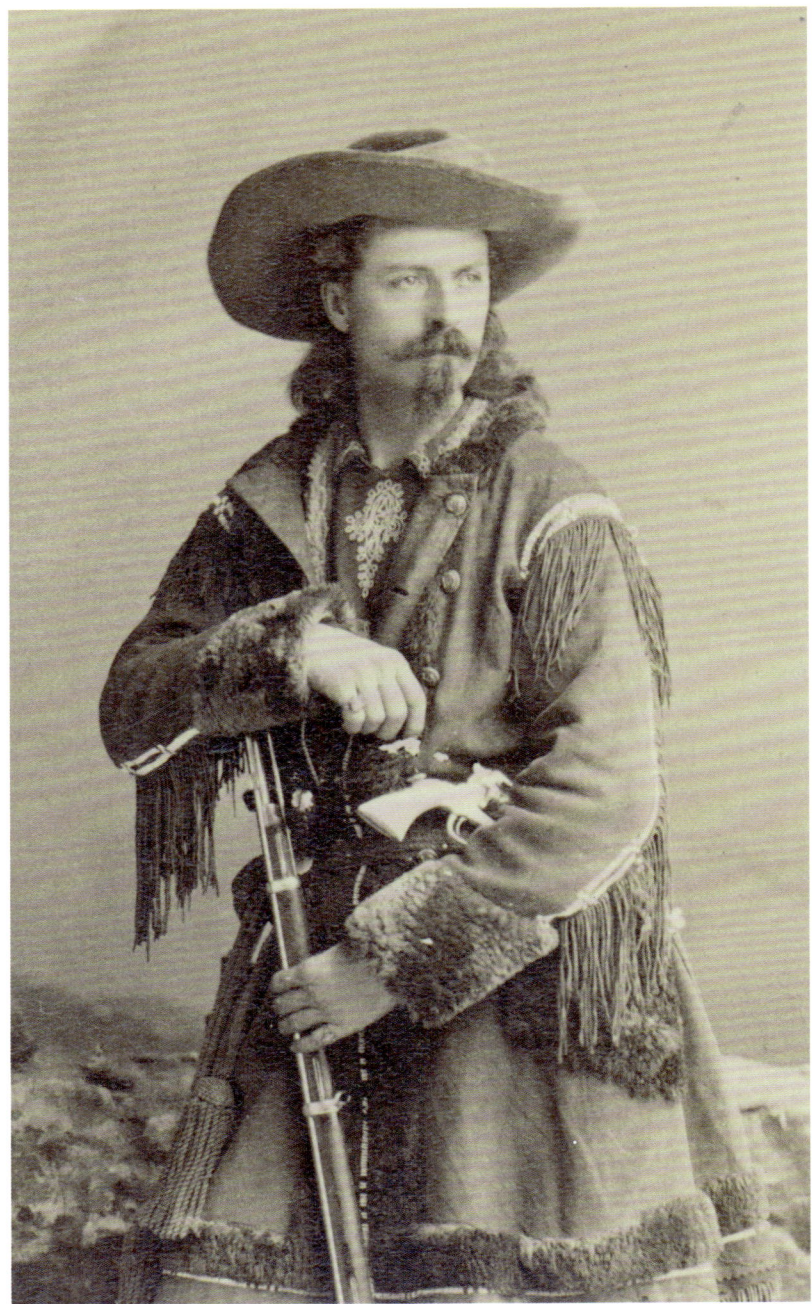

William F. "Buffalo Bill" Cody in 1872. NSHS RG3004-150

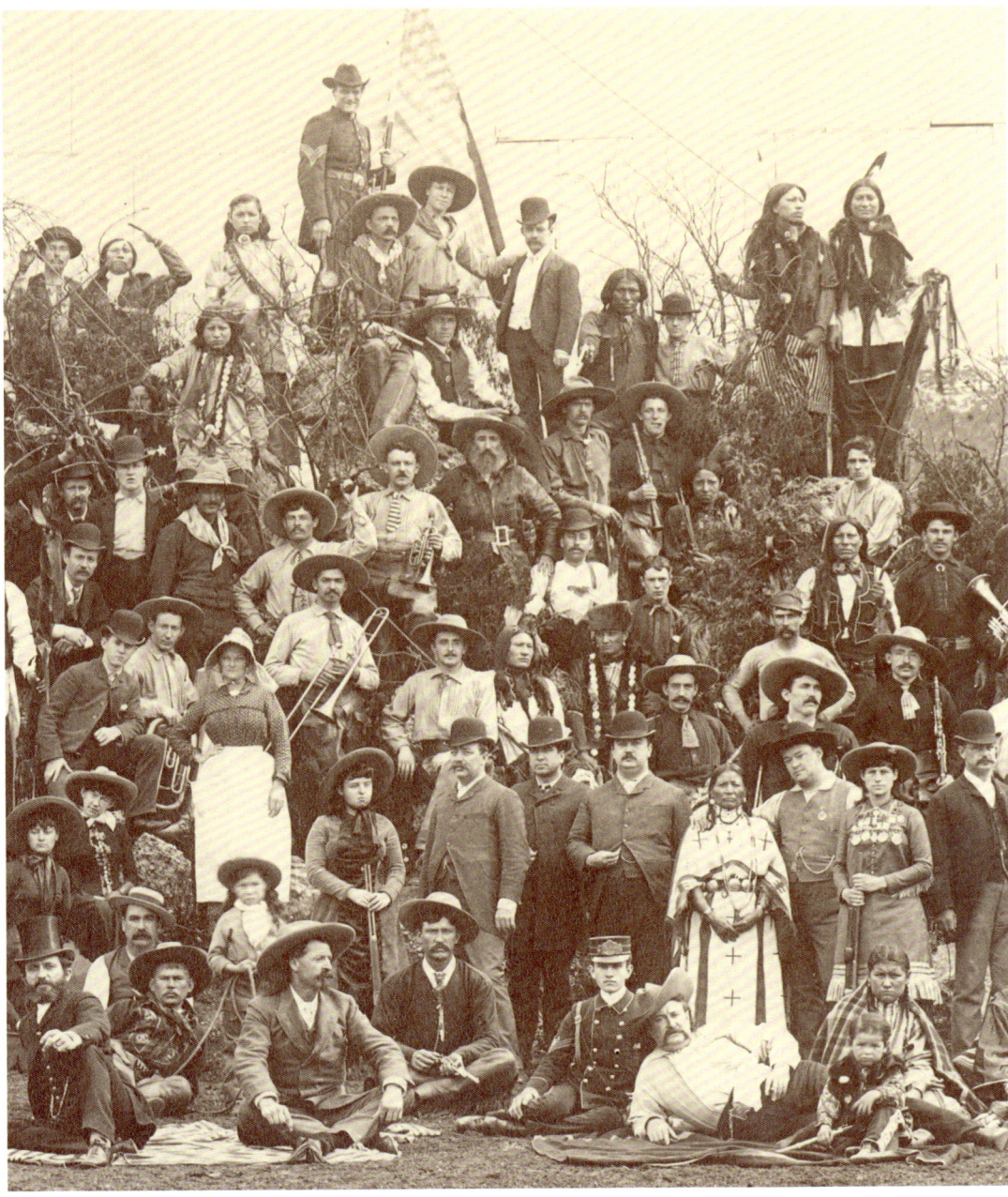

Detail of a group photo of Buffalo Bill's Wild West. Cody is third from left in the front row. NSHS RG3004-32

the North brothers bought a herd of trail cattle at Ogallala, moving them to the land along the Dismal.

Five years later, North Platte's Old Glory Blowout was not billed as a rodeo because it was more than that, and also because at the time rodeo was not a recognized sport. The root word comes from the Spanish *rodear,* meaning to encircle or surround. The genesis is the open range where men gathered and worked cattle, roping and branding them, or took wild, untamed horses, and broke them to ride. Those horses were broncs; the men who tamed them became bronco busters (often spelled "broncho" in the nineteenth and early twentieth centuries).

The skill was necessary on the range. Wild, unbroken horses had to be tamed so cowboys could gather cattle, brand them for ownership purposes, and move them from one range to another, or even to market. The *contest* of rodeo started on the range where one cowboy challenged another, or more often, where cowboys from one ranch or outfit challenged those from another ranch. These contests were spirited, but held without the benefit of "winning" much in the early days; often it was little more than bragging rights.

One of the first recorded competitions of this type took place in 1869 at Deer Trail, Colorado Territory, when the Hashknife, Mill Iron, and Campstool ranches organized a competition among their outfits for the Fourth of July. The ride of the competition took place when Emilnie Gardenshire of the Mill Iron climbed on a bronc named Montana Blizzard. The young Englishman had said he wanted the "worst animal in the pen," and soon found that Montana Blizzard filled the bill. "For fifteen minutes the bay bucked, pawed, and jumped from side to side," reported *Denver's Field and Farm* magazine. Finally the "mighty Blizzard succumbed, and Gardenshire rode him around the circle at a gentle gallop." (In those days the ride lasted until the horse stopped or the cowboy hit the dirt, not the eight seconds of modern rodeo.)

That kind of endurance riding on a bucking bronco earned the cowboy the respect of his peers, who gave him the unofficial title of "champion Bronco Buster of the Plains." As a result of his prowess in the saddle he went home with a new suit of clothes, awarded by the ranch owners.

Buffalo Bill's Old Glory Blowout in 1882 attracted a community audience and was intended as more of an exhibition than the ranch rivalry that had been demonstrated in Colorado. A year later Pecos, Texas, hosted a community rodeo exhibition with competitions for both bronco riding and steer roping. It is Prescott, Arizona, however, that usually gains recognition as the birthplace of rodeo contests. That cowboy town put on a rodeo in 1888—and yes, of course it happened on the Fourth of July. Not only did the Prescott organizers bring in top competitors, but they also charged admission fees of the spectators and ran advertisements encouraging the public to attend.

Prescott established rules for the cowboy competition, including a requirement that any cowboy who entered must be "willing to wear his big hat and boots at all times."

The sport began spreading across the West and by the early years of the twentieth century well-established contests occurred annually at Cheyenne Frontier Days, the Pendleton Round-Up, Calgary Stampede, and the Denver Festival of Mountain and Plain, to name a few. Cowboys and cowgirls competed in Chicago and at Madison Square Garden in New York.

With its roots in rodeo, North Platte many years later would organize and hold the Nebraskaland competitions that continue into the twenty-first century. Omaha got in on the action with contests at Ak-Sar-Ben (Nebraska spelled backwards). But perhaps more important, rodeo spread into the small communities across the state, particularly through the cattle country of the Sandhills.

Born in O'Neill, Nebraska, Clayton and Jimmie Danks grew up in Cherry County but migrated west to Wyoming by the beginning of the twentieth century. There they worked for the Two Bar Ranch at a time when range cowboying was at its final peak. The Two Bar was part of the much bigger Swan Land and Cattle Company, which had holdings extending all across eastern Wyoming and into western Nebraska clear to Ogallala. On that ranch, Jimmie Danks was recognized as one of the best men around when it came to breaking and training young horses. In 1899 a big, black, three-year-old gelding was ready for some work, and Jimmie saddled him then stepped aboard.

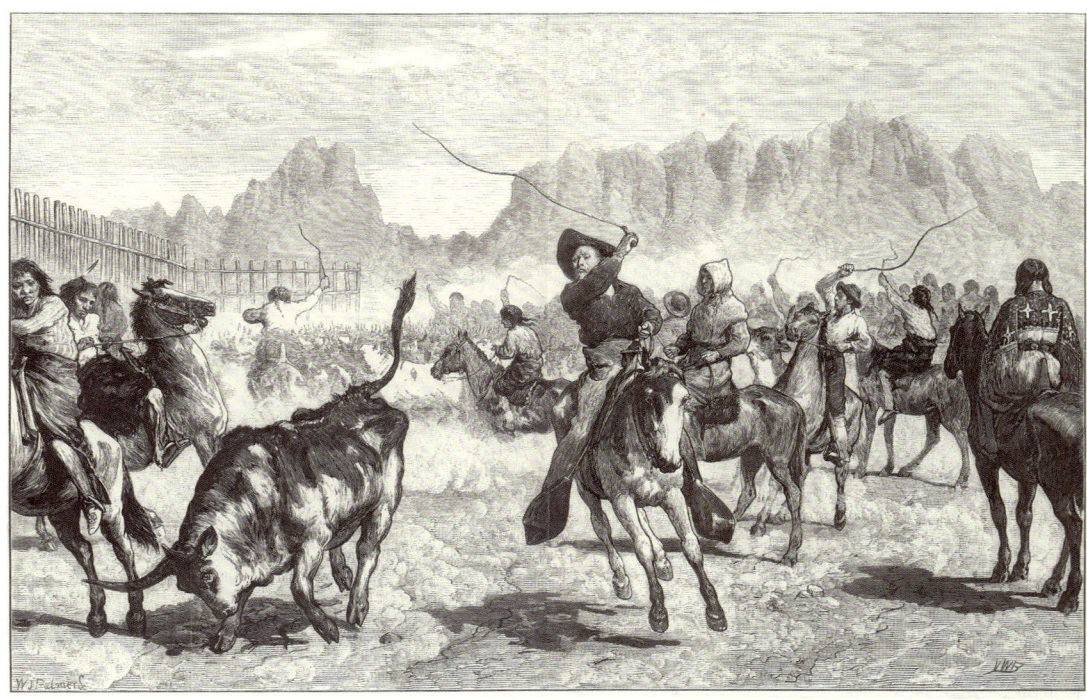

Red Cloud Agency, near Camp Robinson, Nebraska.
London Illustrated News, August 21, 1875

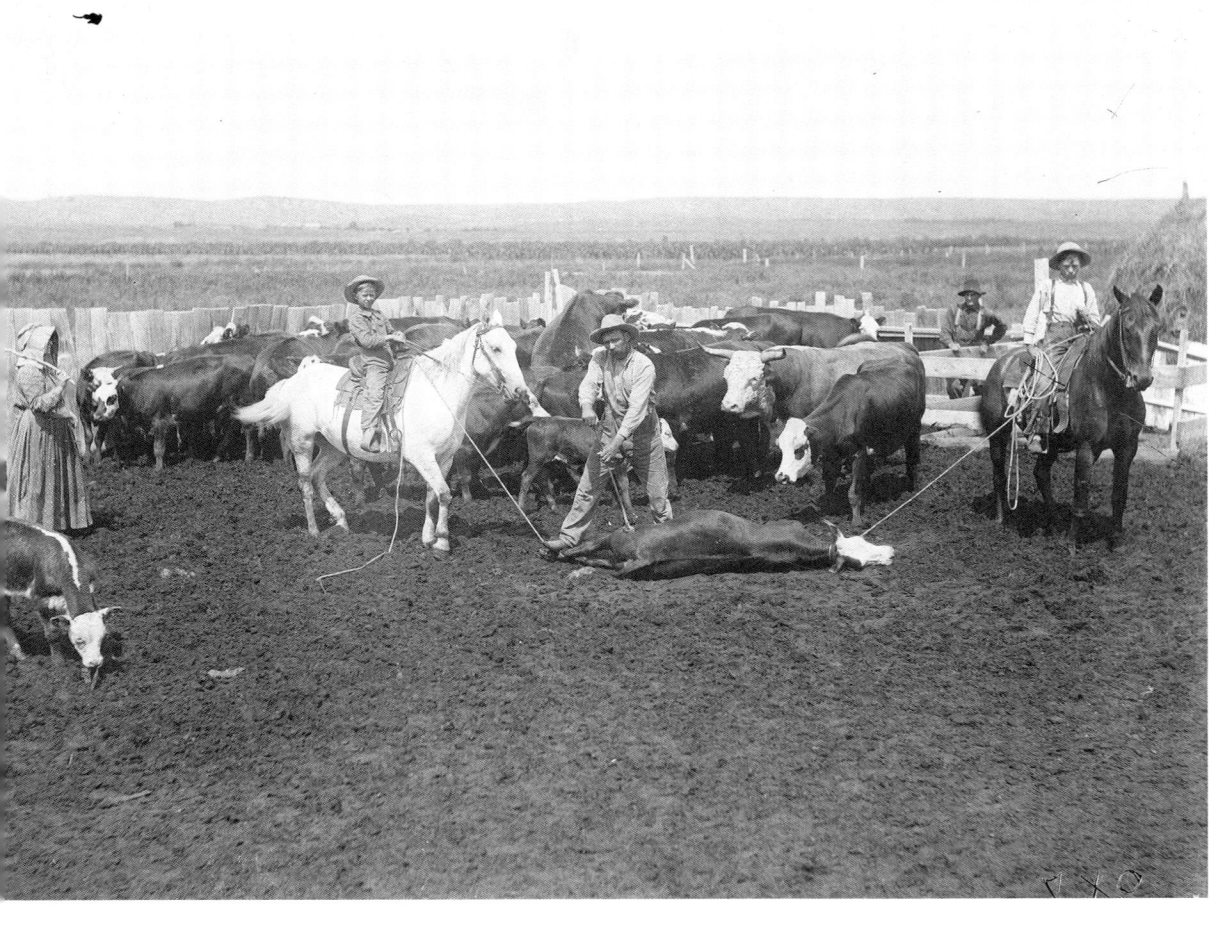

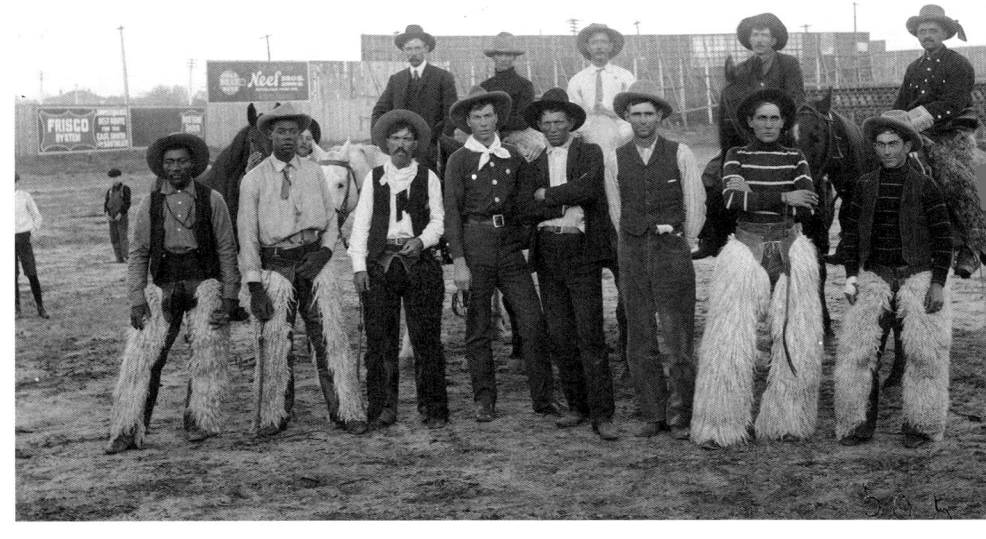

(*above*) Branding at the Cal Snyder Ranch, near the Middle Loup River, Milburn, Nebraska, 1888. NSHS RG2608-1830

(*right*) Pioneering Nebraska photographer Solomon D. Butcher labeled this 1905 photo, "Bunch of genuine old time cowboys and bronco busters at Denver, Colorado." NSHS RG2608-2167a

The horse had three white socks and a sledge-hammer-like ability to come down and hit the ground in an effort to unseat a rider. And when he got to bucking and jumping, he made a whistling sound resulting from a bone in his nose that had been broken when he hit his head while being castrated as a colt. This whistling sound gave the horse his name: Steamboat. Because Jimmie Danks was truly a good cowboy, he might have been successful in breaking Steamboat and making him into a good ranch horse, but the powerful brute's bucking ability instead landed the gelding in the rodeo arena, where he would be used the rest of his life. This horse, one of the five great bucking horses recognized by the National Cowboy and Western Heritage Museum in Oklahoma City, became the symbol of Wyoming—but he was first ridden by Jimmie Danks, a top Nebraska cowboy.

Clayton Danks was as good of a hand as his brother, but while Clayton also worked on ranches, he made his early reputation in the rodeo arena. He was a regular competitor at the Cheyenne Frontier Days in the first decade of the twentieth century. Along with his wife Marie Fitger Danks, also a Nebraska native, he went on the wild west circuit with the Irwin Brothers Wild West Show, which was the business enterprise of C. B. Irwin and his brother Frank. The Irwin Brothers Show promoted cowboys, cowgirls, and billed the bucking horse Steamboat as one of the stars of the show, an early indication that the only reason you had top rodeo cowboys was because you had high-caliber livestock whose job it was to spin, turn, sunfish, buck, and do anything possible to unseat a rider.

Barbara Barnes, the youngest in a big brood of Nebraska children (she had twenty-three siblings), was called Tadpole by her family, a name shortened to Tad. Reared on a ranch near Cody, Nebraska, she spent her childhood riding horses and before long started riding calves. That led her to her first rodeo competition in Gordon, Nebraska, in 1917, when she was fifteen. She married Buck Lucas at age twenty-two. By then she was already riding saddle broncs, and also making a name for herself as a relay racer and trick rider. Tad Barnes Lucas won the trick riding championship in Cheyenne in 1925 and 1927 and added relay race championship titles in 1930, 1931, and 1932,

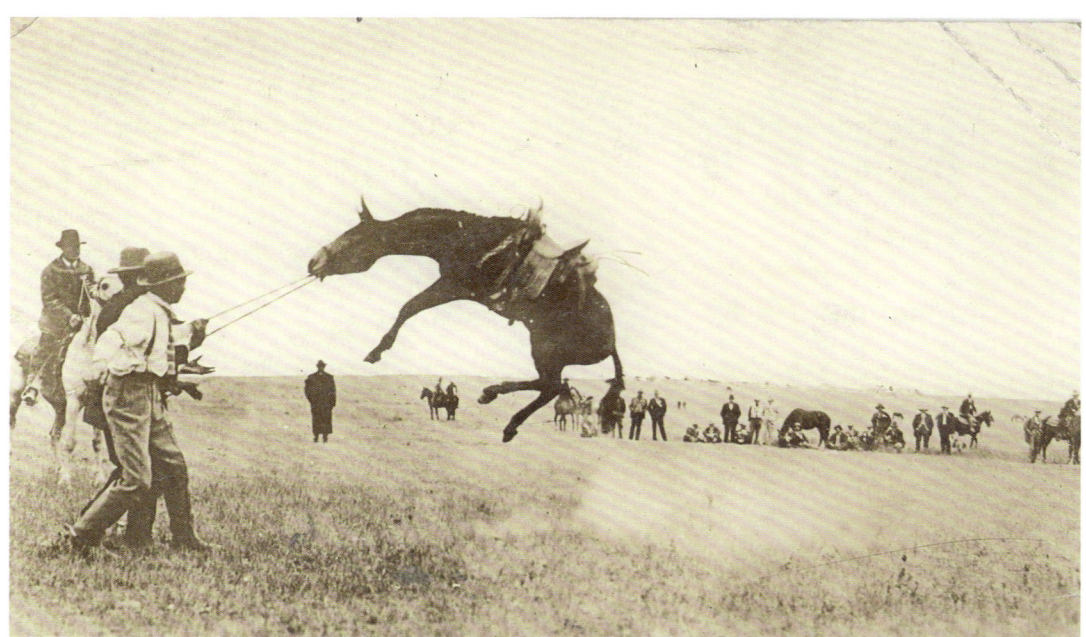

This 1913 photo from Thedford, Nebraska, is labeled, "Easy Money! Want to Try Him?"

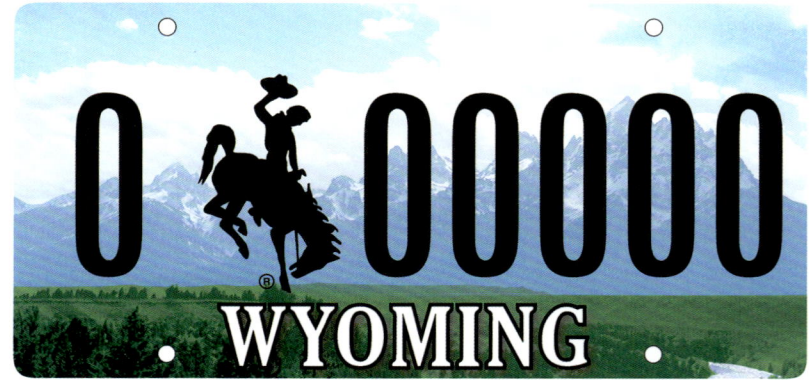

Steamboat, the bucking horse that became a symbol of Wyoming, was first ridden by Jimmie Danks, a top Nebraska cowboy. Courtesy WYDOT.

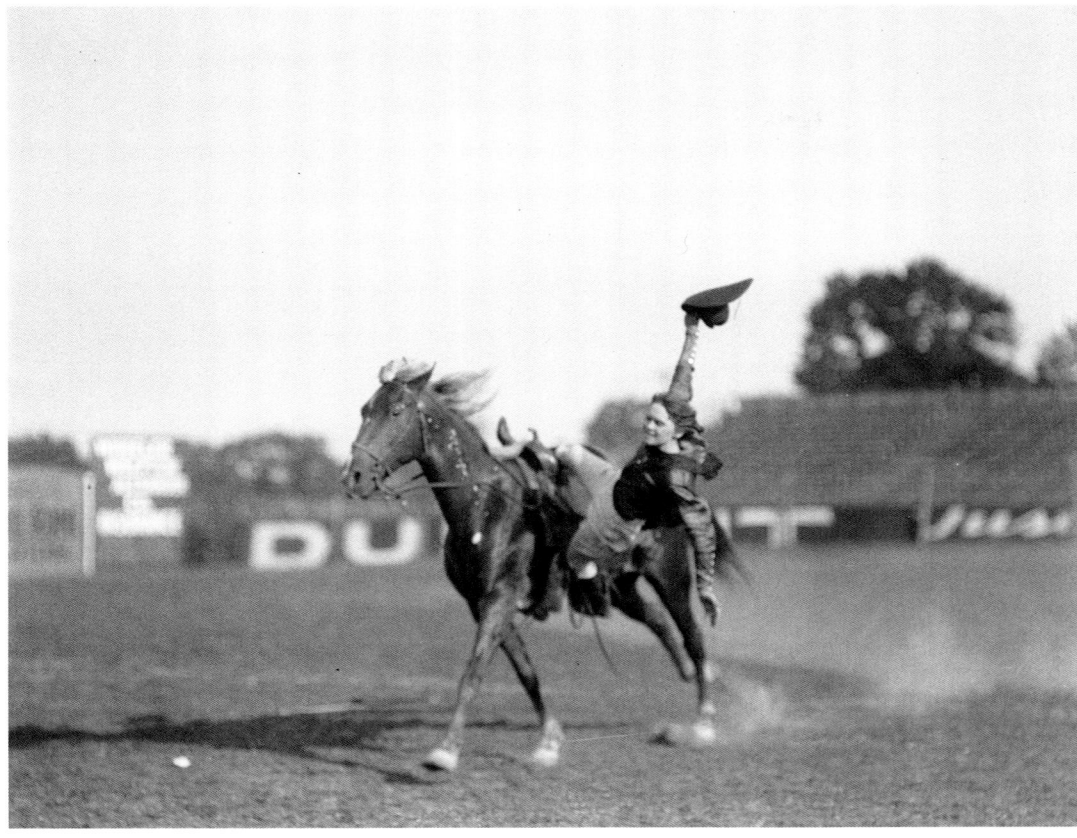

A trick-riding young lady flies by her audience at the Omaha Legion Rodeo, 1924. NSHS RG2478-15.

as well as all-around, trick riding, and relay racing titles in Chicago won from 1925 to 1930.

The best rodeos had the top competitors and outstanding livestock. In addition to Steamboat, top broncs in rodeo's early days included Midnight, Five Minutes to Midnight, and Tipperary. As the sport evolved, the competition would feature not just bronco riding, relay races, and trick riding, but also bull riding and timed events such as calf roping, team roping, and steer wrestling, all of which had connections to the everyday work of cowboys. Women did horseback tricks, rode in relays, and like Tad Barnes Lucas rode bucking horses. Eventually the primarily female competition at a rodeo involved barrel racing, though there would be women like Montana's Jane Burnett Smith and North Dakota native Jonnie Jonckowski who would ride bucking bulls as well as broncs.

There would be other events: wild cow milking, sometimes chuck wagon racing, steer roping (or steer tripping), even mutton busting for the youngsters who got their first "rough stock" experience on the back of a sheep.

Rodeos were competitions and entertainment. Trick ropers, trick riders, the "mutt-riding-monkey act," and clowns who bantered with the announcer kept the action moving along. The clowns—or bull fighters—seemed to toy with snorting bulls, popped in and out of barrels, and served the important role of protecting bull riders. They diverted the attention of angry animals, or ran directly into danger to help free a man whose hand became hung up in his rigging, or who was injured when thrown from a beast that might weigh nearly a ton.

Rodeo evolved from the decades—when Cody first put men on the back of bucking horses—into an internationally recognized but uniquely American sport.

Nebraska rodeos may not be as widely known as the Calgary Stampede, Pendleton Round-Up, or Cheyenne Frontier Days, but they are no less important to cowboys who are either learning the trade, or adding to their winnings in the all-consuming goal of the pro rodeo cowboy to fight his (or her) way to the National Finals Rodeo.

Deep in the Sandhills, a land that is a cattle-raiser's dream, in 1921 Burwell began what is now billed as Nebraska's Big Rodeo™ when the community decided to hold an annual celebration. Whenever good cowboys gather, a crowd usually follows, and that certainly was the case in Burwell. By the 1930s not only did the best cowboys in the country travel for the competition, but also trains from Omaha and Lincoln hauled in thousands of spectators to the small town, which swelled with 20,000 to 30,000 visitors.

Burwell organizers suspended the rodeo during World War II, likely because the cowboys were fighting the war, people had no money for such events, and perhaps they had no fuel or tires for their vehicles. But immediately after the war the Burwell rodeo committee resumed the NBR, attracting even larger crowds and top competitors. Pro Rodeo Hall of Famers Jim Shoulders (winner of sixteen world championships in all-around, bull riding, and bronc riding) and Casey Tibbs (winner of nine world championships in all-around, saddle bronc, and bareback bronc riding) rode in the Burwell arena.

Nebraska's rodeo heritage is a combination of contestants who were born in the state and learned the basics in dusty arenas in their hometowns, and other men and women in rodeo who came to the state for its competitive opportunities. It is a rich history of community celebrations, and a contemporary story of today's rodeo world.

There is an adrenaline rush that bull riders, bull fighters, and rough stock competitors get when the chute opens and an animal lunges out with one intent: throw the rider from its back. While only a fraction of the people at a rodeo have direct contact with that animal, the thrill extends to the crowd as they watch the gyrations of bucking bull or horse and rider.

Like the work of renowned rodeo photographer Ralph R. Doubleday, this collection of images and personal stories brings the sport of rodeo into your living room. Mark Harris climbed out of the stands and into the arena for the chance to capture the action at rodeos large and small across Nebraska. There are intimate moments, like a cowboy's prayer before he slides onto a bull's back and children paying respect to the flag. There are pictures showing pure personal courage—like a bull fighter nose-to-nose with a bull, or a young rider getting a hand up after taking a spill in arena mud.

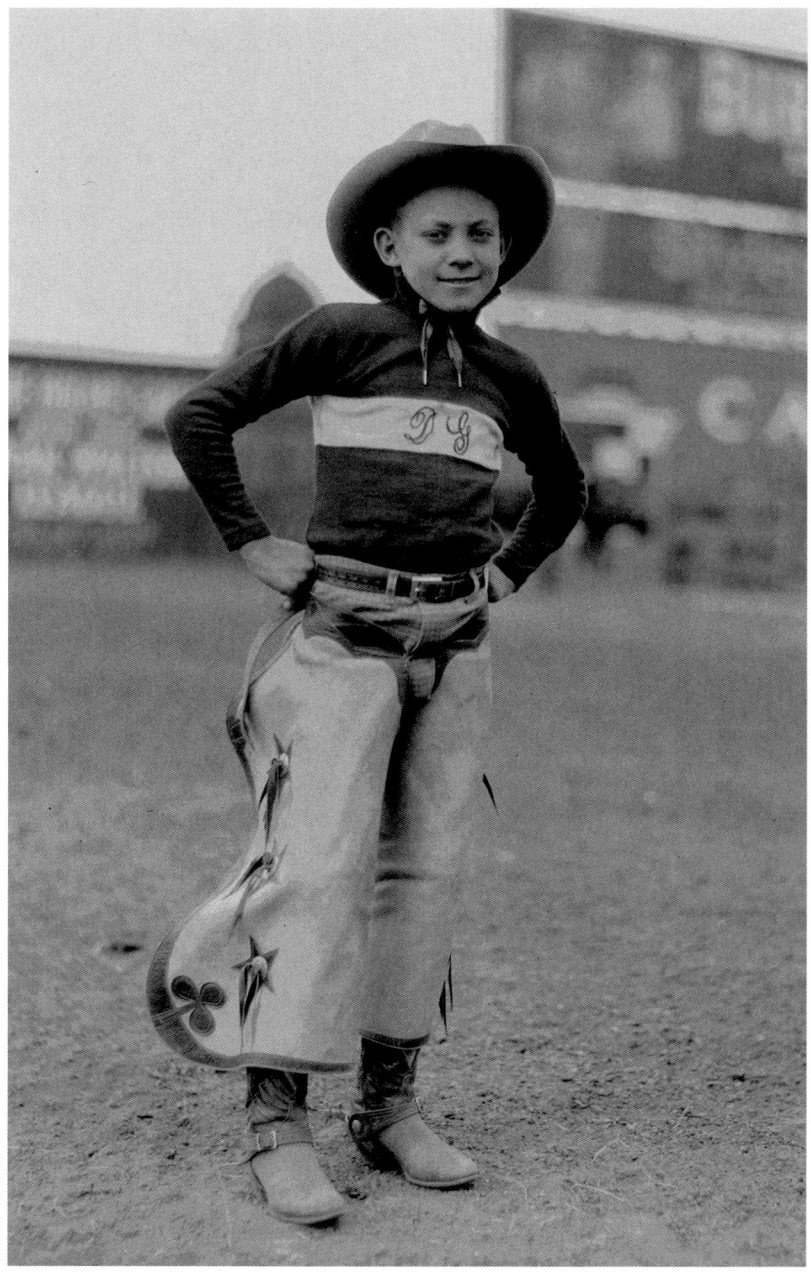

A young cowboy at the Omaha Legion Rodeo, 1924. RG2478-49

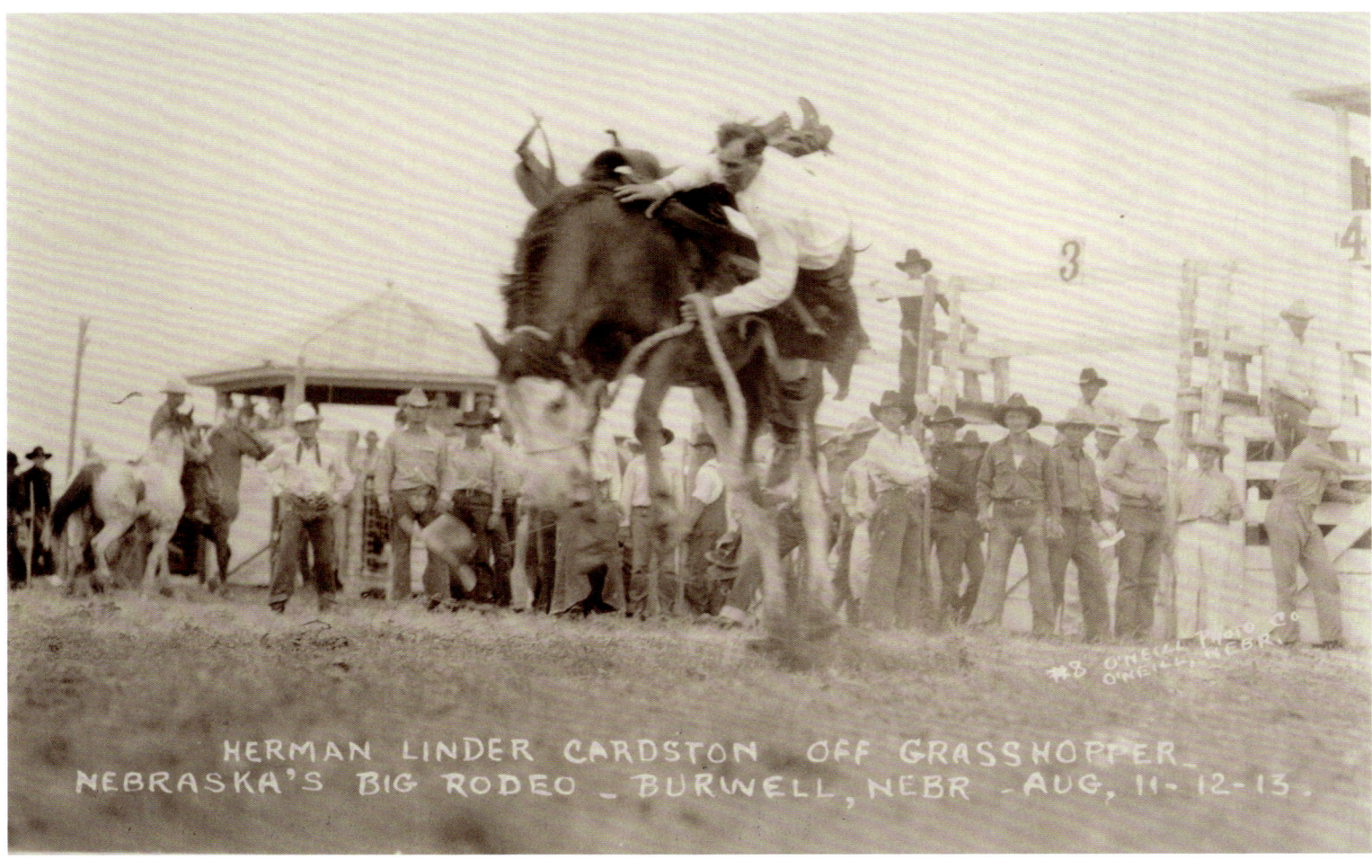

HERMAN LINDER CARDSTON OFF GRASSHOPPER. NEBRASKA'S BIG RODEO _ BURWELL, NEBR - AUG, 11- 12-13.

Herman Linder of Cardston, Alberta, was a dominant bronc rider in the 1930s, one of the big name cowboys who competed at Burwell. NSHS RG3375-2-21

Like the greatest of Doubleday photographs, the collection captures all variety of moments rodeo-related—from classic bucking horses to rodeo wrecks, arena performers, and the crowds who come to watch. Harris also takes you out to the places where cowboys like to play, such as the dance floors where they swing their gals, and the ranches where the great horses of modern rodeo are bred and trained.

You see the concentration of a barrel racer, the determination of young boys on steers, and the camaraderie of cowboys behind the chutes as they protect one of their own from being bashed by a bull, which would rather go up and out, than wait for the gate to open. The close shots of steer wrestlers, calf ropers, snorty bulls, and bucking horses makes it readily apparent that Harris himself is a bit of an adrenaline junkie, daring to get as close as he can with camera and lens while not affecting the outcome of the performance by either animal or human competitor.

The great showman Buffalo Bill Cody had his hand in the roots of Nebraska rodeo, and no doubt he would applaud the men and women who keep the sport alive.

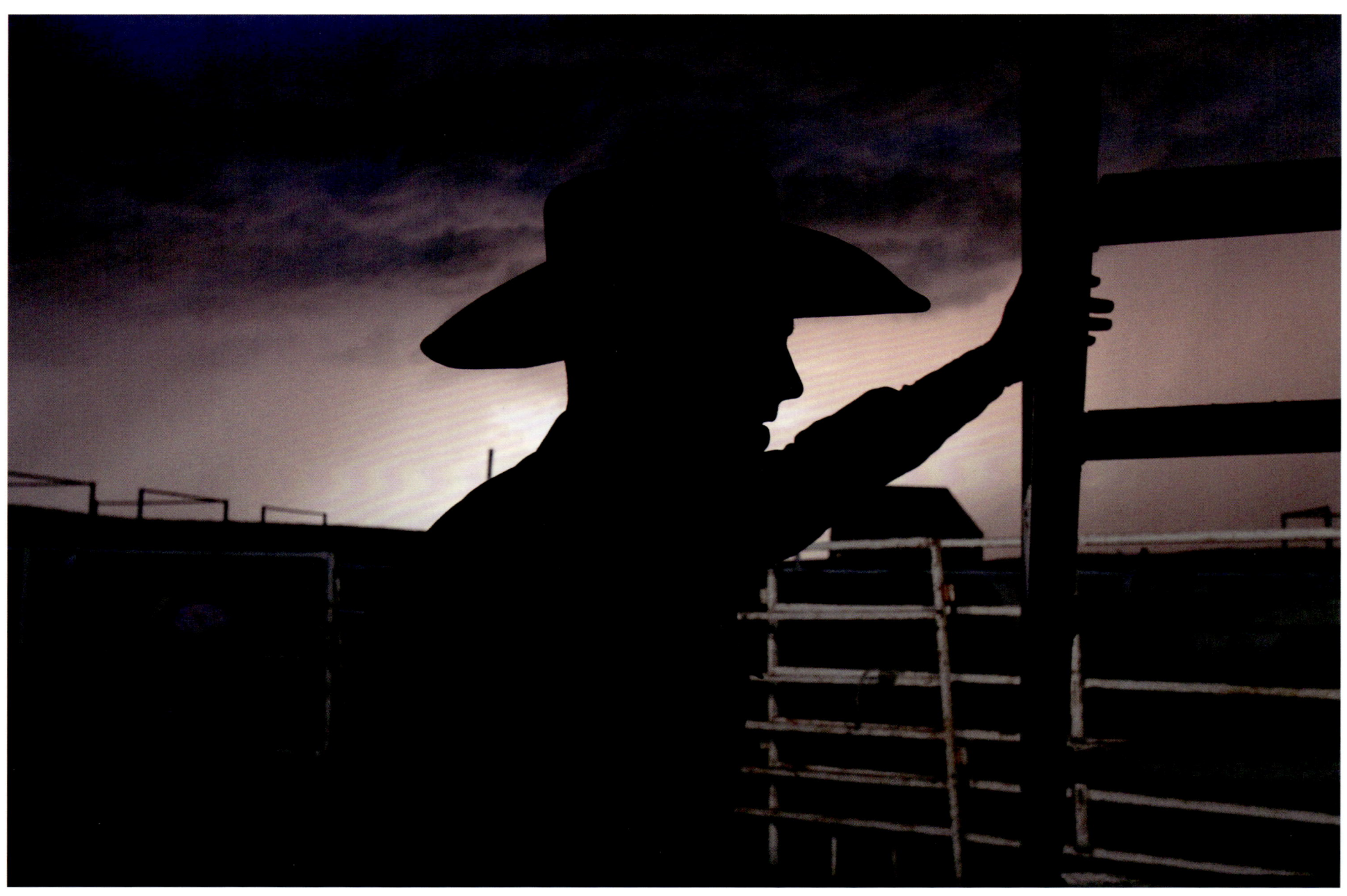

The Nebraska cowboy—in them we see our western heritage. ARTHUR

For the Love of It

The bulls know the drill and they despise it. Brown eyes dilate as shouting stockmen sort them into metal chutes. Smelling of fresh manure, they seethe in tight captivity. Some wait quietly for their chance to explode. Others bellow and slam heads into sturdy bars toward passing cowboys. They want to hurt someone. Years of selective breeding molded them this way, but the cowboys who ride them come from generations of rough stock as well.

Nervous riders stand over the animal they drew. Stretching and jumping, they share encouragements with competitors. They come from ranching families where politeness is deeply ingrained in the culture. With names like Chisum, Tuffy, Dusty, and Rowdy, they say "sir" and "ma'am" to strangers, but cuss like the rest of us when left in each other's company.

The reigning champ jumps up and down, slapping leather chaps in a warm-up routine that bends the old wooden plank beneath. His boot tip deliberately bumps the back of the spotted white bull he drew. Horns spin to retaliate, only to clang against metal, and the rider grins. The bull, trying to escape, throws his head forward into the chute divider. Pens vibrate with the force up and down the line. The bull slams his manure-coated rump backwards with the same effect.

Styles differ. Another rider, thin and young, sits across the chute above his draw, a black hornless bull. He reaches down and scratches its broad hump tenderly, like you would a cat's head. Tiny flies scatter; this bull is their permanent home. "Hey buddy," the cowboy says affectionately. He keeps scratching as he waits his turn. The bull could break his hand with one lurch upward, but this is an experienced bull, six or seven years old, and he knows to hold an even mood until the gate swings.

Hard rock music signals the start of bull riding. Bulls breathe harder and streams of mucus flow from huffing noses. Standing on the plank next to the bull's head I feel its breath, warm and forceful against my leg, and I envision vast lungs serving a powerful heart. Veins widen and muscles fill with blood inside both bulls and men. Another bull bellows—an eerie, belligerent sound. He wants to get on with it.

Bulls are dangerous even within the tight confines of the chutes. As men mount, some bulls try leaping to freedom, some rear backwards, and some lurch down to their knees, but this one remains still with eyes straining backward to see. Black with a white face and long horns, he's done it a hundred times. The bull knows he will succeed in dismounting the man. If he so chooses, he will then have his brief opportunity to crush and maim.

Bull riders compete all summer. The risks are huge and the payoffs are not. They do it for the love of the sport—for the rush it gives them. There is no other logical reason.

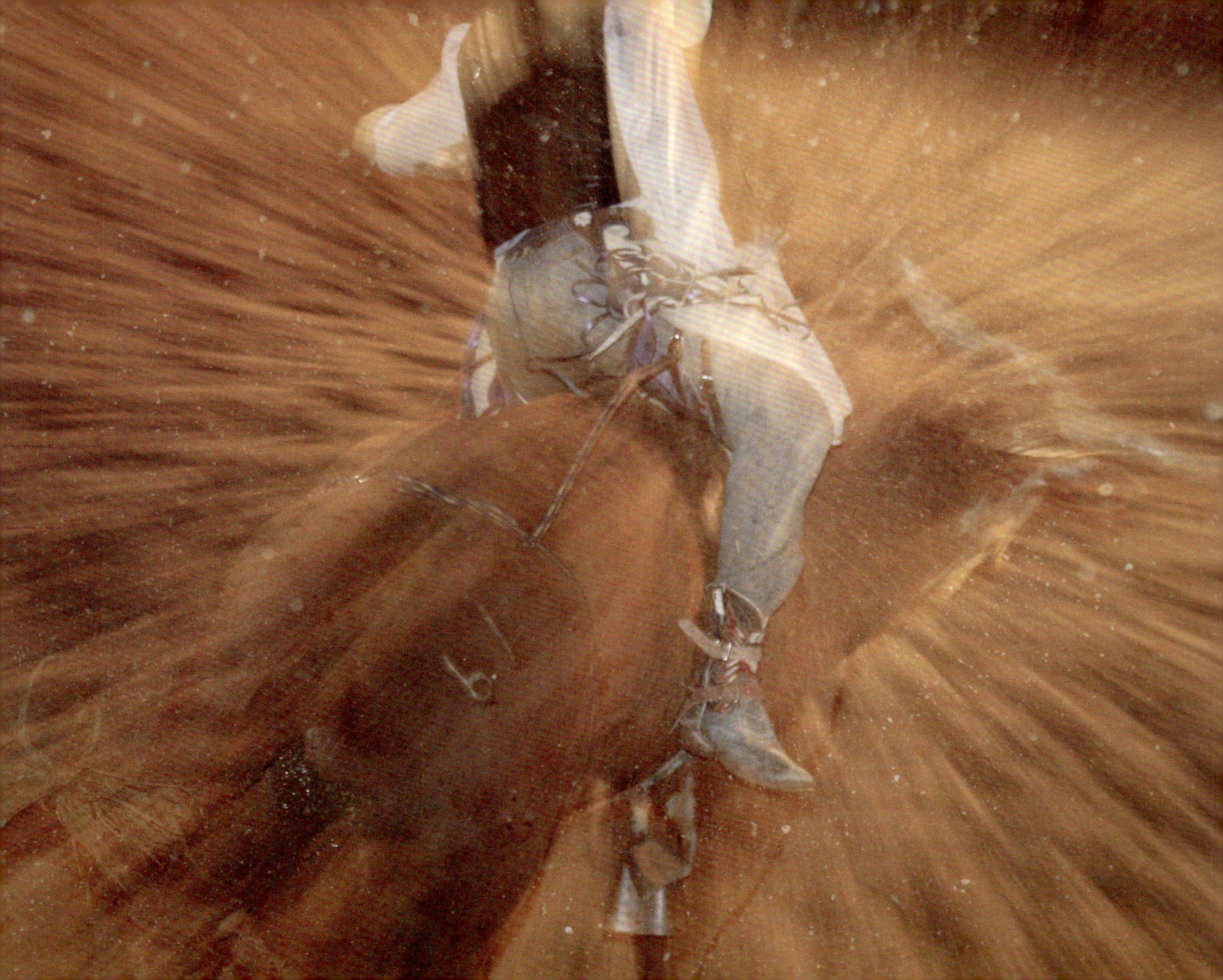

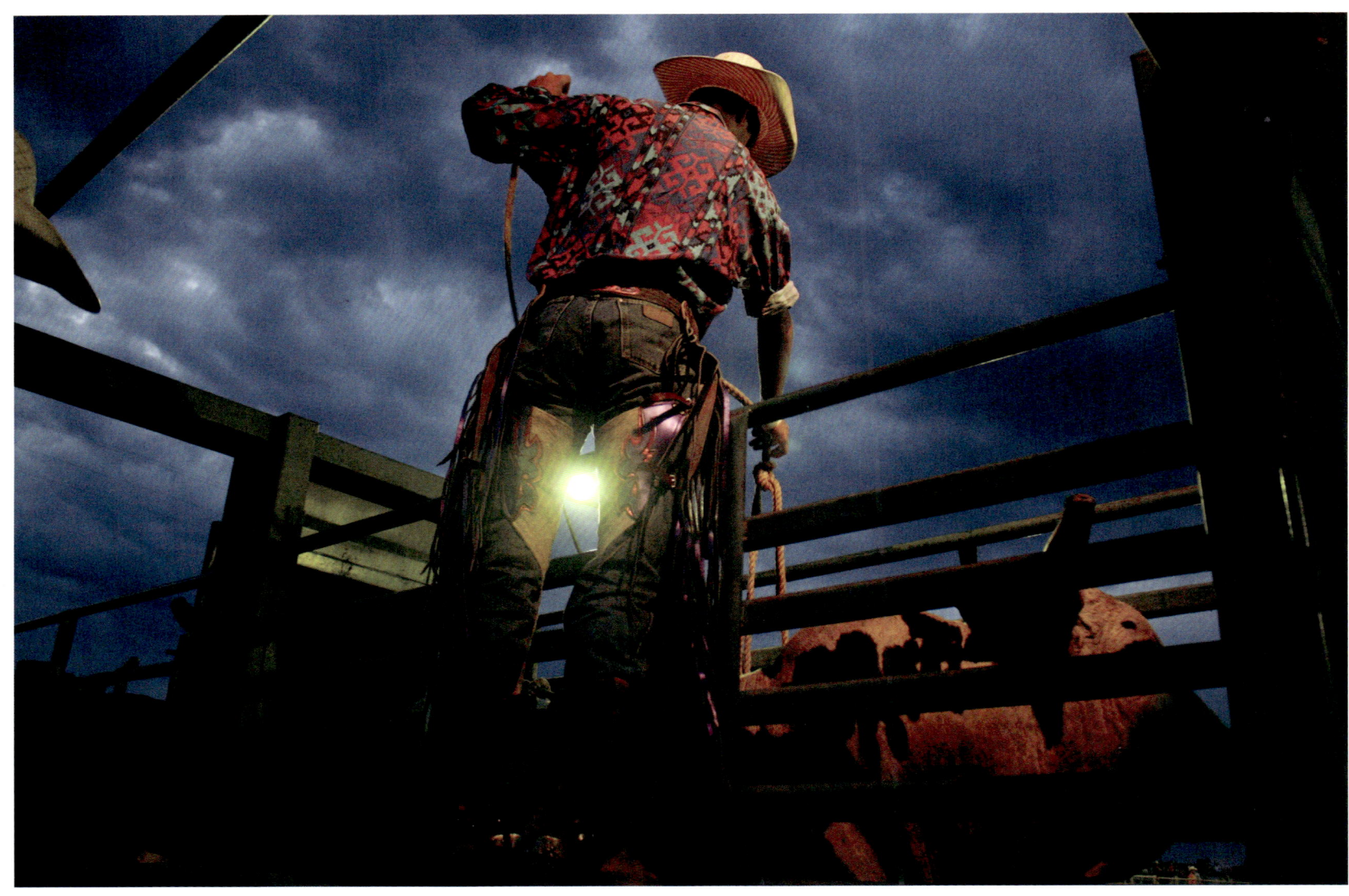

(*above*) Deceptively calm, an experienced bull sizes up the arena as
its rider affixes the bull rope. Minutes later he bucks the rider off,
then flips him head over heels before bull fighters step in. ELWOOD

(*opposite*) Riding a tornado—the bull bell jangles with the power of a
launching bull. MULLEN

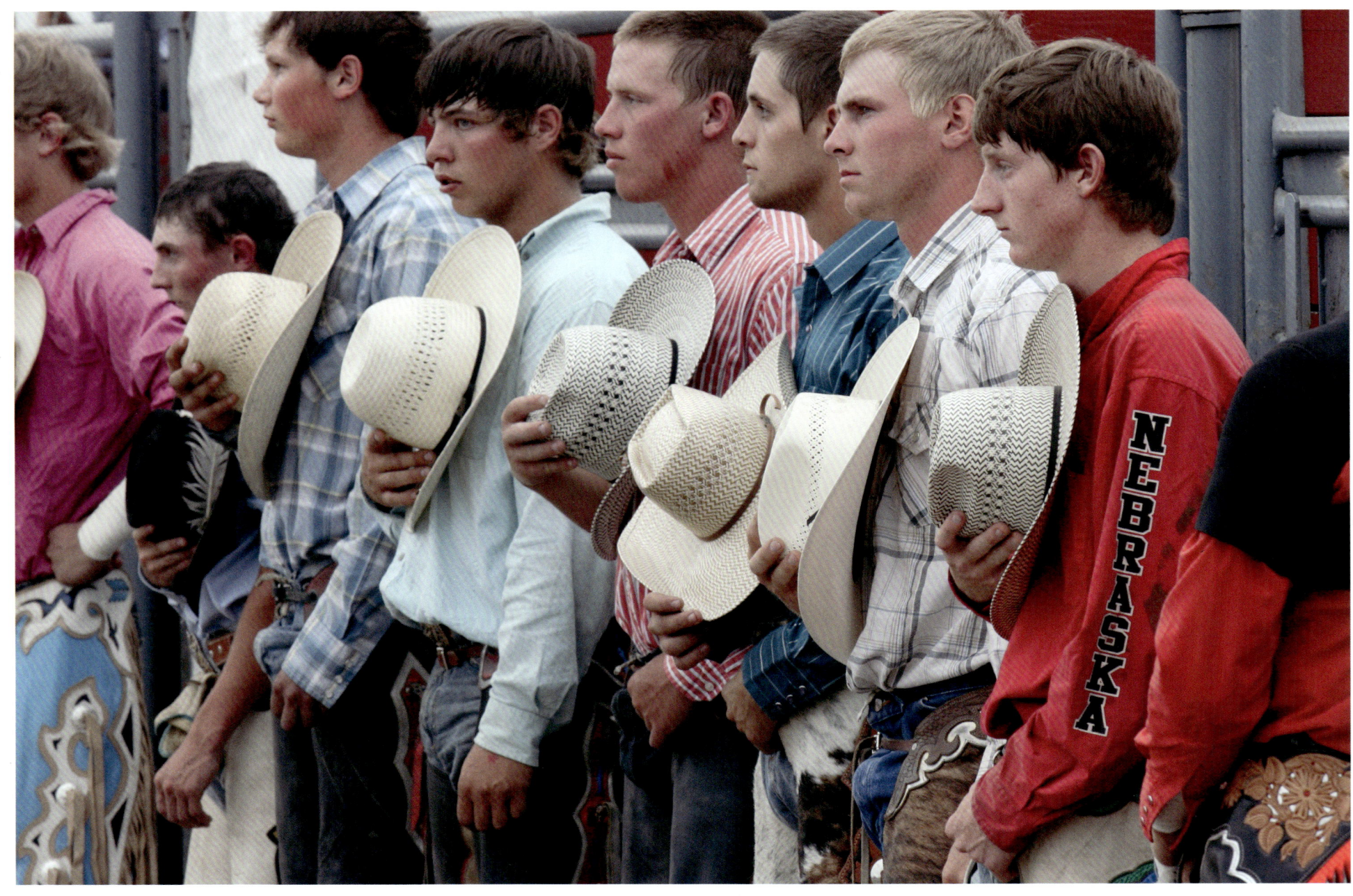

Bull riders face the flag. KEARNEY

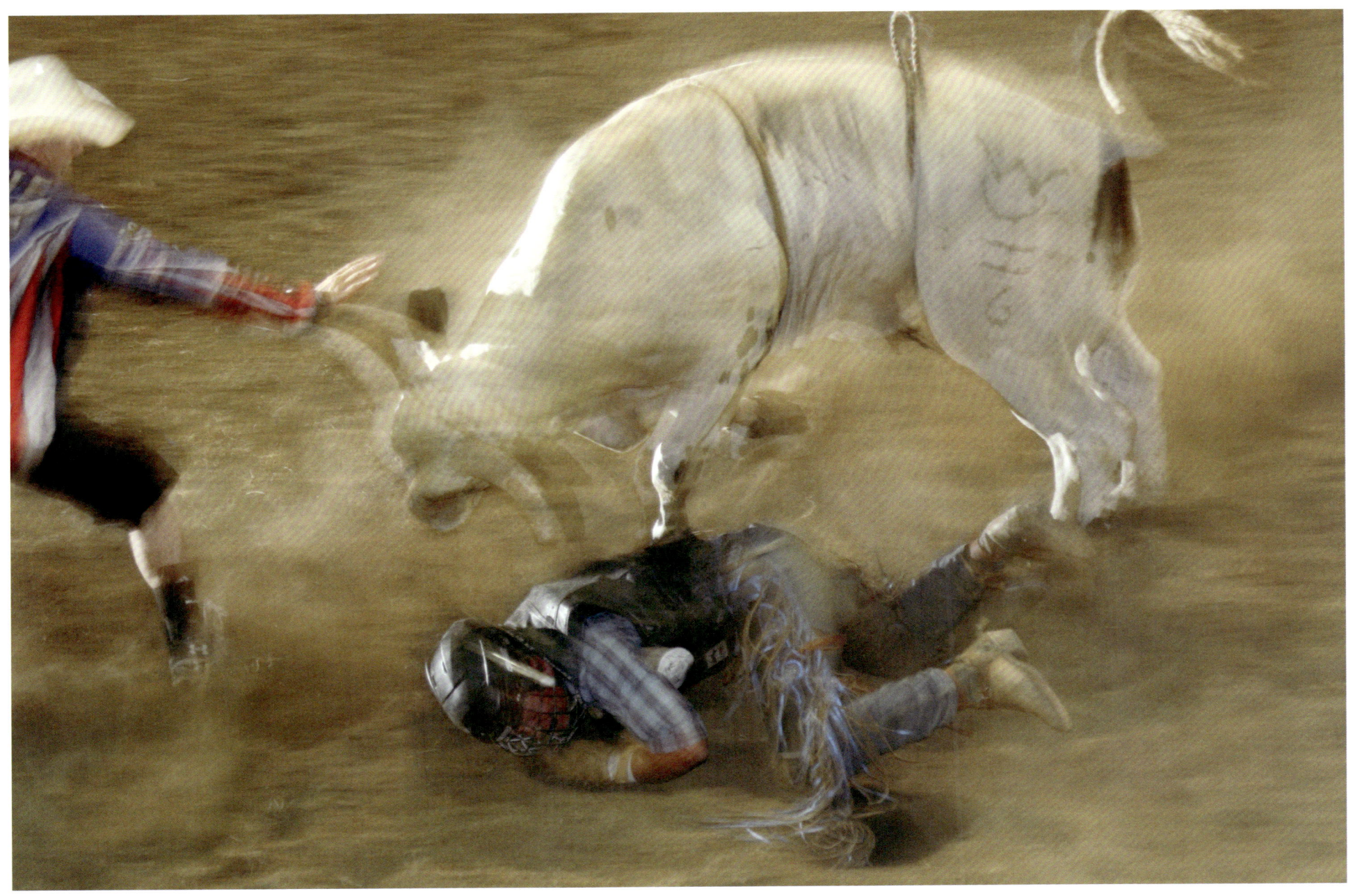

Vengeful bulls have multiple weapons and are experienced in their use. OAKLAND

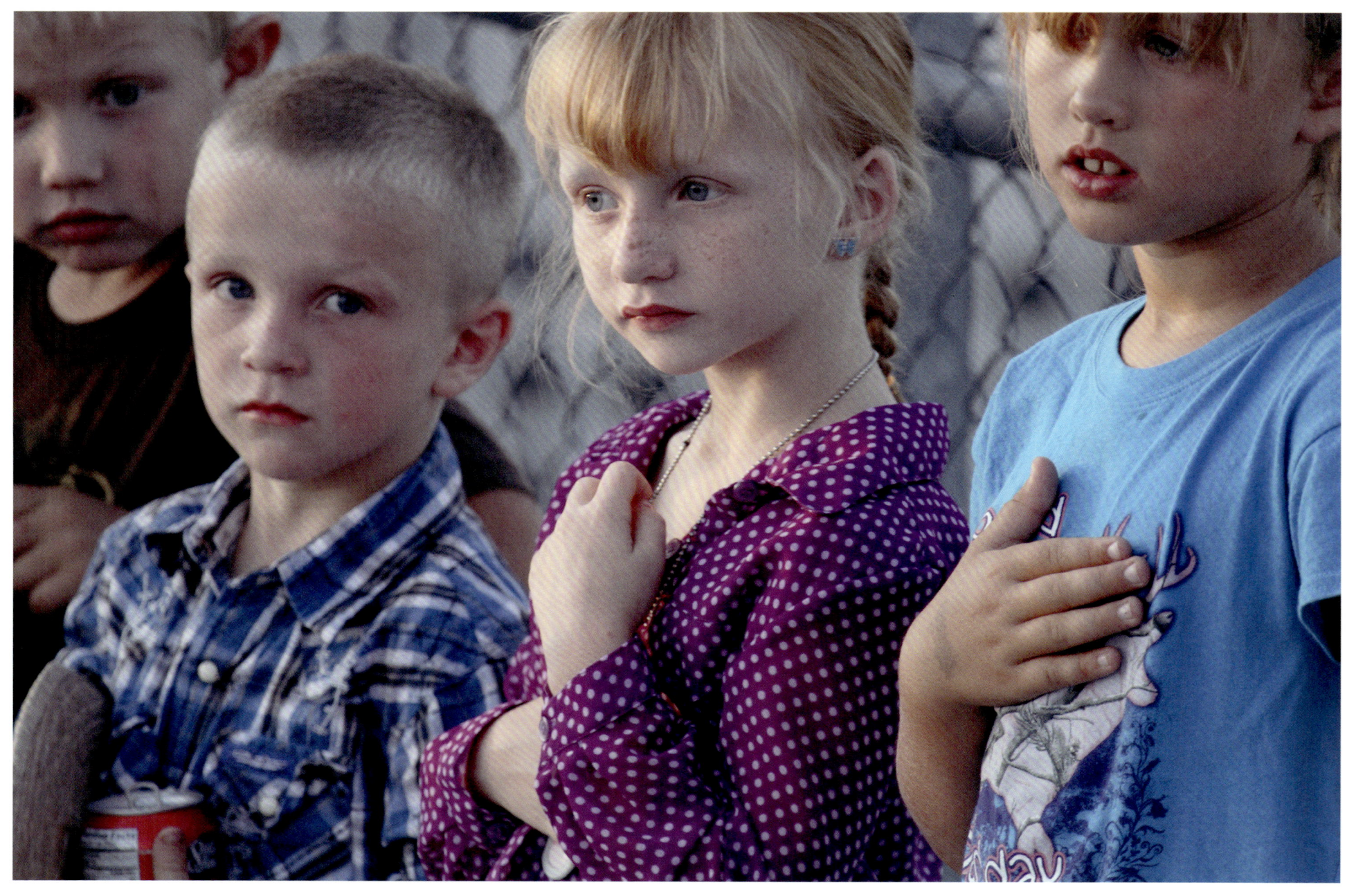

Hands cover hearts as a local singer performs the National Anthem. BENKELMAN

Capturing Chaos and Culture

Growing up in western Nebraska, I occasionally attended the Red Willow County Fair rodeo, but I was usually more interested in who I was with than in the rodeo itself. I held a girl's hand for the first time at the rodeo. I remember how our hands sweated in the summer heat, but I didn't want to let go for fear that I wouldn't find the guts to do it again. And I didn't—it would be years until I held another girl's hand. This was my principal rodeo memory until decades later when, in 2007, I attended my next rodeo with camera in hand.

When photographing rodeos across Nebraska, my original objective was to capture that perfect split-second of chaos which the human eye can't truly comprehend. I did it purely for the love of photographing action. As I amassed photos of lashing hooves and horns, wrecks and fury, I began paying more attention to the people around me. I saw my former self in the young people and began aiming the camera their way. Inside the arena, cowboys and livestock explode into brief battles in which expressions don't range far from anxiety or determination. Outside the arena I found a wide emotional spectrum on the faces of those who came to see the show.

Immersing in the rodeo community, longtime acquaintances began within this group of easygoing, dedicated athletes who belong to a subculture as old as the American West. Though they work ordinary jobs through the week, rodeo is central in their lives. It sets them apart. Through their sunup-to-sundown work ethic and their enduring cowboy spirit they reflect Nebraska's past and I wanted to know what

drives them. They have "a lot of try" in them, as a rancher might say. I wondered what brought them to the sport, what it is like to compete in rodeo, and how the winners got so good.

As rodeos and rodeo culture began filling my summers I realized this was a story worth telling, and the best way I could do that was through photography. I became addicted to shooting this unpredictable sport and got a taste of the excitement competitors crave. I shared their compulsion to improve each time, never fully satisfied with what I did, always looking to the next town where everything might come together perfectly.

Population is no gauge of greatness. Some of the best atmospheres are found in Nebraska's smallest places. These events are often associated with county fairs where brightly-lit carnival rides spin behind rodeo bleachers, and people drive many miles on scarcely used roads to attend. There is a peace and calm about these places and the narrow highways that lead to them. This book is set in these locations because it is here that our rodeo culture is most authentic.

Eight years and fifty-nine towns later, I have captured a glimpse of Nebraska rodeo culture. Relative to our history these years are a blink of an eye, and setting out on the project I wondered how much longer these events would carry on or how they would change. What will rodeo look like in 100 years? Rodeo is a lifestyle implanted early or not at all. How many more generations will sustain it? Whatever the answers may be, all I could do was look through the lens and stop moments of time. And what I saw was spectacular.

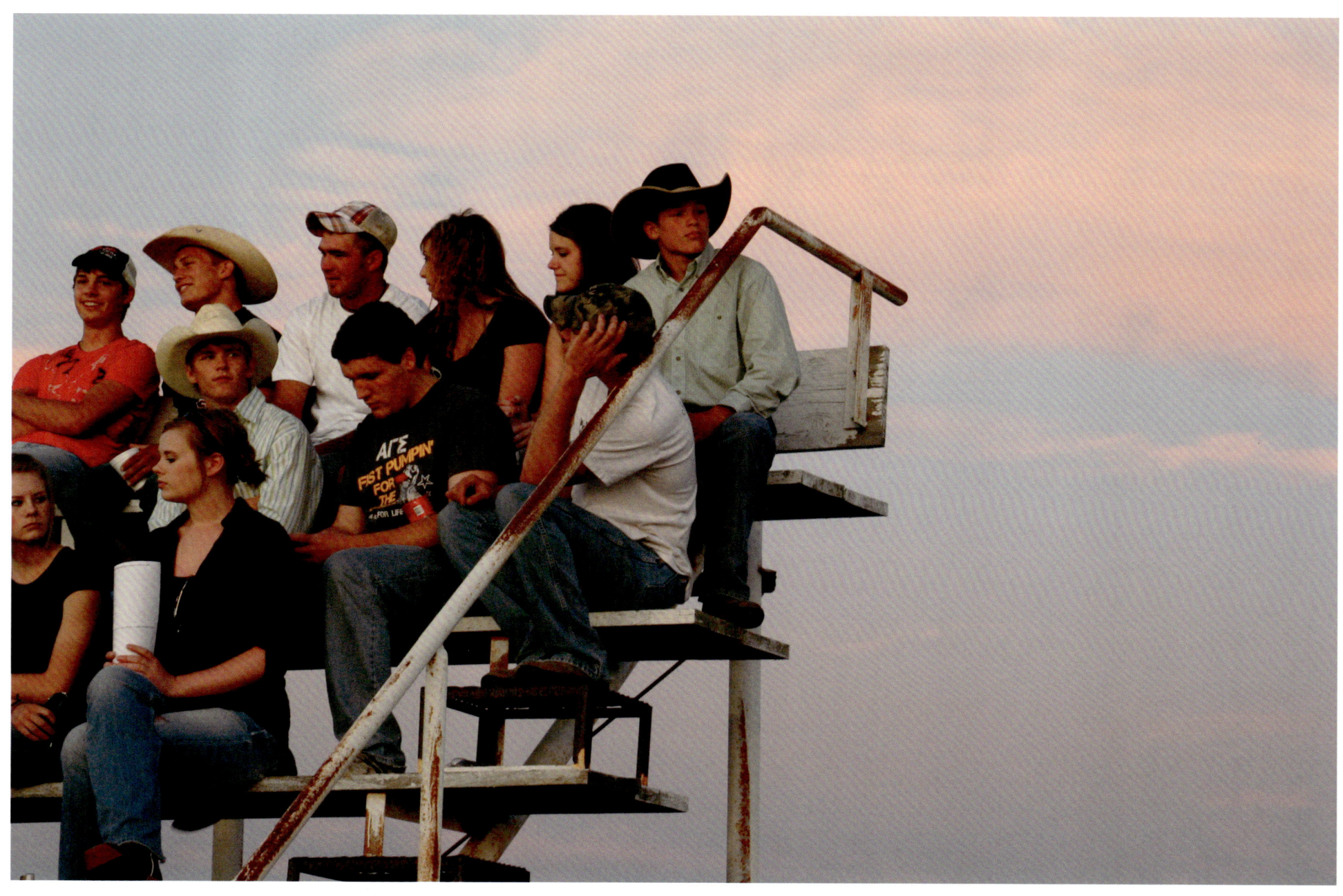

Photographing the younger crowd, I remember my own
youth and yearn to go back. CALLAWAY

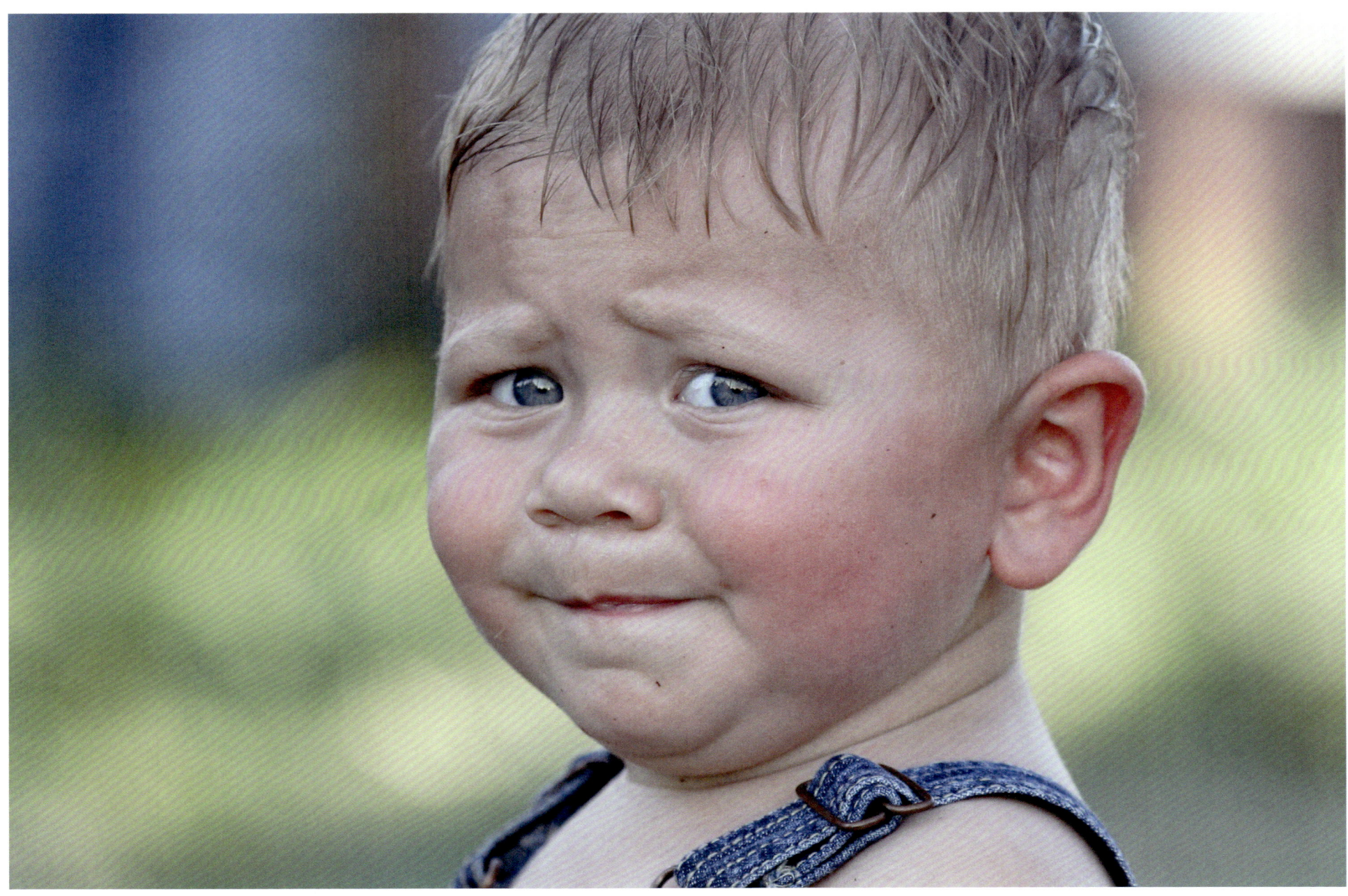

Squeezin' dirt! Jackson crushes fistfuls of dirt under the grandstands, mustering strength deep from within. He's known for his dirt squeezin'. BLADEN

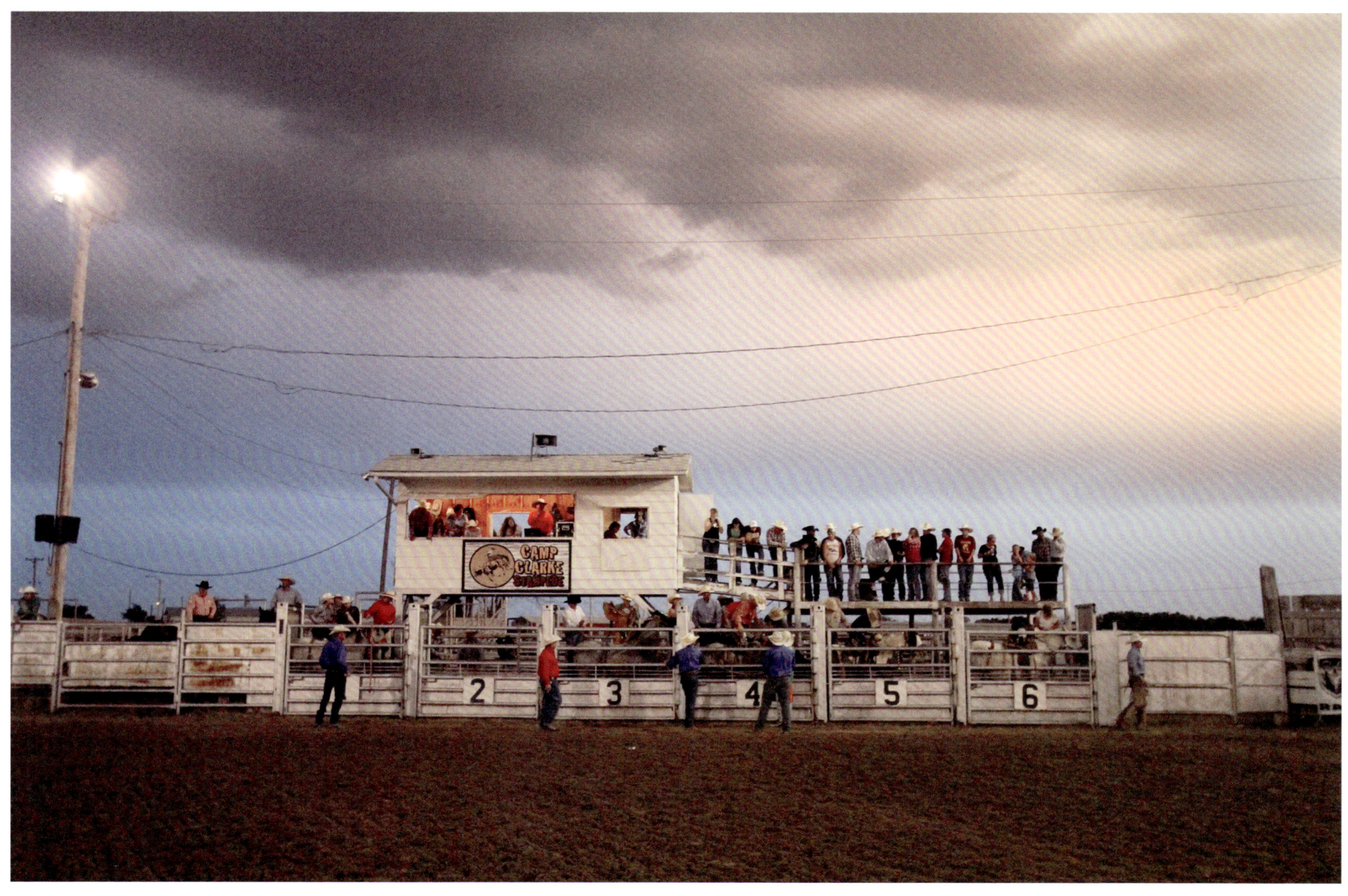

Bronc riders prepare their mounts as a storm approaches
on a sticky July evening. BRIDGEPORT

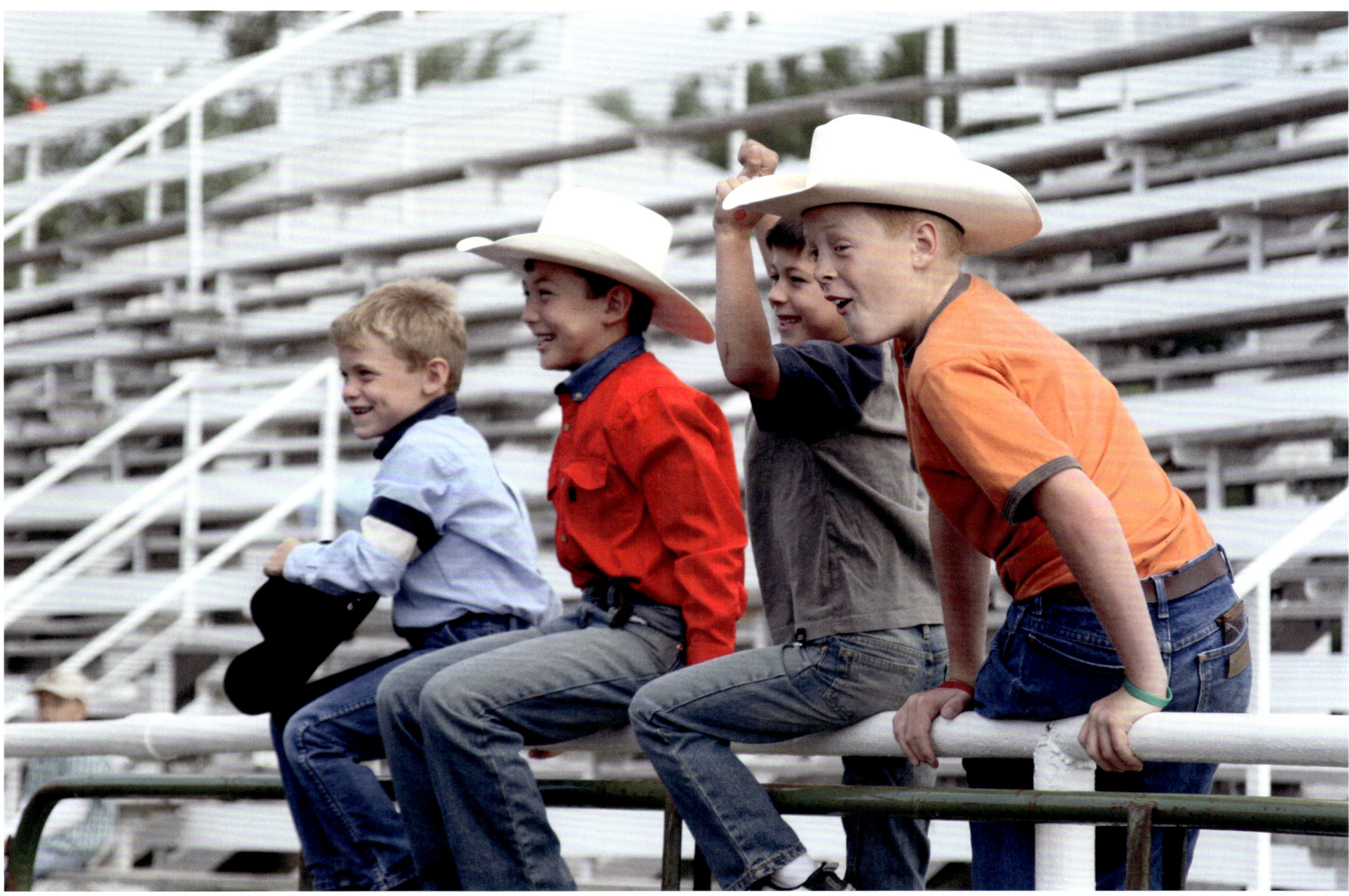

As a water truck dampens the dusty arena before the rodeo, local boys react as a playful waterman sprays at their feet. CLEARWATER

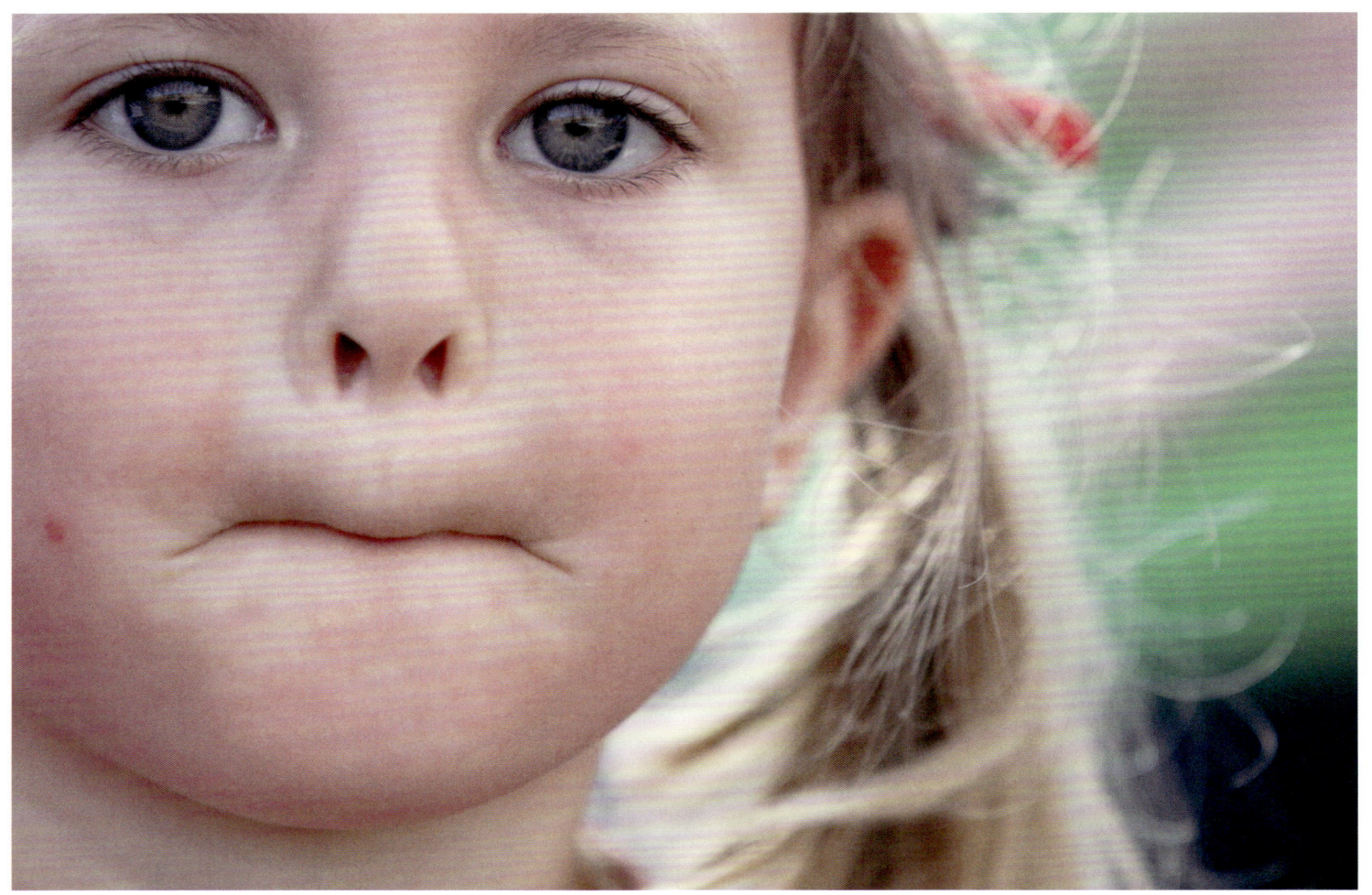

(*above*) Kids and competitors are similar camera subjects: both move quickly and both end up in the dirt. SCRIBNER

(*opposite*) Determined to know what drives these rodeo competitors, I follow the circuit. Fifty-nine towns later, I'm as obsessed as they are. PITZER RANCH, NEAR ERICSON

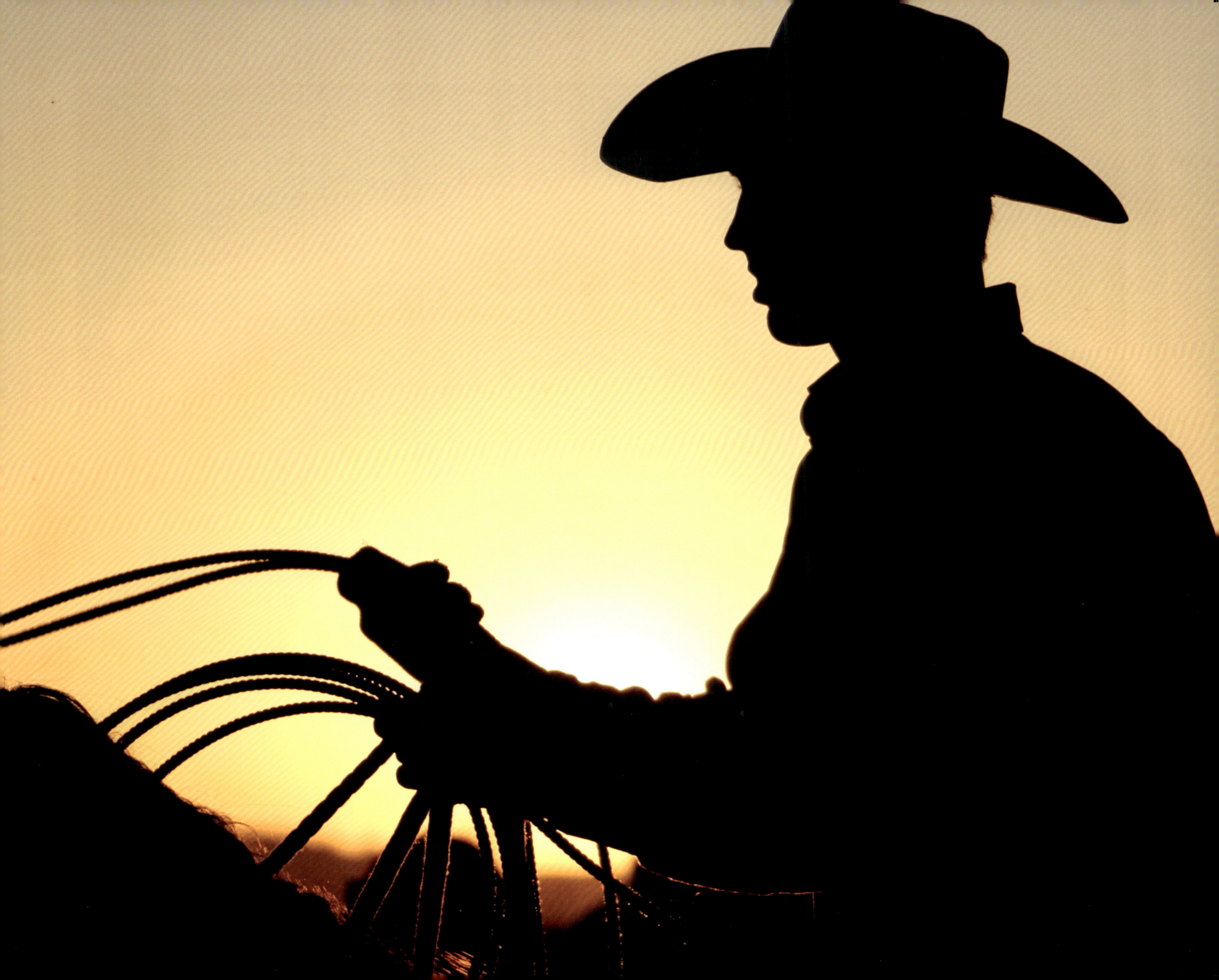

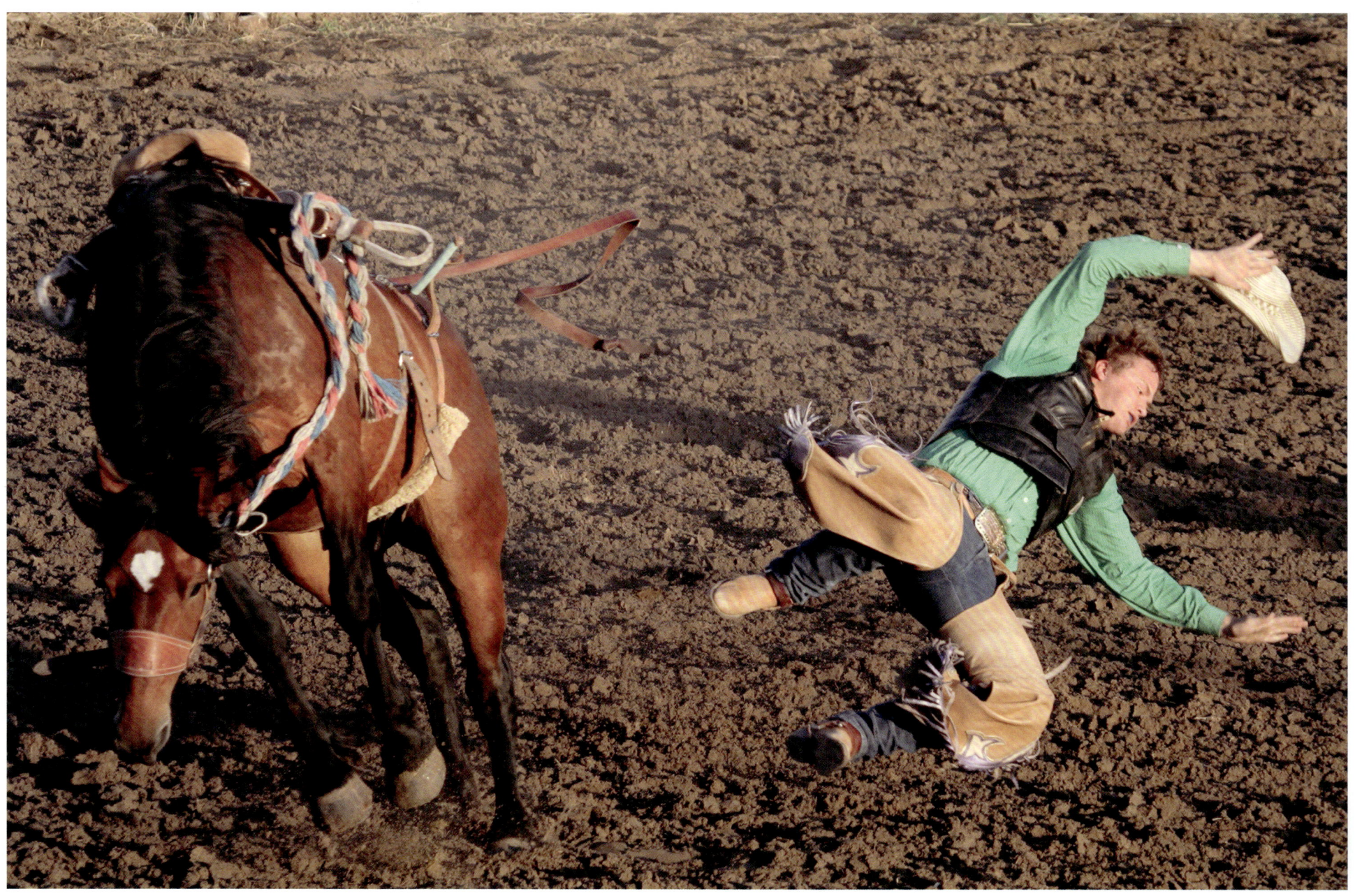

Asked what he was thinking at this moment, Drew Spencer of Mullen said, "That I should have lifted my rein and got back down in there! You got to scratch, claw, or bite. You do whatever it takes not to get thrown." BRIDGEPORT

Tuck Your Chin and Brace for Hell

BRONC RIDING

Unlike bulls, bucking broncs don't hold grudges. Anxiety replaces fury. They only want the man off their back and out of the arena. Bronc riders are still at risk but they don't face the threat of attack by the animal that threw them. Bucking broncs are generally larger than an average horse and madly averse to people controlling them, and they are primed to explode when the gate opens. Some fall into a pattern of violent but predictable straight-line bucking. Men on their backs usually make the ride. Others gyrate in mid-air and land with erratic jackhammer bounds. Their riders often get a face full of dirt.

Fewer riders compete in bareback than in saddle bronc, especially as summer wears on. It works like natural selection, weeding men out as ligaments are torn and bones broken. Atop a saddle bronc one rides more or less upright. Bareback contenders lean backward on a bed of rock-hard vertebrae with a horse-hip pillow. Rider and bronc slam backbone to backbone as the horse fights to rid itself of its human parasite. Horses grunt with wide nostrils and untrimmed manes flowing like tassel.

Zane Smith is a young cowboy from Broken Bow, Nebraska. His trademark is a decades-old derby hat, which belongs to his dad. Zane is smaller than most riders, but toughness isn't measured by height or weight. Like most bronc riders, he's had his lumps. "I've been stepped on and kicked in the head and knocked out a couple times," he says casually. Knowing that, one might expect to find nervous, fidgeting men behind the chutes. Instead, one hears jokes and lighthearted conversations. "Goofing off is part of most people's routine," Zane says. "You try not to think. You try to get out of your brain. There's no time to think anyway, it's all reaction."

Saddle bronc riding is about balance, finesse, and an intimate knowledge of horses and riding. Every cowboy comes with a lifetime of ranch riding under his belt. Most began riding further back than they can remember and they began their competitive careers in the high school rodeos that are common in rural Nebraska.

A saddle bronc competitor sits atop the mount with feet in stirrups and spurs high on the horse's shoulders. One hand holds a thick rein; the other hand is held high. Spurs are blunt, that is the rule in modern rodeo. At the nod of his head the gate swings and the horse bursts into the arena. Wide-eyed and panicky, inexperienced broncs are easy to spot prior to launch. Some rear and kick prematurely, punching the air, grunting, and pounding metal chutes with hooves. I sometimes catch an odor like that of burnt hair from the friction of hooves against metal.

It seems to me that Zane Smith gets more than his share of crazy horses. After one incident where his bronc went vertical and became hung up by its "armpits" on top of the cage before saddling time, I ask Zane if this sort of thing bothers him. "Yeah, I don't like it much when that happens." He looks at the ground as he speaks, and I know this horse has gotten into his head. But the experienced horses, the "old campaigners" as they're called, seem relatively calm. They know when to wait.

Young or old, once the gate opens the horse rockets out of the chute and time starts. Judged as a pair, same as bulls and bull riders, the horse generates points for bucking and the man earns points for how he rides. By rule, spurring must begin above the horse's shoulder and the rider's free hand must not touch either the horse or himself. Judging is subjective based on style, spurring action, and fluidity. It's about control—not control of the horse; it will do what it wants—but rather the rider's ability to control his rhythm with the horse's bucking style.

Bareback riding is sitting on flesh and bone with no place to put your feet. Riders have nothing but a small handle strapped behind the horse's shoulders to hold one-handed. "Bareback riders are nuts." That's what saddle bronc men tell me. To compete here is to lean back and brace for hell. Colten Blanchard is a bareback rider and a student at Chadron State College. Placing consistently in Nebraska's elite, he plans to go pro—the national rodeo circuit. Colten has no illusions about the risks. He has taken his beatings and knows a rodeo career can change with one wrong move. Broken ribs, punctured lung, cracked skull, a shattered eye socket—those are just the big ones. Bareback injuries are second in frequency only to bull riding; it's a nasty eight seconds.

Colten recounts sitting in the back of an ambulance, bloody napkin in each hand, one for his nose and one for his mouth. Dazed, he wondered why he had candy in his mouth. Turned out it was part of his tooth. A year later he's winning again and has his sights on the national stage. "It's the biggest adrenaline rush you'll ever feel," he says. "Strapping yourself to a 1,200 pound animal, moving with that animal, then walking away from it. It's about accomplishment."

Adrenaline—that's the word in this sport. Ty Kenner, from Wood Lake, Nebraska, is a perpetual winner in the Men's All-Around, which is any combination of winnings in any men's events. Most win with a combination of timed events, such as roping and steer wrestling.

Ty does it with bareback and saddle broncs and that's rare. He's durable and obsessed, which defines the best in bronc riding. "It took me a while to learn to make the switch in my mind from one to the other," he says of riding the two events back to back. "The balance is similar."

So are the injuries. Broken bones and dislocated shoulders haven't stopped him. A bareback rider's arm and shoulder take enormous stress, and one ripped ligament can end a career just as fast as a broken skull. Bareback riders often suffer dislocations from the arm held high in the air, caused by whiplash from the horse's bucking. "You've gotta keep your chin tucked or when your head snaps back you get knocked out," Ty explains. What keeps him at the top of the game? "It's no different than any other sport. You stay as healthy as you can. You have this competitive drive."

Corey Evans, of Valentine, Nebraska, is currently the oldest and best bareback rider in the state. What Corey does, and the frequency involved, is almost beyond imagination. He is forty-six years old and has diabetes. He takes his insulin pump off only for the arena. Considering his age, health challenges, and that he's number one year after year—Corey is an aberration. He often grabs top spots in South Dakota and Kansas as well. That's about eighty rodeos a year in addition to working on a cattle ranch full time. "I seem immune to pain until the season ends," he explains, "and then I'm sore as hell." I ask him how he practices and he laughs. "I don't! If I don't know how to do it by now I might as well quit!"

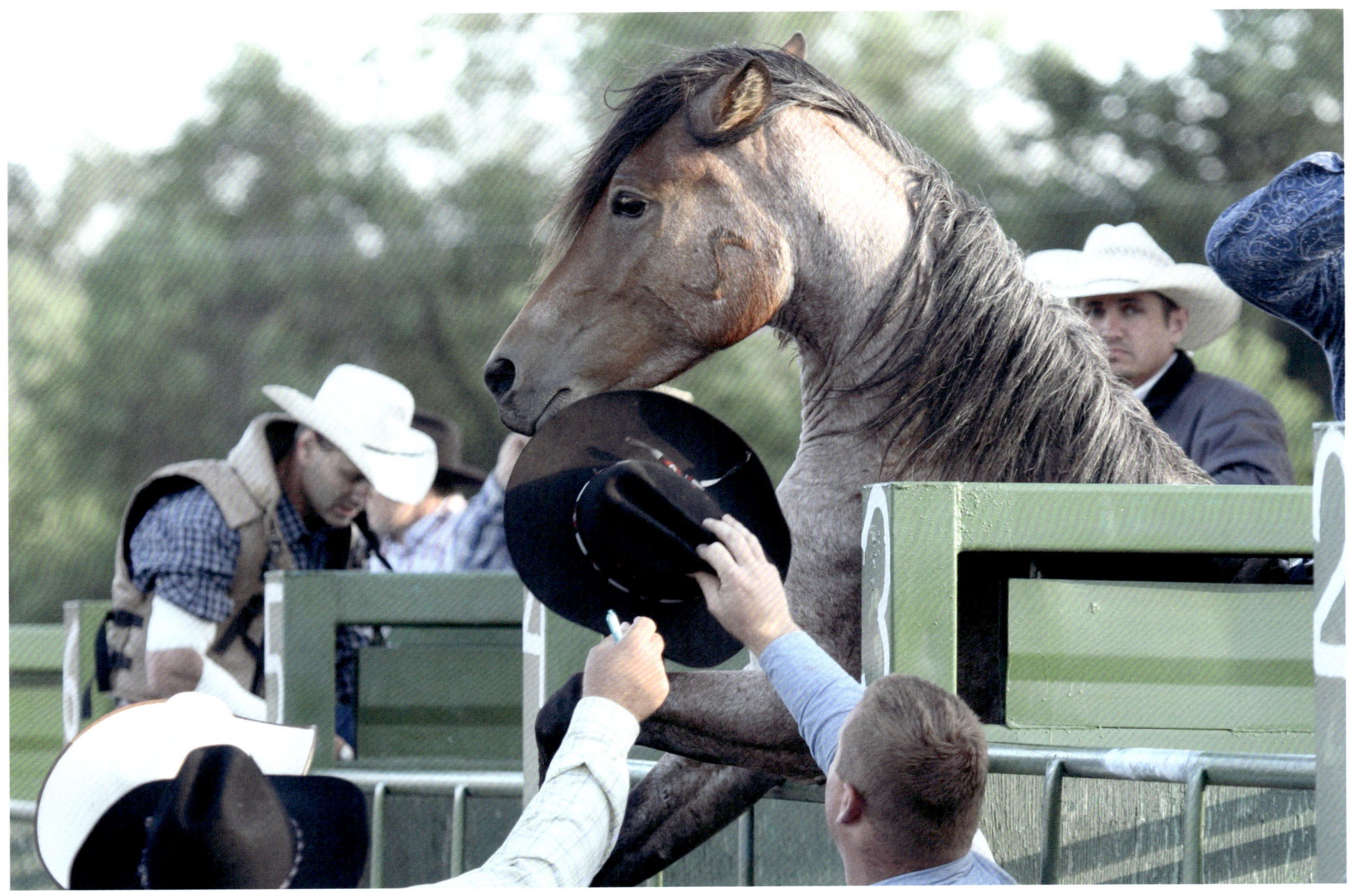

Unnerved in the chute, a bareback bronc wants out. Its frantic
energy assures a wild ride to come. CLEARWATER

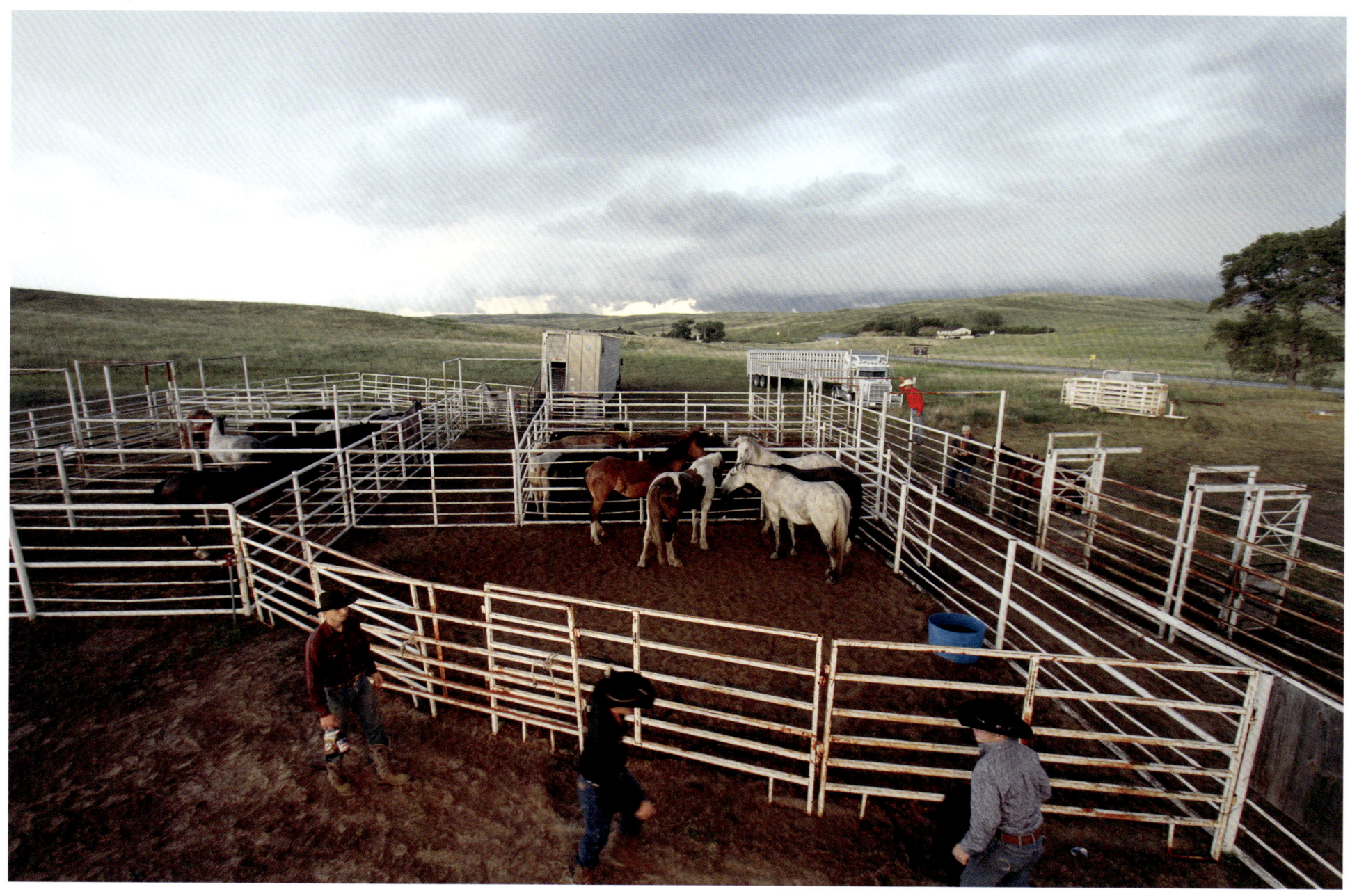

Sandhills frame stock pens at the Arthur County Rodeo. Well north of Interstate
80's monotonous glimpse of the state, this is rolling, scenic Nebraska. ARTHUR

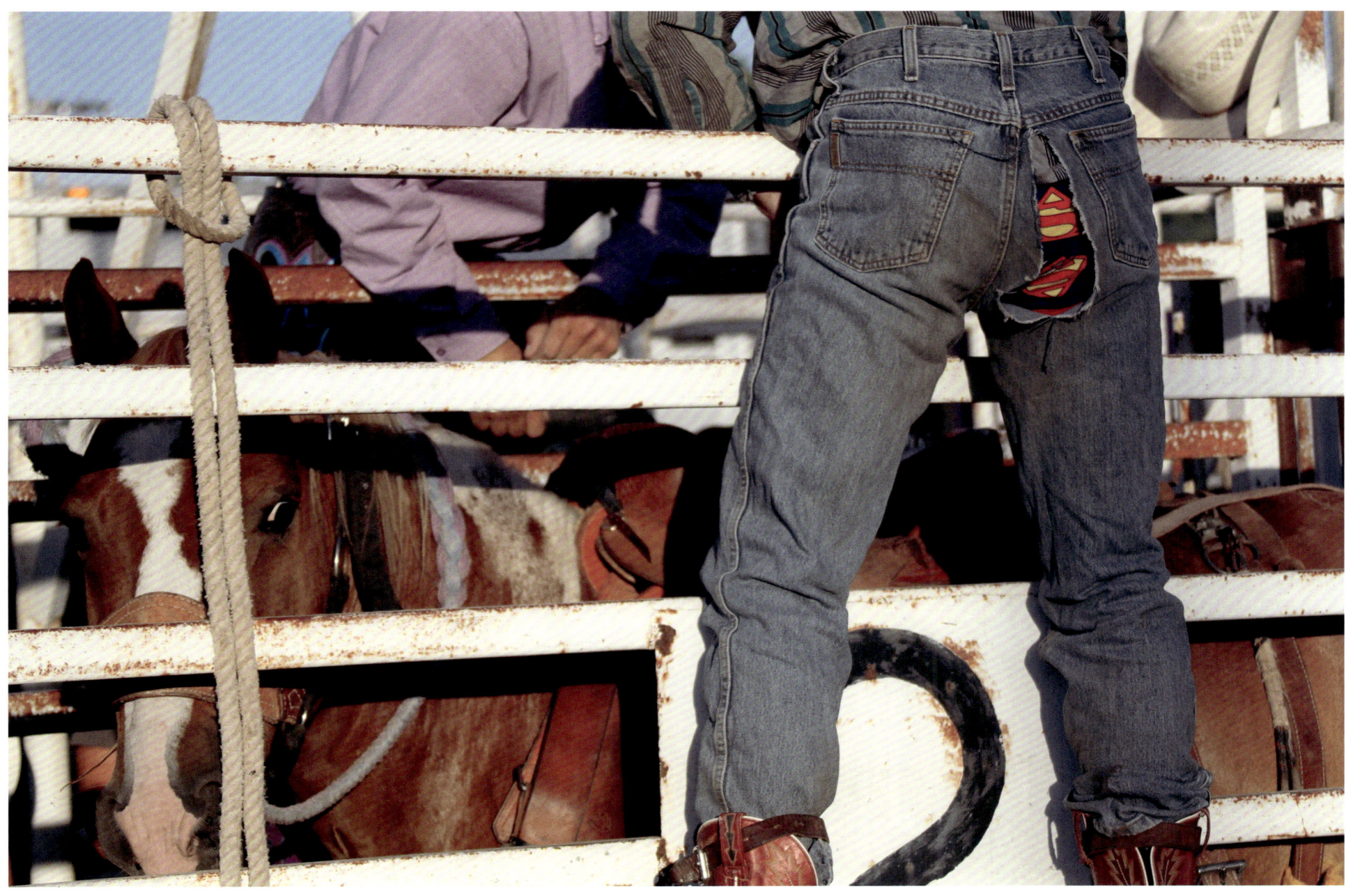

"Old Campaigners," the experienced broncs, take things
in stride until the gate swings. CRETE

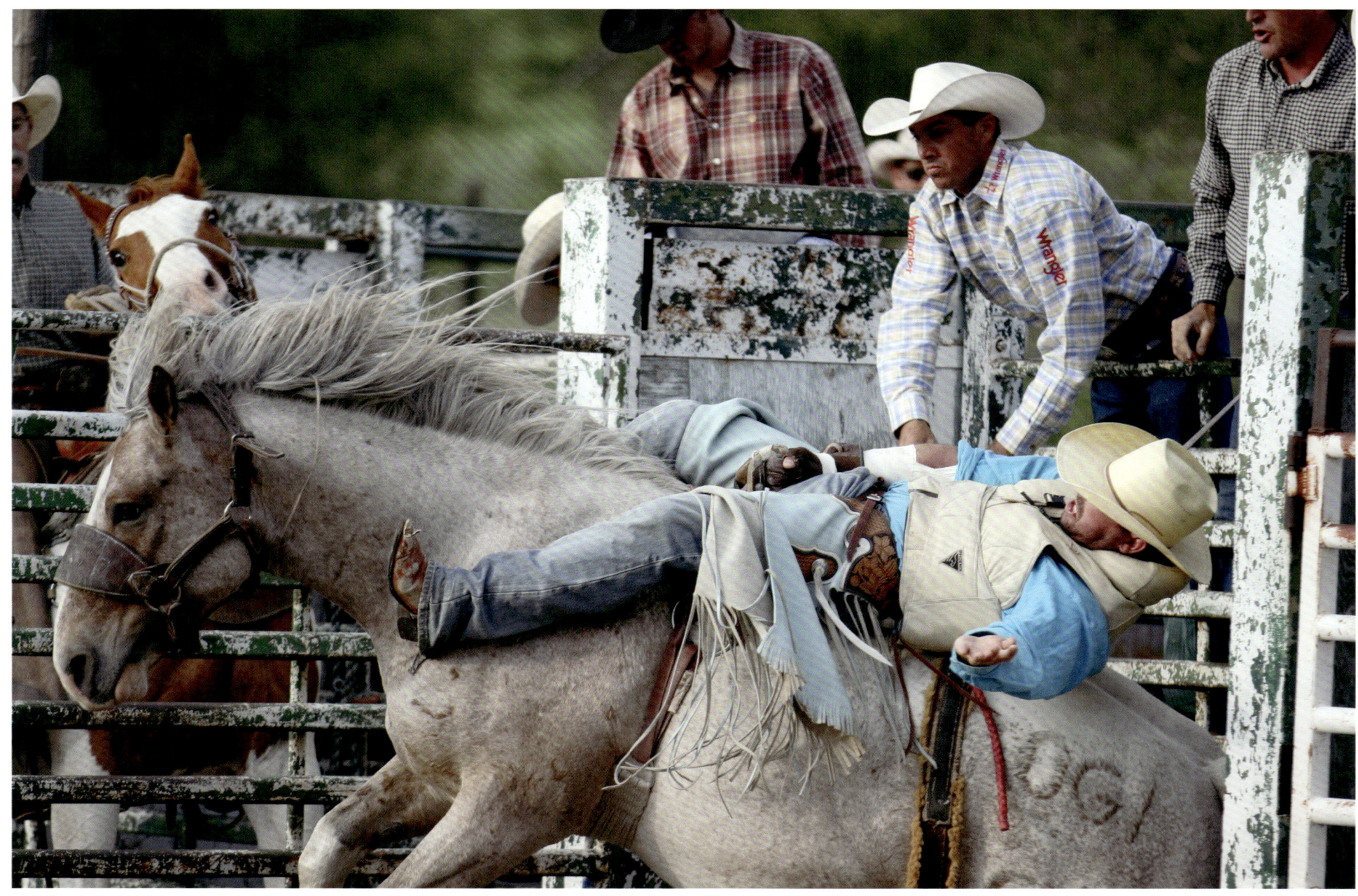

"Bareback riders are nuts." That's what saddle bronc men tell me. EDDYVILLE

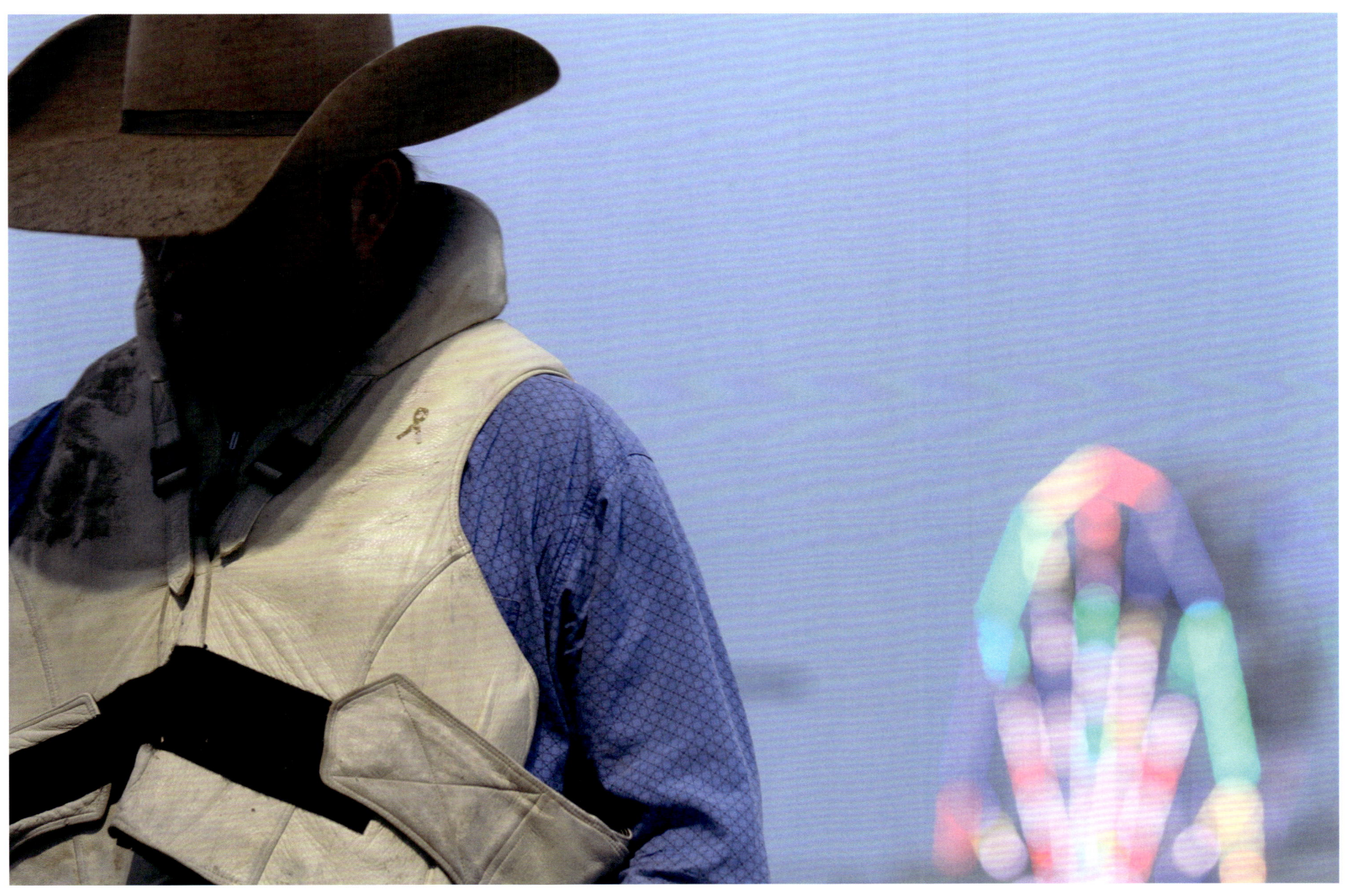

Backlit by the Red Willow County Fair, a bareback rider prepares to ride. MCCOOK

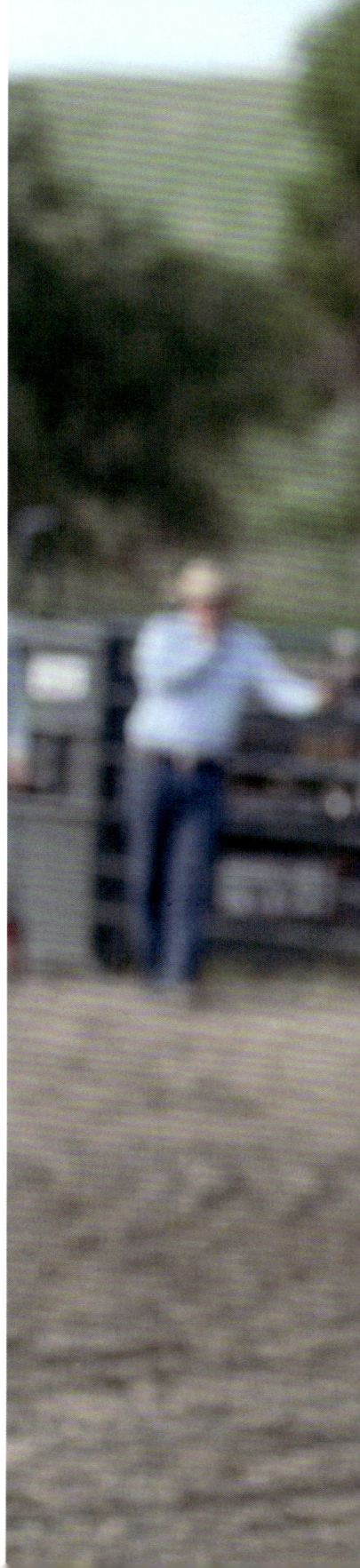

(*above*) Rider and bronc go down. Inexperienced broncs might sacrifice their own balance to ensure that the rider is thrown. FORT ROBINSON

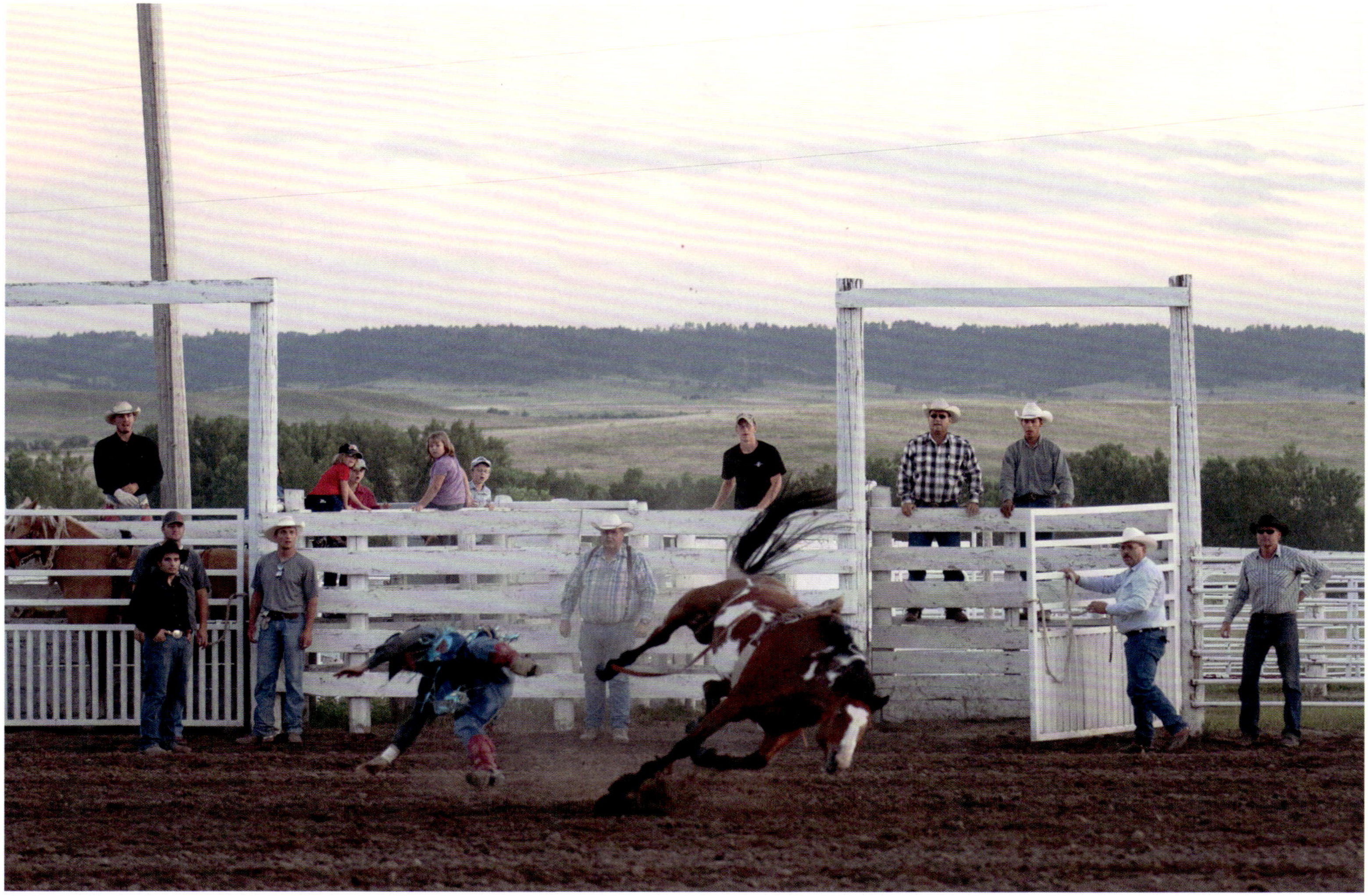

(*opposite*) "It's just another day," says bareback rider Colten Blanchard when asked what he is thinking behind the chutes. Taking second place at this rodeo in 2011, the following year he will fracture his face and skull on a bronc, only to return as a top competitor in 2013. EDDYVILLE

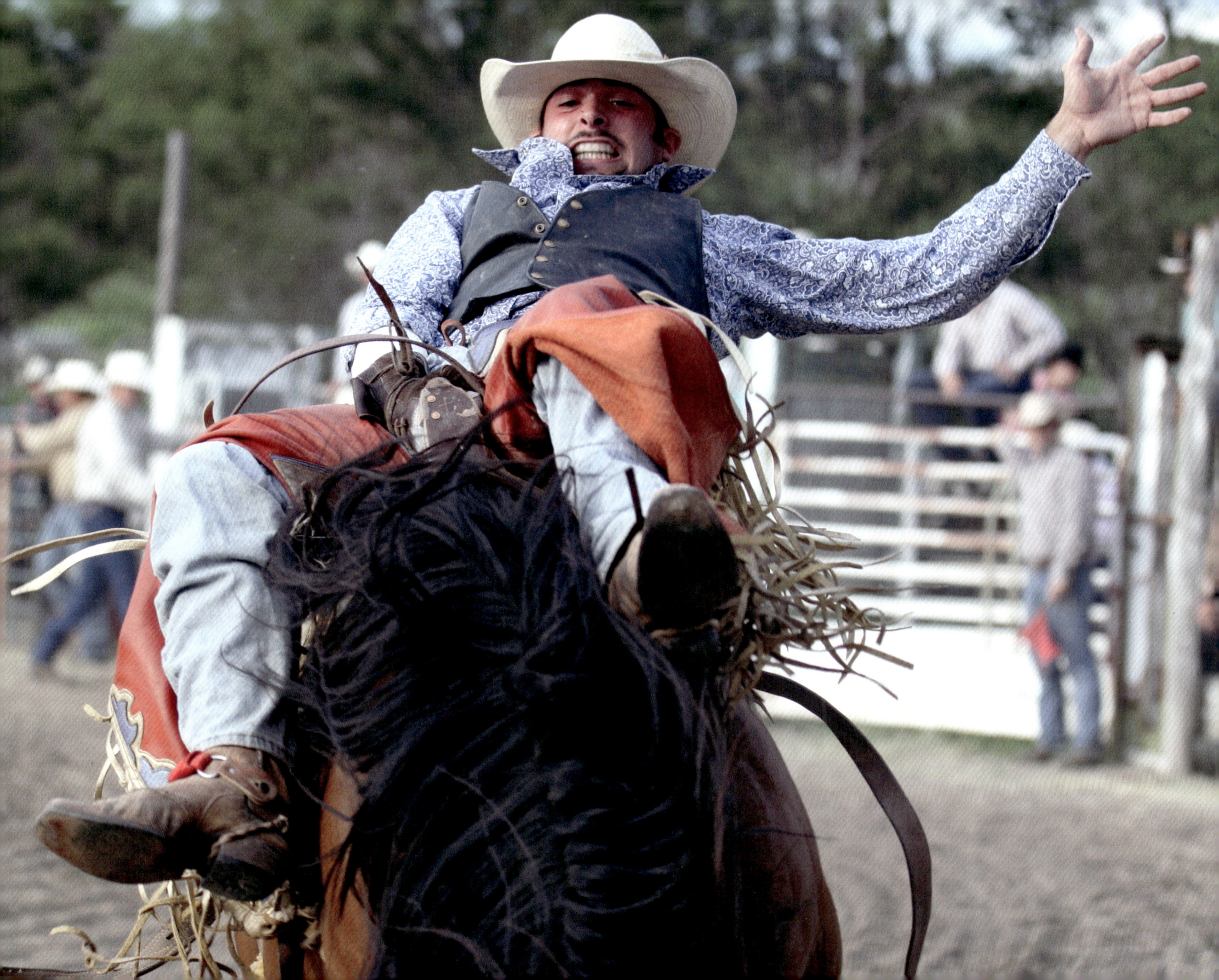

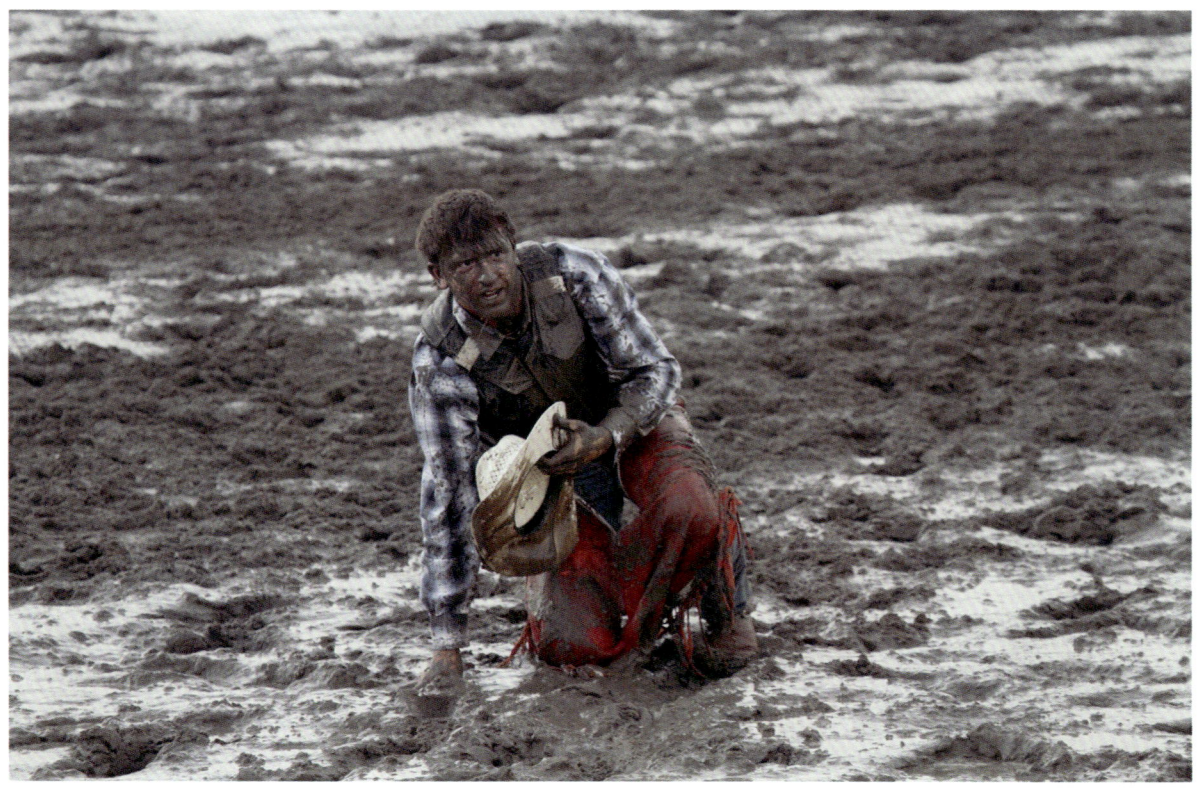

A torrential downpour just before the rodeo makes this bronc rider's landing softer but uglier. VALENTINE

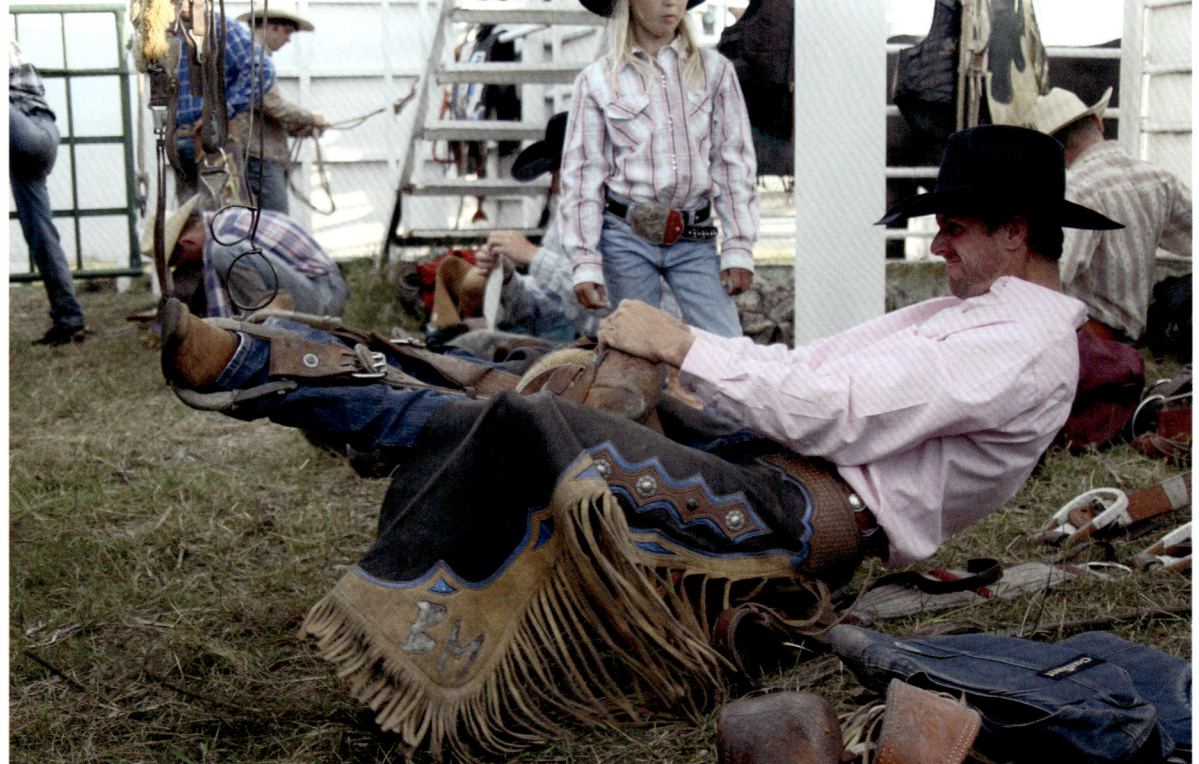

Champion Brad McCully of Mullen travels with one of his two daughters on the rodeo circuit every summer weekend. Before his ride, this daughter watches her dad check and adjust his bronc saddle. CLEARWATER

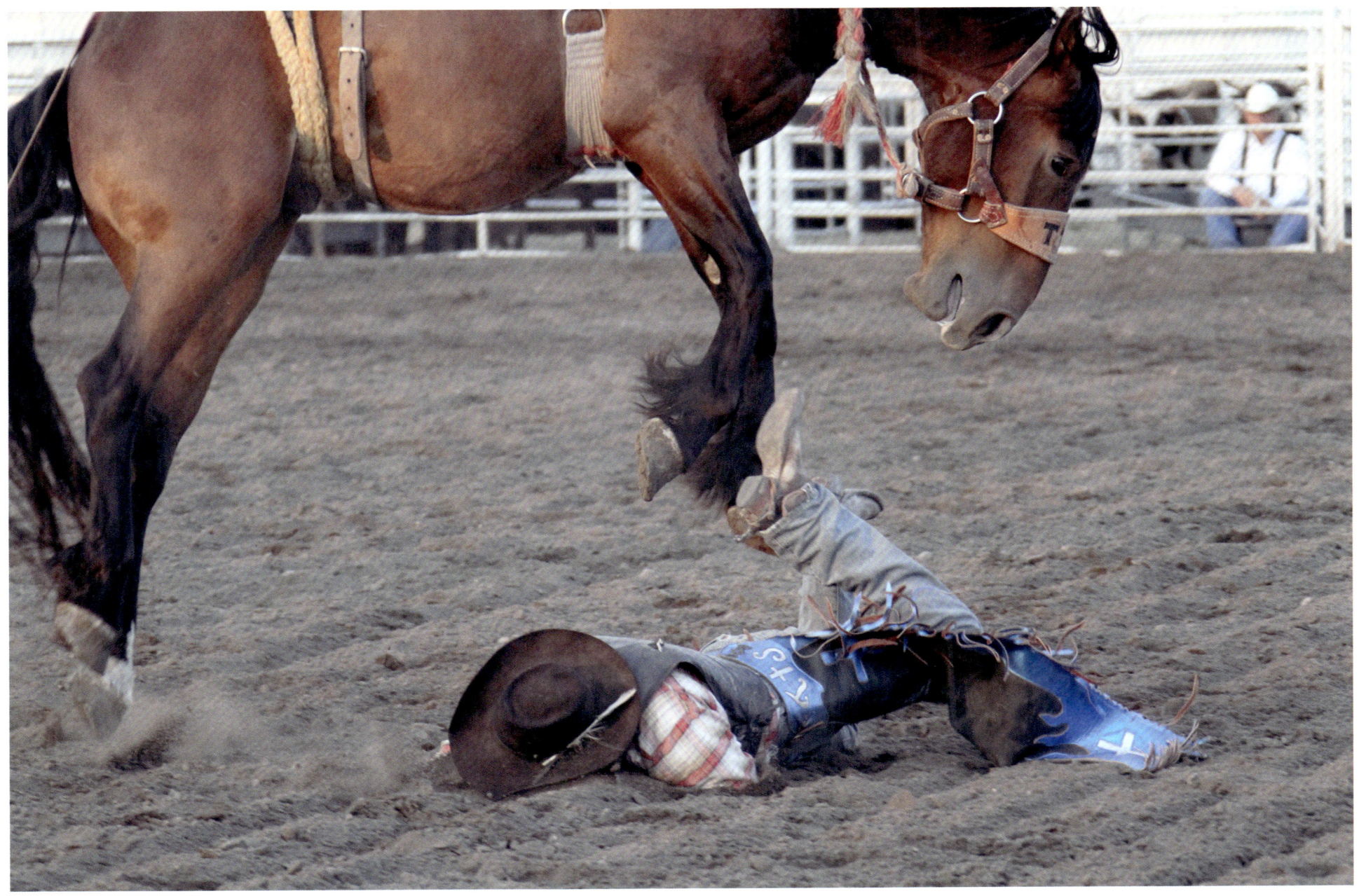

Bronc riders face many risks, but not the threat of attack by the animal that threw them. Broncs only want the man off their back and out of the arena. SUTHERLAND

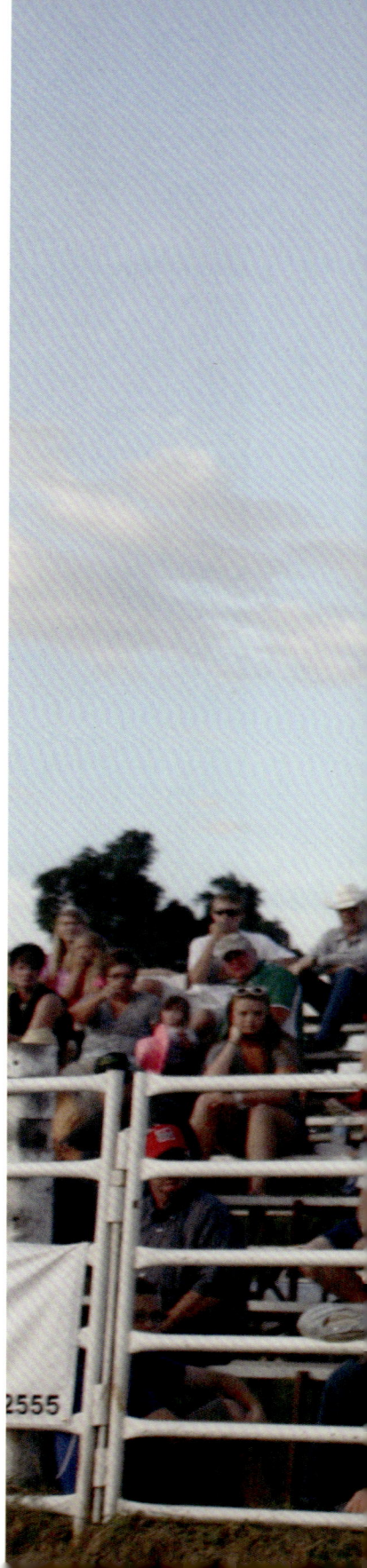

(*above*) "These are wild horses," says one bronc rider. "They get the same feeling we get in the chute. They're just anxious and want to go! It's kinda like the feeling you get right before a fistfight." CLEARWATER

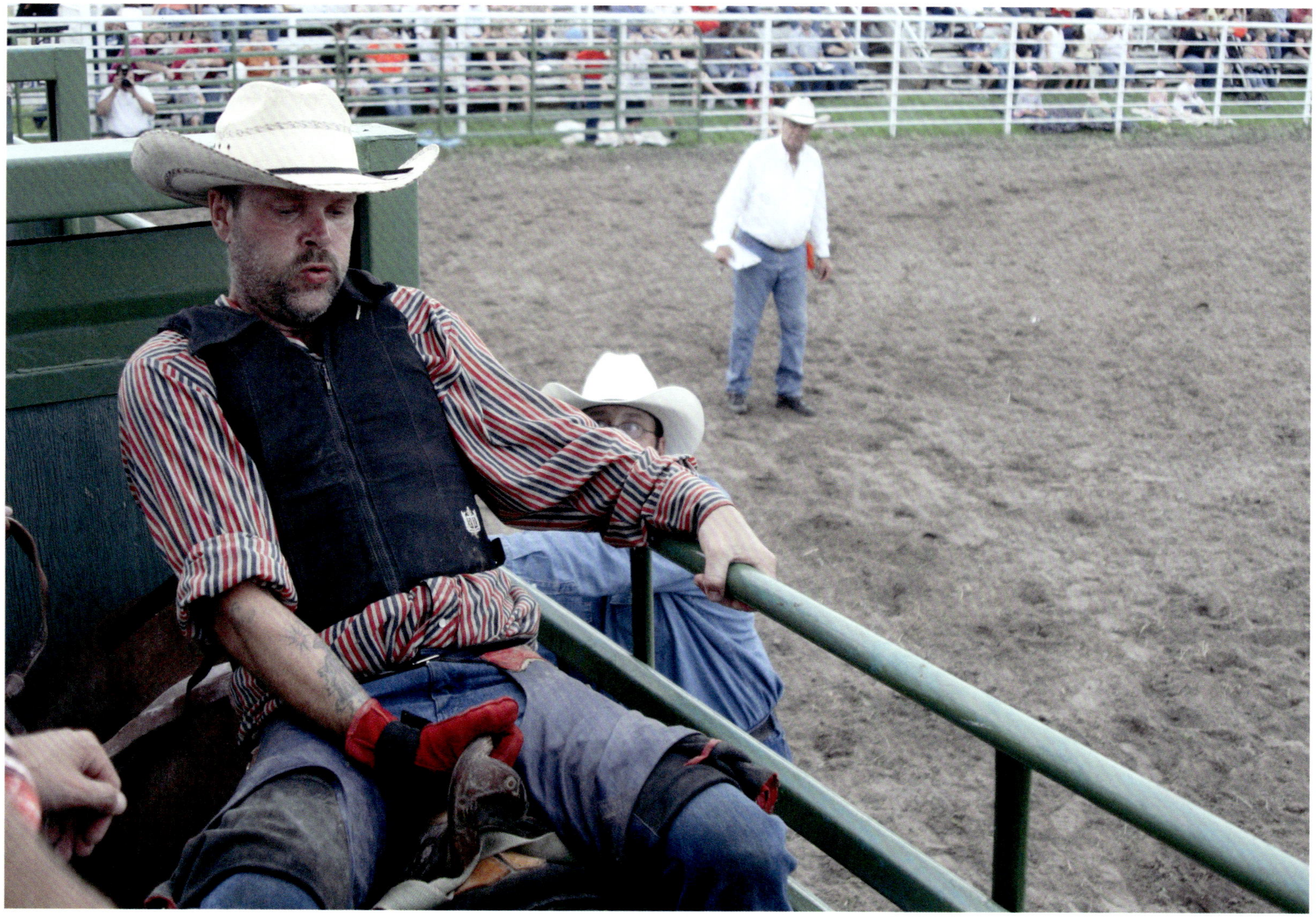

(*opposite*) "Objects are closer than they appear." Wide angle lenses give a false sense of distance, and though that fact is always in the back of my mind, yards quickly turn to inches in bronc riding. My hurried tripping and tumbling for safety only adds to the show. GREELEY

2555

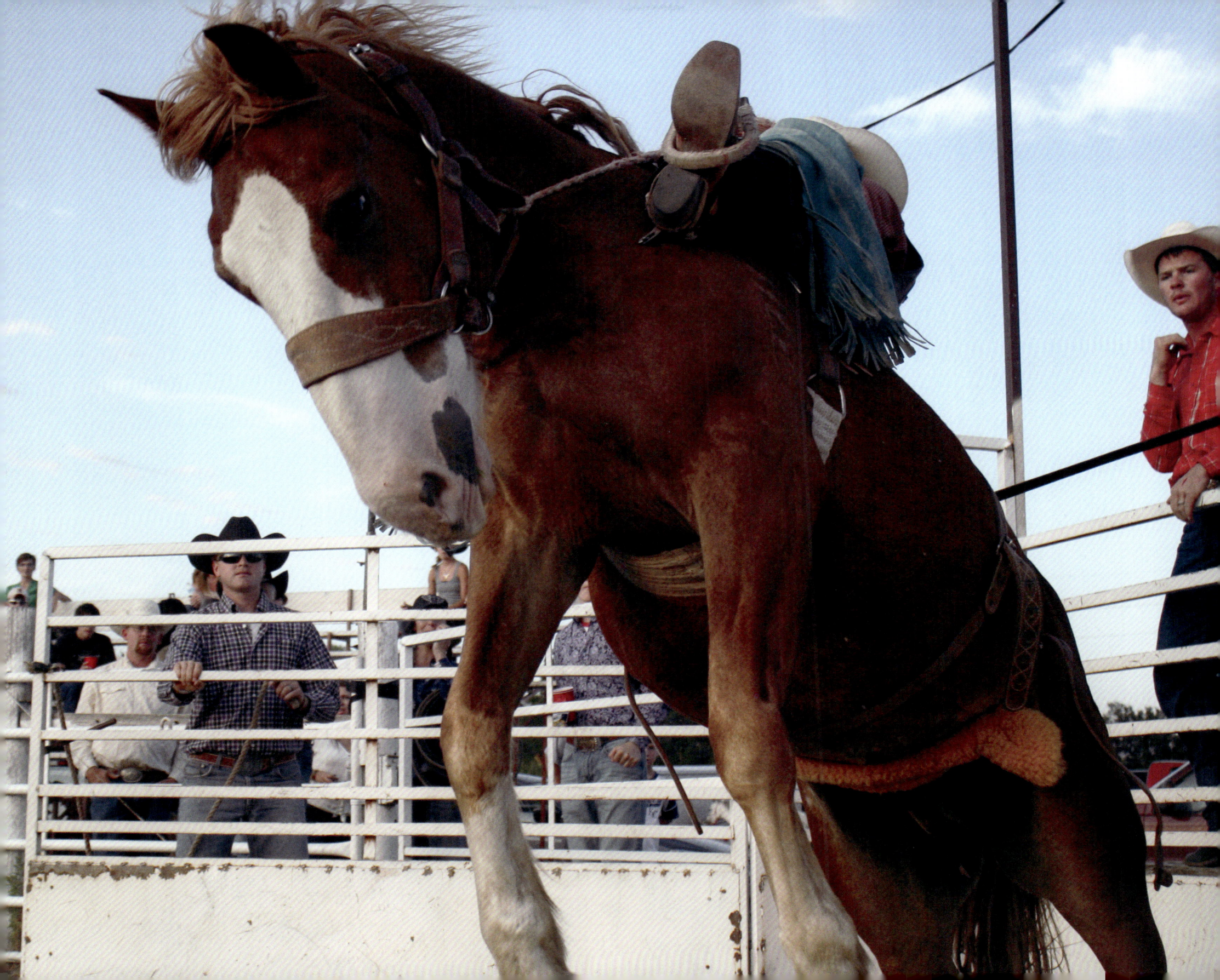

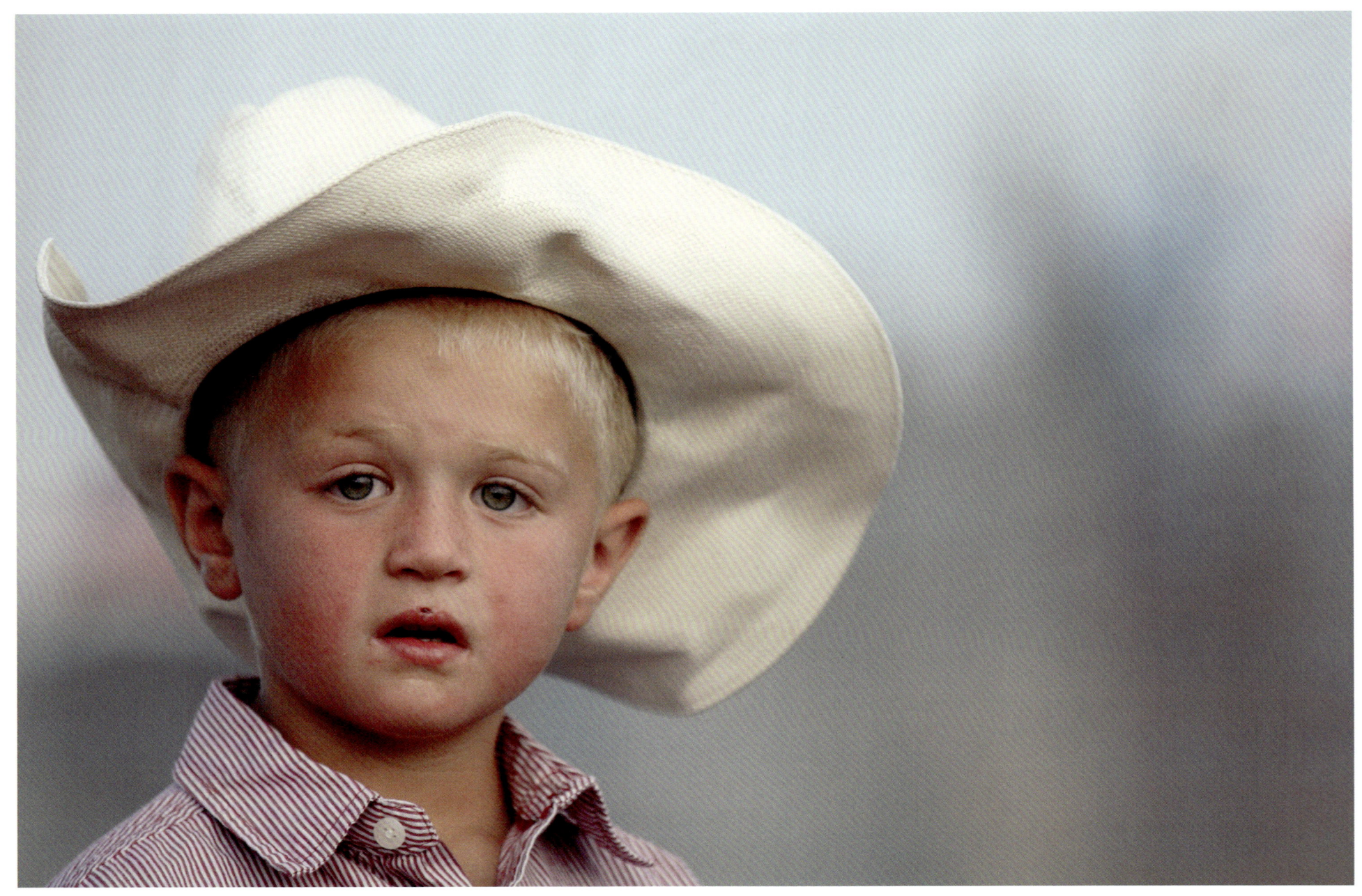

This is cowkid country. Rough stock doesn't look so rough through a ranch boy's eyes. ALLIANCE

Innocent Eyes

When I think of small town Nebraskans I think of blue irises inherited from northwestern European ancestors—Germans, Czechs, Swedes, Danes, and Irish. Genetically recessive blues and greens noticeably outnumber browns, contrary to the state's metropolitan areas. My lens captures brilliant hues, some flecked with gold. Kids' overt joy is charming and I gravitate toward their innocent eyes, wishing I were one of them again just for a while.

In tiny towns like Callaway and Hyannis, lawn chairs unfold in pickup beds backed up to the arena. Policy is loose. Civility is standard in these places; it feels safe and kids have more liberty to roam. Like wandering monkey troops, they play around rodeo bleachers and climb arena fences. Uptight horses speed past and thrilled little voices cry out when dirt clods rain down. Friendly announcers warn the monkeys away and they comply for a while.

Children love the camera and adults dodge it. Gregarious grown-ups are few at rural rodeos other than the inevitable man saturated in beer. Point a camera toward a group of kids and each individual presumes to be the central subject. They relish that role, sometimes ten at a time. Aim squarely at an adult and they move out of the way, looking behind to see whose limelight they're spoiling. Targeted older women are mortified without fail, with male counterparts tickled by their wife's concern.

Small, ultra-rural crowds like that at the Arthur rodeo are composed of two main communities: the locals and the competitors. Like a traveling roadshow, I see familiar faces of riders and their families across the state. My son befriends a boy named Cash whose namesake father will later ride a bull. Goofing under the grandstands is the top attraction for Cash and other riders' kids who attend more than their share of rodeos. Frolicking rodeo kids lure local youngsters from their seats. It's fun watching this fusion and I'm often torn between photographing competitors or kids. They are similar subjects: both move quickly and both end up in the dirt.

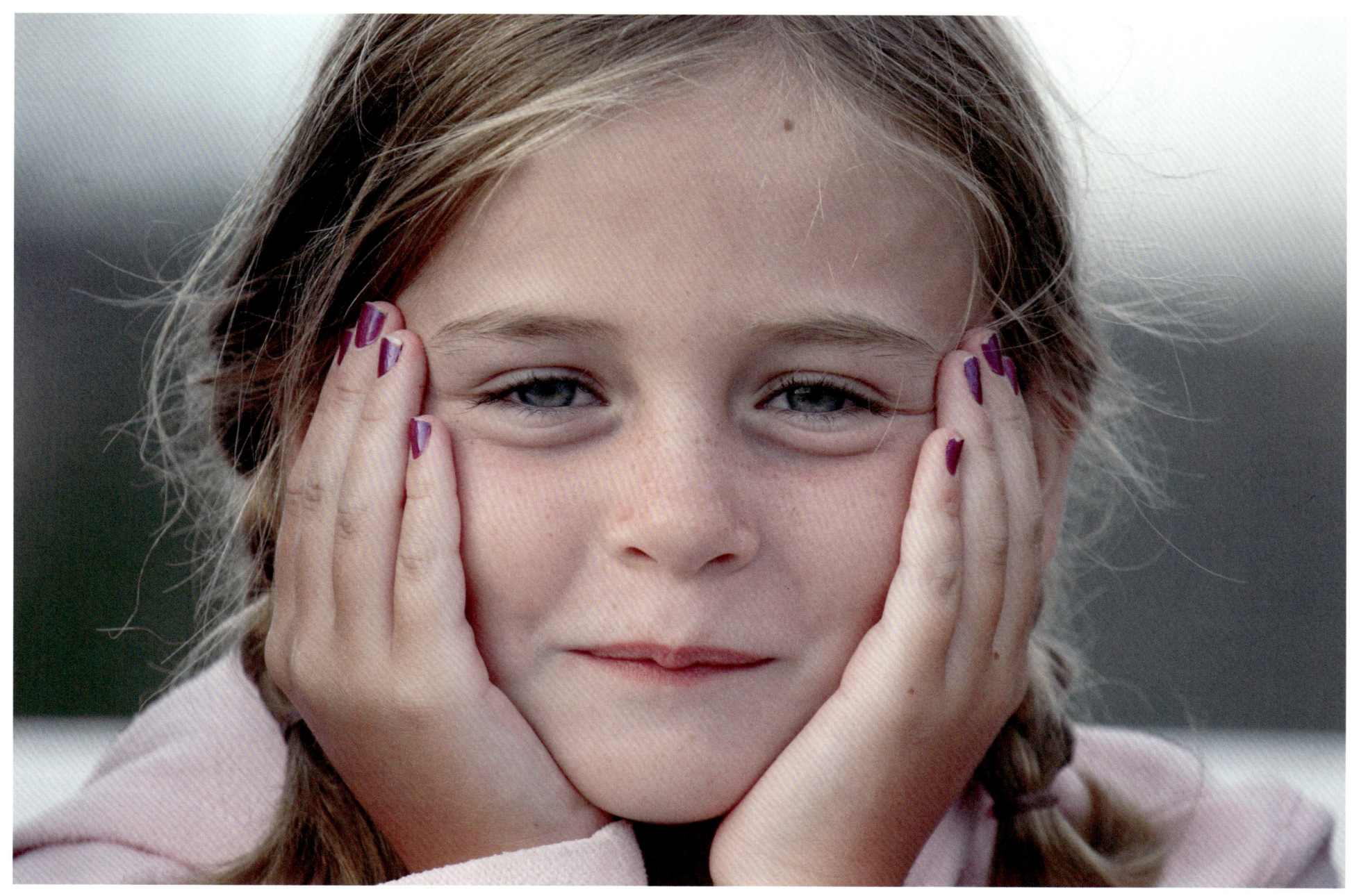

With a wink and quick zoom, a moment is shared. The camera loves kids. FORT ROBINSON

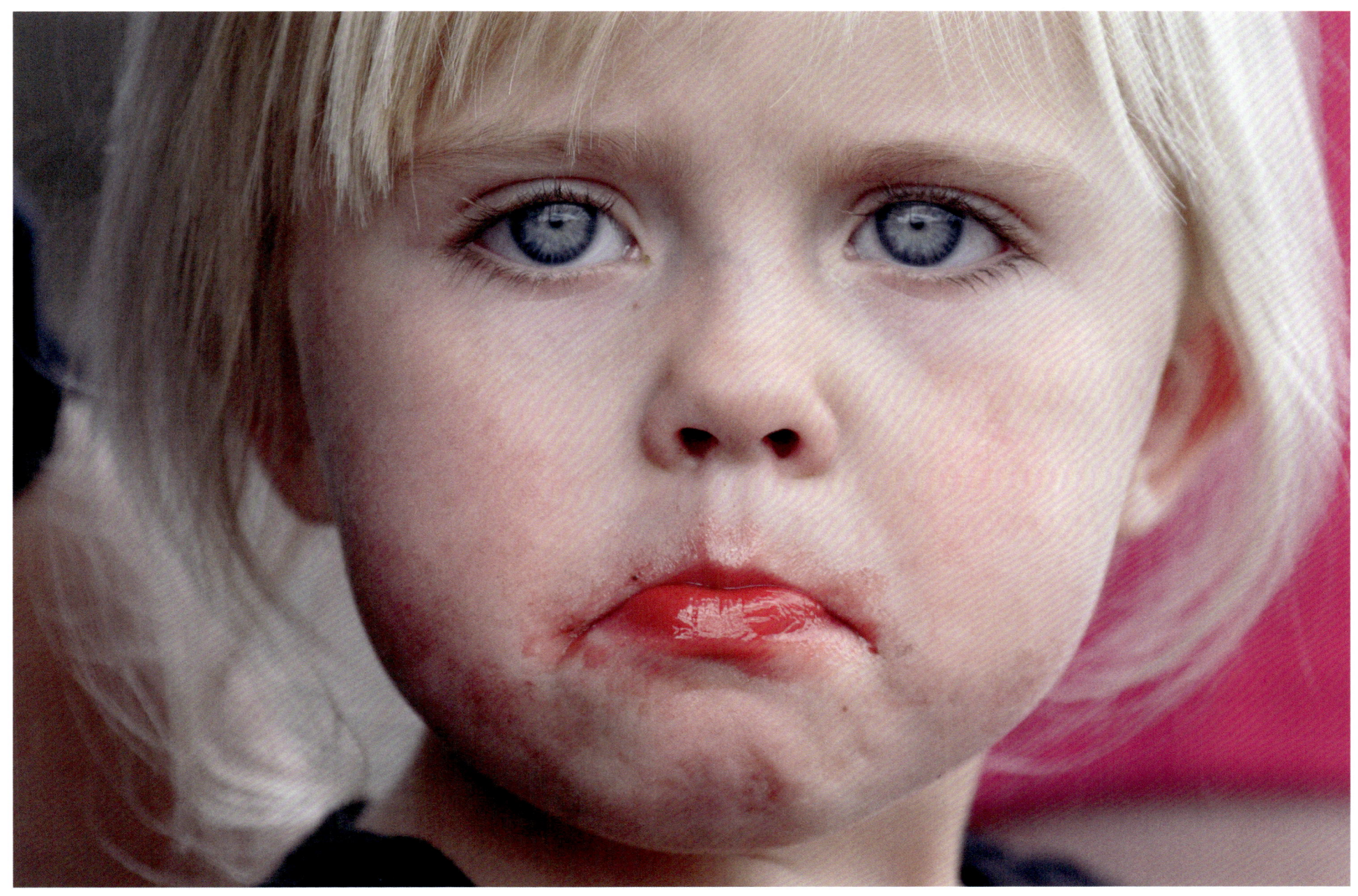

Stained from a cherry slushy, this sadness lasts only seconds
before the joy of youth reboots. ARTHUR

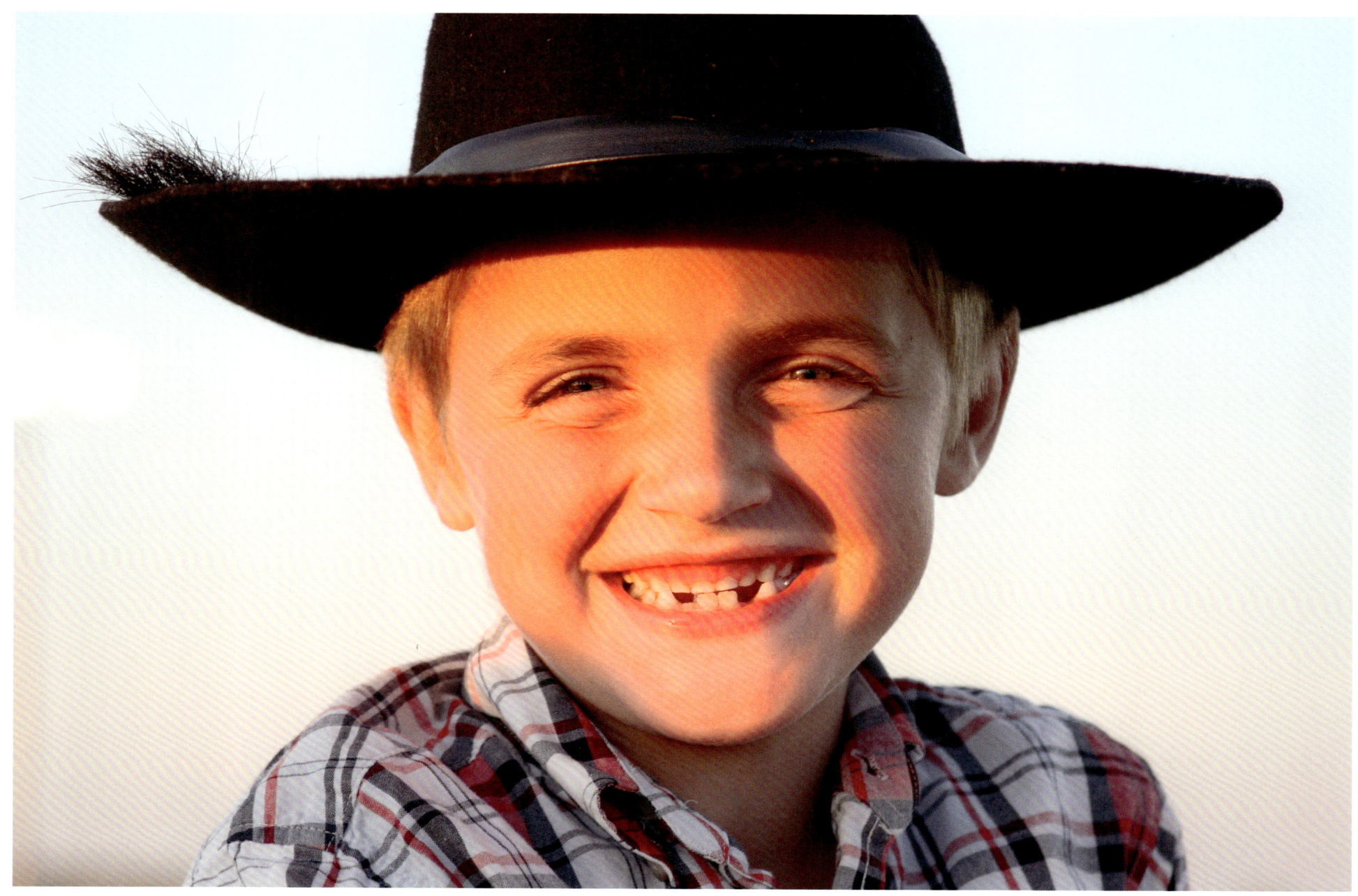

Parents usually encourage a smile when my camera swings their kid's way, but feigned smiles spoil the shot. Ribbing from his pals about future photo fame brings a genuine smile to this country boy. CALLAWAY

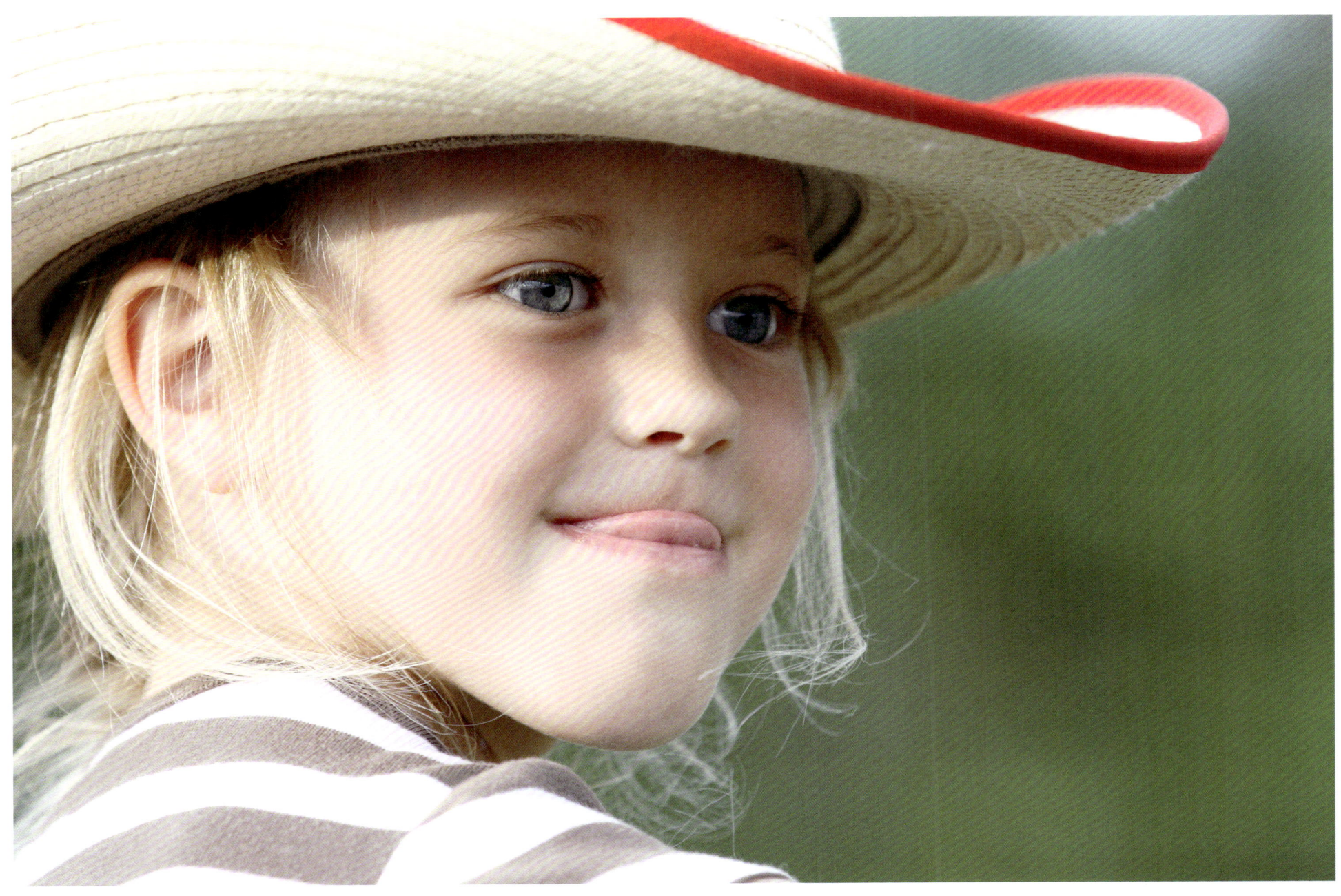

Grasping high on the arena fence, a local girl anticipates the
next breakaway roper's launch. EDDYVILLE

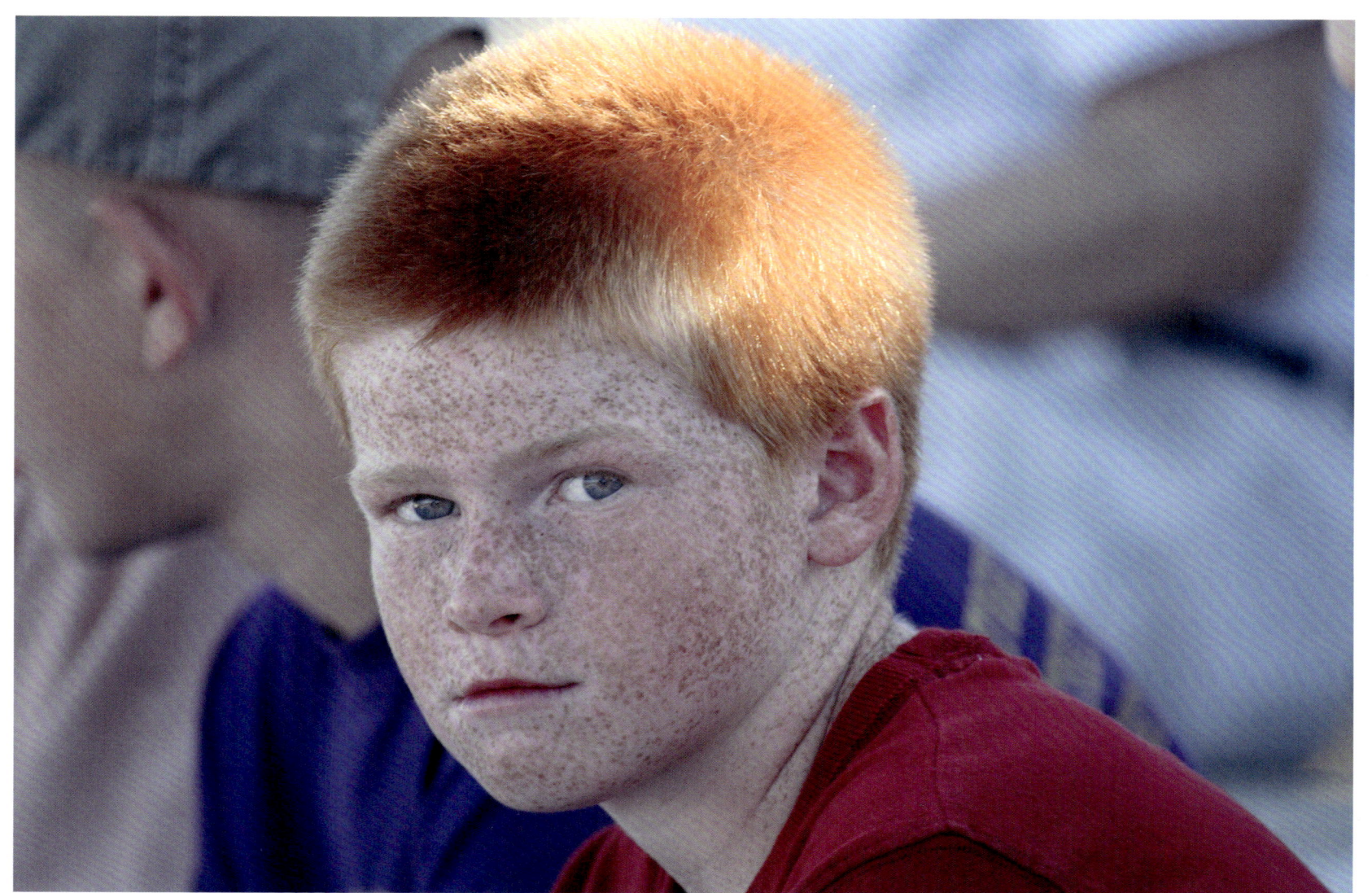

(*opposite*) Inherited from northwestern European ancestors, blue and green irises outnumber browns in rural Nebraska. FORT ROBINSON

(*above*) KEARNEY

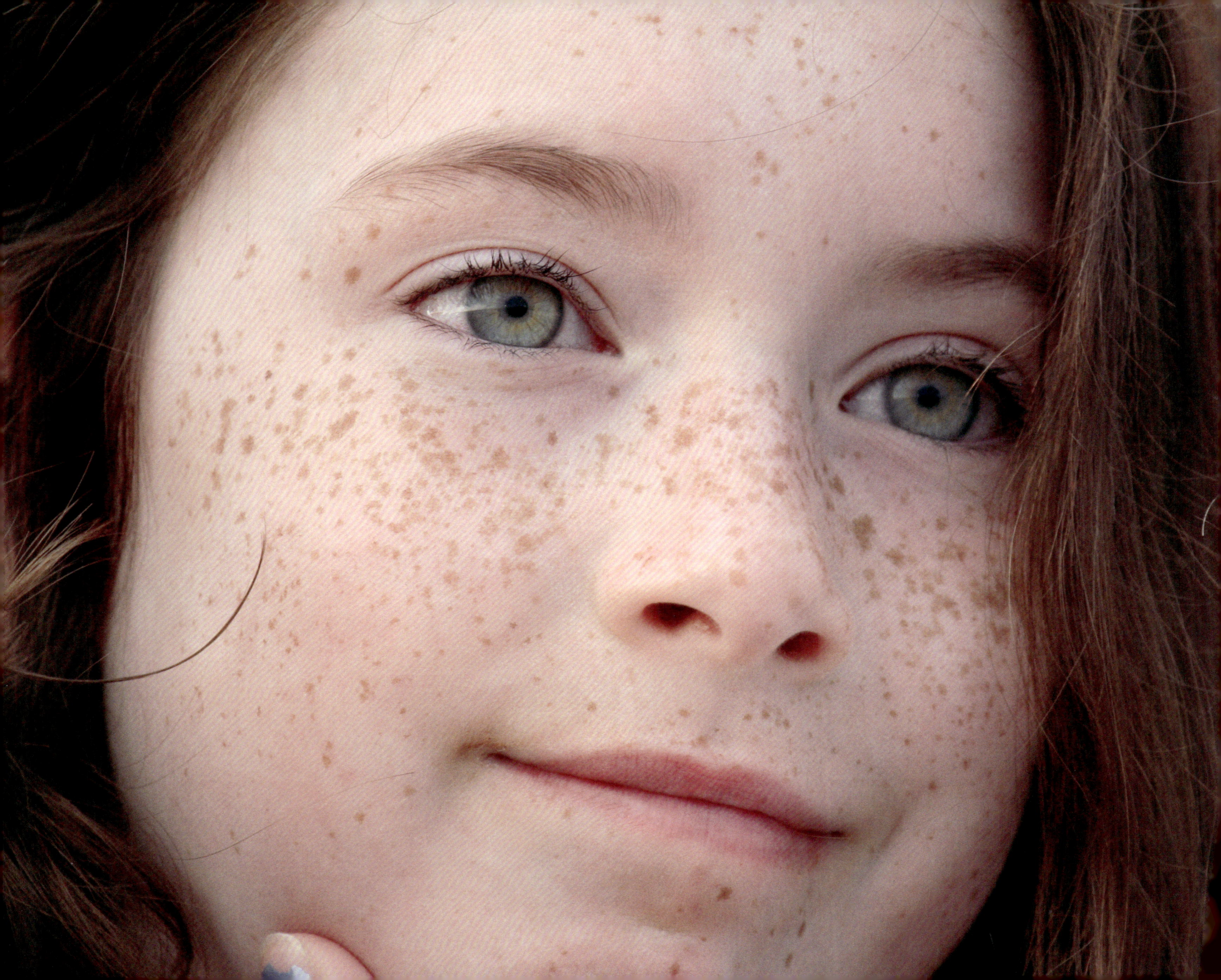

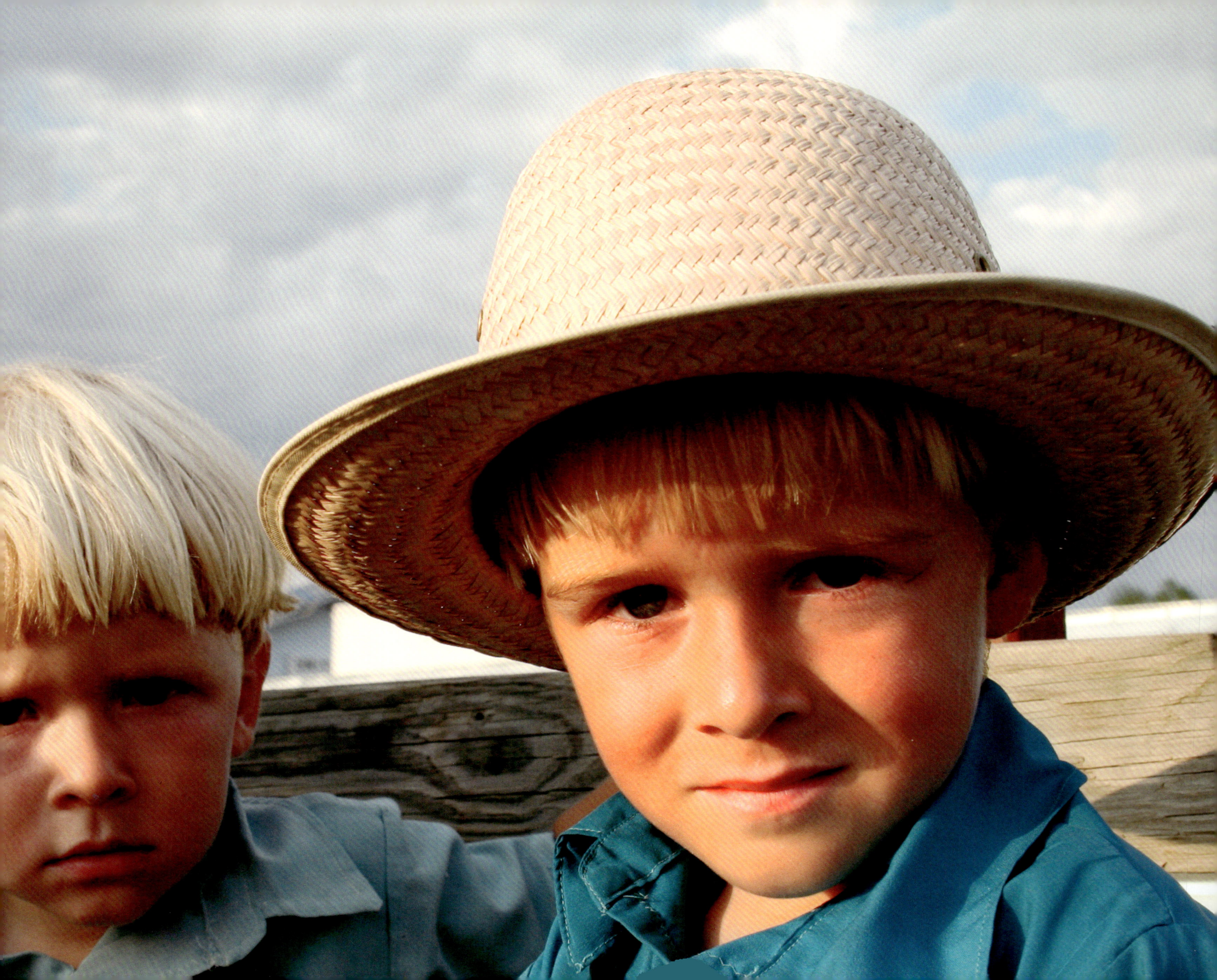

Far southeast is Nebraska's Amish country. Black horse carriages park next to double-cab pickups on grass parking lots. PAWNEE CITY

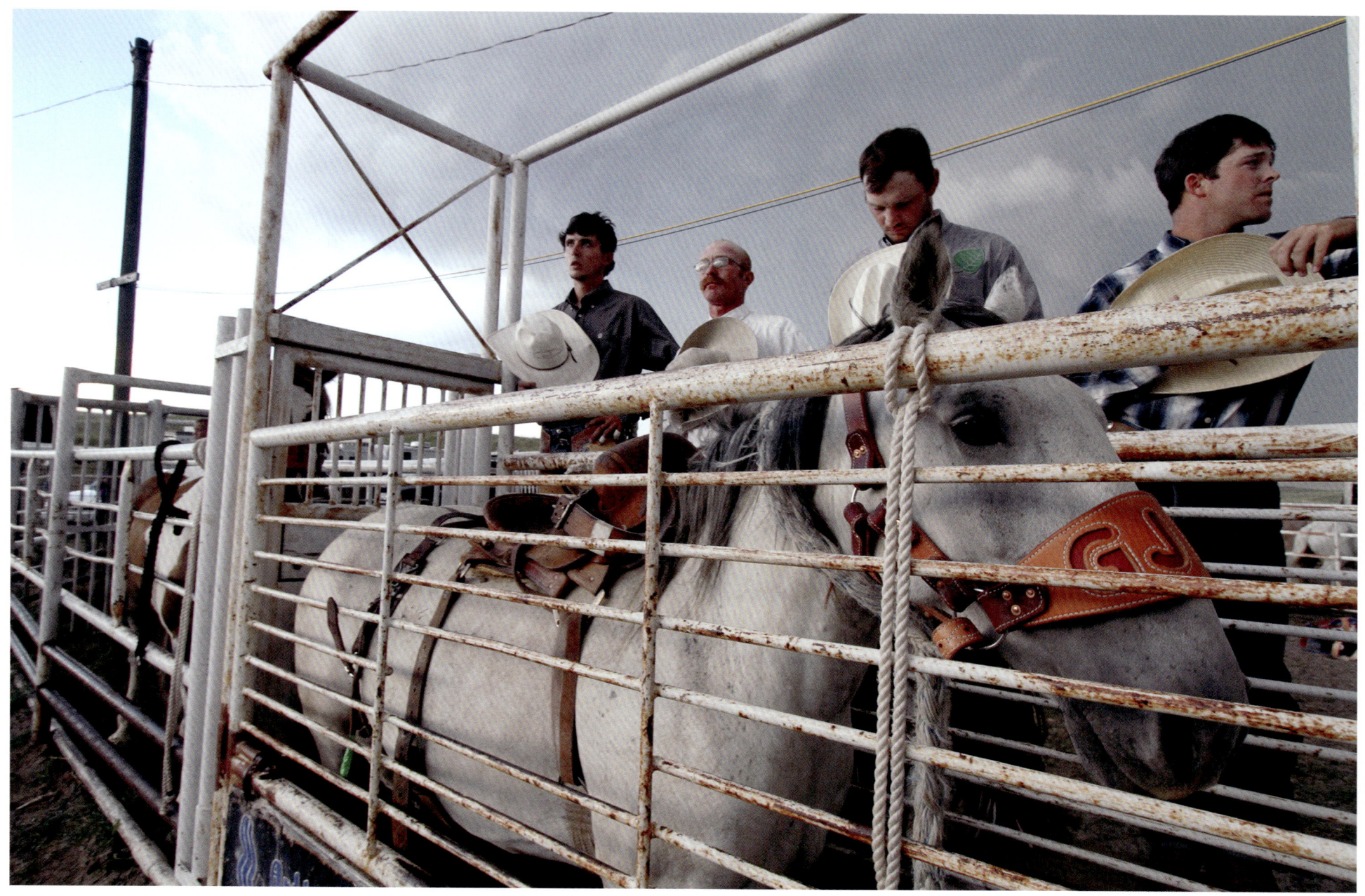

From the herd of stock contractor Kenny Kramer, saddle bronc Desert Storm waits his turn to buck during the National Anthem. Nervous but contained, the horse knows what's coming and what to do. This is his only job. ARTHUR

The Frantic and the Focused

PICKUP MEN AND BRONC CONTRACTORS

When a bronc rider makes the eight-second horn, in ride the pickup men. These bowlegged cowmen work for the company who brought the rough stock. With horseback skills matched by few in the world, these men know each bronc's quirks. Sandwiching the bronc between their pickup horses at a gallop, the first man reaches back to grab the rider's belt, and then the rider lunges for that pickup man's waist. Swinging his body off the still-bucking bronc, the rider aims to slide across the pickup horse's rump to the opposite side. There he hangs for a few beats while the procession slows. If done right his boots hit the ground running, but failed timing at high speed leads to nasty dismounts. Riders occasionally miss the lunge entirely, which is like shooting off a waterslide into a pool of dirt.

Contrary to bulls, which stop bucking once free of their rider, broncs keep bounding along, hack rein flopping, until a pickup man releases their flank strap. Dismounted bulls immediately seek a human target or the exit, not much concerned with the still-tightened strap. Perhaps panic has been mostly bred out of bucking bulls; they focus better under stress, channeling retaliation or retreat without short-circuiting their brain. Horses remain haywire until back with their herd.

Grabbing the bronc's rein at high speed, pickup men then lead the bronc out. Obstinate broncs run several laps before settling down. It is grand entertainment for the crowd, clods of dirt peppering the closest seats. Rodeo clowns incite laughter with mock horse-racing commentary, and cheers erupt when the bronc is finally penned. Poker-faced pickup men have heard it a hundred times.

I tell a bronc rider how it seems pickup men have the hardest work at the rodeo. "I wouldn't take their job for nothin'," he replies. That sounds peculiar coming from one who mounts wild horses every week, but while contestants might spend fifteen seconds from the swing of the gate to the end of their night, pickup men grind on in hot, dirty conditions all evening. In unspoken unison, they work at breakneck speeds on horses that need little guidance. It's odd when pickup horses converge with broncs: two highly trained, well-groomed animals scuffle to pen a dusty maniac of the same species.

Kenny Kramer is a rough-stock contractor and pickup man. Middle-aged, mustachioed, and cowboy capped, his actions in the arena are programmed by years of hard riding. On a sunny January afternoon I visited Kenny's Sandhills ranch west of Stapleton.

As we bounce along in Kenny's pickup, the trained horses raise their heads high to watch us. Kenny lures them with the daily feeding call: "BOYYYYS!" They gather around the pickup bed, finding only spilled dog food instead of the expected grain. Some sample it, producing sour faces with splayed lips exposing yellow teeth. They look stouter and wilder in their thick winter coats. A few extroverts seek attention but the others would rather not be touched. They know human hands might mean a saddle and then work.

Paul is a massive red roan with a bit of draft horse in his genes. He wants attention and doesn't care if it might mean work. Paul's size is unusual for a pickup horse. He forfeits some speed for mass, so in the arena Kenny steers to intercept at angles rather than simply chasing broncs down. Paul's large hooves throw twice the dirt as he thunders by. You can feel him running. "There isn't a bull he can't drag out on a rope," says Kenny.

Pickup horses undergo heavy training. Theirs is specialized work requiring courage and intelligence. The horse must continue to do its job even if the reins are knocked out of the rider's hand; actions must become muscle memory. But running shoulder to shoulder with a kicking bronc does not come naturally. Kenny and his wife, Angie, train by repetition. Atop a trainee, Angie chases down a seasoned horse ridden by Kenny. She steers the beginner until her leg is touching the shoulder of Kenny's horse, then she reaches back for Kenny as he grabs her waist and slides onto the rookie's rump as a bronc rider will do. Once a student learns to tolerate this chaotic nearness plus a man sliding around its hind quarters, it's ready. Novice horses are high-strung in their first real show. There is no simulating the violence a wild horse brings to the game.

Kenny is nearing the end of his career as a pickup man—two more years if all goes well. The legs take the biggest beating. Heavy quarter-inch leather chaps provide some protection from flying hooves, but uncovered body parts are at risk. Kenny has had frequent ankle breaks, his back takes a pounding, and thumb jams are common from releasing flank straps on unpredictable broncs.

Choosing studs carefully from around the U. S., Kenny and Angie have started their own breeding program with seven pregnant mares. Before breeding their own stock, they purchased bucking horses at regional sales where horses are bucked and then auctioned—the better the bucking, the better the price, from $250 to $3,000. Bucking bulls are sold the same way, buck then bid. Bulls that don't buck sell cheap and often become hamburger. They are livestock, which is a key word in this industry. As Kenny puts it, "Buckers are truly stock, versus our trained horses where lifetimes are spent together."

Kenny Kramer (*right*) grabs the bronc's rein as his partner reaches to free the flank strap. Horses collide then turn toward me, and in wet sand I trip into a backward somersault. Kenny turns hard left, pulling the ruckus barely by. The crowd loves it when I fall. Inevitably a devilish snicker arises. "Did you get a good shot of that?" ARTHUR

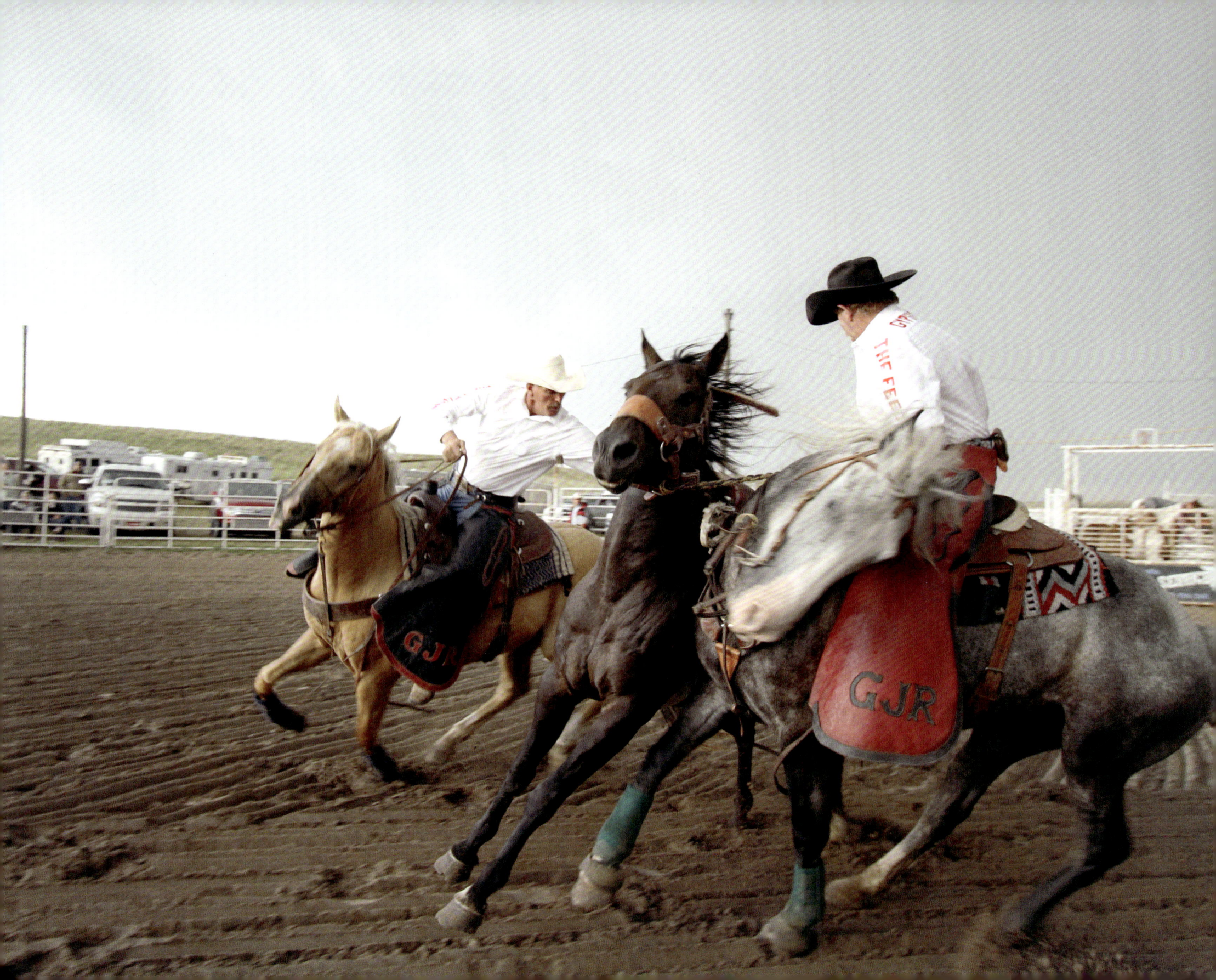

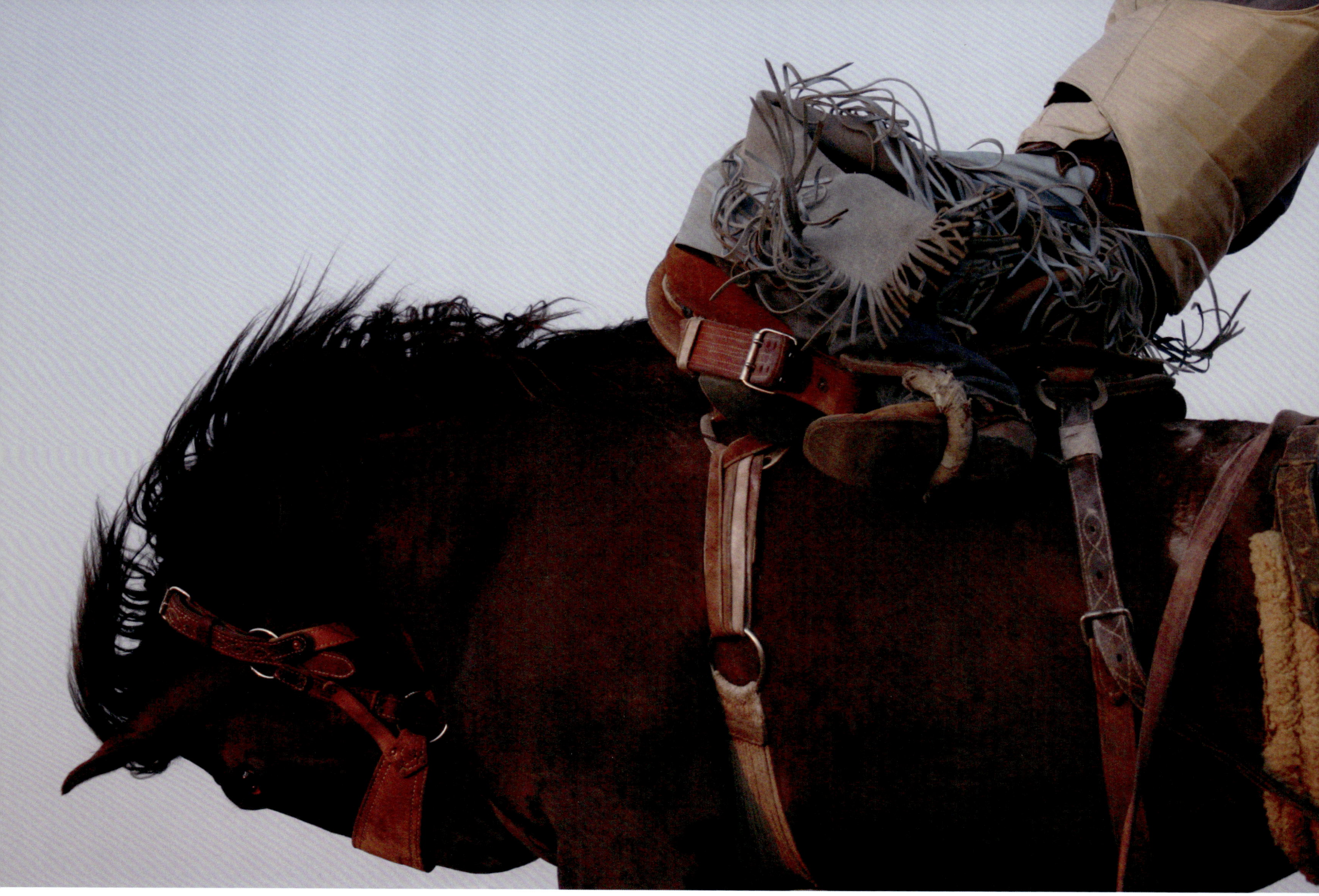

Moving into the adjacent pasture, separated by barbed wire fence, we visit Kenny's broncs. They gather around the pickup more readily than the trained herd did and without being called—they don't do ranch work so a pickup truck brings only good things. This herd is different though: they are warier, jumpier, and most don't let me near. Only one, named Fletch, allows a touch to his nose. He nudges for attention one minute and becomes uneasy and lurching the next. When I ignore him to photograph the others he bites my back—not to hurt me, but to get my attention so I might pet his nose again.

Broncs' eyes are wilder, their manes more tangled, and they are generally larger than the trained herd. Names fit markings or personalities, such as Icicle, Arrow Head, and Rockin' Chair. There is Gloria with a long, messy mane like a woman on a bad hair day. Gun Smoke was one of their first; he is beloved, but even favorite broncs are not family pets. When their usefulness ends their next stop is the sale barn, which is the typical last stage in any American ranch horse's life. Expenses trump sentiment. But broncs live great portions of their lives in leisure compared to regular ranch horses. Enduring a few minutes of arena panic twice a week each summer is the price they pay not to work cattle year-round. "These are our equine athletes," says Angie, "and we take good care of them. What most people don't realize is that those buckin' horses get treated better than most saddle horses."

The broncs' pastoral dispositions at home contrasts starkly with rodeo night, where they become violent, grunting beasts, tongues hanging in exertion. Fights are prevented by keeping tame horses separate from broncs at all times. "Sometimes when corralled before the rodeo, the broncs and pickup horses stand up to each other across the fence," says Kenny. Prickly stare-downs occur, like fighters before a match. A few rivalries are ongoing. Blue Duck, a notorious blue roan bronc, has a grudge against Kenny's horse, Paul. Blue Duck does what he can to harm Paul when Kenny rides in—kicking, biting, and throwing his head like a hammer. Paul knows it will come but he does his job without flinching, same as Kenny. It is the cowboy way.

A bronc's power is unimaginable to those who haven't ridden rough stock. Riders get to know each bronc and how they behave. Says one champion, "If you don't know the horse you draw, then you find a competitor who does and he'll share the horses' quirks with you. On paper it's between you and the competitor, but it's really you against the horse." BERTRAND

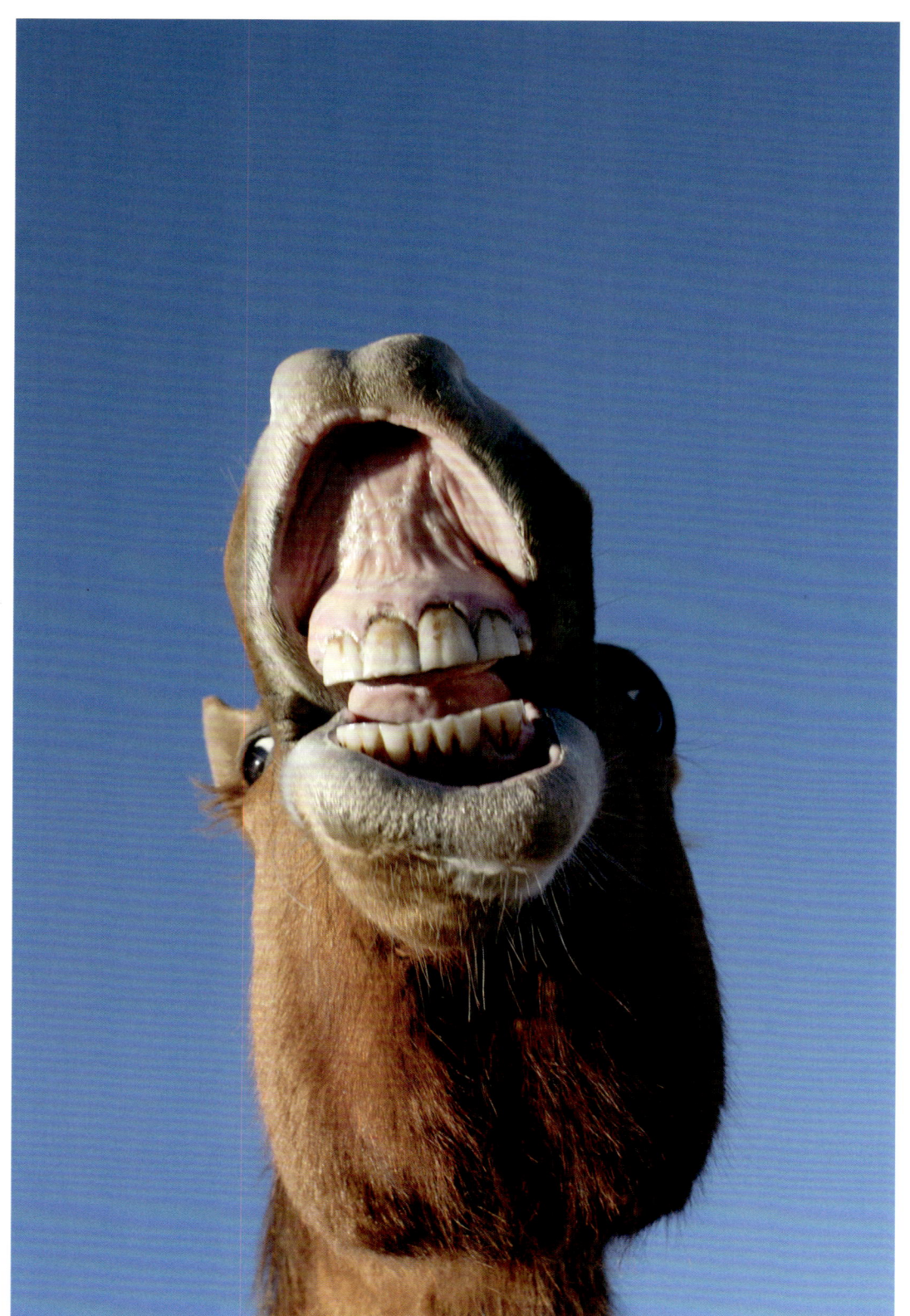

The universal face for "Yuck!" Reaching into the pickup bed in search of grain, this bucking bronc finds spilled dog food instead. KRAMER RANCH, NEAR STAPLETON

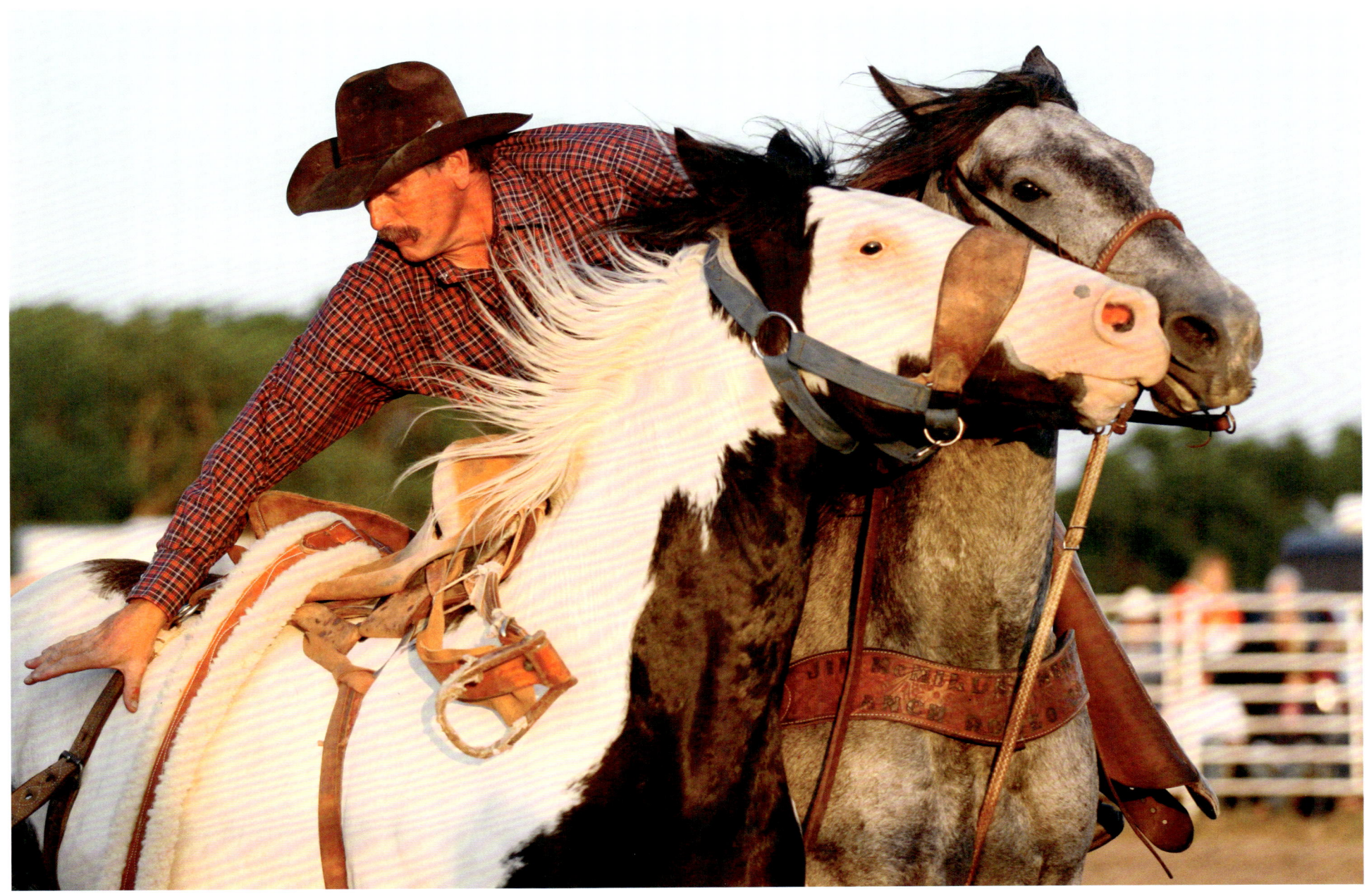

I always find it odd when a pickup horse converges with a bronc: a highly trained, well-groomed animal scuffles to pen a dusty maniac of the same species. CALLAWAY

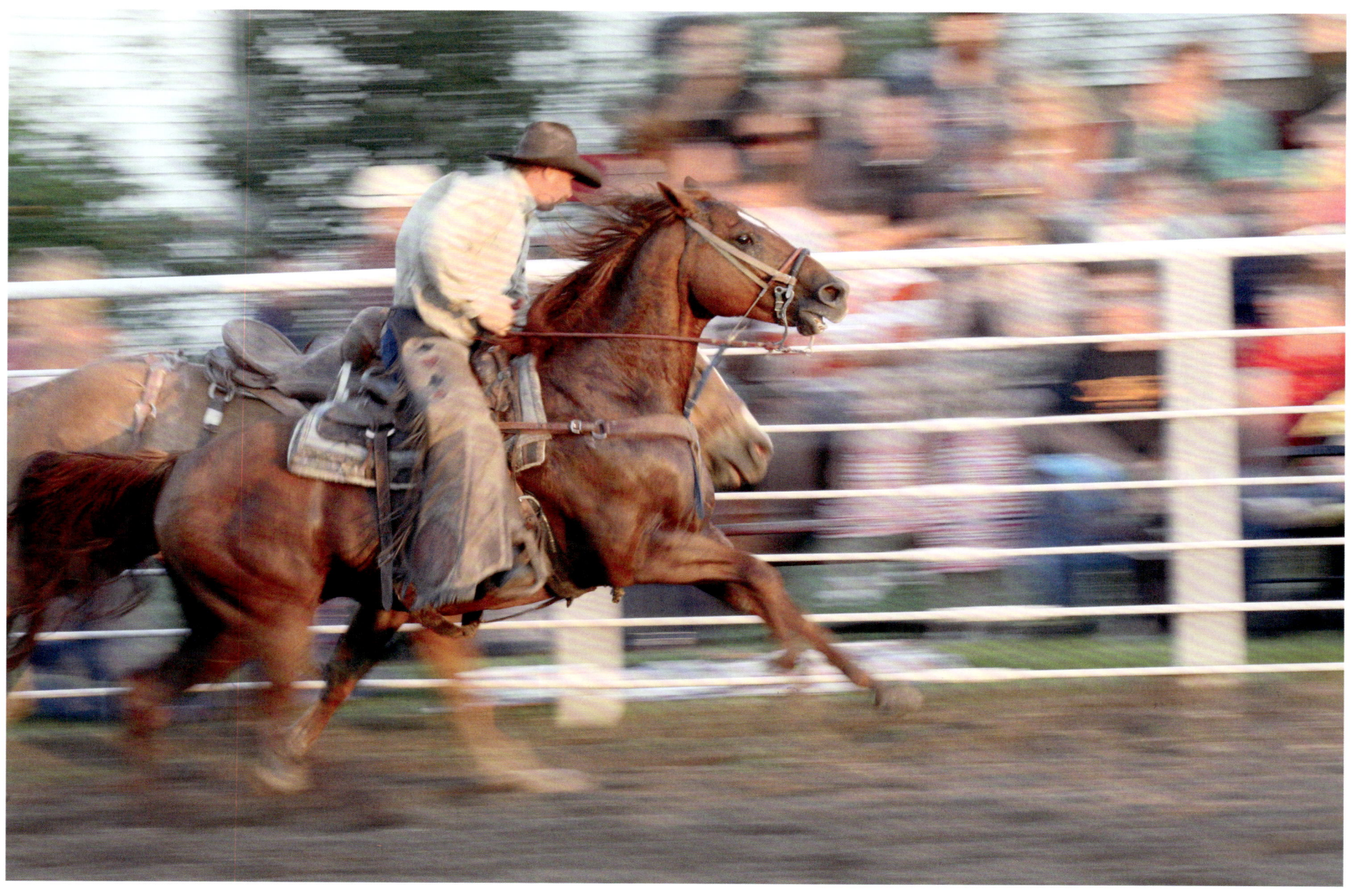

"I wouldn't take their job for nothin'," says a bucking bronc
rider about pickup men. CLEARWATER

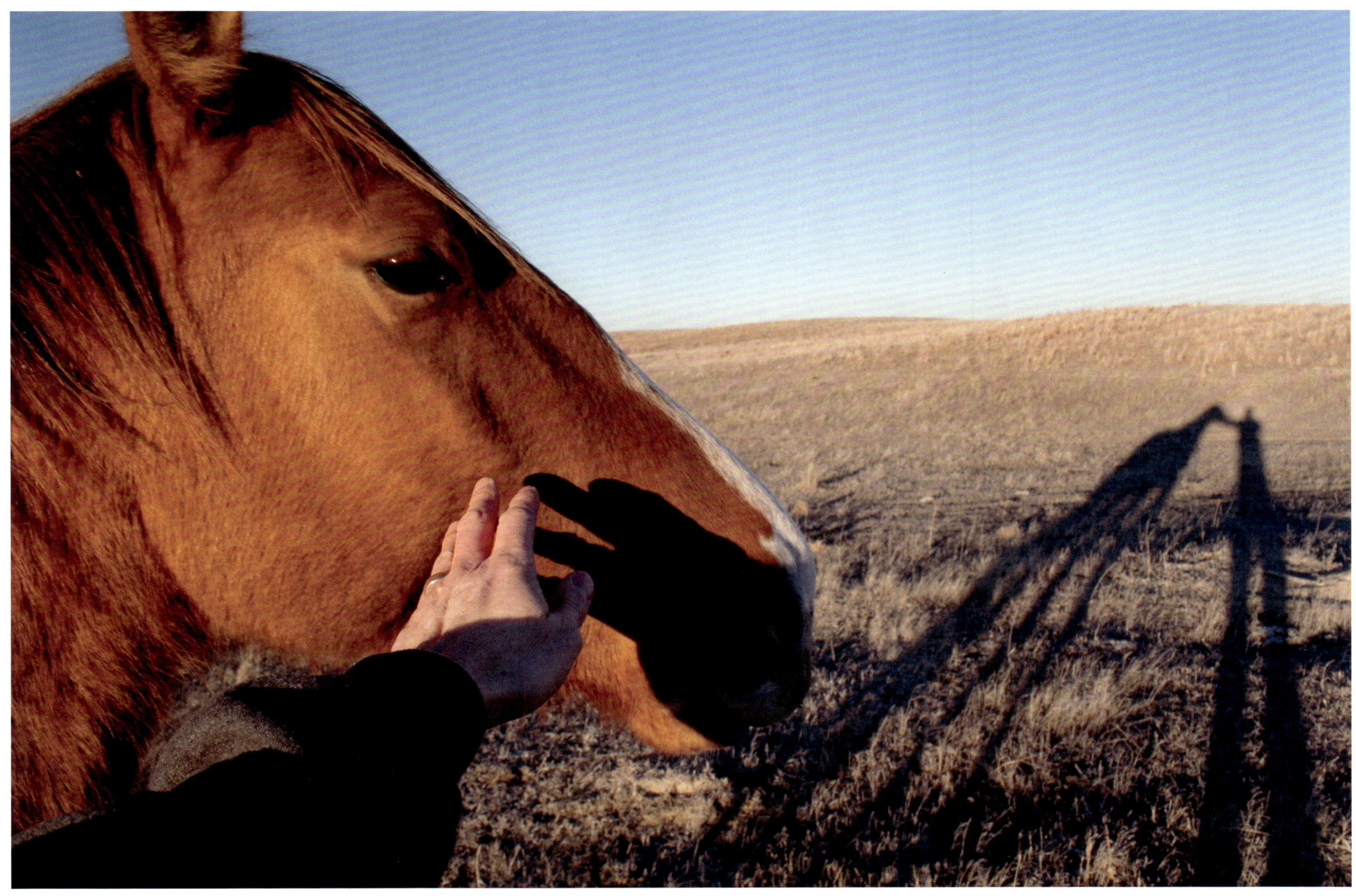

In the bucking broncs' home pasture, only Fletch allows my touch, but he does so with a strange combination of affection-seeking and jumpiness. When I turned from him he bites my back—not to be nasty, but to prompt me to pet again. KRAMER RANCH, NEAR STAPLETON

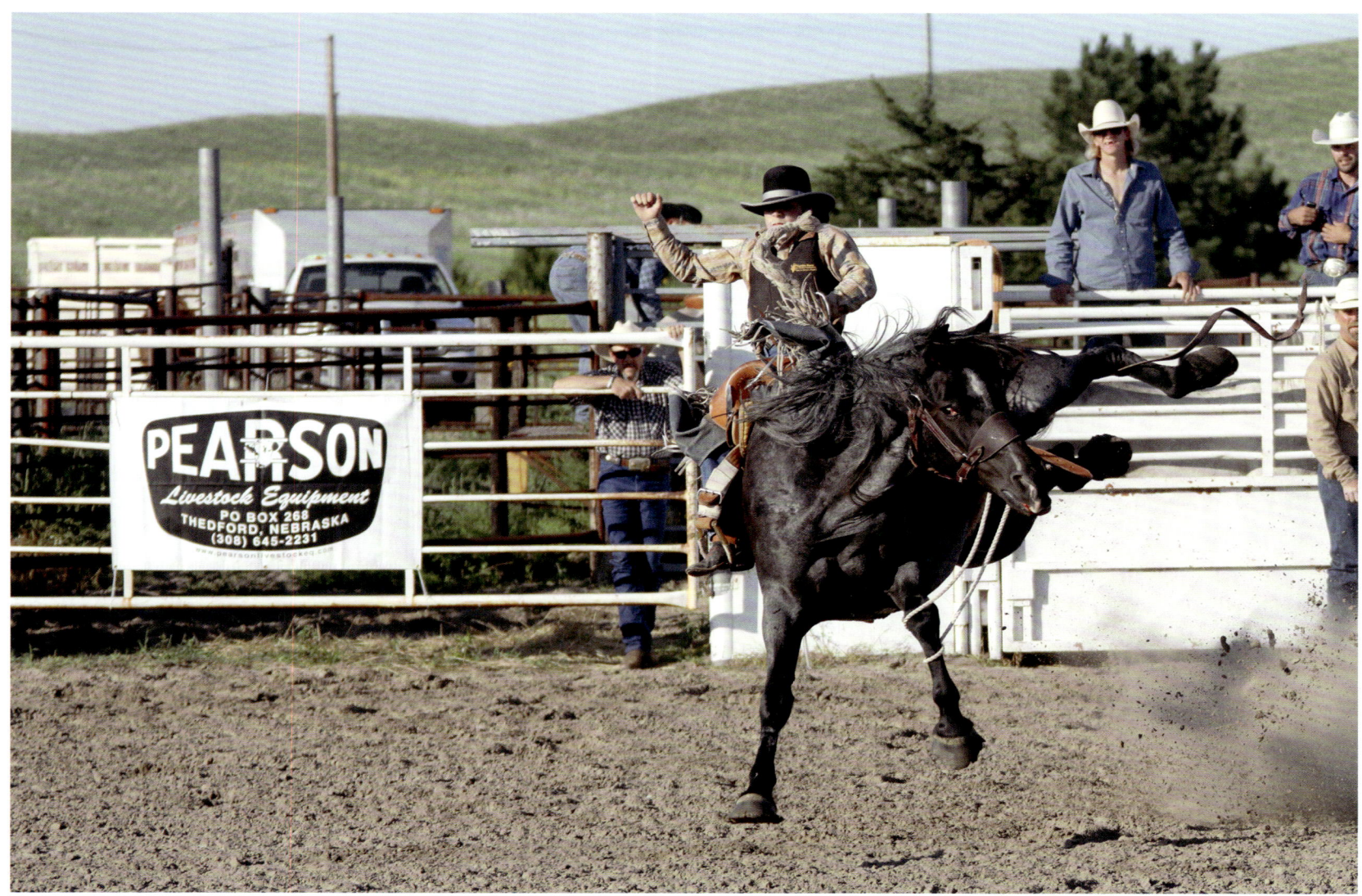

(*above*) Zane Smith experiences the wrath of Blue Ridge, one of Kenny Kramer's craziest horses. Blue Ridge will recover from this contortion—barely—and Zane will ride eight seconds and take third place. What's the worst part of the rodeo circuit? "You don't get time to heal up," says Zane. "You're always ridin' sore." THEDFORD

(*opposite*) One of the Kramers' first broncs, Gun Smoke, performs his single role on earth. Other than these brief moments in the arena every summer, Gun Smoke's life is that of pastoral leisure. And though Gun Smoke is loved, he is still considered stock; he is not a family pet. STAPLETON

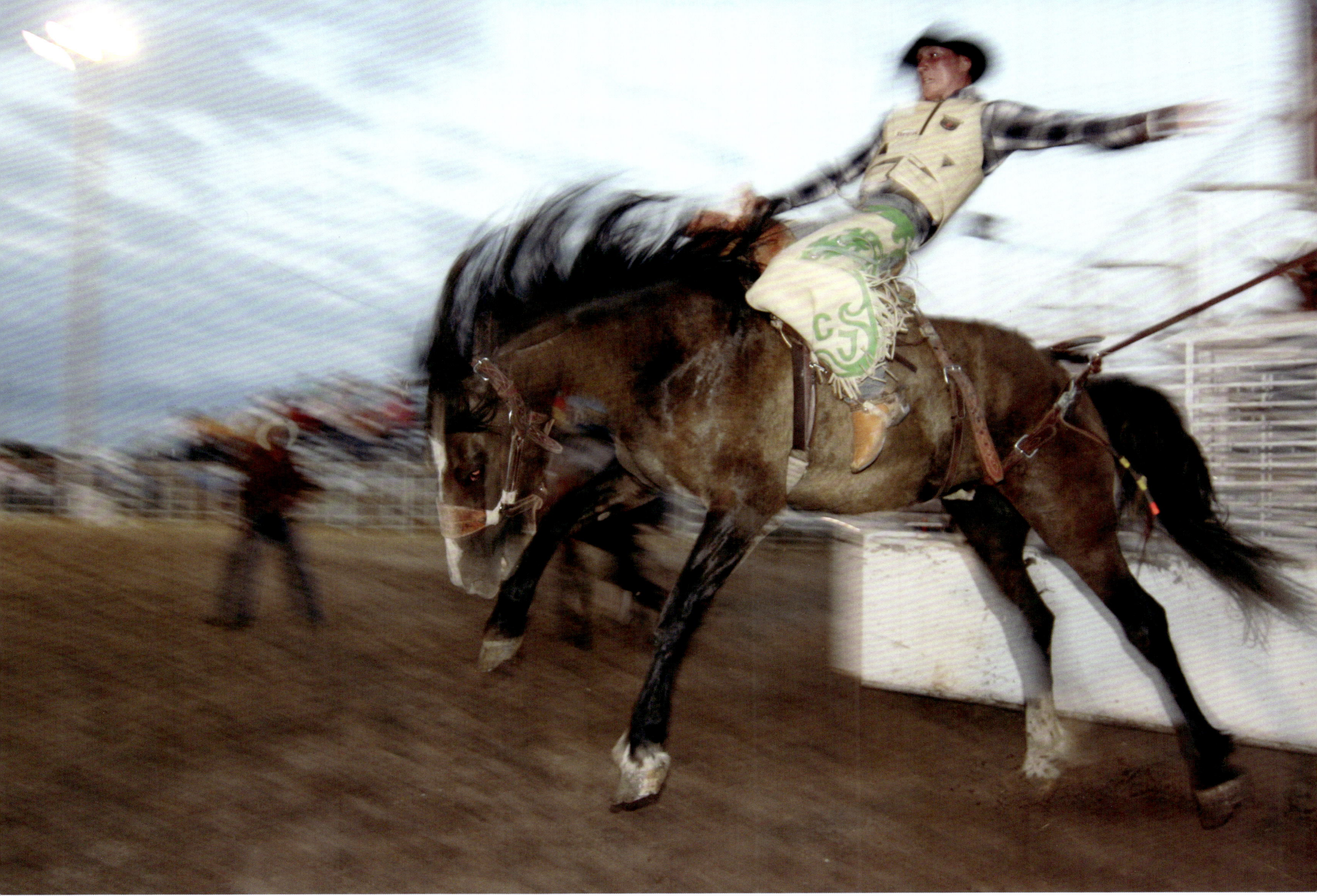

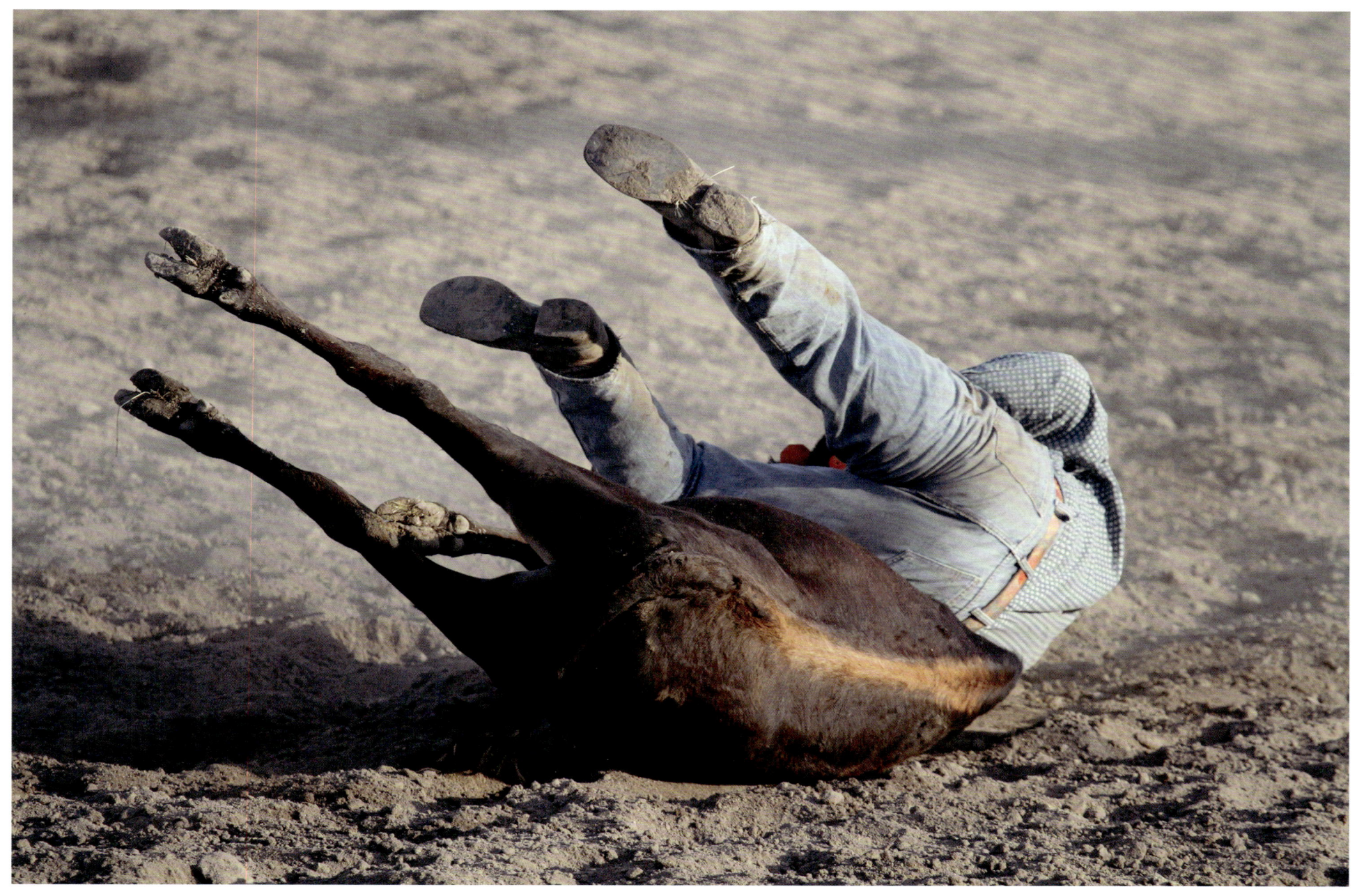

Steer wrestling is for rodeo arenas only; no sane cowboy does this on the job. NELSON

"I'll be ropin' 'til I can't get on a horse no more"

MEN'S TIMED EVENTS

Few closer partnerships exist in any sport than the timed-event rider and their horse, anticipating each other in fluid motion. Waiting on horseback near starting gates, competitors try to focus their minds before they rope, wrestle, or race. Fractions of seconds matter in timed events.

Stockmen jostle wary calves through a funneled fence toward the chute where a trip rope encircles their necks. Hesitating calves soon find a large man shoving their rear end. The roper backs his twitchy horse into the far corner of the starting box as the calf fidgets in the chute. Horse and rider need every inch; ten-second penalties come from breaking their starting box's bungee barrier before the calf breaks its trip rope. A jittery horse doesn't settle well, and a patient rider guides it with slight movements of rein and knees while the horse circles like a dog looking for a place to lie. A nod signals the chute operator to slam the release lever. Horses seem catapulted into the ring at the lever's loud clunk. Calves never hesitate; they want out. They run without strategy toward open ground and escape.

The lasso spins high as the rider leans over the horse's mane. On calm nights the rope rips through the air with an audible whoosh. Champions are made by decades of practicing quick, subtle motions; youngsters don't fare well in this event. Modesty and respectfulness guide behavior after a ride. Never does one outwardly celebrate a good performance in Nebraska speed events, nor does one fuss over failure. These competitors see one another week after week and many are friends and relatives.

Garret Nokes of McCook, Nebraska, is a rancher, tie-down roper, team roper, steer wrestler, and a regular winner. Cattle and horses define him. Like most who succeed in timed events, he is a veteran who takes the sport seriously. At it since age ten, Garret is now thirty-eight. Steer wrestling, also known as bulldogging, is hard on the body; it is a younger man's sport. Garret has lost teeth against a steer's horns and had pectoral muscle torn from the bone in a recent steer-wrestling mishap. This signals the end of his steer wrestling days. Now he's focused on roping, saying, "I'll be ropin' 'til I can't get on a horse no more."

Garret used to buy his roping horses, but now he breeds his own. A fully trained calf-roping horse, a "finished" horse as they're called, costs $30,000 to $150,000 depending on their lineage. Pros on the national circuit buy those. In regional rodeo, cowboys are more likely to buy a partially trained horse and finish the training themselves. Young men getting started might buy a more affordable older finished horse with three to five good years left in it.

Training a tie-down horse is intensive work, but this is a sport where a good horse makes all the difference. "The only time we control the horse is setting them up in the box and telling them when to go," Garret says. "As soon as you throw the rope the horse does the rest on its own, including knowing when to stop." And stop they do! Though a roping horse's quickness is purely natural, its halts are extraordinary. Once the rope catches a calf's neck the horse straightens all four legs at an abrupt forward angle, digging into loose, deep arena dirt. Clouds of earth billow upwards and some horses nearly drag their rump straining for traction. Using the last bit of the horse's forward momentum, the rider vaults off the saddle then runs the length of the rope to the calf.

Flipping the two-hundred-something-pound calf to its side, the cowboy then grabs a tie-down rope held in his teeth. He loops and cinches three legs, and then raises his hands to stop time. Winning times are under nine seconds on a good run. Trained to hinder the calf's escape attempts, the horse keeps tension on the rope until the rider remounts. Then the rope is slackened and the calf is granted six seconds to wiggle free and ruin the roper's day.

Steer wrestling is explosive. It takes a big guy to bring down a 500-600 pound animal, and it takes guts to do it off the back of a sprinting horse. Like so many events in rodeo, the event leaves city slickers asking, "Why would anyone do that?" The cowboys have the answer: "Because that's how you wrestle a steer."

No animal can dodge a rope—ropes seem to come from nowhere—but a man approaching alongside on horseback is avoidable, and the steer wants only to avoid. That's where the hazer comes in. It is the hazer's job to gallop along the steer's opposite side and block it from veering. If all goes well then everything stays on a straight path as the steer runs between horses like a car caught between two semi-trailers. Moving thirty miles per hour, the bulldogger dives off his horse and onto the horns. Dirt spews from boot heels, digging into the arena while the cowboy tackles the steer to its side.

More judo than tackling, it's about upsetting the steer's balance in flowing motion; where the head goes, so goes the body. Some steers'

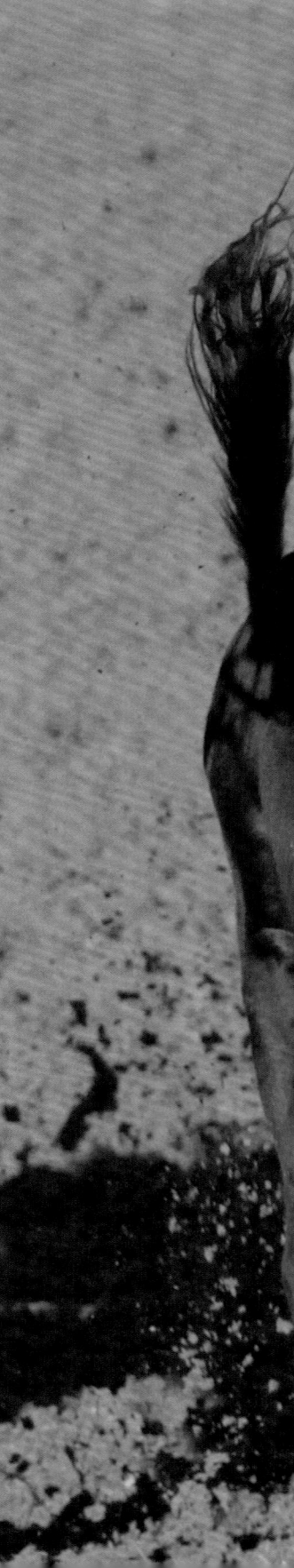

Positioned perfectly here, the wrestler drops off his highly-trained horse and onto the steer's head. Bearing one of my favorite cowboy names on the rodeo circuit, Goober Snider is the prototypical bulldogger. CLEARWATER

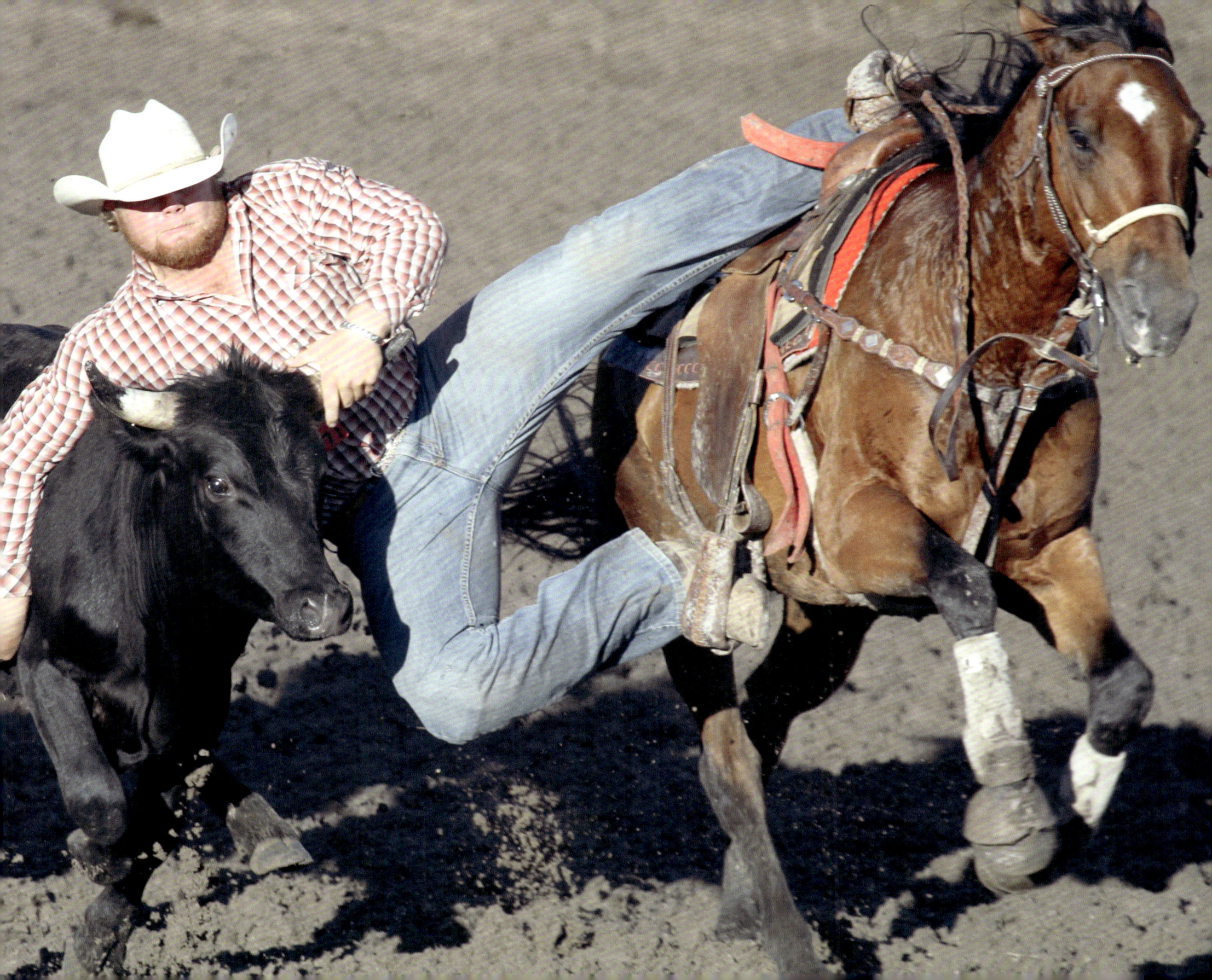

necks seem rubberlike. A failed first attempt results in a wrestling match, but by then it is about pride, not winning. Surprisingly few wrestlers are seriously hurt in this most dangerous timed event. Those making it look easy have years of experience and a phenomenal horse.

"Some of these steer wrestling horses are as fast as any horse in the world for the first fifty feet," Garret Nokes says. To catch a speedy steer a horse needs what cowboys call top-end speed, that finishing push. Pro-level horses with that quickness help cowboys win consistently in Nebraska rodeos. "You look for the lineage that brings you what you need in every event," he says, "but you never know. The best horse I ever had came out of a pen headed for the stockyard."

Top steer wrestling horses are trained only for steer wrestling. "Some of them are so specially trained they're not good for anything else," says Garret. "They're hard to ride around the pasture because they just want to sprint." If there is trouble with the horse it is normally in the starting box. Like sprinters before the gun, their energy is hard to confine.

Team roping brings another traditional ranching skill to the arena. If there is reason to catch and restrain a large animal on a ranch, then that is a two-person job. Two men, or a man and a woman in mixed team roping, each has specific duties. One ropes the head and the other the back legs: a header and a heeler. Horses are specialized in heads or heels as well. Casual rodeo fans might hit the concession stand during team roping; each attempt goes more or less the same, but team roping is a big deal in the rodeo world. Most cowboys and cowgirls in the crowd have team-roped at some point in their life. Team-roping-only events have grown exponentially during the last twenty-five years after national roping associations created a handicapping system similar to golf, in which ropers compete against people only as good as they are. This system allows everyone in the family to compete and to have a fair chance of winning big money in their division. Longtime roping relationships include family teams of fathers, mothers, sons, daughters, cousins, aunts and uncles.

Capturing and subduing a large steer solo is possible, but doing so requires an unusual skill. Steer roping, or steer tripping as it is sometimes called, is an event not commonly seen at rodeos. One man, one horse, and one steer enter the arena at full speed. Horns are snared and with a quick turn of the horse, the steer is tripped to the ground. Imagine a team jump-roping error with one end of the rope held by the steer's horns and the other dallied to the saddle horn. With the rope powered by 1,000 pounds of horse, the steer's back legs are tripped. If done correctly the steer ends up on its side and the cowboy races over to lash three legs before it can rise. The horse plays a key role by keeping the rope taut, hindering the steer's ability to stand.

Stewart Allen of North Platte is a seasoned steer roper who knows what makes a roper successful. "Perpetual winners practice relentlessly and they also have the best horse," he says. "And the horse must have the desire to rodeo." Some of Stewart's horses can't wait to get in the trailer. "You have to consider how special these horses are. They stand in a bouncing trailer for hours at a time. They have to keep their balance in there. It's hard for them to rest. Then they may have an hour out of the trailer before they compete, then they get right back into the trailer for the next destination." Top horses thrive in this ever-moving rodeo life just as top men and women do.

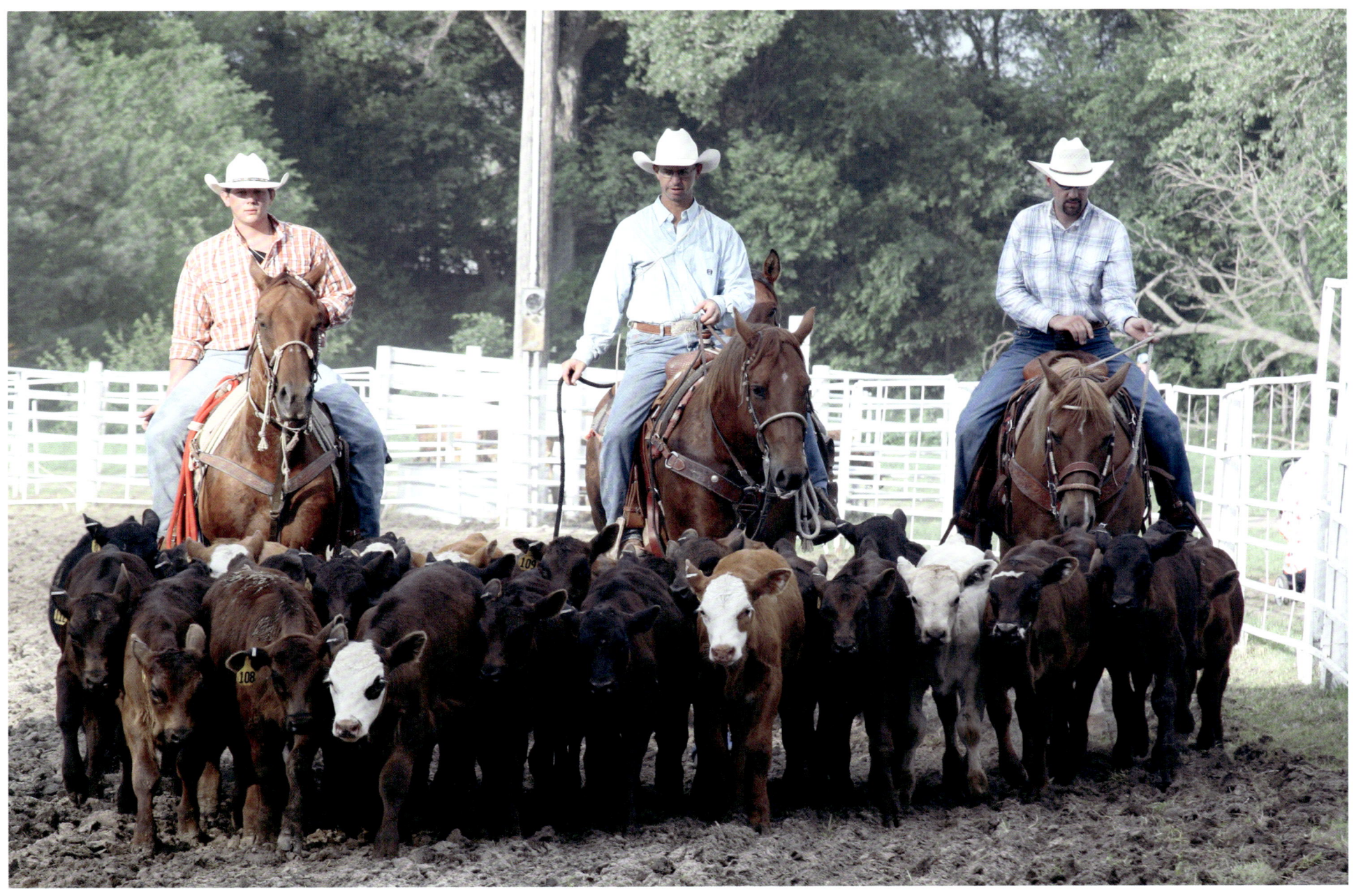

Herded from the corrals across to the chutes, this is the scene before
every rodeo as calves are readied for roping. WOLBACH

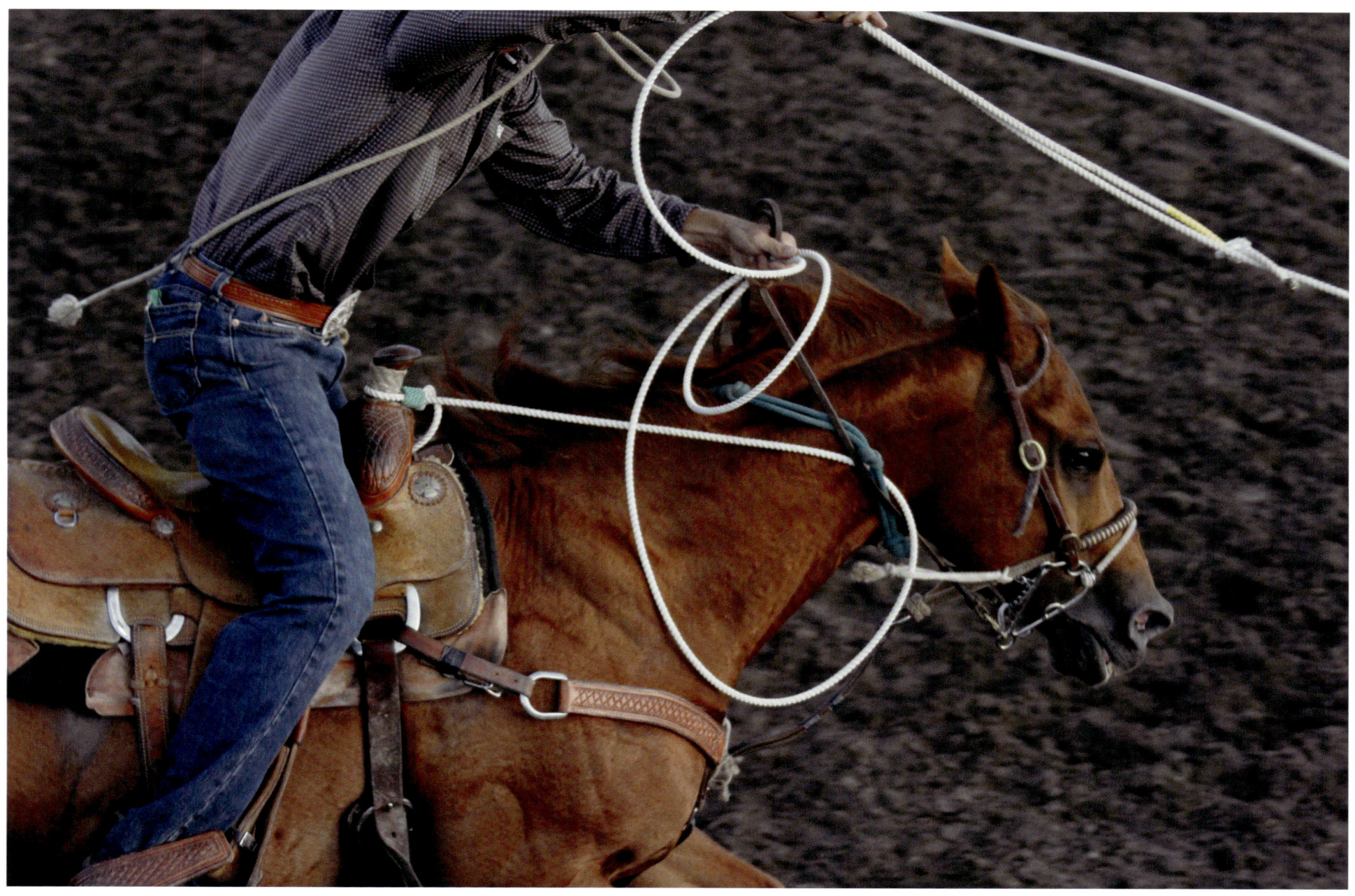

It's all about the horse, say the ropers. Like a Labrador obsessed with retrieving birds, these horses want to chase down livestock. A trained roping horse with strong desire might sell for $150,000. CRETE

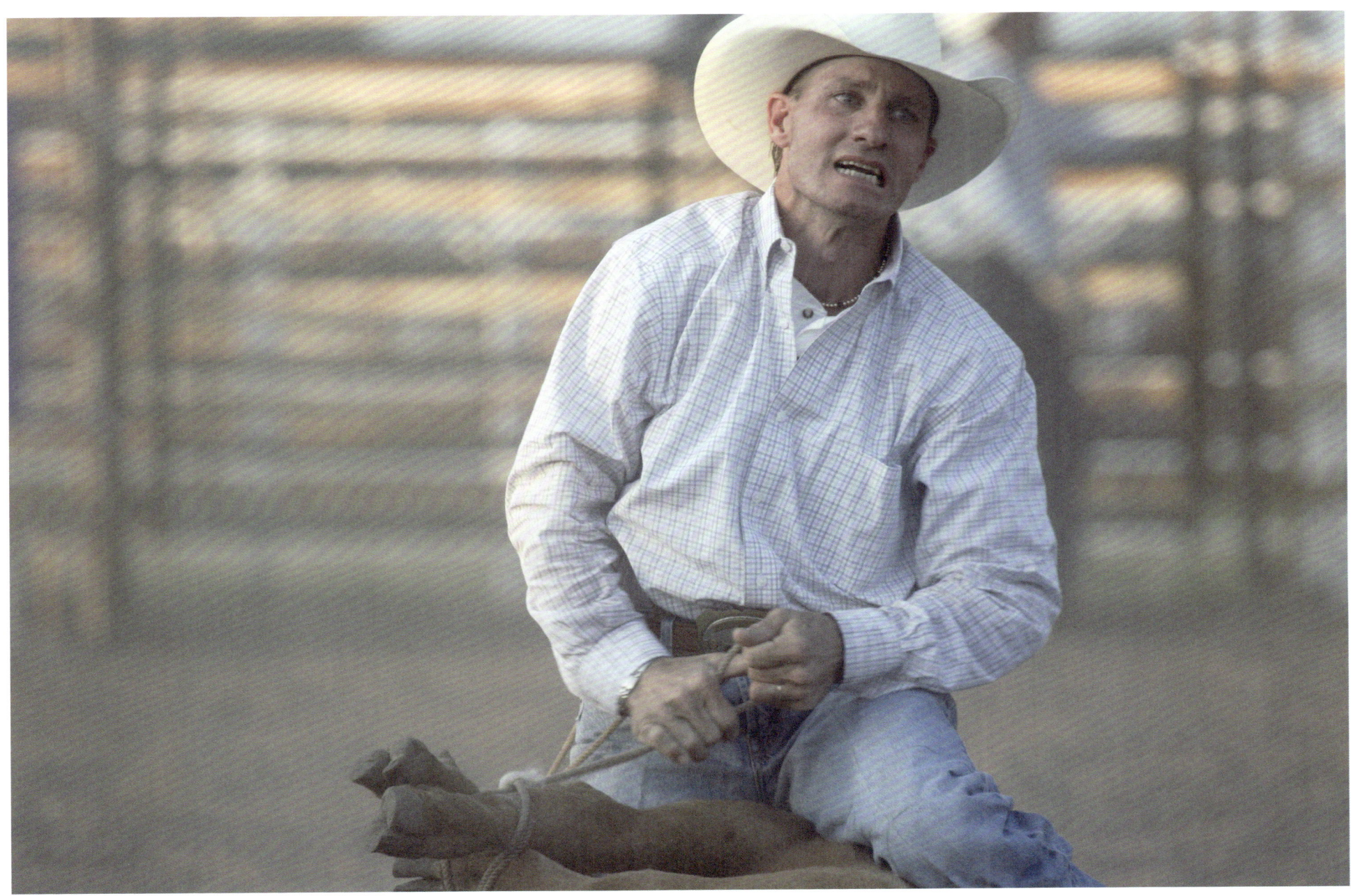

Enveloped in a cloud of dust, this roper can tie three legs of a calf faster than you can tie a shoe. Like little brother pinned by big brother, the calf doesn't resist much at this point; it just wants it over with. FREMONT

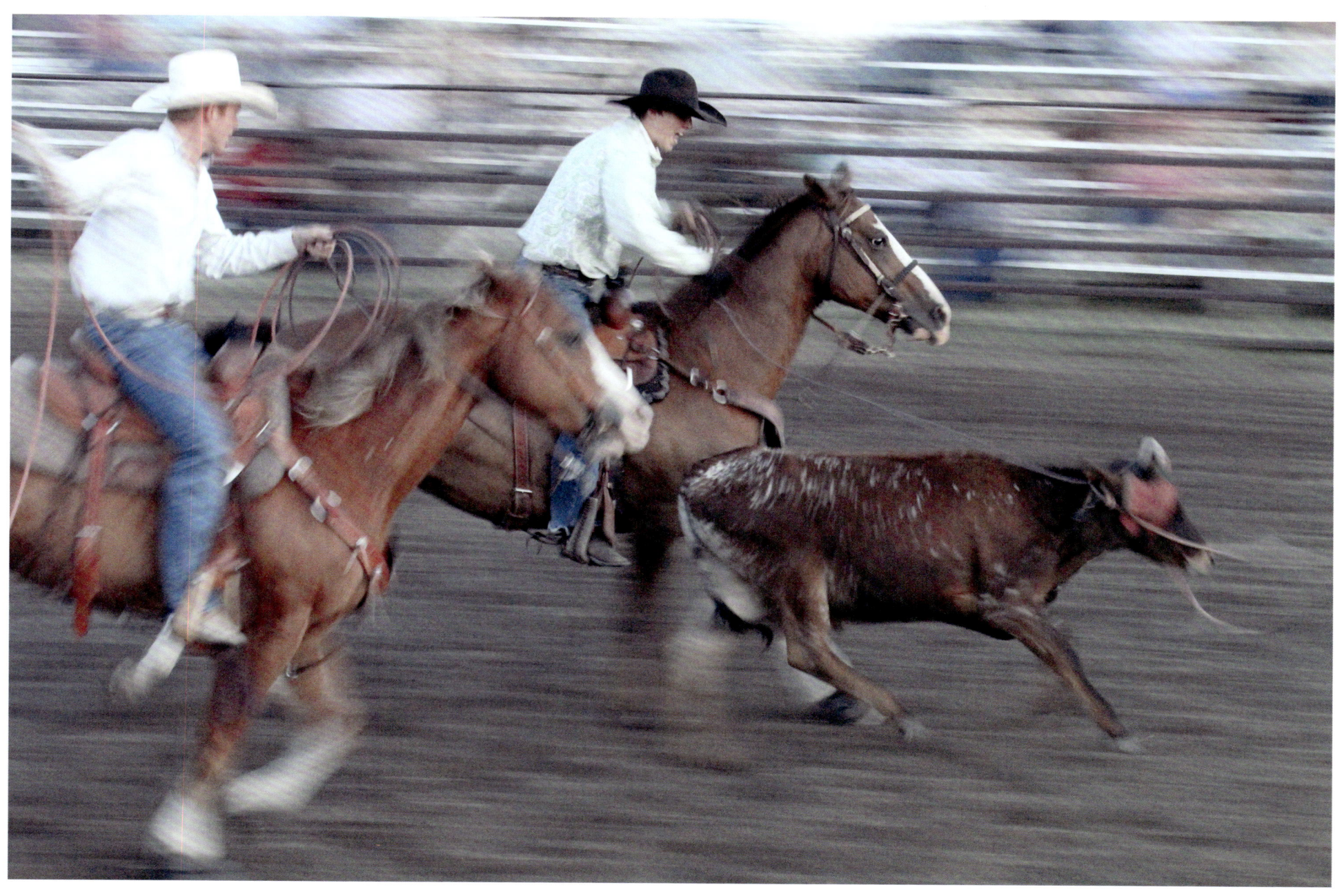

Team roping is rodeo's biggest, fastest growing sport. Roping-only events with massive jackpots quietly proceed across the U.S. year-round. NORDEN

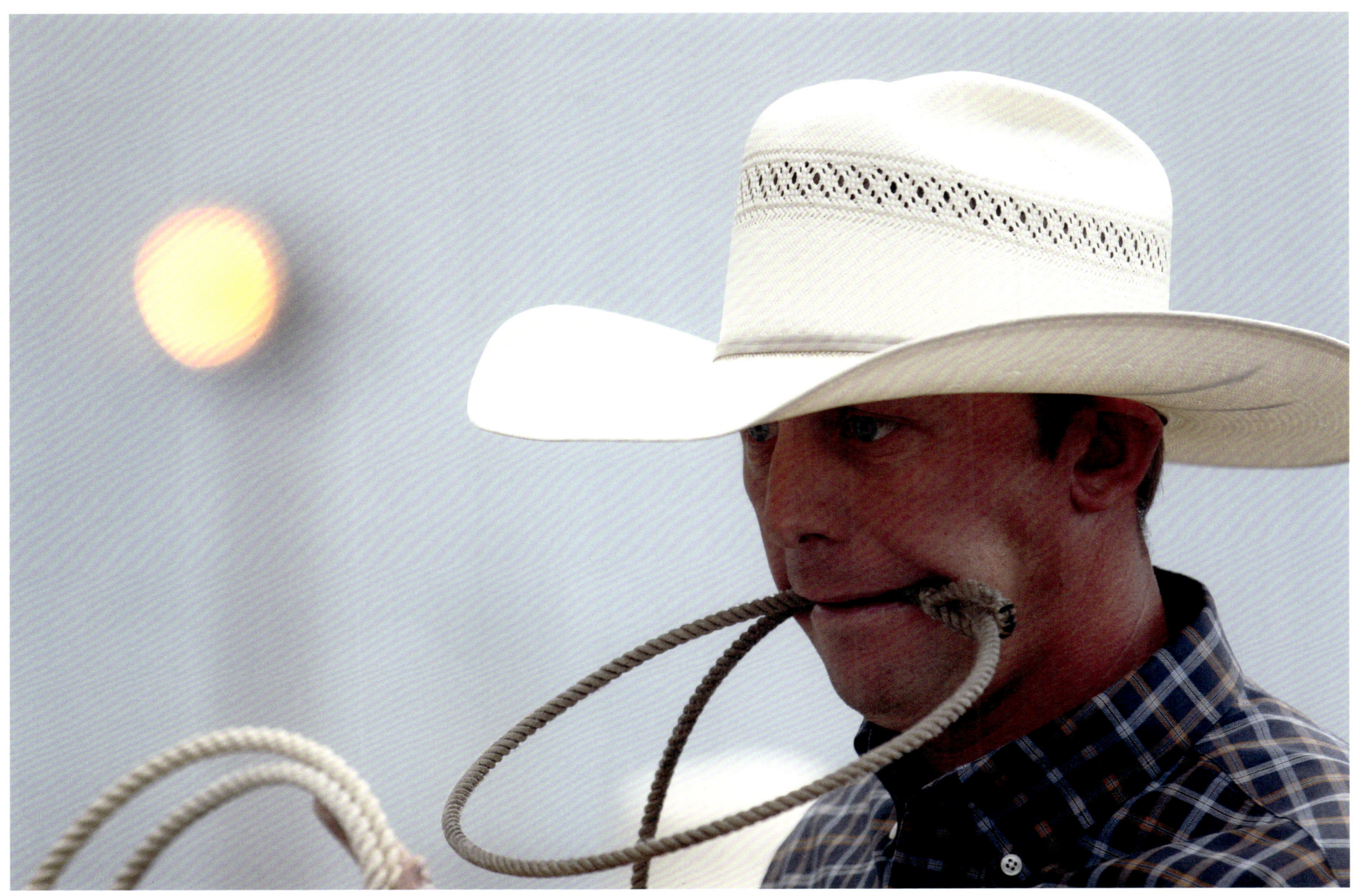

Hands busy with rope and reins, this is where the tie-down rope goes before the chute swings. SUTHERLAND

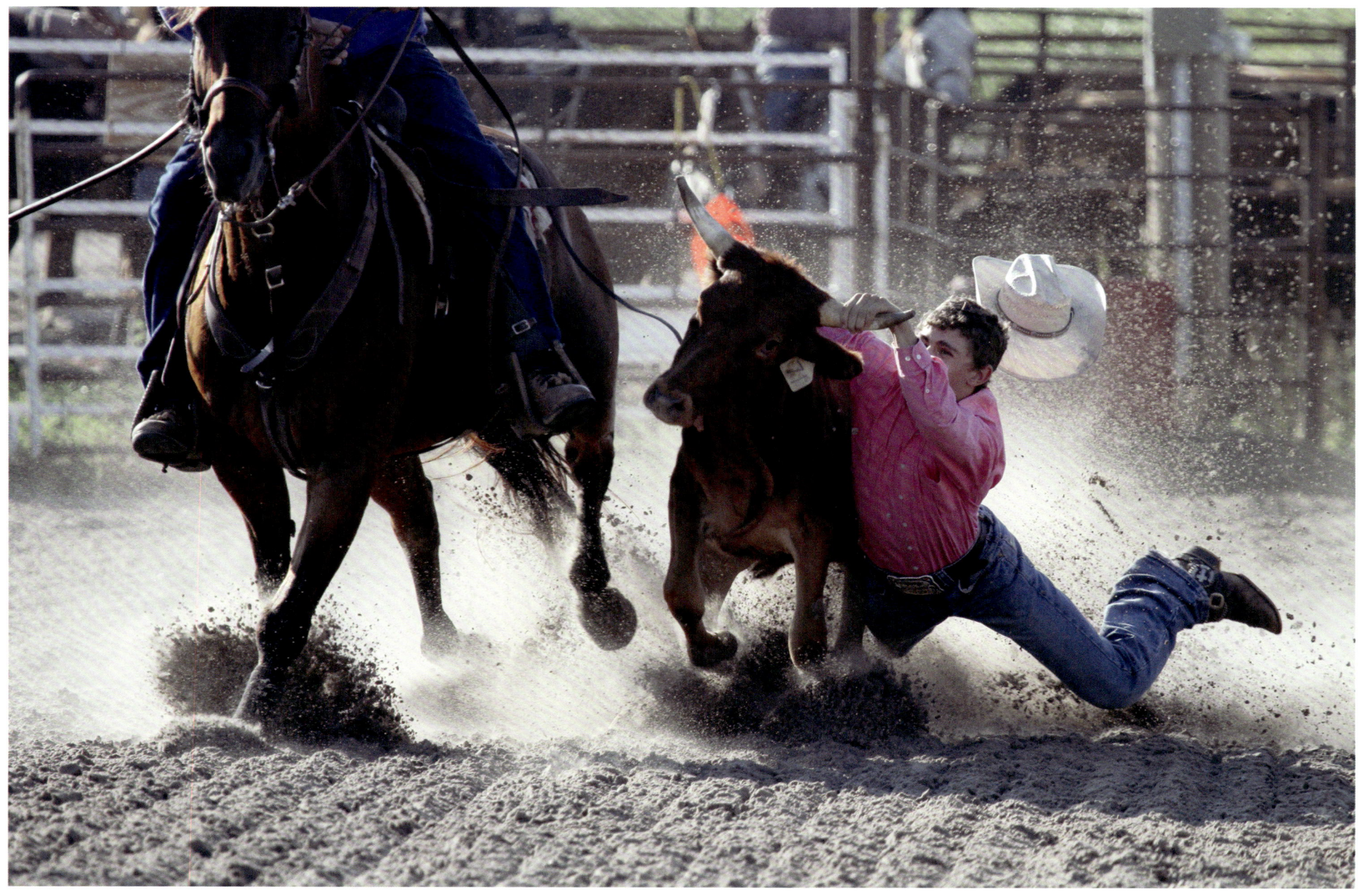

Never give up! That's the theme in bulldogging. Dragged a ways and dirtied up, this wrestler will swing his heels out front, brake the steer to a stop, and then take it down. THEDFORD

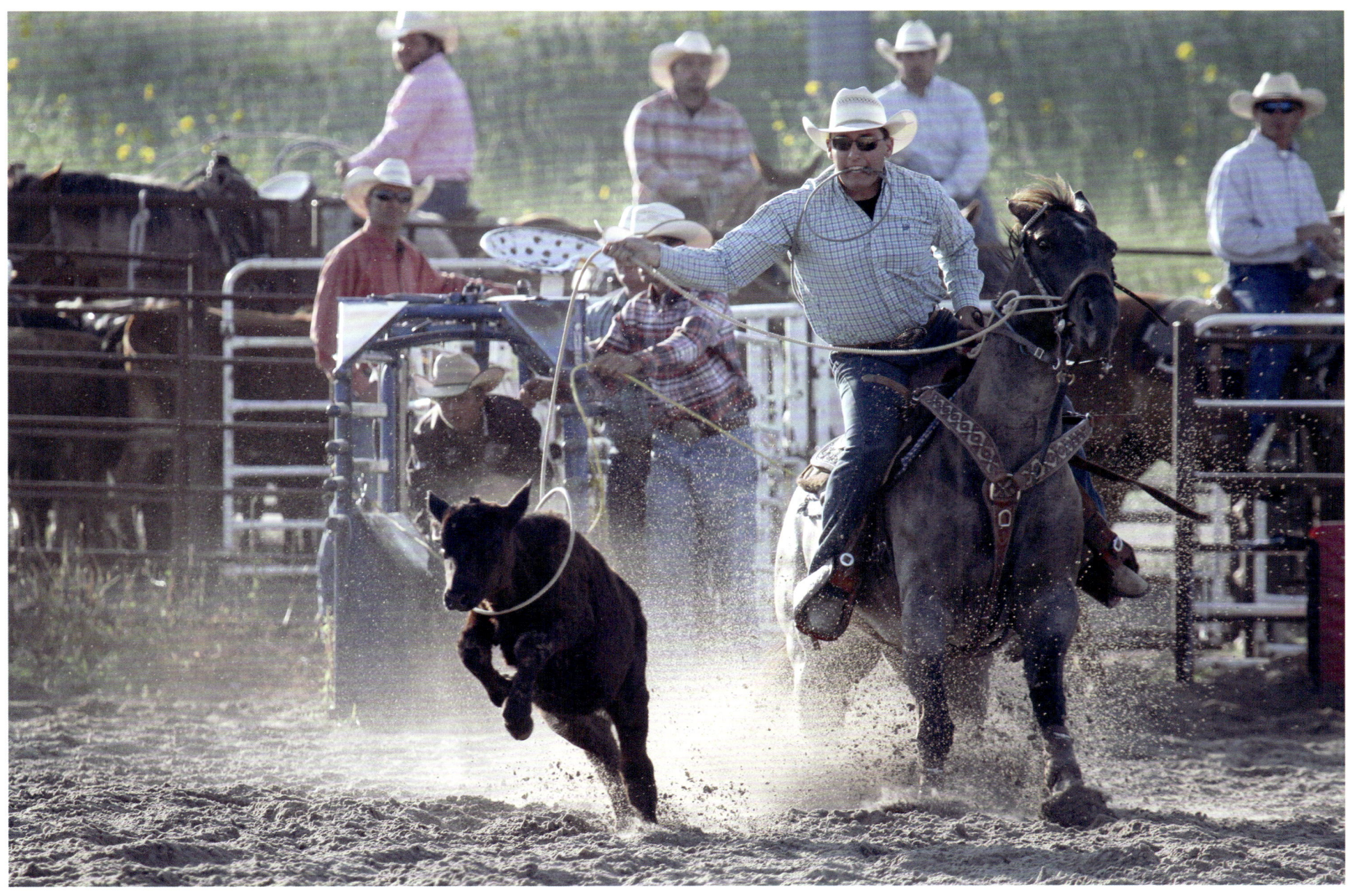

Young men don't win calf roping events; nothing less than a couple decades of roping makes the best contenders. THEDFORD

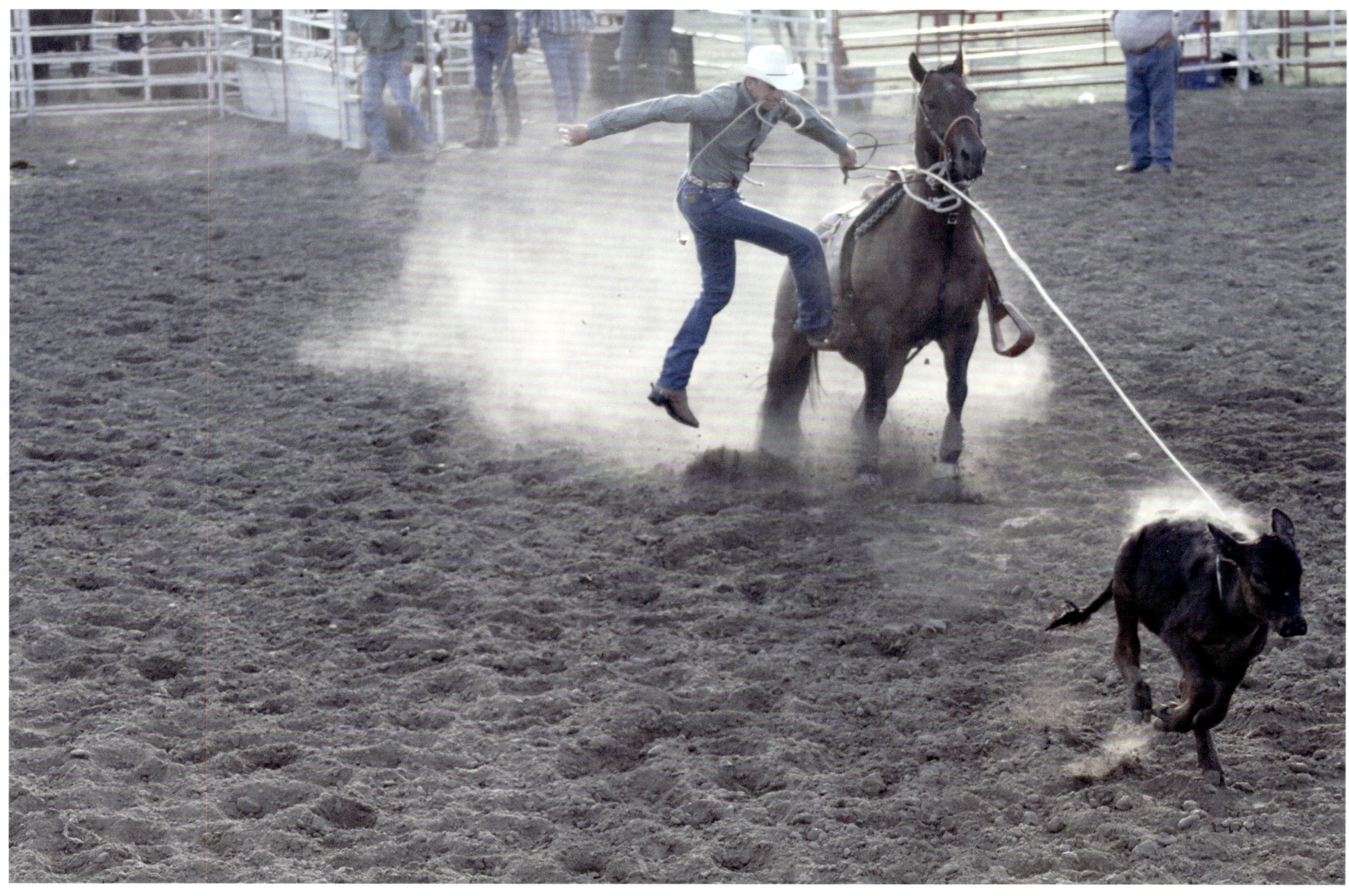

At the wrong end of a physics equation, this calf will spin as the horse skids to a stop. The roper uses forward momentum to close distance quickly in this money-winning run. TRENTON

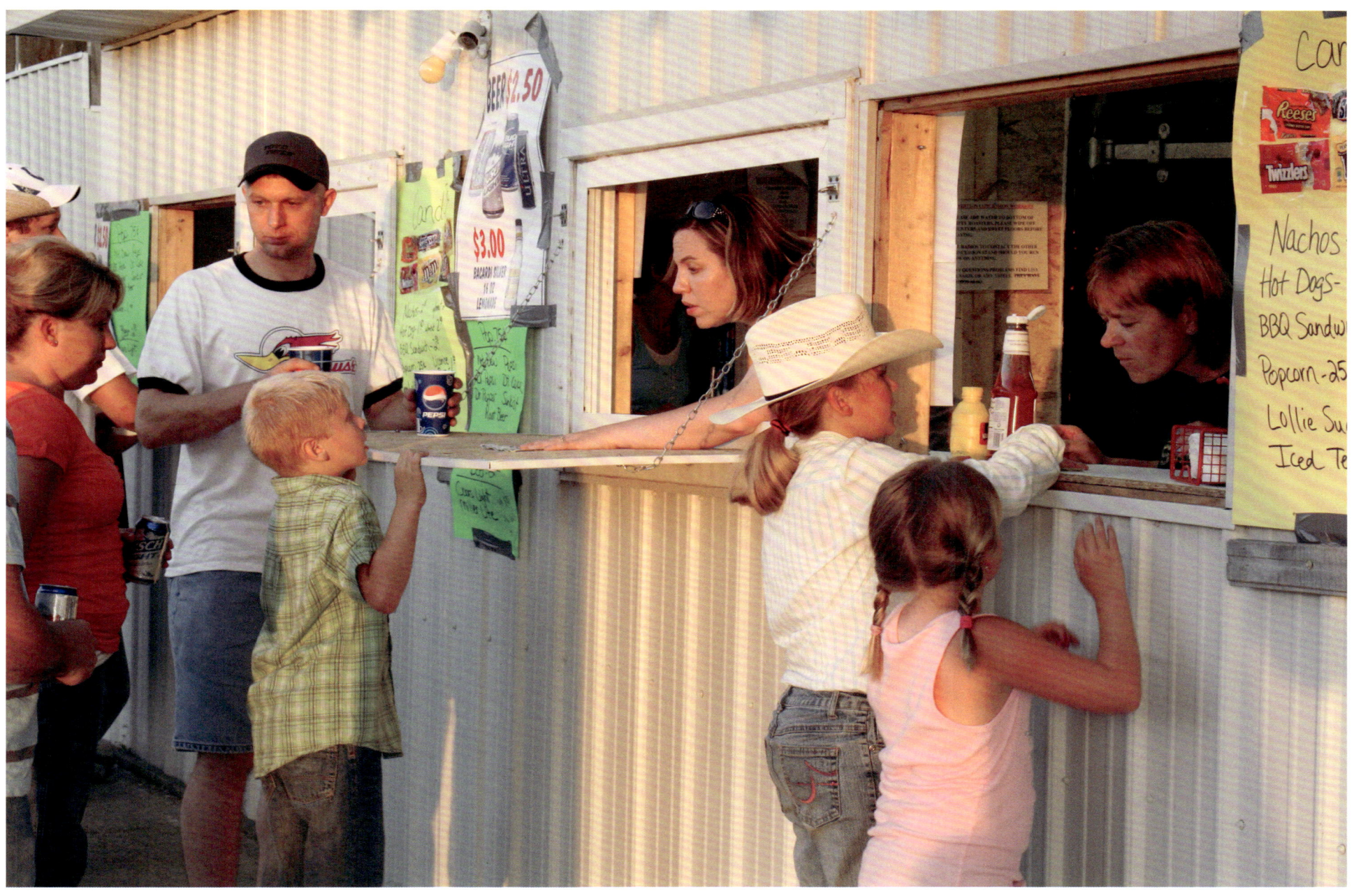

Midway through the rodeo, snack time often comes at roping time. The grandstands smell
of popcorn, the chutes smell of manure; both smell good to the cowboys. CLEARWATER

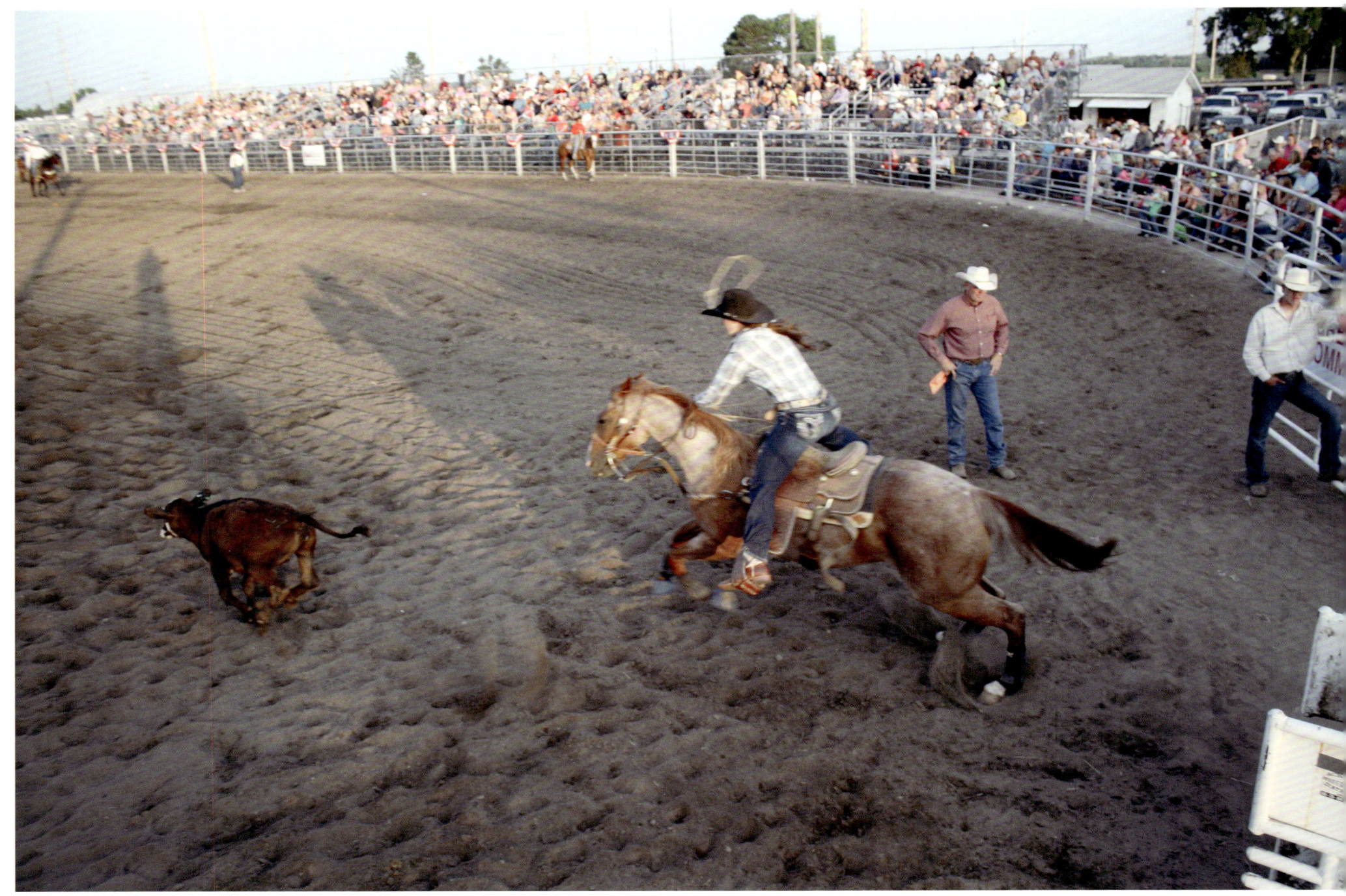

The Cowgirls

WOMEN'S TIMED EVENTS

Man against beast is a recurring rodeo theme but horsewomen are equally competitive and just as obsessed. Women pat their horse's neck after a good run and men usually don't, which is one of few notable differences. Women lasso calves in breakaway roping competition but, as the title suggests, their rope breaks free when the horse stops. There is no tying down.

Both genders are stoic as they wait their turn. Huddled together on horseback watching others go before them they seem almost indifferent, but they are not. This is their chance to absorb information and to strategize. Split seconds matter, so factors are weighed; planning is crucial. How big is the box? Is the ground hard or soft? What size is the calf? Is the chute V-shaped or flat? Is it a new chute that opens immediately or old and clattery, resisting the gatekeeper's push? These dynamics help determine where to place a horse in the box and when to tell it to go. It's about gaining maximum momentum with minimum risk of barrier penalty. The start means everything; neither horse nor rider can err. Waiting competitors exchange brief greetings but conversations lag as they retreat into their heads.

There is no Nebraskan better than Ginalee Tierney in the combination of breakaway roping, barrel racing, and team roping. Badger is her breakaway horse, Payday is for team roping, and Chester runs the barrels. Born, raised, and trained on the family ranch in

Ladies' ropes break away once a calf is snagged; there are no women's tie-down events in Nebraska rodeo. As the sport evolves it will likely come. SUTHERLAND

Nebraska's hilly midlands, her red roan horse Badger is especially loved. At age nineteen he is approaching retirement so Ginalee is training new horses, but Badger won't easily be replaced. "He loves his job and he's still doing awesome," she says. "It will be a long time before a young horse can hold a candle to him." With just two to four years of competition left in him, sometimes she gives Badger a break and takes a rookie to Nebraska's smaller rodeos where the payouts are less. It is on-the-job training and, as Ginalee says, "If they goof up it doesn't matter much."

Minimizing the mental trap that super-specialized horses can fall into, Ginalee adds variety to their lives by giving them ranch work, although she admits being leery of injury when taking a finished horse into the pastures. "Sometimes when driving cattle I put my mom on one at the very back of the herd, because I know she's not likely to go chasing after cattle all the way back there," she says laughing.

Barrel racing horses require much more training than those for breakaway. "Breakaway is in a straight line," Ginalee says, "but in barrels you're asking them to run as fast as they can then break their body down to make a very tight turn three times in a cloverleaf pattern with a sprint to the finish." Breakaway requires precision in exiting the box whereas barrel racing is won and lost by how quickly you turn around each barrel. Knock the barrel over with too tight of a turn and you've lost, though the ladies never quit. Ginalee explains, "When a barrel falls you're always headed away from it, so it's hard to tell if it fell. If you hear the crowd cheer then you know you're good; if they go 'OHH' then you know you're not. Sometimes I'm so focused I don't hear anything at all."

A beginning horse needs more help knowing when to turn than does a seasoned vet, but all these horses want to run. Like a dog set free in the park, this is what they live for. Ginalee loves the challenge of helping younger horses improve, and like great competitors in any sport she craves the action. Striving to achieve thoughtful self-imposed challenges as every year goes by—this is how Ginalee wins.

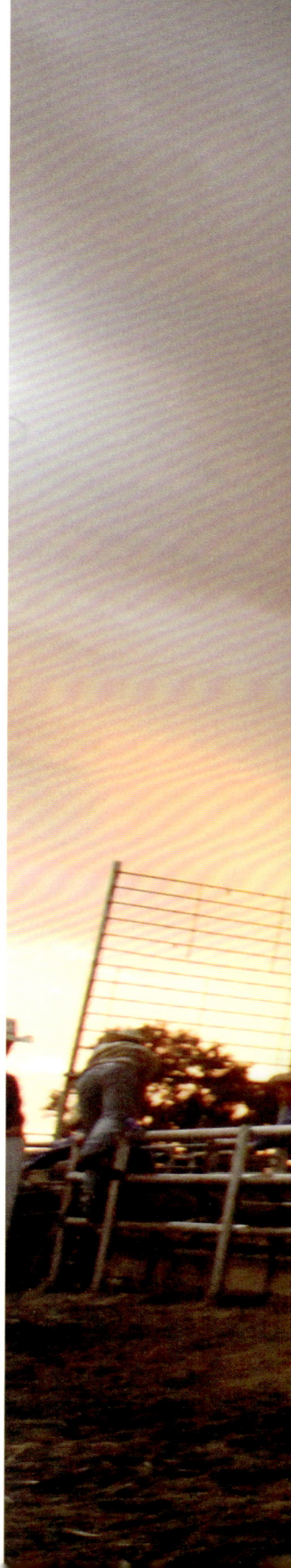

A good run means a good start. For the first fifty feet these horses are as fast as any horse in the world. BRIDGEPORT

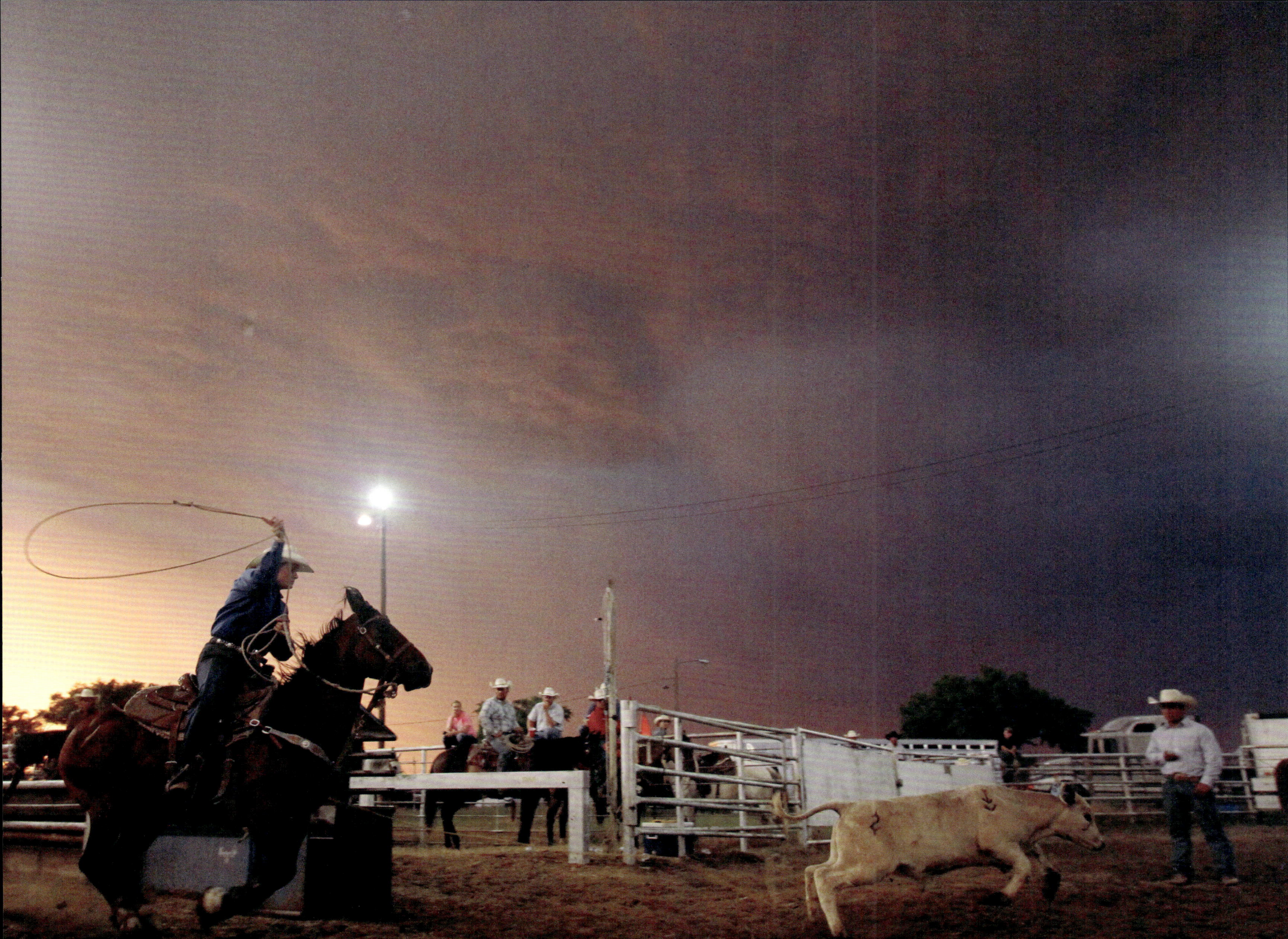

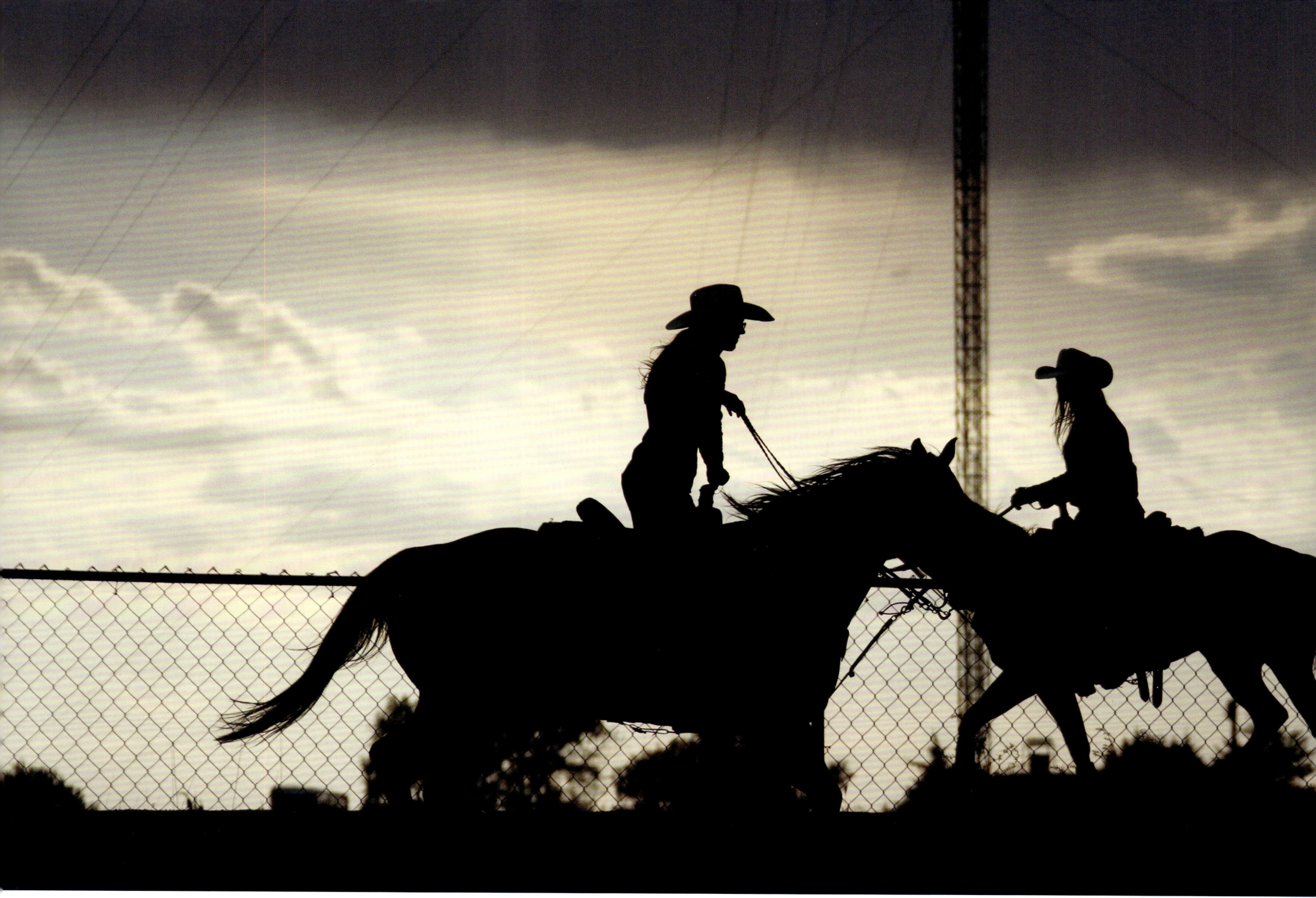

During bronc riding the ladies limber up their horses nearby. ELWOOD

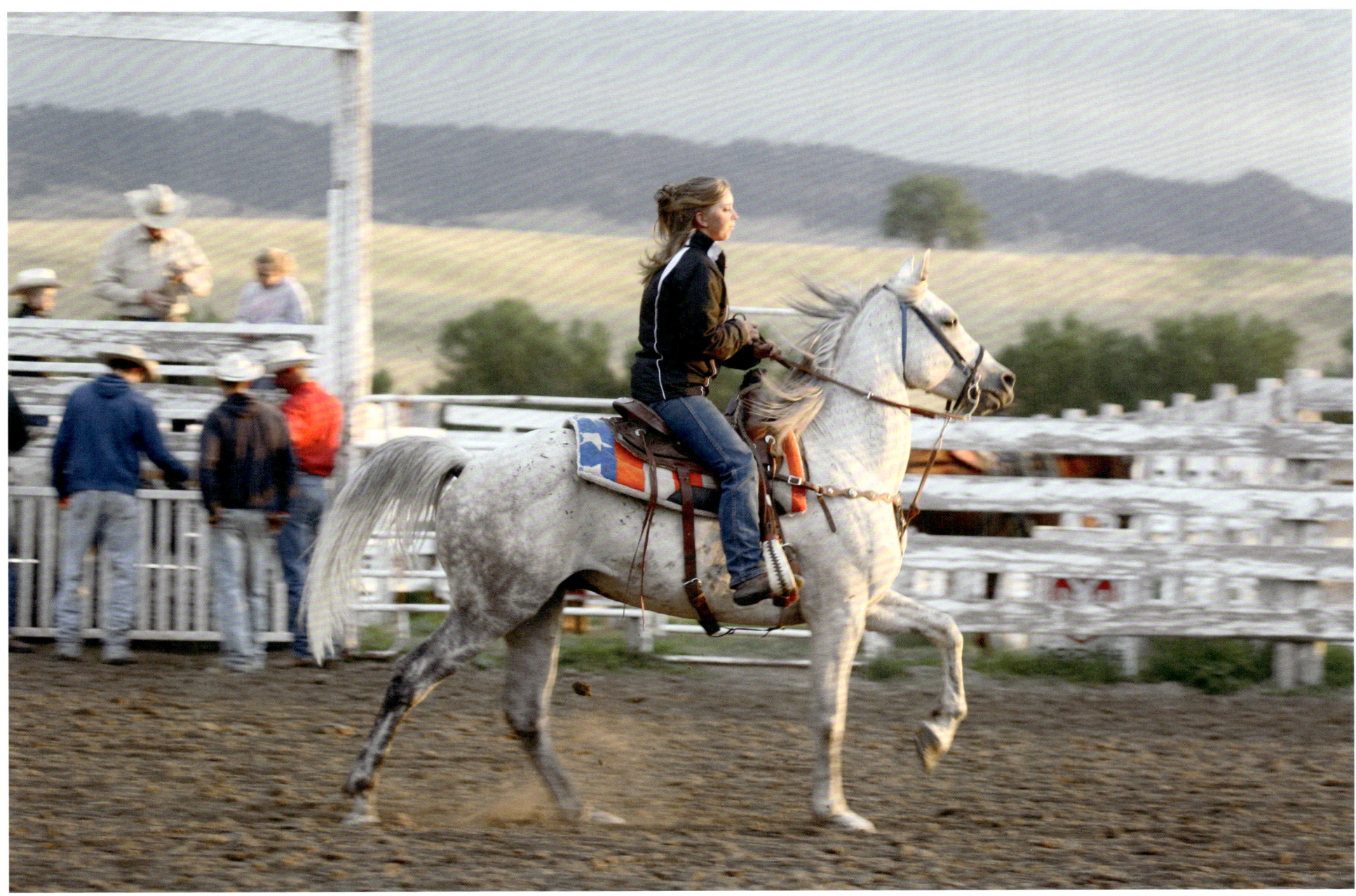

Fort Robinson State Park wranglers and other staff provide weekly rodeo entertainment for park visitors. Women compete with men in team roping. Other events include: musical chairs, saddling races, tag-you're-it on horseback, and a cowboy in drag feigning a wreck to be rescued by a horse wearing a flashing red light between its ears. FORT ROBINSON

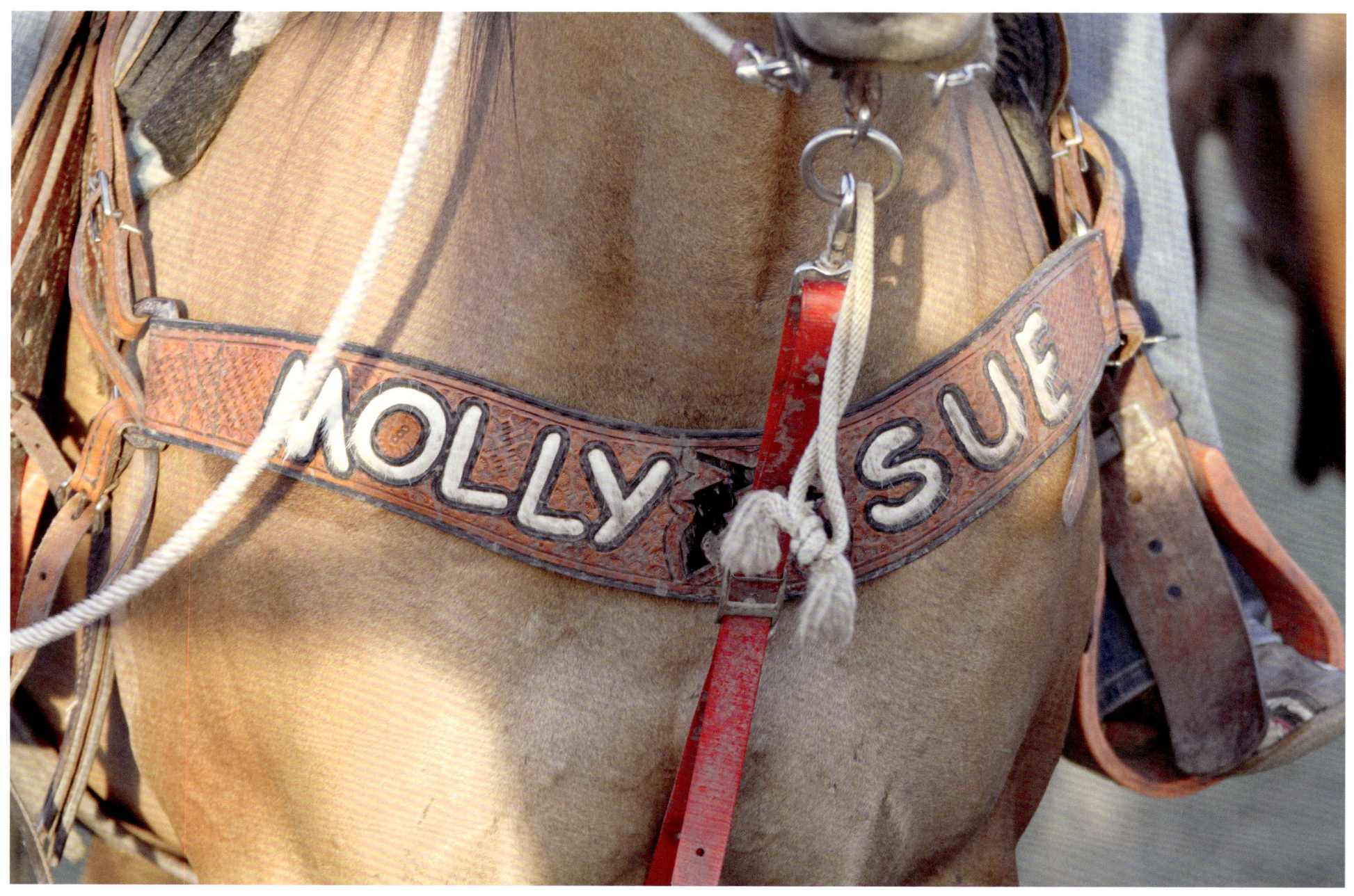

Waiting for her roping run, Molly Sue is loved by her female rider. There are few human/animal relationships stronger than that of a woman and her horse. NORDEN

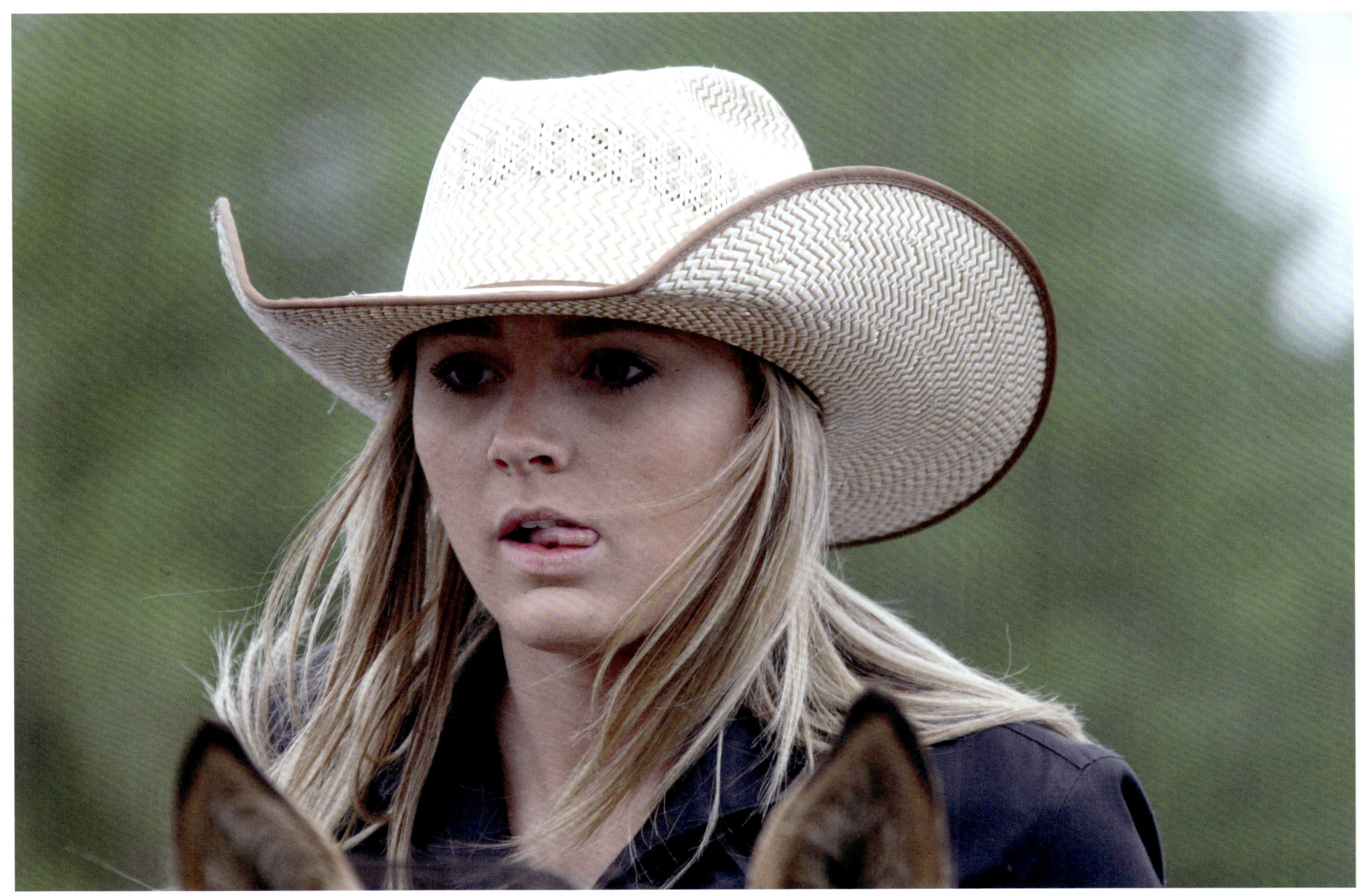

Horse and rider are on high alert just before the calf's chute opens. They have traveled many miles for these few hectic seconds. TEKAMAH

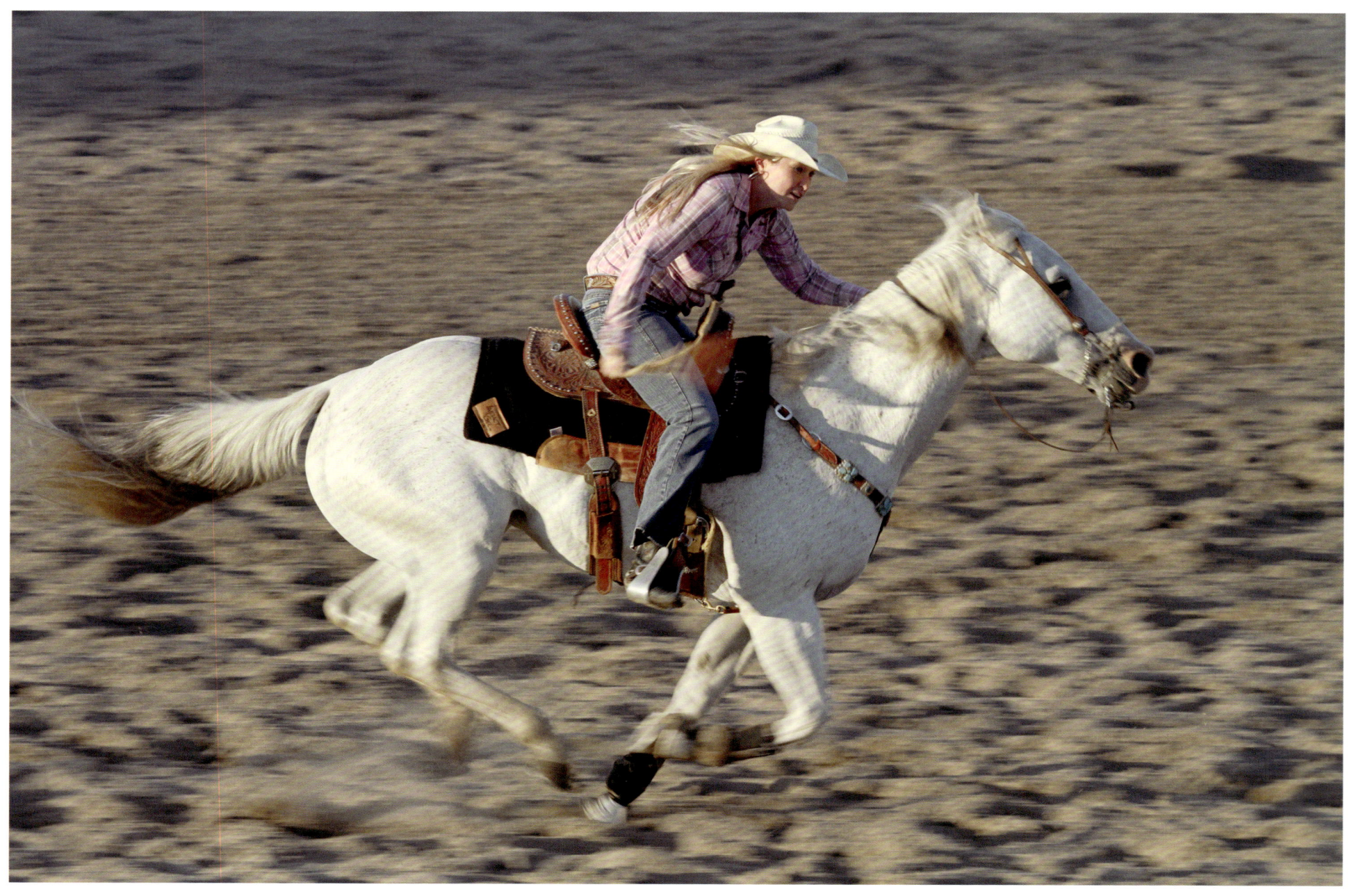

Born to burn! As with all speed-event horses, barrel racing horses are specialized.
This is all they do until retirement, and they love their jobs. THEDFORD

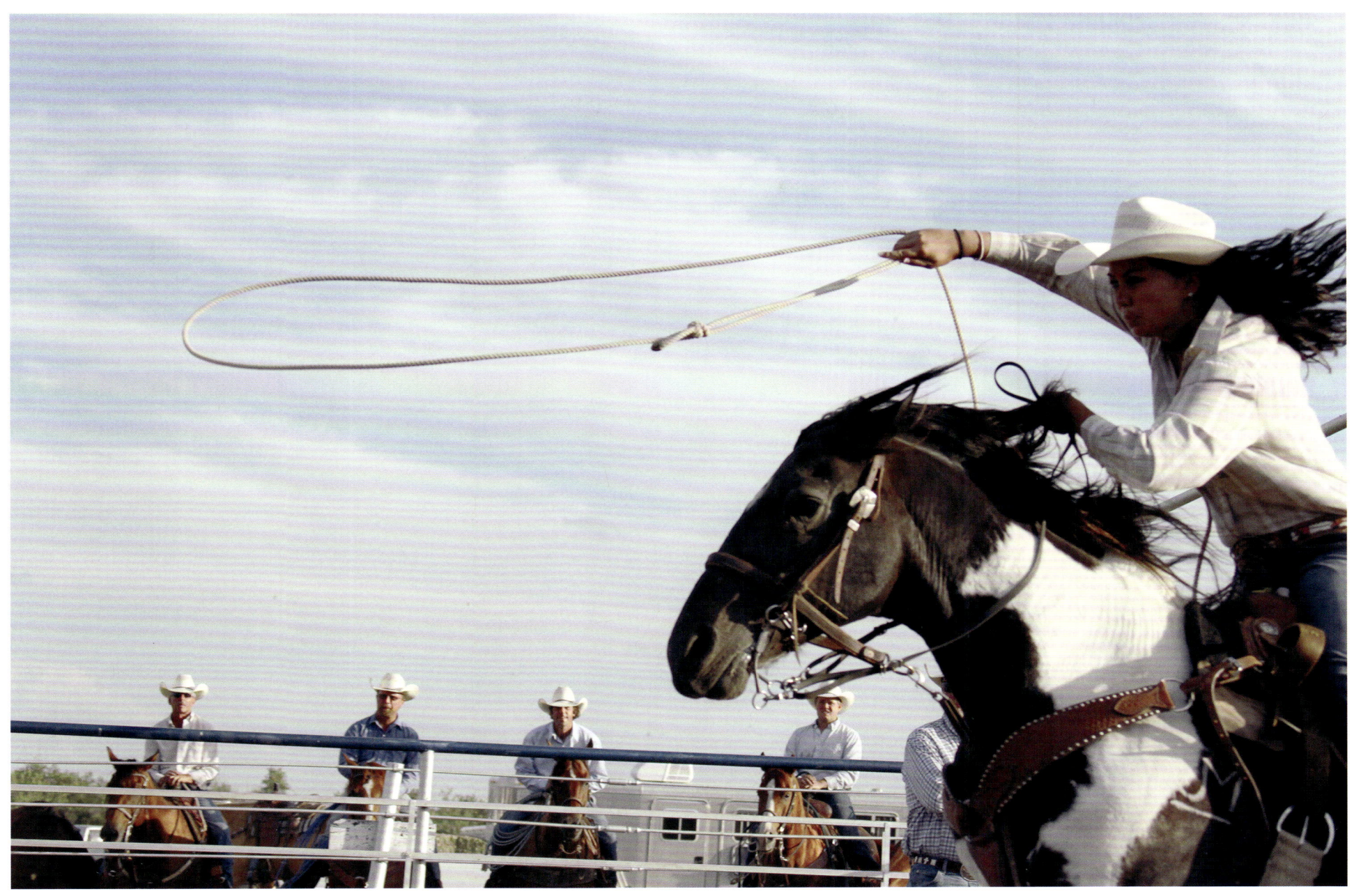

Waiting on horseback for their turn to compete, husbands and wives watch each other's performances, hoping one or the other ends up in the money. TRENTON

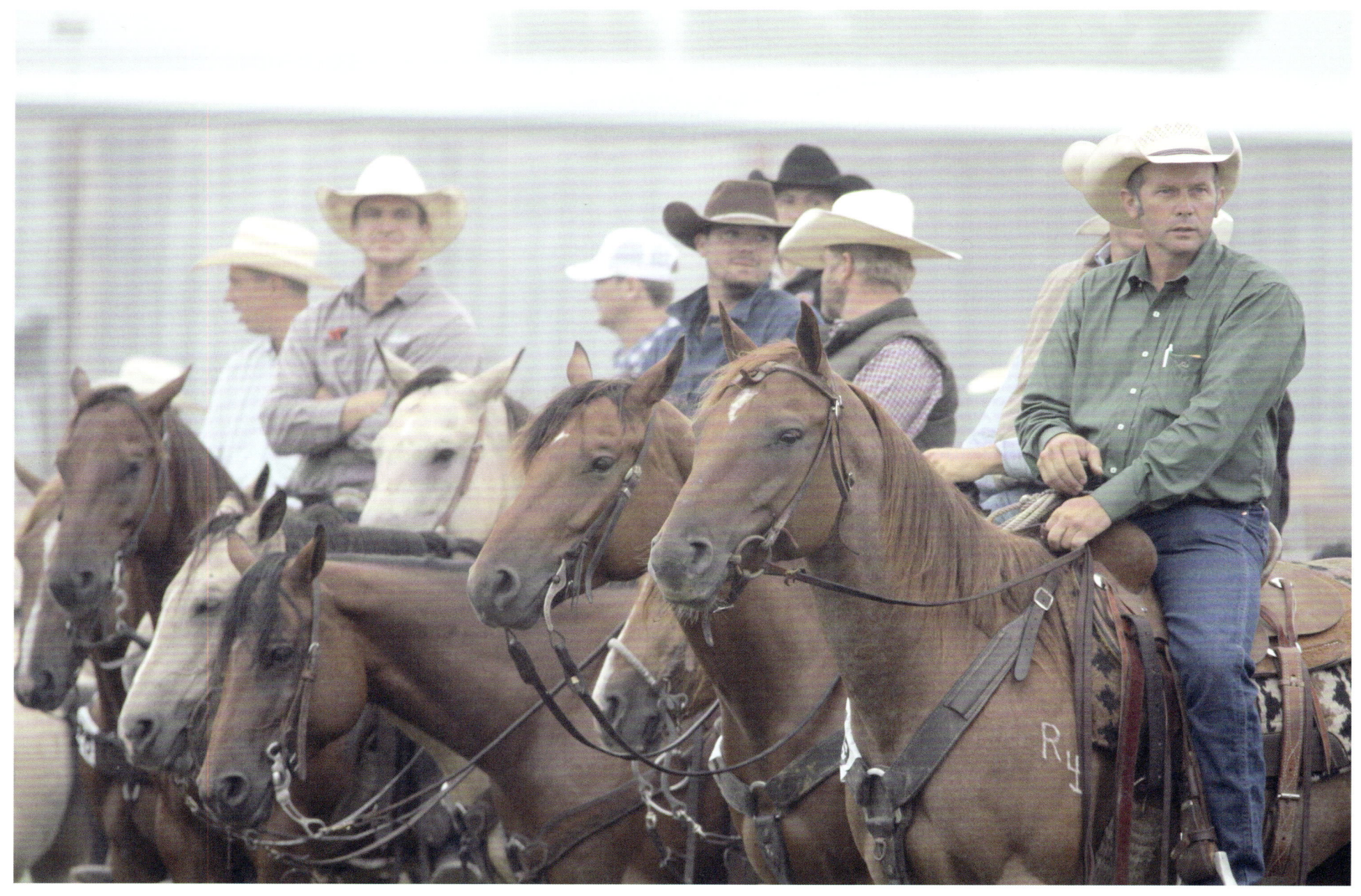

At the Pitzer Invitational obstacle course, horses watch their kin
race before their turn. PITZER RANCH, NEAR ERICSON

Sandhills Speedsters

SPEED-EVENT HORSES

Casual rodeo fans don't think twice about speed-event horses; a horse is a horse. But these horses are not the typical pasture-grazers one sees along Nebraska's highways. They are bred to be high-end athletes. Where do they come from and what makes them phenomenal? These questions led me to the Pitzer Ranch, a quiet powerhouse in the horse breeding industry where an average of 240 little speedsters are born each year.

Near the town of Ericson in Nebraska's Sandhills, the Pitzer Ranch spans rolling grassland split by the clear, sandy-bottomed Cedar River. The Pitzers have been honing their vision of the perfect quarter horse here for generations. The pedigree traces back to a single legendary stud, Two Eyed Jack. He sired 1,416 foals by the end of his time. A dozen studs with direct lineage to Jack now impregnate 350 to 400 mares annually, half naturally and half via artificial insemination. I sympathize for what science has done to the studs' sex lives, but controlling Mother Nature adds precision to the processes; recipes are written for twenty-first century horse herds. Regardless of how they came to be, beginning in May, bright-faced foals arrive eager to take on their new world.

Grandson of ranch founder Howard Pitzer, the family's current patriarch, Jim Brinkman, and his wife Tanna have that easygoing niceness required in a word-of-mouth industry. Touring the pastures with Jim one May evening I mindlessly state, "So I imagine you're pretty selective about what stud gets what mare." "Well . . . that's kind of everything," he says with a grin. "That's the whole deal."

They often purchase mares to keep bloodlines fresh, but the better Pitzer fillies are kept around to breed one day. Certain physiques and personality make the cut. "We breed for about 15 to 15.1 hands high (60 to 61 inches at the withers) and around 1,200 pounds or a little heavier," Jim says. "That's right in the middle of quarter horse size." Breeding for color is a factor as well. Certain colors sell better, such as buckskin, roan, palomino, and grey.

Disposition is also central. "We're looking for the ones that act like a Labrador puppy," says Jim. "There aren't as many cowboys in the world now so our horses have to be calm and quiet. It's no different than breeding dogs. You look for the traits you want to make dominant. We've been weeding them down for over six generations." Analyzed yearly, colts are narrowed to a small group that might be kept and then those are further assessed to see which may become a Pitzer stud. As this cycle continues, offspring become quicker and more receptive to training. Trainability trumps physical qualities in a rodeo horse; as in people, the best athlete in the world must train well to perform at an elite level.

Caught and led around the training pen for twenty minutes, foals have their first human contact when they are three to four months old. Other than occasional hoof trimmings, this is the only close human interaction they receive for the first two years of their lives. School starts two years later. Lane Larreau, Jim's son-in-law, is one of four trainers who work the youngsters year-round. "We start with a lot of petting. Everything is slowly introduced," Lane says. "This all leads to getting them comfortable with a saddle and then a rider. I think the fillies pick up on things a little quicker, they seem to mature earlier like human girls do."

Rest is the best reward for a trainee according to Clayton Schlenger, a young, lanky trainer with a mild manner conducive to teaching horses. "I like to let them almost fall asleep in there so they think it's easy," he says. All new horses get the same start. Standing in the center of a small round pen the trainer prods the horse to run circles around the perimeter. As Clayton raises his arms and cuts off their path, the horse first learns to "WHOA!" Once they understand to stop at that command, the next stages follow with much petting and rest in between: halter, saddle blanket, saddle, and finally rider. A novice two-year-old learns all this within two hours—much less time than most people imagine. Contrary to typical western movie scenes, training is a loving process. Though a horse occasionally goes ballistic, says Clayton, "Once I get on top they realize it isn't that big of a deal."

Arena riding follows immediately and soon Clayton and beginner are out riding the hills. "I like to make their first day a big one," he says. After their first training day they are set loose with the herd and left alone for a full year until ranch training begins. By exposing a horse to everything in ranch training, quirks are exposed and trainers begin to alter the horse's behavior. "Every horse is different," Clayton says. "Some are afraid of the rope. Heck, some are afraid of cattle!"

What is the best part of a horse's day? "Sleepin'!" he says. "The point when you're done riding them." All colts and fillies get the basics in ranch work, but those displaying superior abilities or eagerness to work will move on to specialty training. "Working a horse a month on then a month off and so on, we can finish a horse in about a year," Clayton explains.

How are horses chosen to be trained for rodeo? "You let the horse tell you," says Jim Brinkman. "If they're good at certain things you go

that way. Some want to be sport horses and some want to be family pets—the trail horses." Everyone in the Pitzer family regularly rides new horses to keep them sharp and to look for traits. Promising horses train for calf roping, barrel racing, steer wrestling, and the Pitzers' specialty: team roping. Team-roping jackpot events dot the country all year. The competitor base is huge and so are the winnings. Jim says, "Spending $50,000 on a horse is no big deal to some folks because they may win it all back the next weekend." A finished Pitzer rodeo horse can sell for up to $150,000. A good trail horse costs much less, about as much as a brand new pickup. "Ranchers, hobby riders, and competitors all run in the same circles," Jim says. "Riding horses is entertainment for most folks out west. They don't go to the mall or the movie house. They ride."

Those owning Pitzer lineage have the chance to show what their horses are made of at the annual Pitzer Horse Ranch Invitational. In early September, seventy-some horses and their owners come from around the U.S. to compete in a series of diverse events. Half are standard rodeo speed events, but the biggest sensation is the Ranch Trail Course. Like a back-country steeplechase mixed with ranch tasks, the course is designed to test the physical and mental limits of horse and rider.

Horses call out to each other in the early morning mist as they arrive by trailer on event day. A horse whinnying at full throat is not just heard, but felt. Deep chests release trumpeting vibratos through flared nostrils, and then they wait prick-eared for responses. This is a homecoming for most of these horses; their mothers are here.

The course changes yearly, so contestants never know exactly what to train for, but one quality is always needed: speed. One by one they

Hamming to the crowd with a loud hoot near the end of his run, this rider inadvertently startles his horse into a dangerously high river-entering leap. The landing will be extreme, but neither horse nor rider falls. PITZER RANCH, NEAR ERICSON

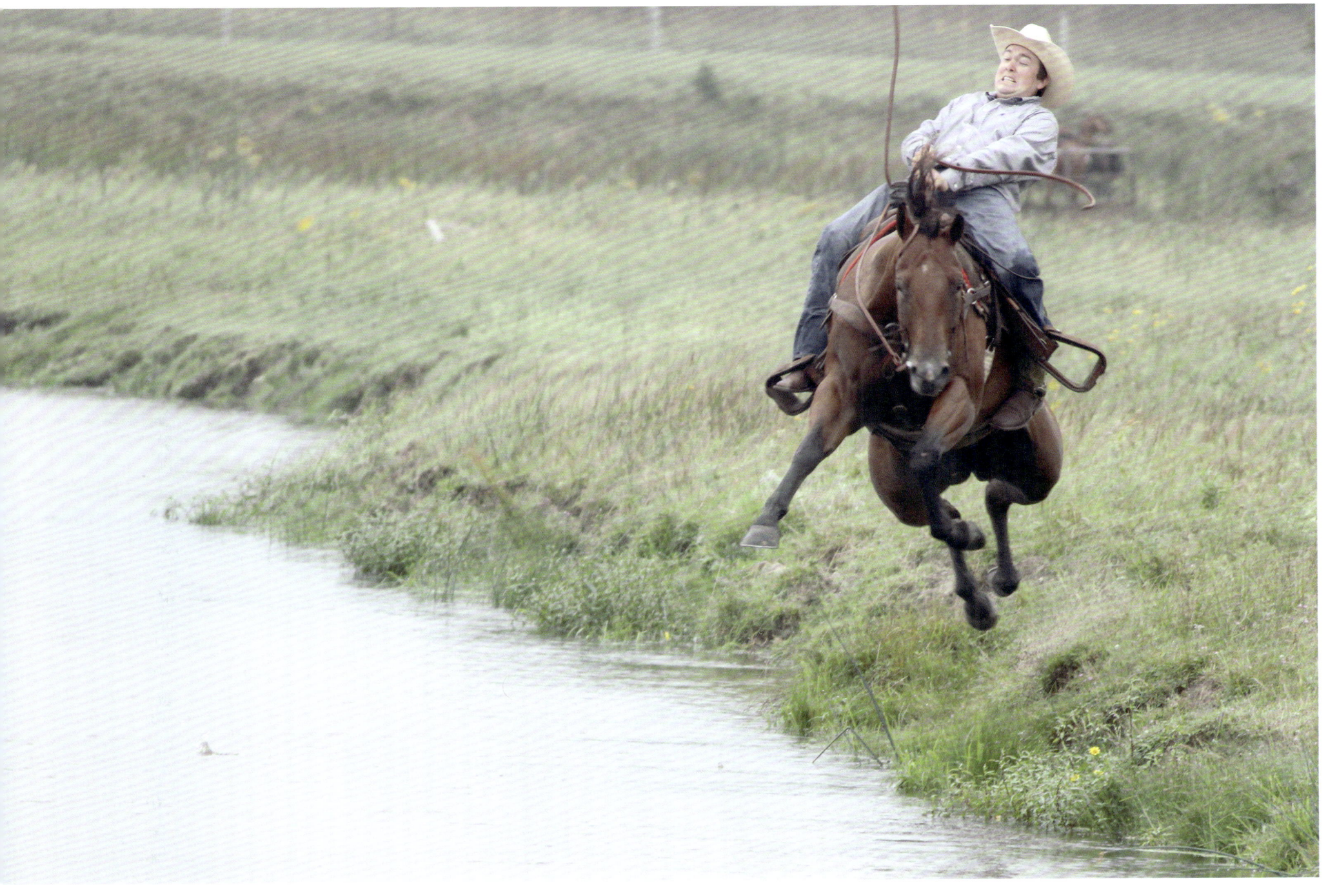

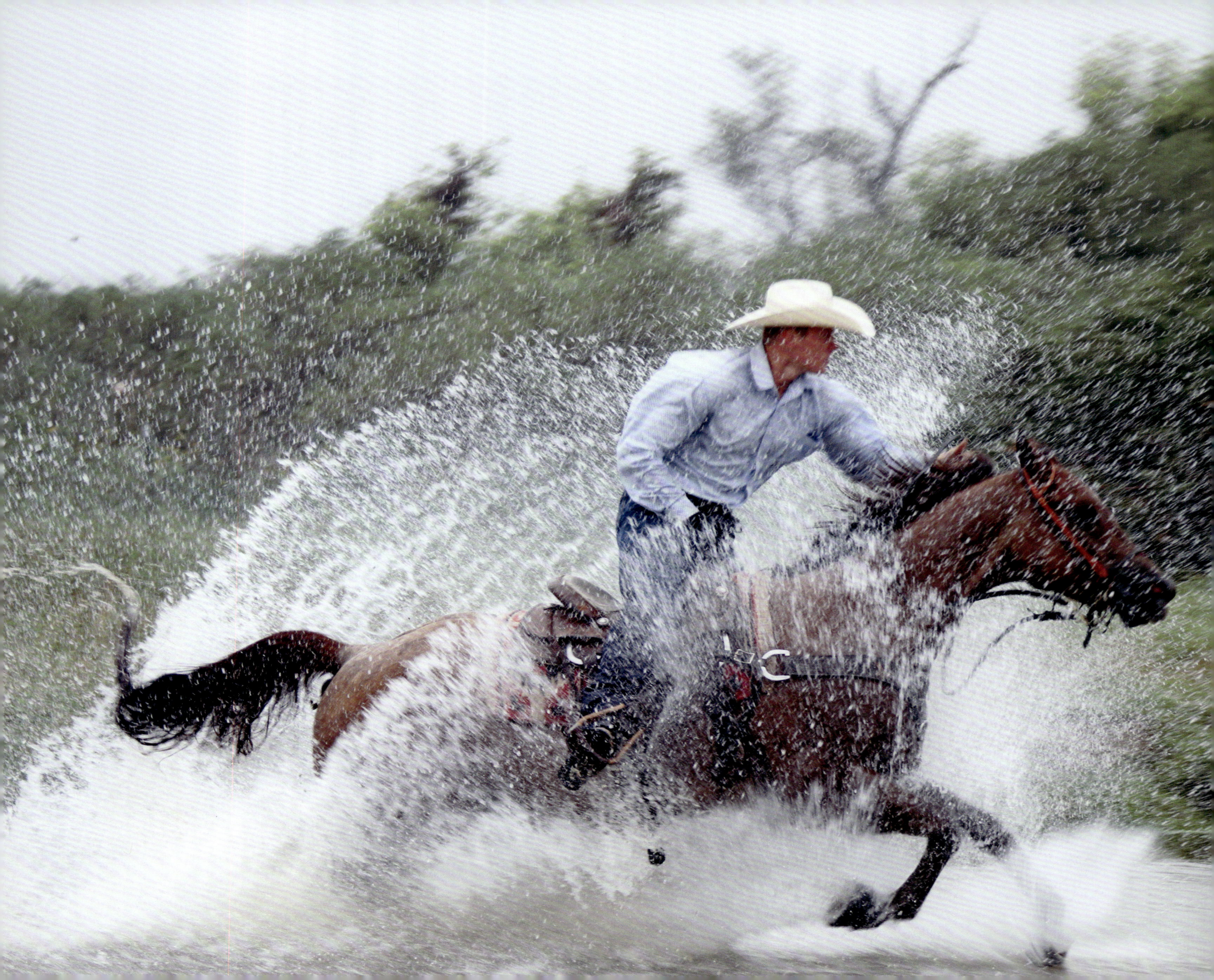

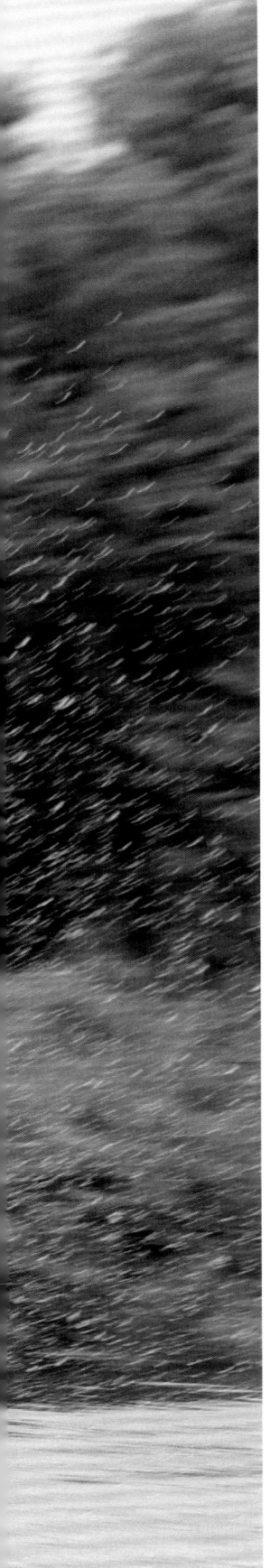

compete: load a massive log onto a trailer, cross the Cedar River, traverse a small wooden bridge, skip through a pile of dead trees, jump a ditch, splash through a marsh, drag a caged goat from point to point (goat looking equally confused each turn), cross the river once more, then push through a metal gate next to a fire-spitting branding iron oven. Add full-on sprinting between each challenge and that's a ranch trail course.

Locals line the river in folding chairs to watch. Some horses wreck crossing the creek, but riders grasp the saddle horn and float alongside their flailing horse until its footing is solid. Then the rider slides back onto the saddle and both rise together wet but undaunted. There are no practice runs; horses trust that their rider won't point them toward any obstacle they can't conquer.

Men compete against women on this course. This is fair—the horses are the stars. Their grace and speed is astonishing. Shea Bailey of Berryville, Arkansas, wins the event with a thundering two minutes flat. Second place goes to Lakota Pappan of Steelville, Missouri, on her red roan horse named I.D. Smaller than most Pitzer horses, I.D. is a barrel racer, but Lakota trained her hard for all Pitzer Course contingencies; pedigree means nothing without practice. I.D. ran as if for her life but was barely winded afterward. Receiving my compliments, Lakota smiles, pats her mare's neck and beams, "She's my baby." That gesture sums up everything I have ever witnessed about women and their horses.

I ask Jim Brinkman how the horse business has changed since he was a young man. "There are fewer true horsemen than there used to be," he says. "We spend more time now educating people about what makes a good horse: their structure, their biomechanics, their conformation." And as in all industries, technology brings change.

"Artificial insemination started around the '60's, but today's techniques make it a much bigger factor in what we can do." In the future, Jim predicts, "We'll end up with more hobby people, more folks that want to experience this lifestyle. We'll have to lean more toward vacationing people. Rodeo jackpots will keep getting bigger, so that will stay strong, but generally horses will need to be gentler," he said. "Compare it to lap dogs versus coon dogs. We'll have to breed less for ability and more for personality. The traditional rancher/cowboy style is fading; these cattlemen don't need horses to control their herds as much with today's four-wheelers. But there will always be that one cow they can't catch and that's when they call us. We'll always have the horses and dogs that can get that stubborn cow in."

Memories of my youth and of Wyoming cattle drives come to mind where skilled horsemen with brilliant cattle dogs brought large herds down from mountain-valley pastures, and I wish Nebraska had more cattle lands where four-wheelers could never enter.

Clayton Schlenger, one of the Pitzer Ranch's trainers, rides a trainee at top speed through the Cedar River at the end of his obstacle course run. PITZER RANCH, NEAR ERICSON

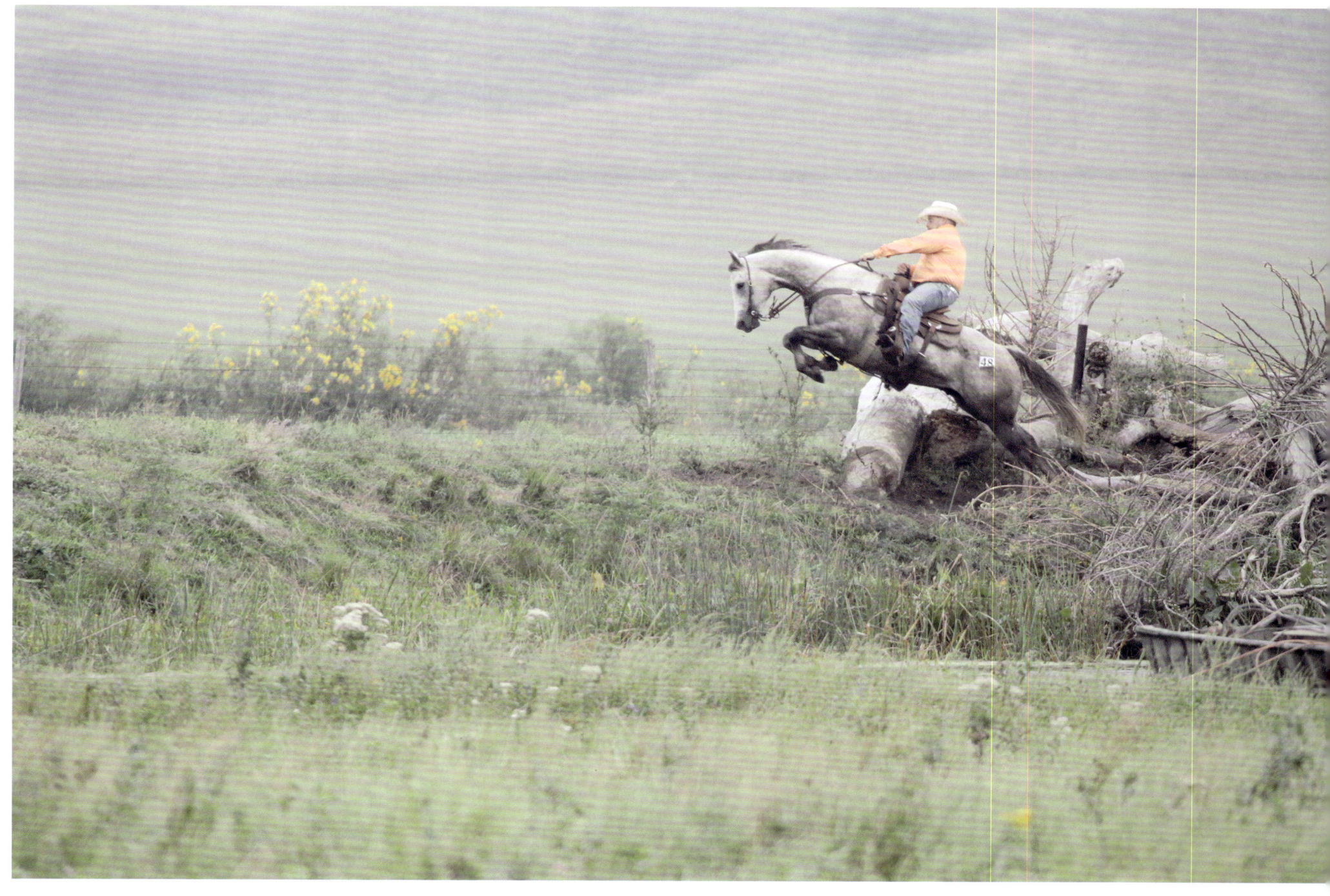

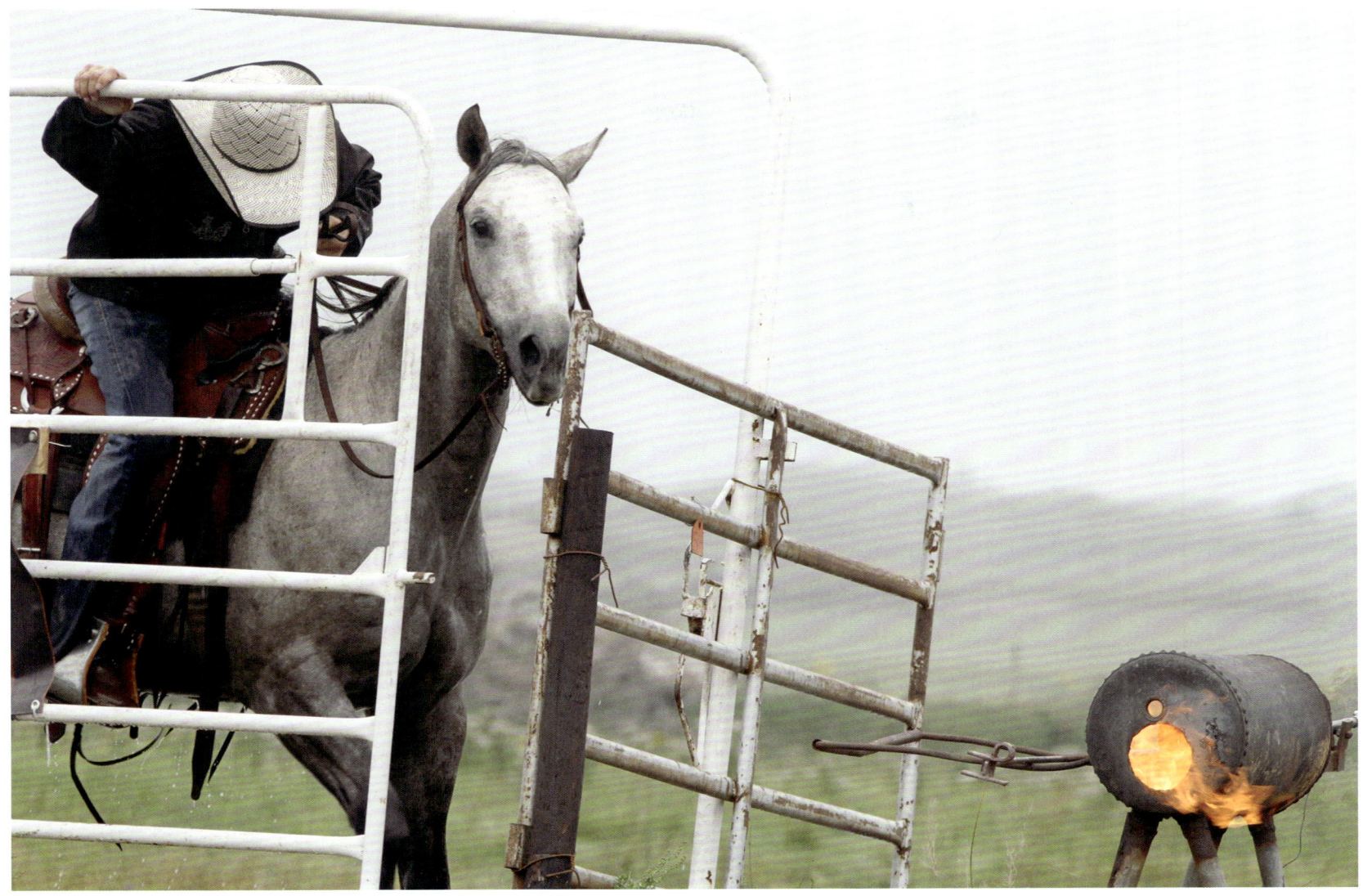

(*above*) Great ranch horses trust their rider. A branding iron oven roars next to the finish line at the Pitzer Ranch's obstacle course, but not one of seventy-some competing horses hesitates. PITZER RANCH, NEAR ERICSON

(*opposite*) Exiting a log maze midway through the Pitzer Ranch Trail Course competition, this Quarter Horse shows off the qualities for which it was bred: speed, agility, adaptability, toughness, and power. And embedded within all that: the temperament of a sweet Labrador pup. PITZER RANCH, NEAR ERICSON

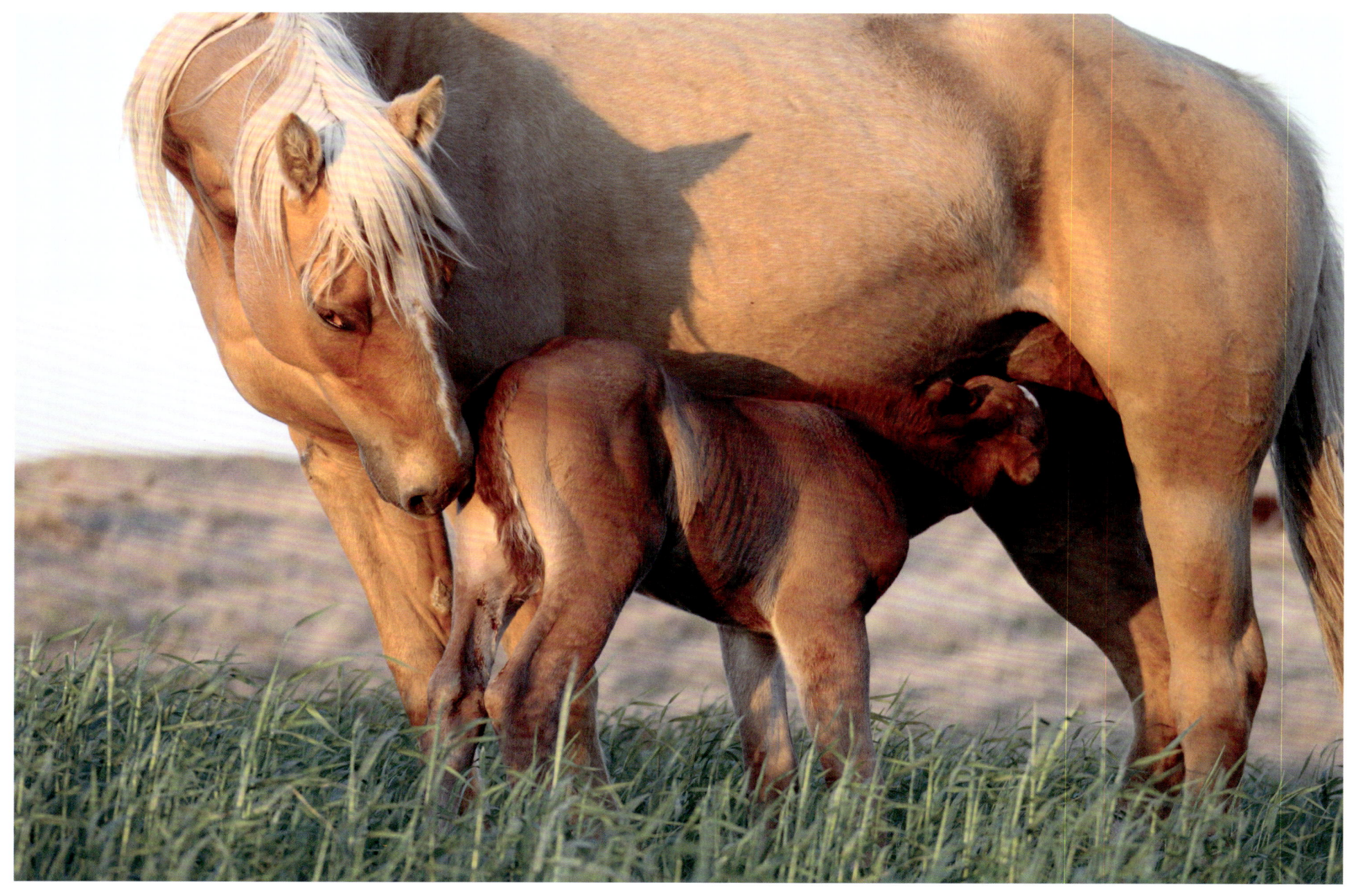

A days-old Pitzer foal nurses in a field of rye. PITZER RANCH, NEAR ERICSON

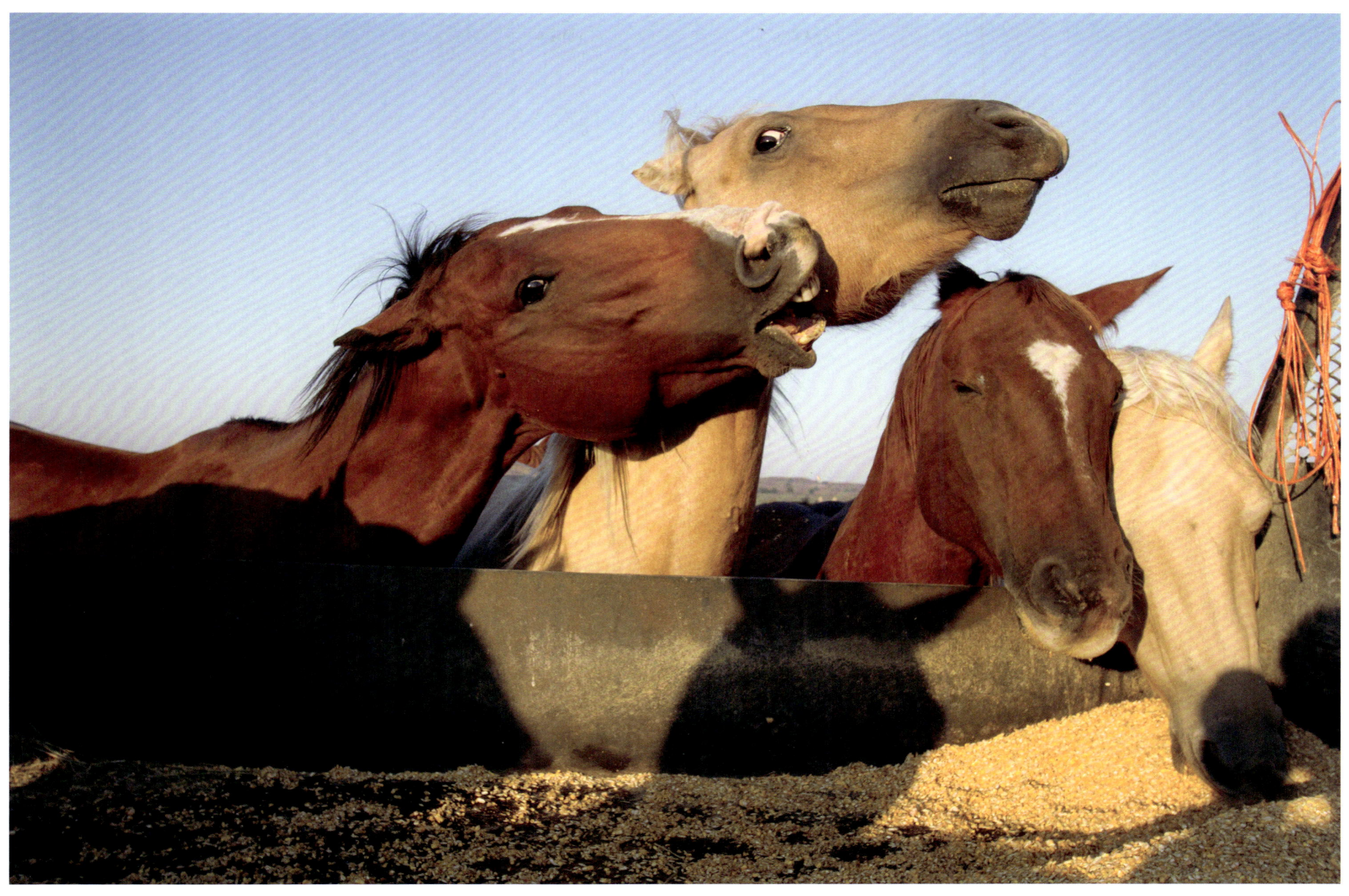

Feeding time makes obvious the dominant mares. PITZER RANCH, NEAR ERICSON

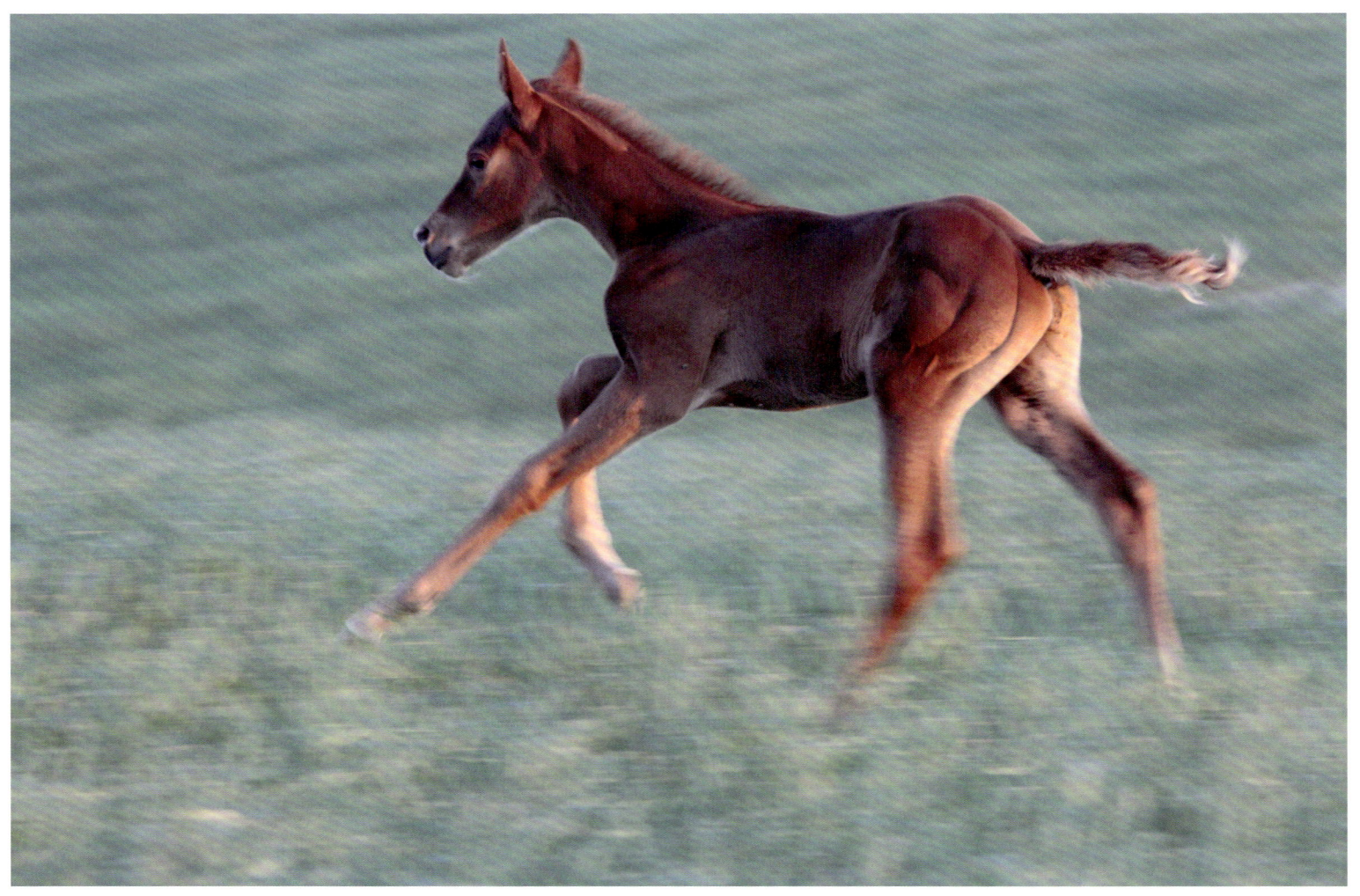

(*above*) Encouraging this foal to play, just as I would my dog in the backyard, this one-week-old gets the message. Sprinting past repeatedly, it eyeballs me as if I should join in. PITZER RANCH, NEAR ERICSON

(*opposite*) Mares and foals lead the way; they know where the grain will be shoveled. PITZER RANCH, NEAR ERICSON

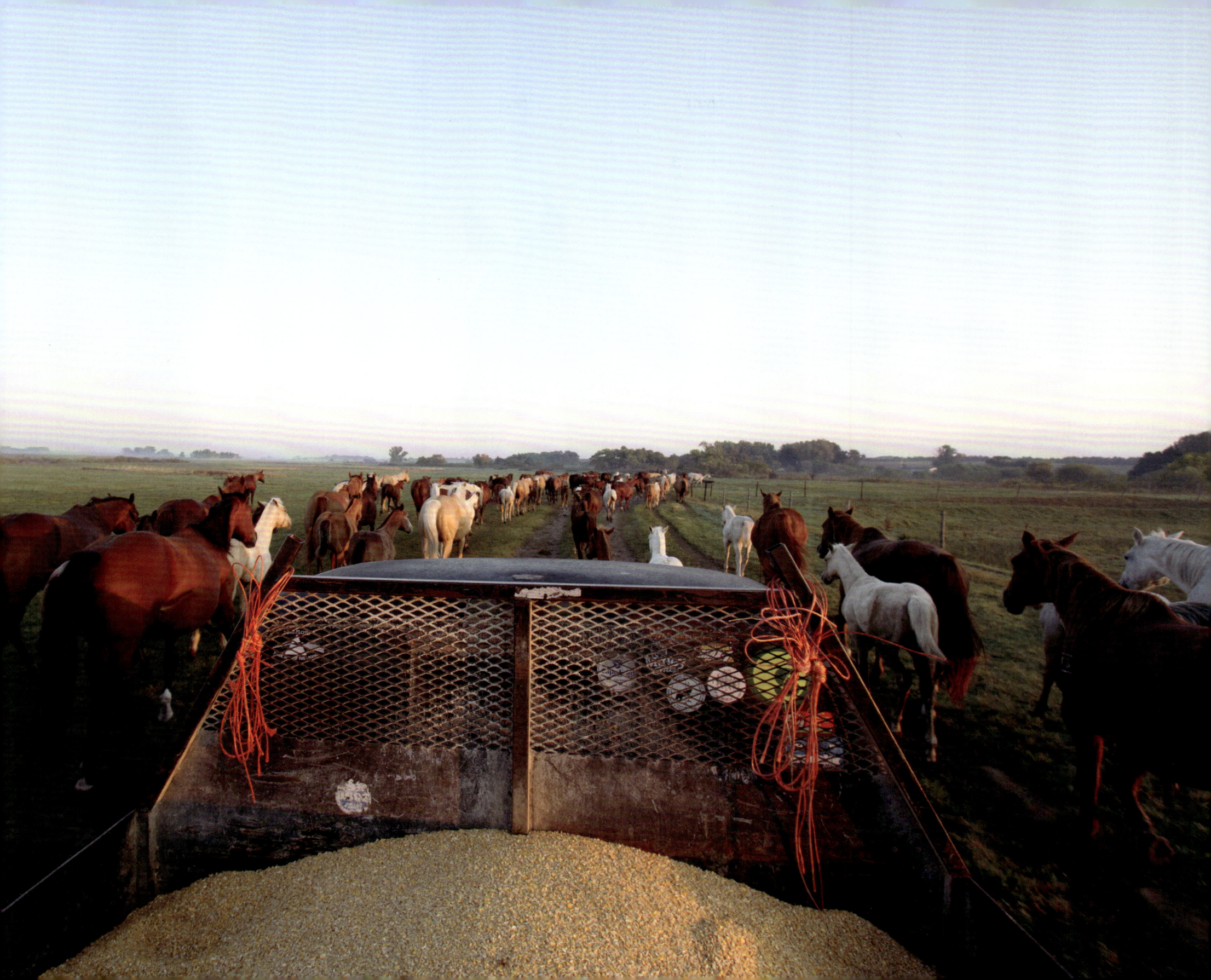

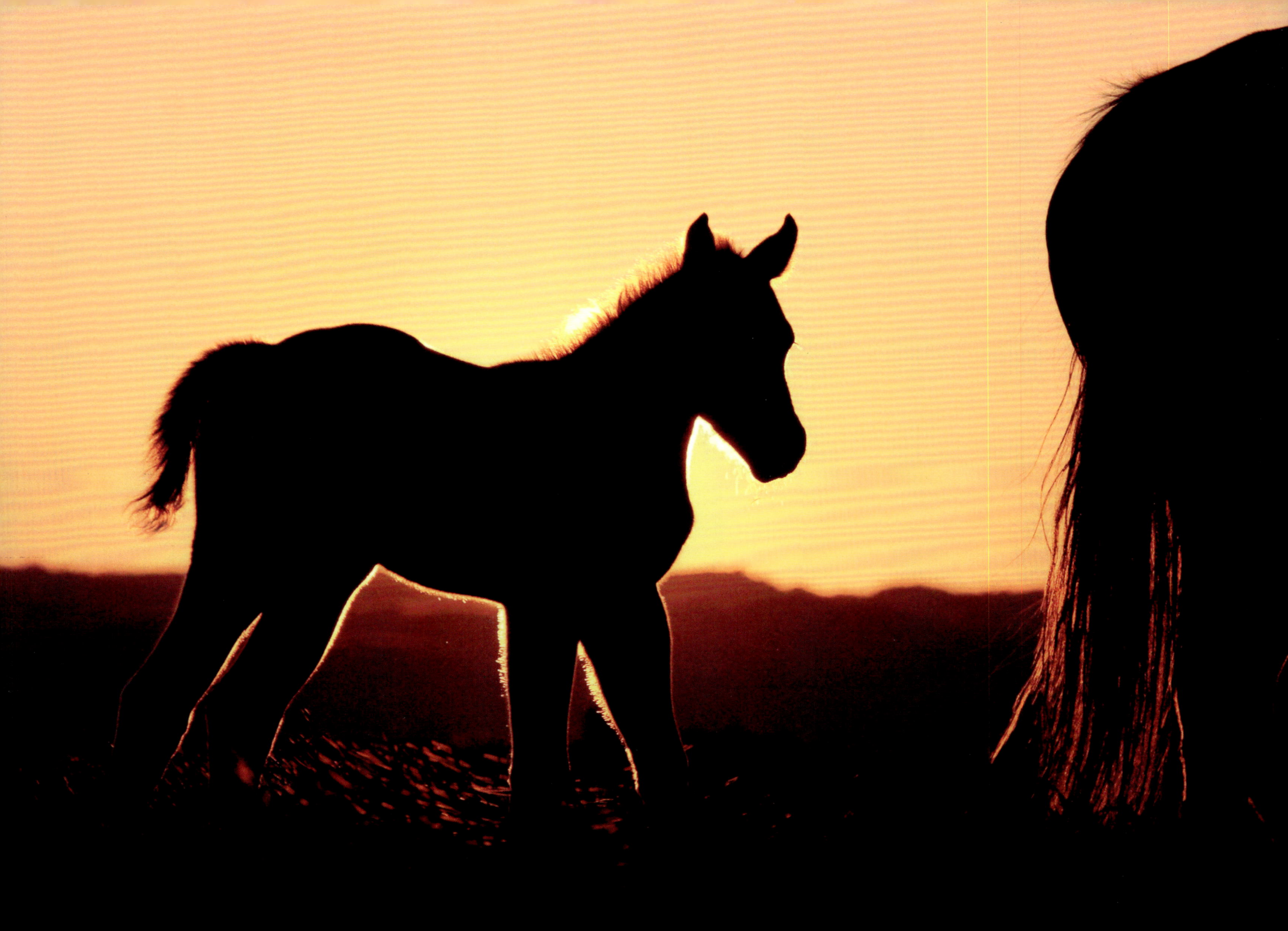

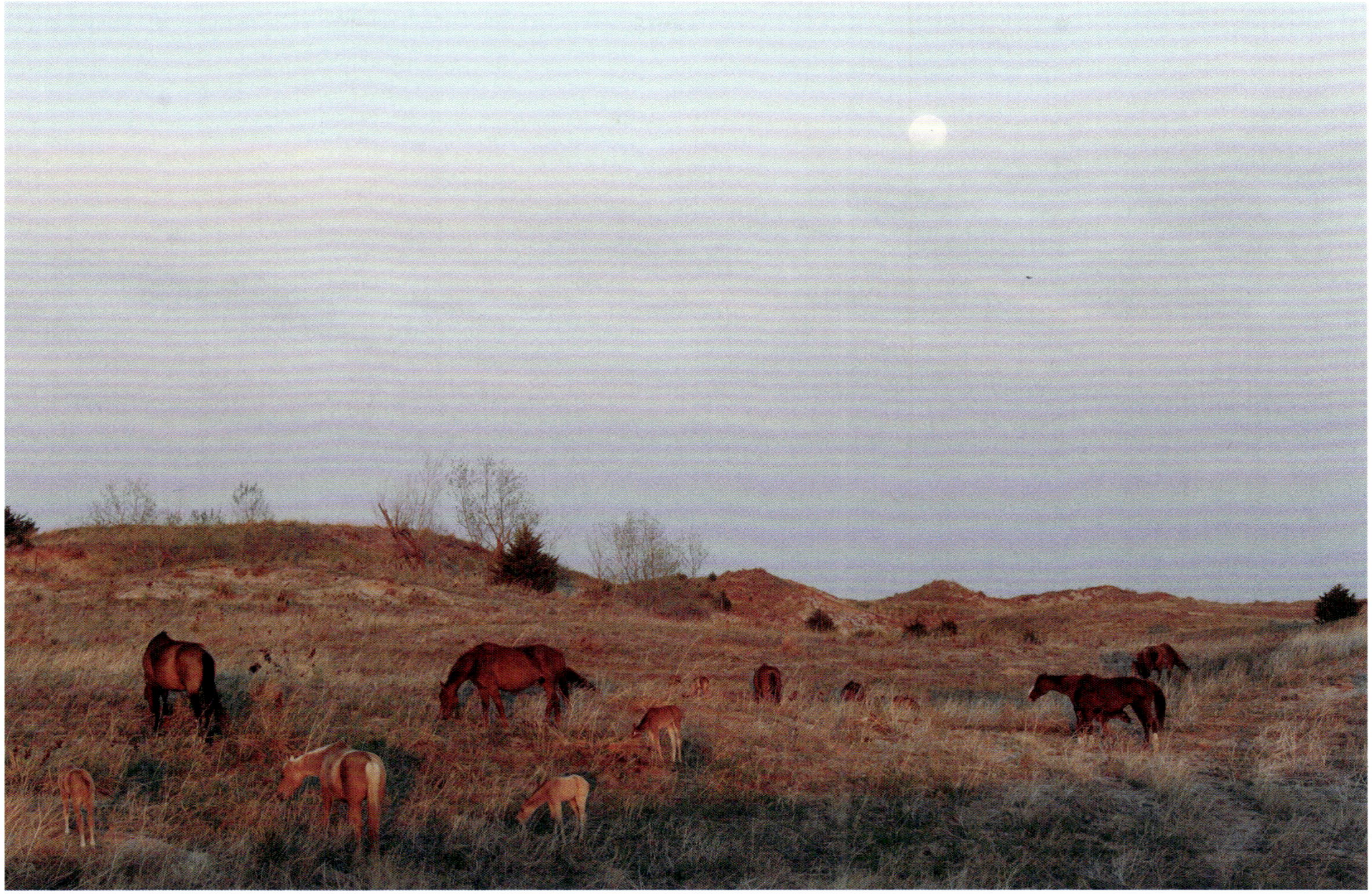

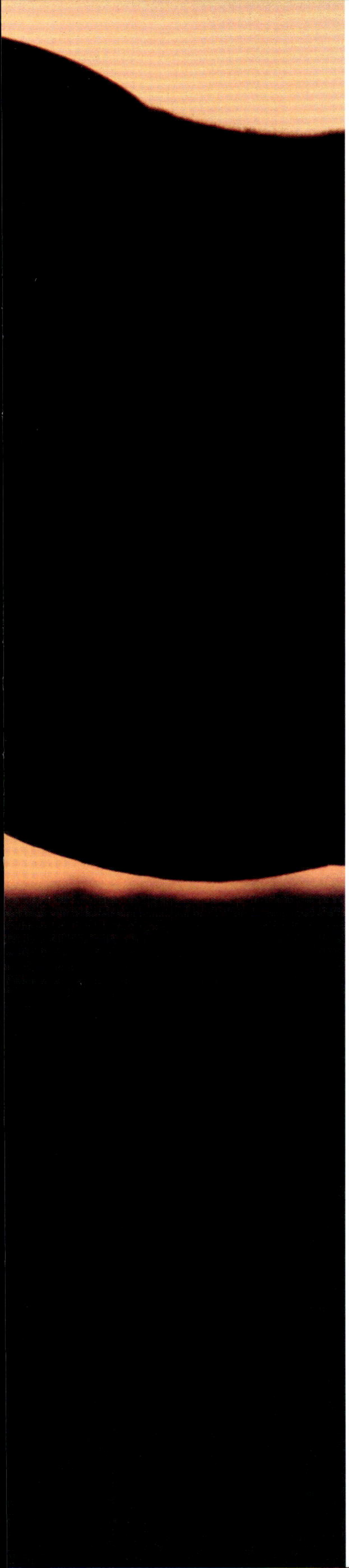

(*above*) PITZER RANCH, NEAR ERICSON

(*opposite*) This youngster might sell for as much as $150,000. PITZER RANCH, NEAR ERICSON

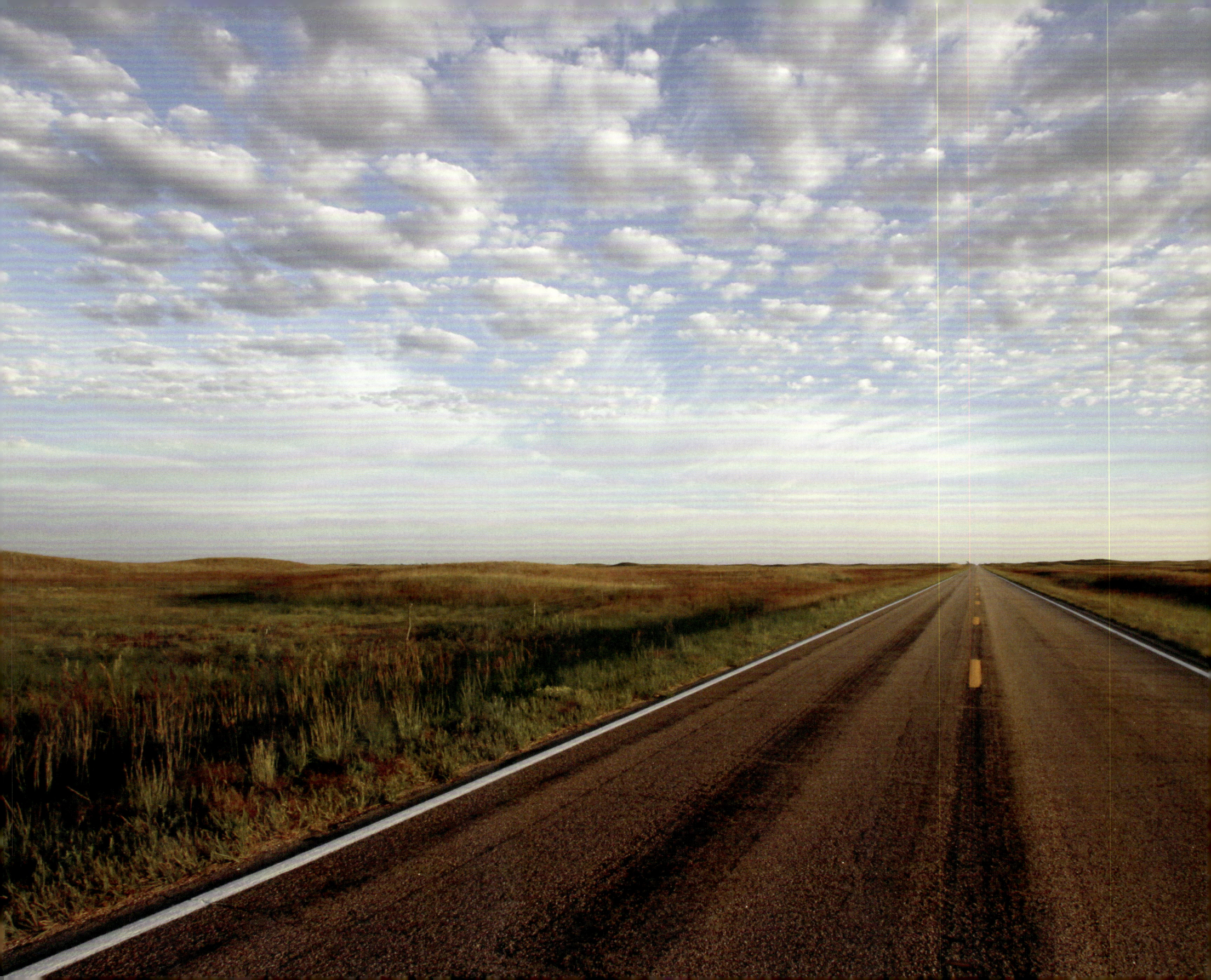

Rodeo competitors love Nebraska's rural highways just as I do. Long white trailers hauling well-trained horses crisscross these roads all summer. LOUP COUNTY

Lonely Roads and Where They Lead

I don't need directions to small-town rodeo arenas; dually pickups pulling horse trailers show the way. In summertime I share rural highways with these shiny six-wheeled pickups hauling long, white horse trailers topped with air conditioners and bales of hay.

Traveling rural routes gives me a sense of freedom I haven't found elsewhere. Rodeo competitors know this feeling. I have love affairs with certain Nebraska Sandhills highways. Other folks love them too but there is roadway enough to avert jealousy. The road rolls and winds like a Formula One track, but on either side lies Nebraska as the bison once knew it—grassy with occasional ponds speckled with migrant birds, and maybe thirty miles without passing another human, maybe fifty. I forget about the other world for a while and imagine it has forgotten me.

Cruising locals will likely wave. Where I live, drivers pass hundreds of strangers daily, but these travelers' next passerby may be a distant neighbor. Closing speed doesn't allow time to recognize acquaintances so everyone gets a wave just in case. Or maybe it's that strangers are worthy of a wave too. A few fingers upstretched from the steering wheel—maybe just the pointer finger—and passing drivers acknowledge we are briefly sharing this spot on earth. My hands grip the wheel low and out of sight; I'm always unprepared for wavers so a head nod must suffice. That is a mediocre trade for a finger wave and I feel deficient. Flashing past them I wonder who they might be, though I'm glad they are gone.

My name is penciled on desk calendars in tiny motel offices, reserved by word not by credit card. Appearing from their living quarters behind the office, owners might guess who I am as I enter. "Yep, that's me." Then I'll pet the owner's dog if one comes around. In my room an '80's-model tube TV aims toward an ultra-firm bed which must be shoved askew to reach the hidden electrical outlet. Some owners operate their business with love and it shows. If a place is dated, but clean and quaint, I make a mental note to stop back sometime. Others, secluded too many years, long ago stopped noticing all the little flaws that compose a motel from hell. It's a bad omen if I spend the first five minutes killing flies.

County seats host summer fairs, some of which hold rodeos sanctioned by state or regional associations. Generations of competitors region-wide have written the names of these towns on their kitchen calendars. Larger towns have carnivals with glowing midways; smaller towns simply have old-fashioned ribbon-giving events with entries ranging from grandma-jarred pickles to youth-raised pigs. Families and bands of teenagers are drawn by G-force-altering rides, funnel cakes, and maybe a concert. Boots and stroller wheels pass over electrical cords spider-webbing all directions from throbbing generators. Each fair has its own charm but each stands abandoned at rodeo time.

Too old to goof on the dance floor and too young to dance, this cowboy is content observing. BRIDGEPORT

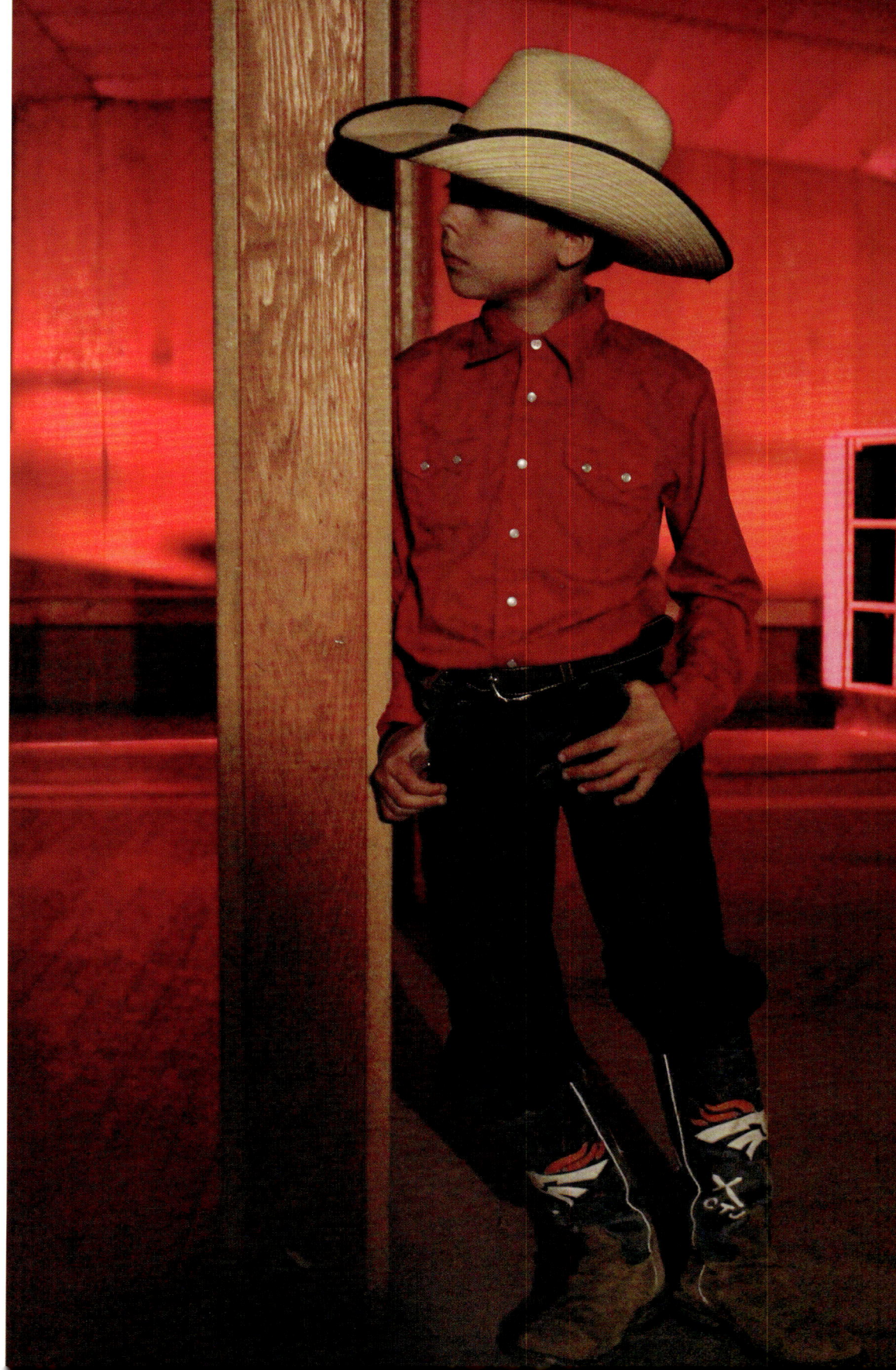

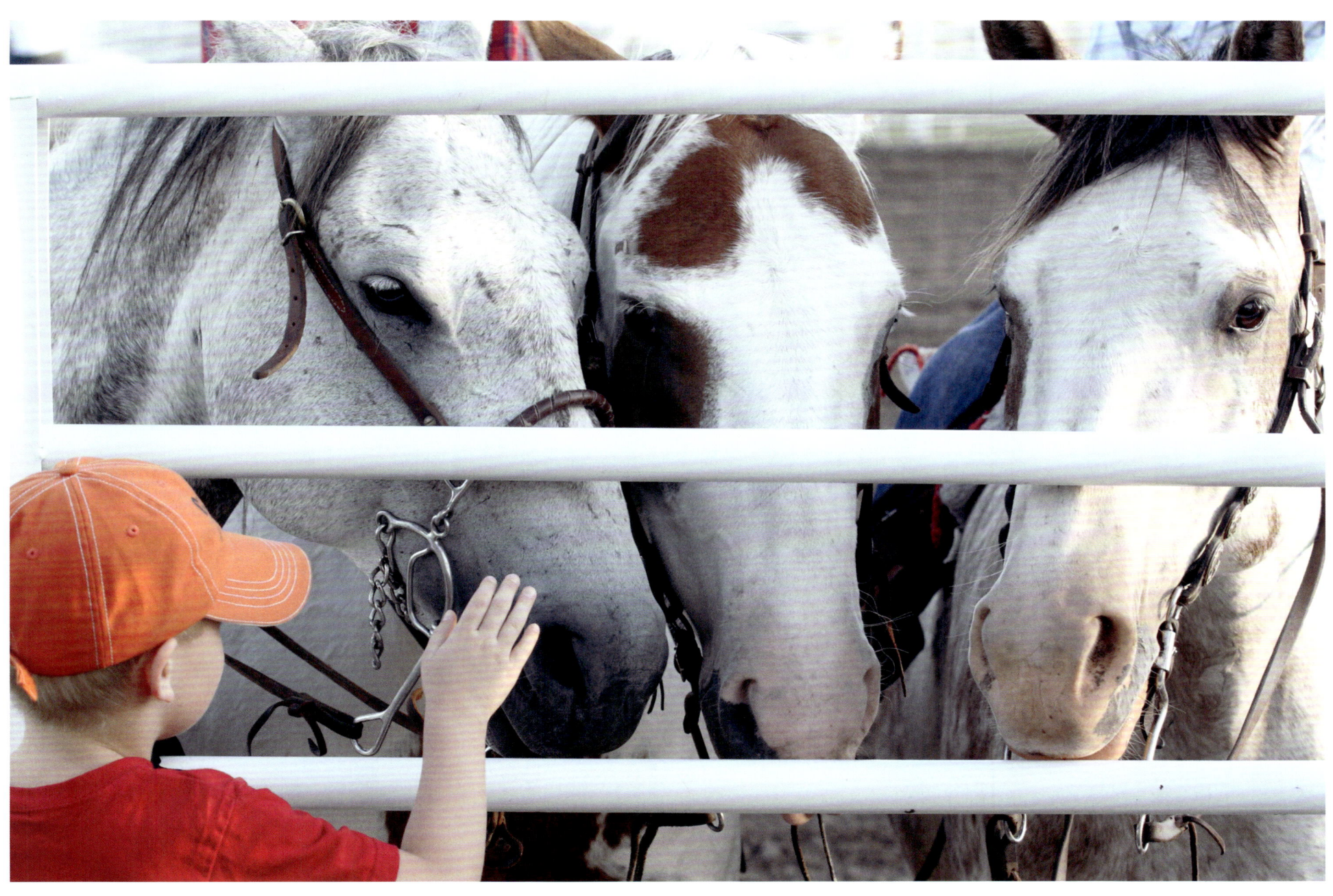

A city kid touches a horse for the first time, experiencing the animal's immensity, its smell, the heat and might of its breath, the sound of tails swishing at flies. FORT ROBINSON

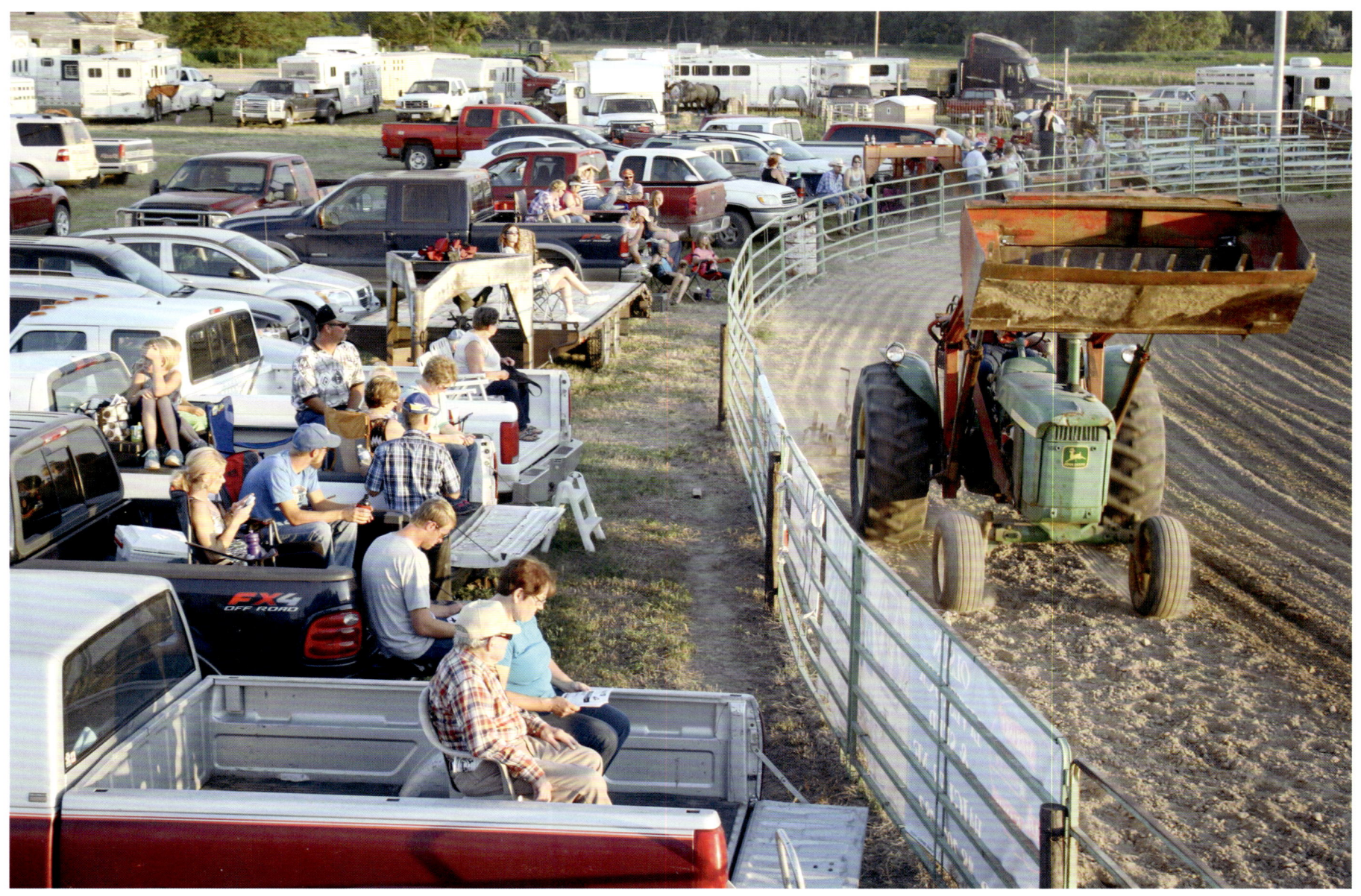

Early arrivals get arena-side seating at some small-town rodeos. Community members watch a tractor smooth dirt before the rodeo begins. BENKELMAN

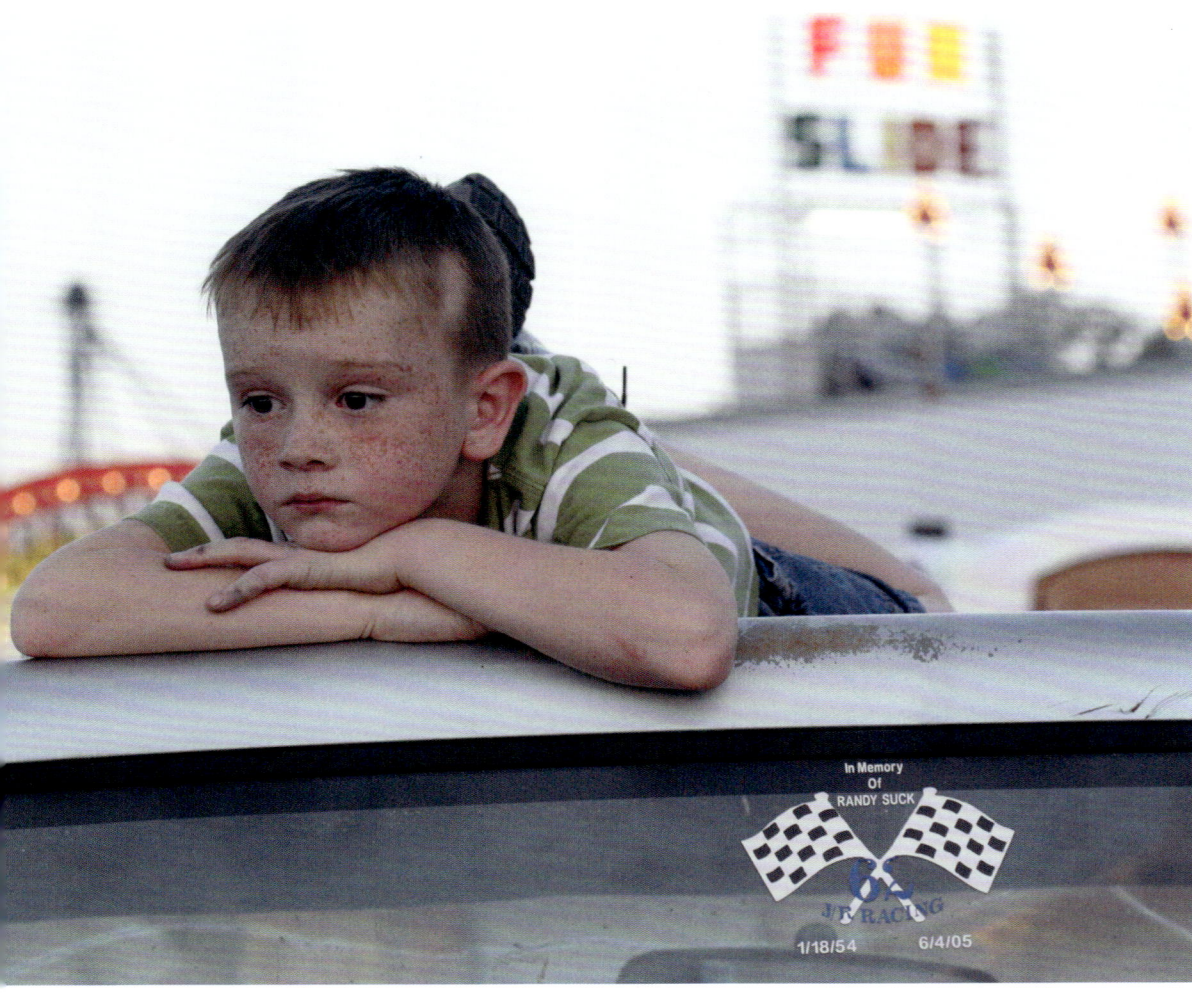

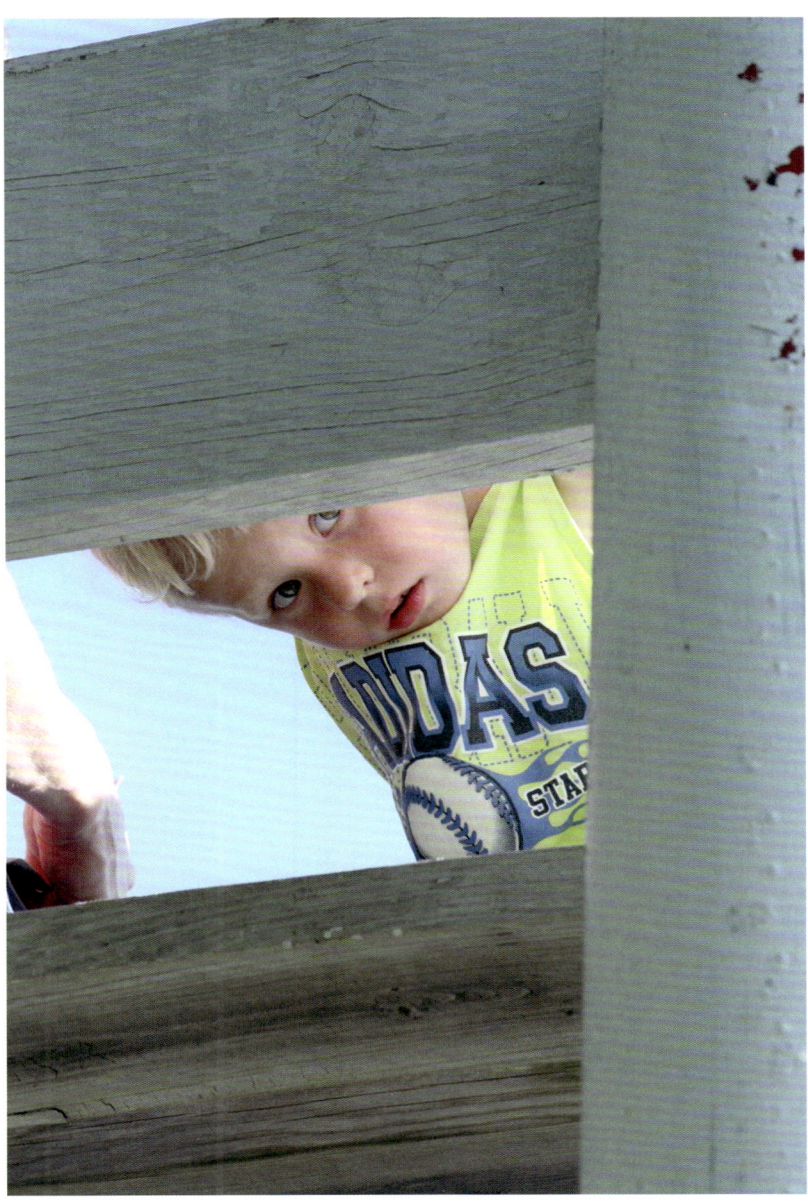

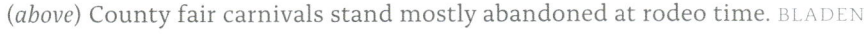

(*above*) County fair carnivals stand mostly abandoned at rodeo time. BLADEN

(*right*) As opposed to older women, who are consistently mortified by
my camera's attention, kids draw toward it. An occasional shy kid will
duck and hide, as this boy will do after one shot. O'NEILL

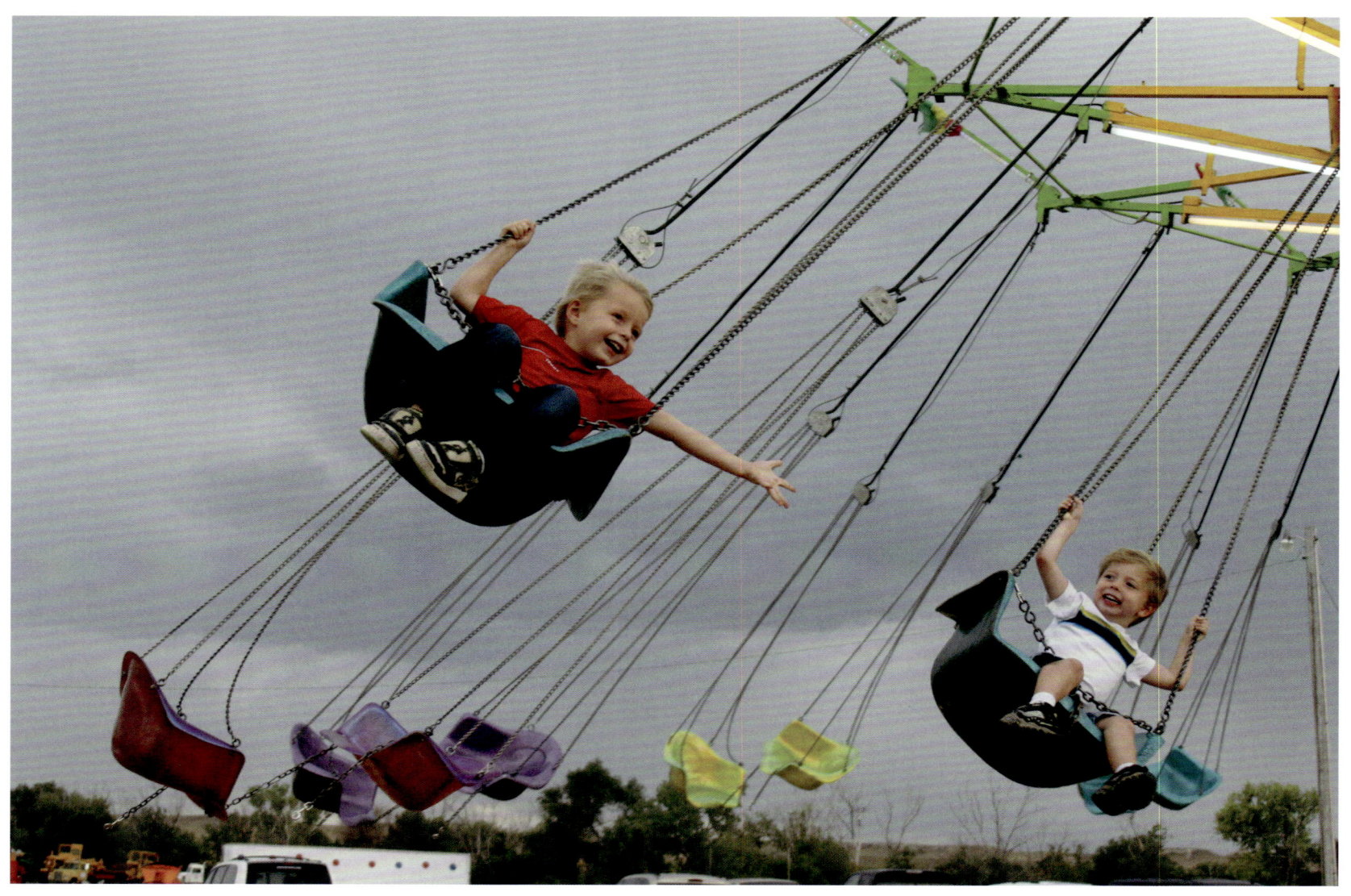

(*above*) A lasting memory is formed. SIDNEY

(*opposite*) SIDNEY

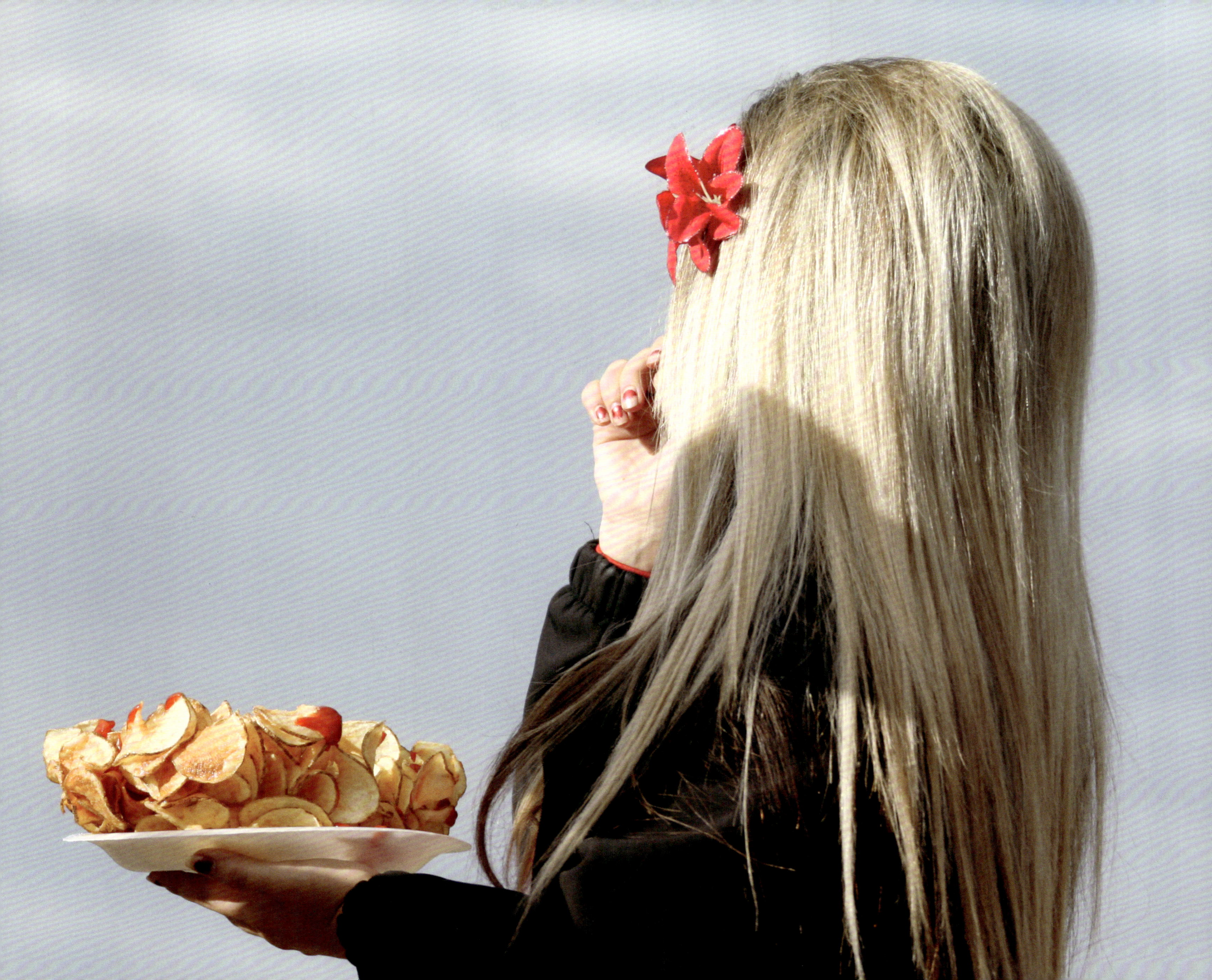

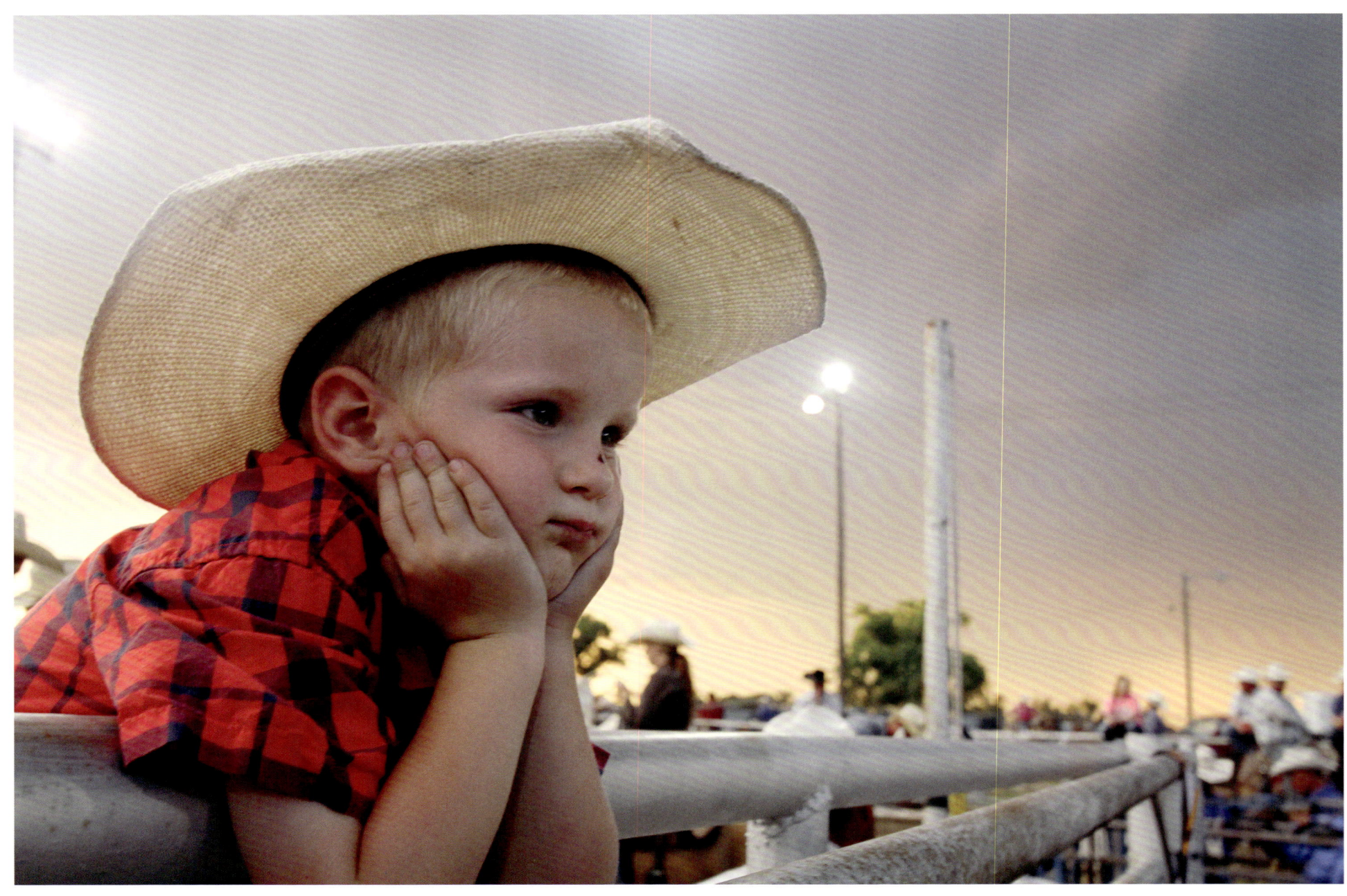

Policy is loose at small town rodeos; kids have liberty to roam. BRIDGEPORT

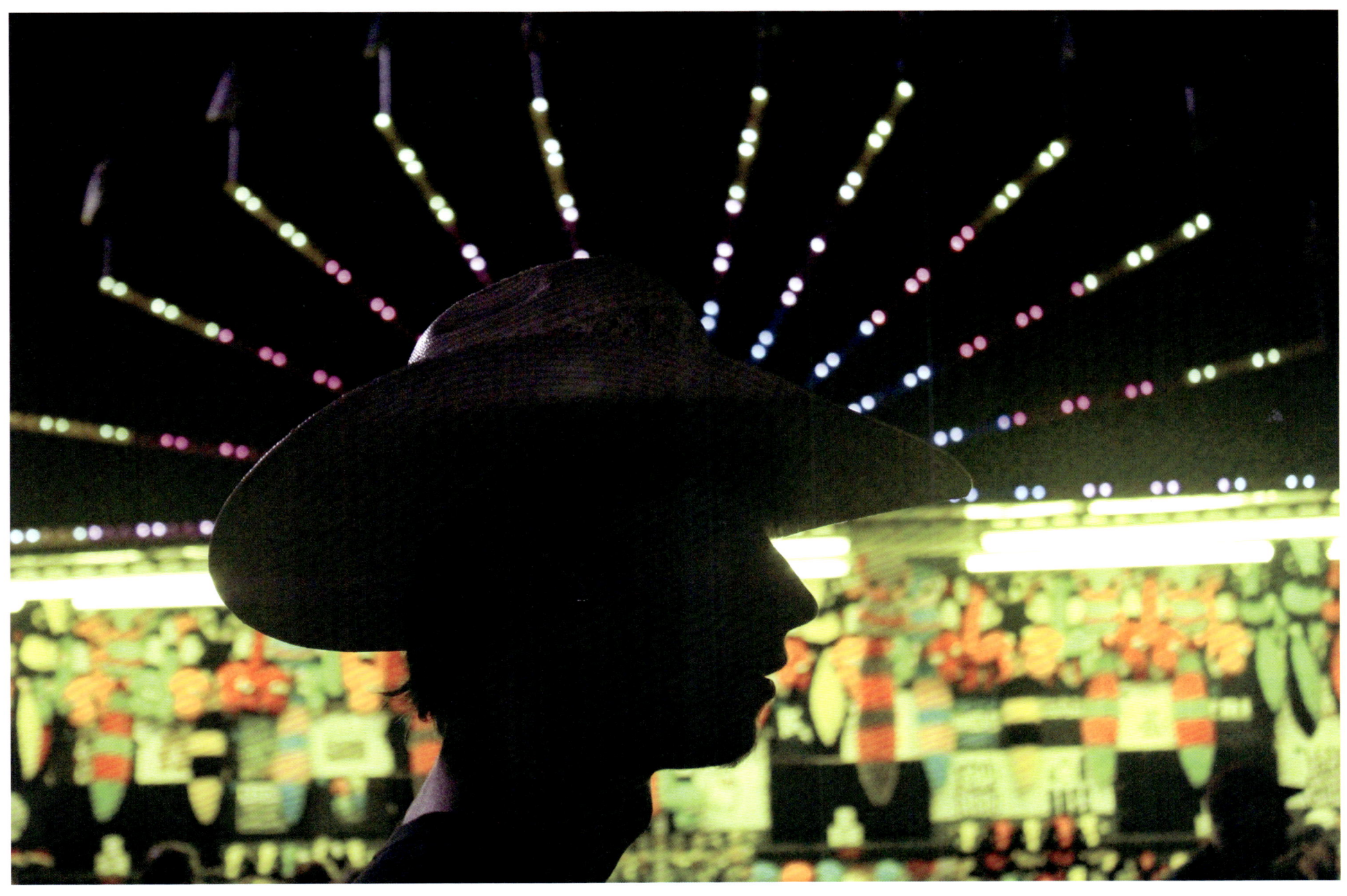

Cruisin' the midway with pals after bull riding ends. BLOOMFIELD

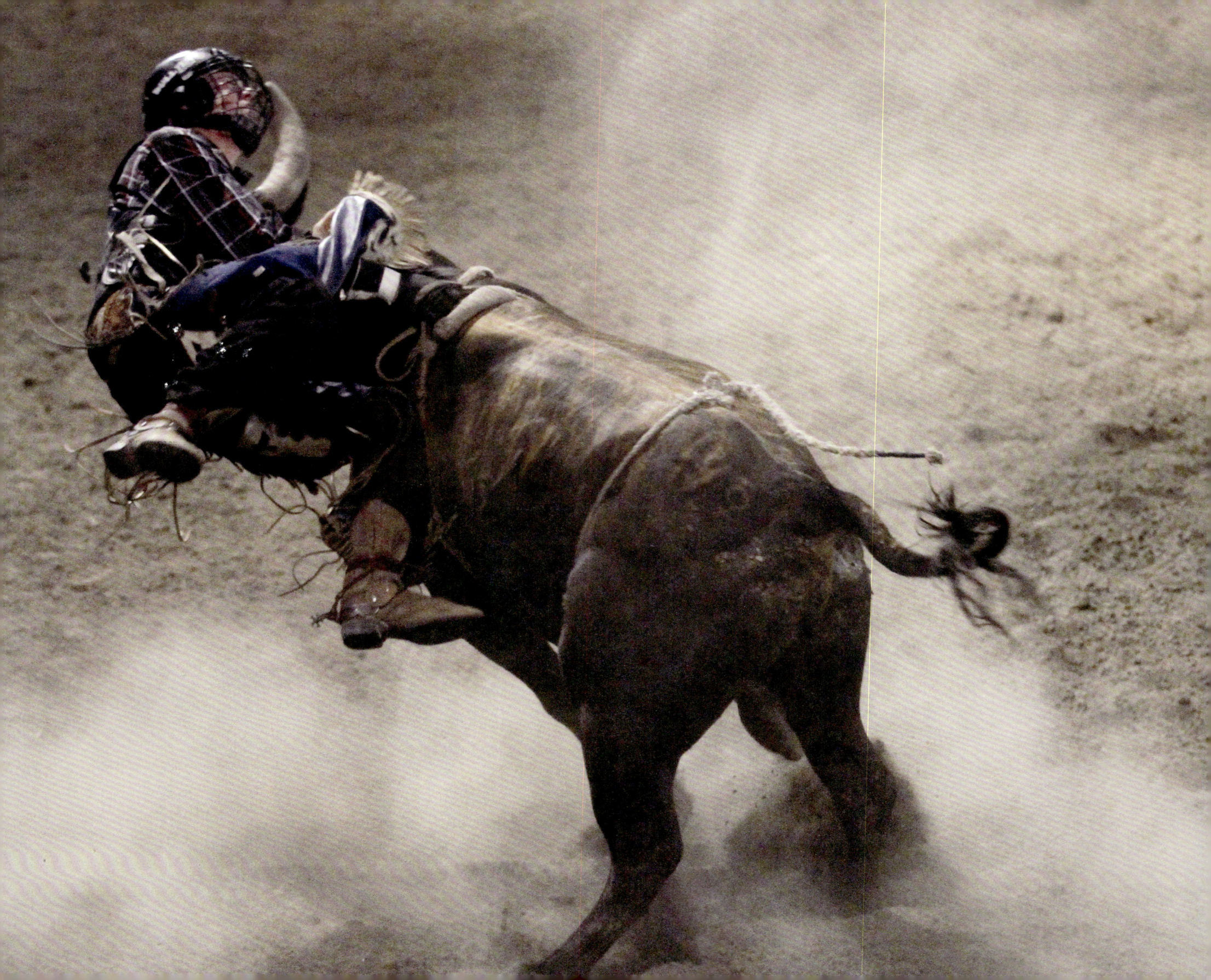

Hooves, Horns, Wrecks and Fury

BULL RIDING

Bull riding is electrifying. Illuminated by stadium lights, keyed-up fans have high expectations for the rodeo's last event. Men with nothing more than plastic swatters enter pens to shoo agitated bulls into narrow pathways leading toward chutes. The bulls' colors and sizes vary broadly. Some are horned and some not. Extra-long horns are ill-fitted for tight pathways, hitting vertical bars as they clang left horn, right horn all the way through. Some bulls need a persuasive slap in the hindquarters to enter the bucking chutes; others move too quickly, causing bottlenecks. Slaps and boot toes only strengthen a stubborn bull's resolve, until a stockman with a pocket zapper jolts their rump. The show must go on. Once they are in the right spot, cowboys slam dividing doors between bulls and they are trapped. Several bulls retaliate, kicking back or ramming forward. Metal dividers clang, wooden ones thwack and bow and I wonder how they have held up so long. Colliding bull horns are blemished with paint, like car grills from a fender bender. The bulls average 1,700 pounds, with some well over 2,000, and they are quick to anger. For that they are bred.

People don't just wake up one day and decide to become a bull rider. They come from agricultural backgrounds; they are raised as cowboys. Starting young, they ride sheep, then calves, then steers, and of course ride horses throughout their lives. A cowboy's sense of balance on a moving animal is well tuned, but it takes a certain type of young man to take the final step and get on top of a full-grown bull.

Like most bull riders, Jordan McAllister grew up around the sport. His uncle rode bulls. Jordan showed a genuine interest, so his dad sent him to bull riding school. This is common training for rookies, or even for veterans wanting to brush up their skills. Living in Gering, Nebraska, Jordan has attended several of these intense training camps during his career. He brings seriousness to bull riding because failure can be ugly. One principle of training: once you're thrown you get movin' because the bull may be comin' to squash you. After being thrown ten feet in the air and landing on his head, Jordan followed that rule at one fateful event, but after reaching the fence he knew something was wrong. His whole body shook uncontrollably.

"It took me seven months before I could get back on a bull after I broke my neck," says Jordan. That sentence sums up the abyss between bull riders and everyone else on the planet. I'll never truly understand them.

"Wrecks," as they are called in bull-riding lingo, can be so violent that it makes pro football seem like child's play. Heath Zuellner, of Cozad, Nebraska, lost three teeth in his high school rodeo days. That's the only lasting visible effect, but the same wreck also knocked him unconscious for four hours. Though great portions of Heath's memory from that day and the following day were deleted, when he woke in the hospital he knew where he was. He recognized the X-ray machine from the previous year's wreck. Stopping by the rodeo the next night to watch the competition, he overheard talk of his rumored death.

Why do smashed-up bull riders persist in riding? The answer doesn't vary: adrenaline. Camaraderie is a factor, as are cheering crowds, but it boils down to chemicals. "It's an adrenaline rush you can't experience anywhere else," Heath confesses. "I need that fix when I haven't been riding for a while. I get cranky." Money is not a factor. Most are happy winning just enough to pay their travel costs. Moods may worsen when finances wane but that won't stop them. "You get into a slump and you're not winning, and then the money gets low and it gets into your head," Heath says, "but then a good weekend comes and it all turns around." Most summer-circuit riders compete on fifty to seventy bulls per season so they will eventually win something, but sooner or later they will also be hurt.

Beer before a ride? Most wouldn't, but if anyone does it's likely a bull rider. ARTHUR

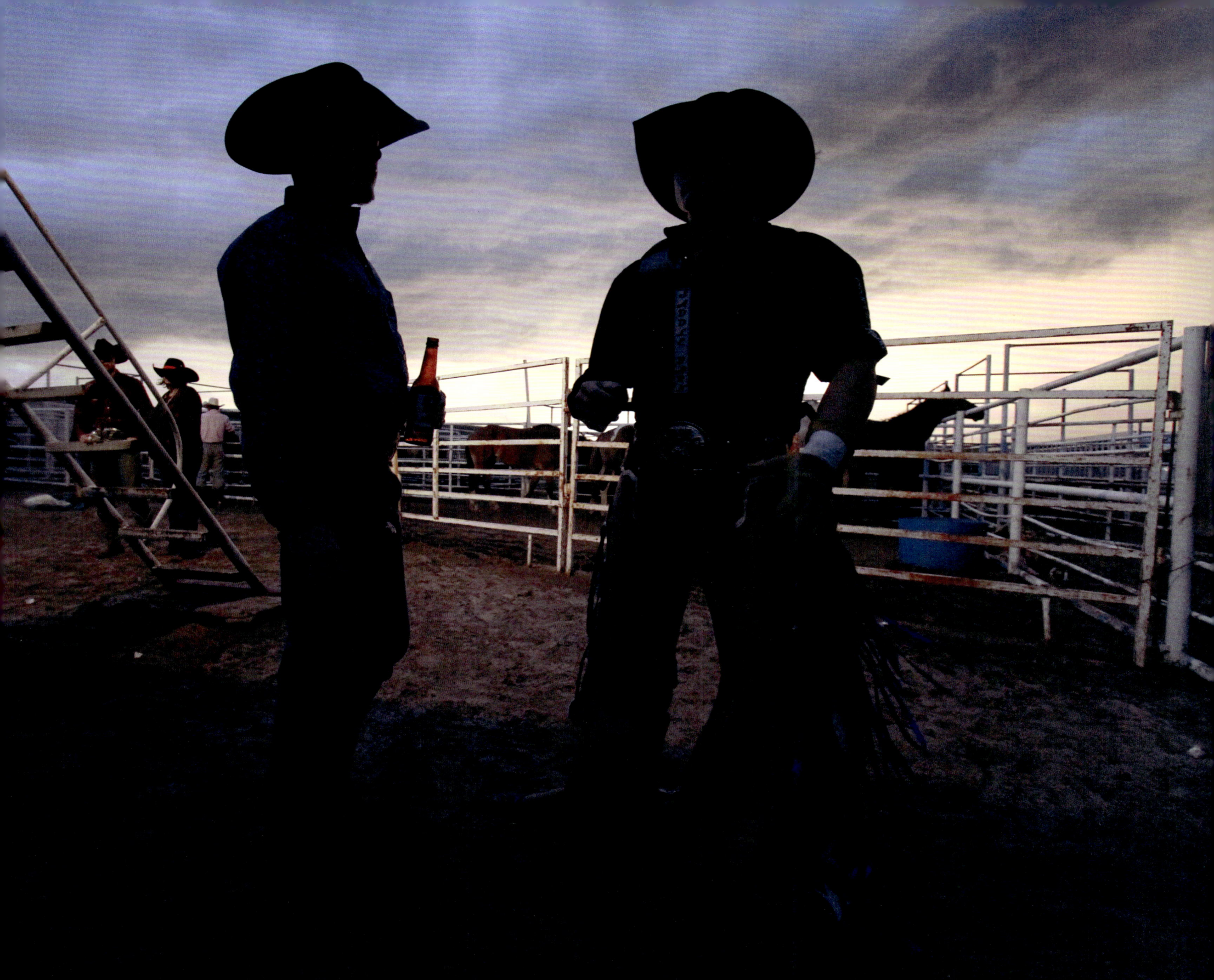

Dewey O'Dea of Johnstown is regularly at the top of the regional bull-riding standings. For twelve years he competed professionally in the Pro Rodeo Cowboys Association until children reprioritized his life. Now it's a family affair. His wife, Heidi, competes in barrel racing, and three-year-old Zoey often hangs out with Daddy behind the chutes. Zoey knows where not to be in this hectic environment and Dewey finds a fellow rider to watch her during his ride. Their family rodeo expedition is typical in Nebraska. Mom and Dad work all week, load the horse trailer on Friday, travel, compete, and then come home Sunday weary and worn but prepared to work the next day. They do it all summer.

Goals can be elusive in a sport where eventual injury is guaranteed, but all good bull riders form long-term aspirations. Performing at a high level means everything to those at the top. "If I aint winnin' and placin' then I'm not hitting my potential," Dewey says. "It's one of those deals where you know you do it good and there's no feelin' like that in the world."

Dewey had no intentions of riding bulls in his younger days until accompanying a bull-riding pal to practice. His friend wasn't keen on mounting a particularly nasty bull so Dewey ribbed him. Frustrated, the friend challenged Dewey to either shut up or get on himself. Dewey got on. "It felt good. I had a knack for it." At 5' 8" tall and 170 pounds, Dewey has the perfect bull-riding physique. Smaller guys, wiry but strong, do best in a sport where low center of gravity and a light frame benefit. There is one other noticeable common denominator behind the chutes: youth. At thirty, Dewey is nearing the end of his bull-riding career. He sees himself roping in the near future, a retirement plan of sorts.

In addition to rodeos, many riders compete in bull-riding-only events which pop up across the state in late summer. Pens, chutes, bulls, and sound systems emerge like traveling carnivals in little towns like Emerson, Scribner, and Worms. Torn down and packed up the next day, on it rolls. These events offer more prize money than average rodeos, so riders travel from afar.

Bull riding events often give audience members the chance to cash in by bidding on riders who are auctioned off like livestock in a sale barn. If your rider wins first or second place, you're in the money. Before the final round, bulls are also auctioned off as a group—if nobody rides eight seconds then the bull bidder wins. Bidding is driven by emotion, not logic, and can rise into the hundreds. Based on my years of observation and some math, those bidding on riders have terrible odds. Though they might quadruple their bet with a win, this probability is only about 10 percent, with just a 20 percent chance of any return at all. With an average bid of $270, that hurts. Savvy gamblers bet on the bulls in the final-round. This bid can be in the $400's and winning will triple it. Betting on the bulls means your odds of winning first or second place are about 80 percent.

Every rodeo and bull-riding organization requires various skill levels, but most Nebraska events are neither professional nor amateur; they are something in between. Many highly skilled regional competitors could make the transition to pro, but, as Dewey O'Dea found, one often can't spare the time between family and jobs to do so. Competing at a high level within their area is enough to feed the addiction. These rodeos sanctioned by regional or state associations do award prize money, just not nearly as much as in professional circuits.

To move to a professional rodeo association, one buys a permit for a few hundred dollars to compete with the pros for a year. You are then a "permit holder." If you win at least $1,000 in pro events that year then you become a "card-holder," a pro. If one doesn't hit $1,000 in prize money during a pro year then they must buy another permit to compete the following year. It's a tougher world in pro rodeo. Times are faster in speed events and bucking animals are fiercer. However, regional rough-stock breeding programs have taken great strides recently, and some animals buck as wickedly in Nebraska as in any pro event—a dangerous formula with less-experienced riders. It's not uncommon to see ten bull riders bucked off in a row at any given Nebraska rodeo. But for those who persist, there is decent money to be made and large wells of adrenaline to tap.

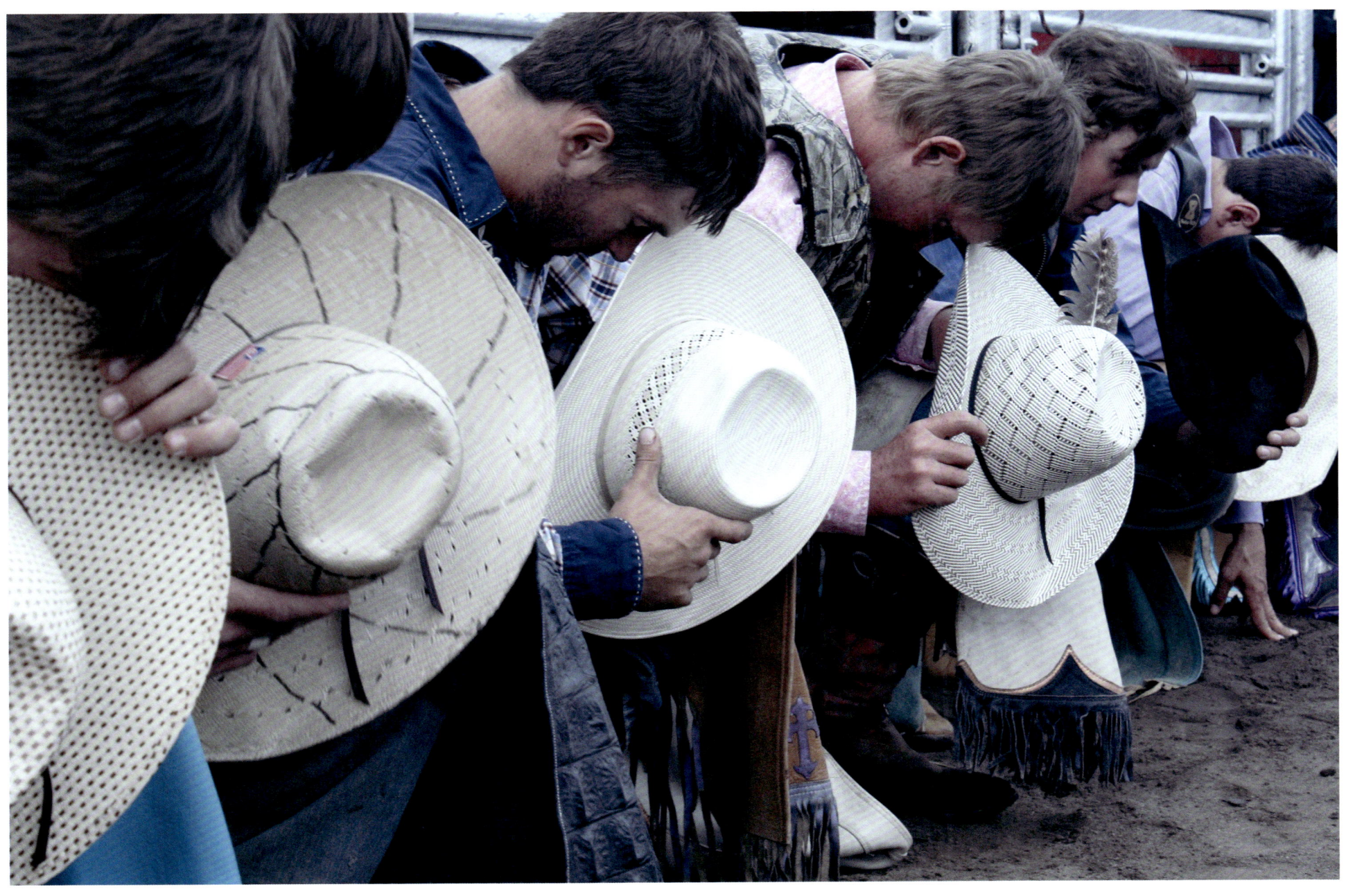

A cowboy-themed prayer over loudspeakers precedes every rodeo. BROKEN BOW

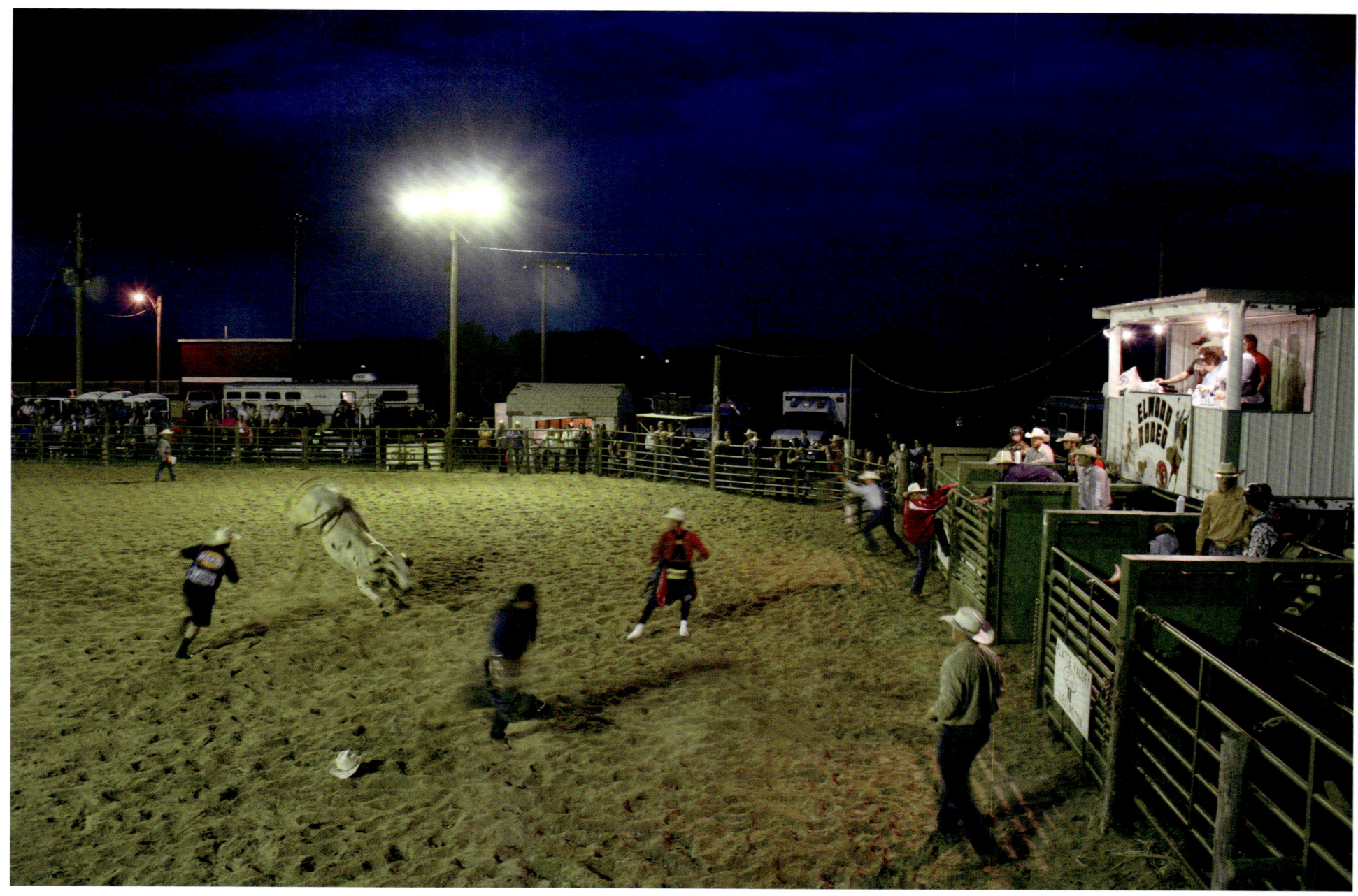

A bull rider runs for safety as the bull fighters mind the bull. ELWOOD

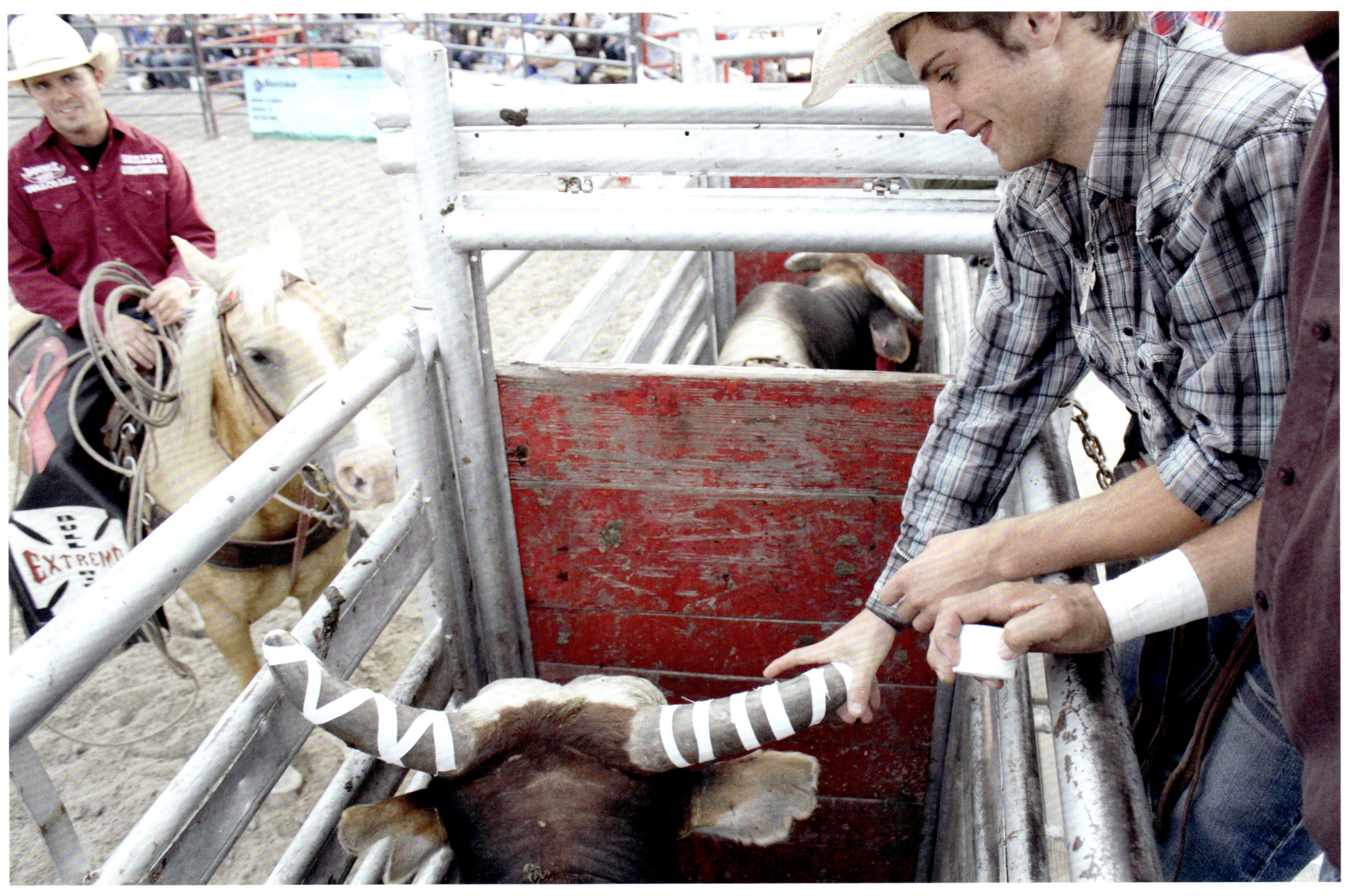

Passing time before their rides, bull riders decorate a cooperative bull's horns. GENEVA

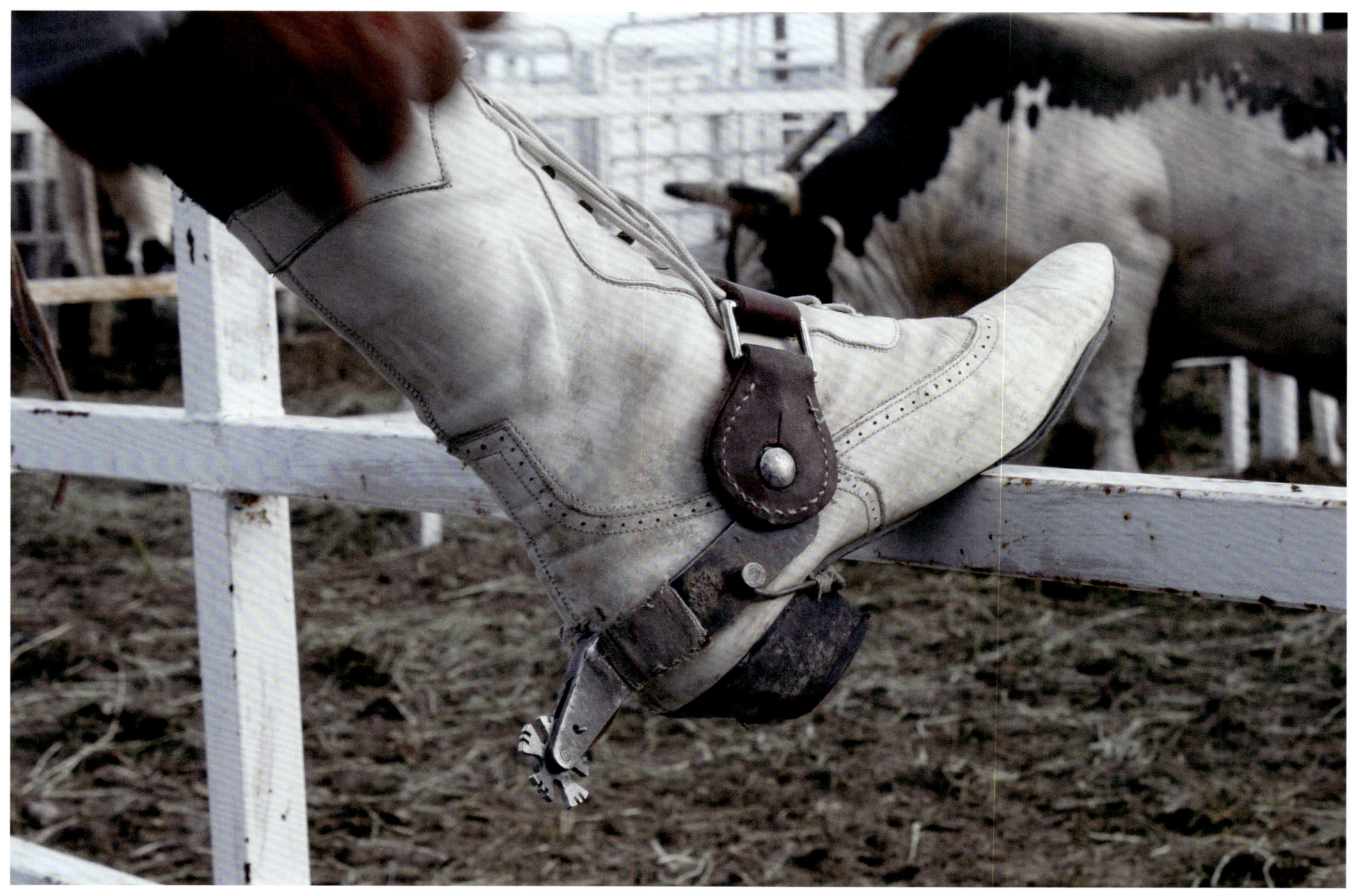

Quirky boots bring bull rider Trey Kerner good luck. Every year I rib him
about his boots and every year he just smiles and wins. SIDNEY

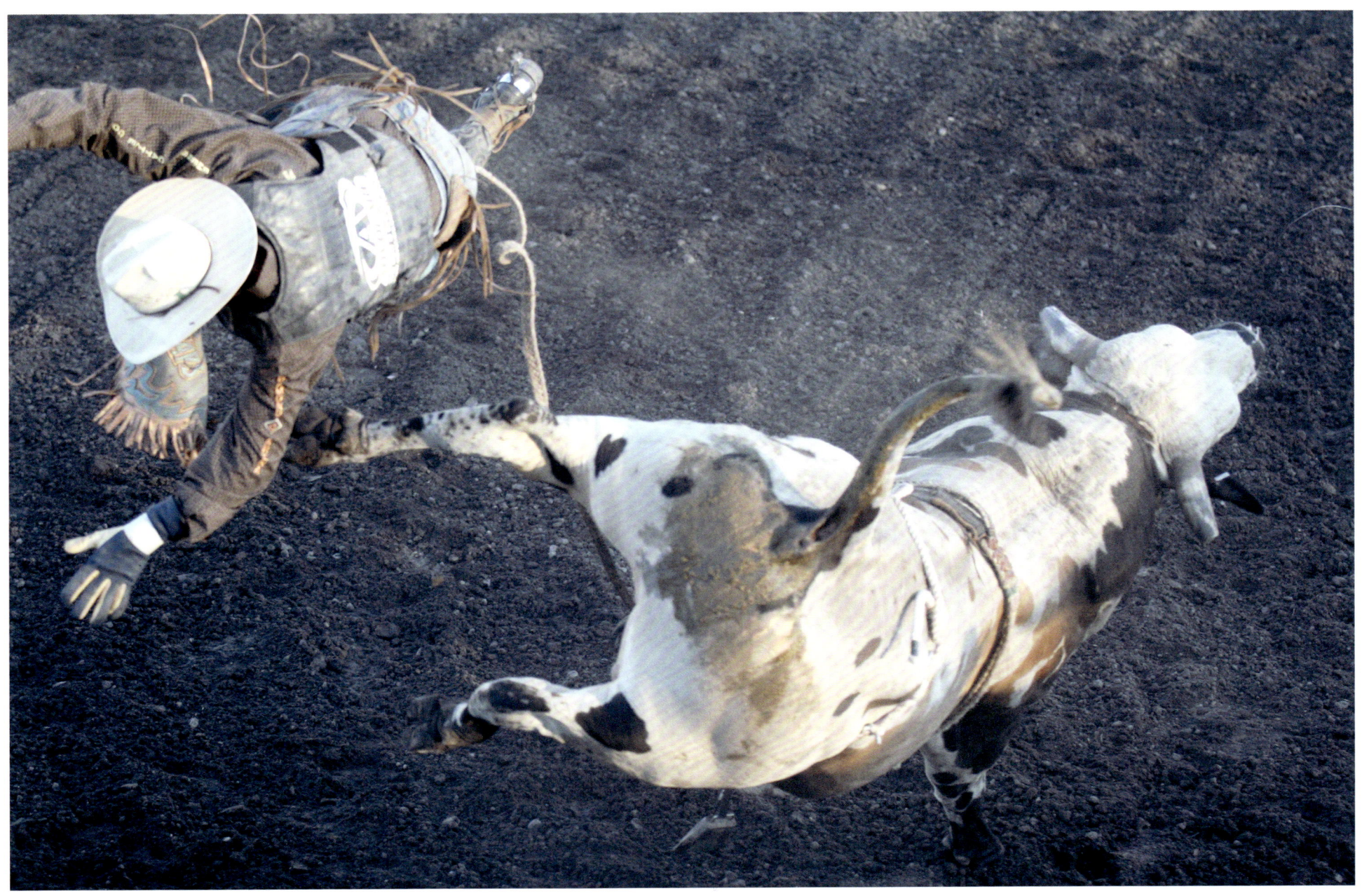

It's seems to me that bulls are about 10 percent anxiety and 90 percent anger. Bull rider Jordan McAllister agrees but adds, "I think the oldest bulls just want to get it over with. Either way, they all know how to buck." SIDNEY

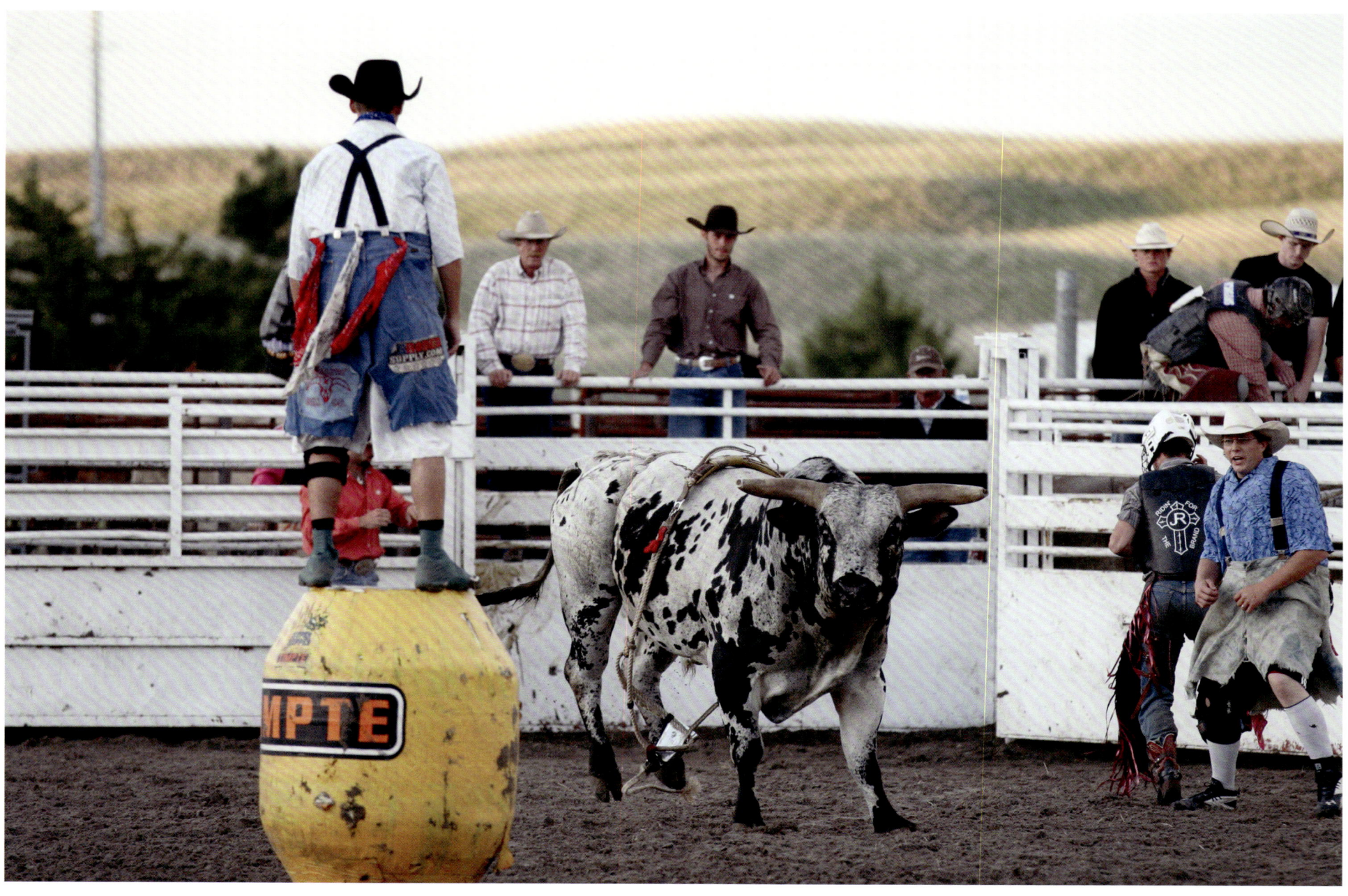

A bull glares at the barrel man before he attacks. The man will
leap from the barrel just before impact. THEDFORD

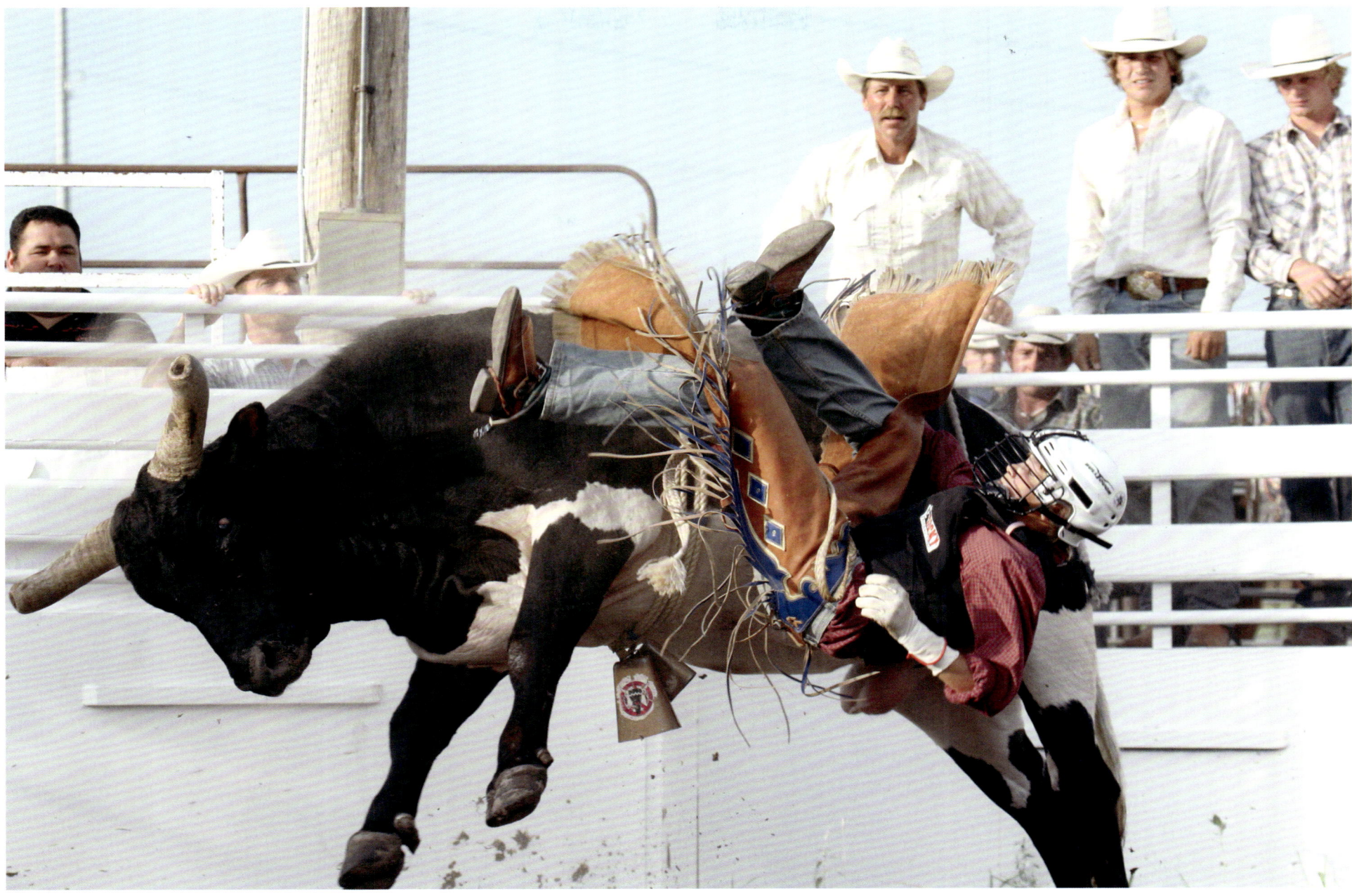

THEDFORD

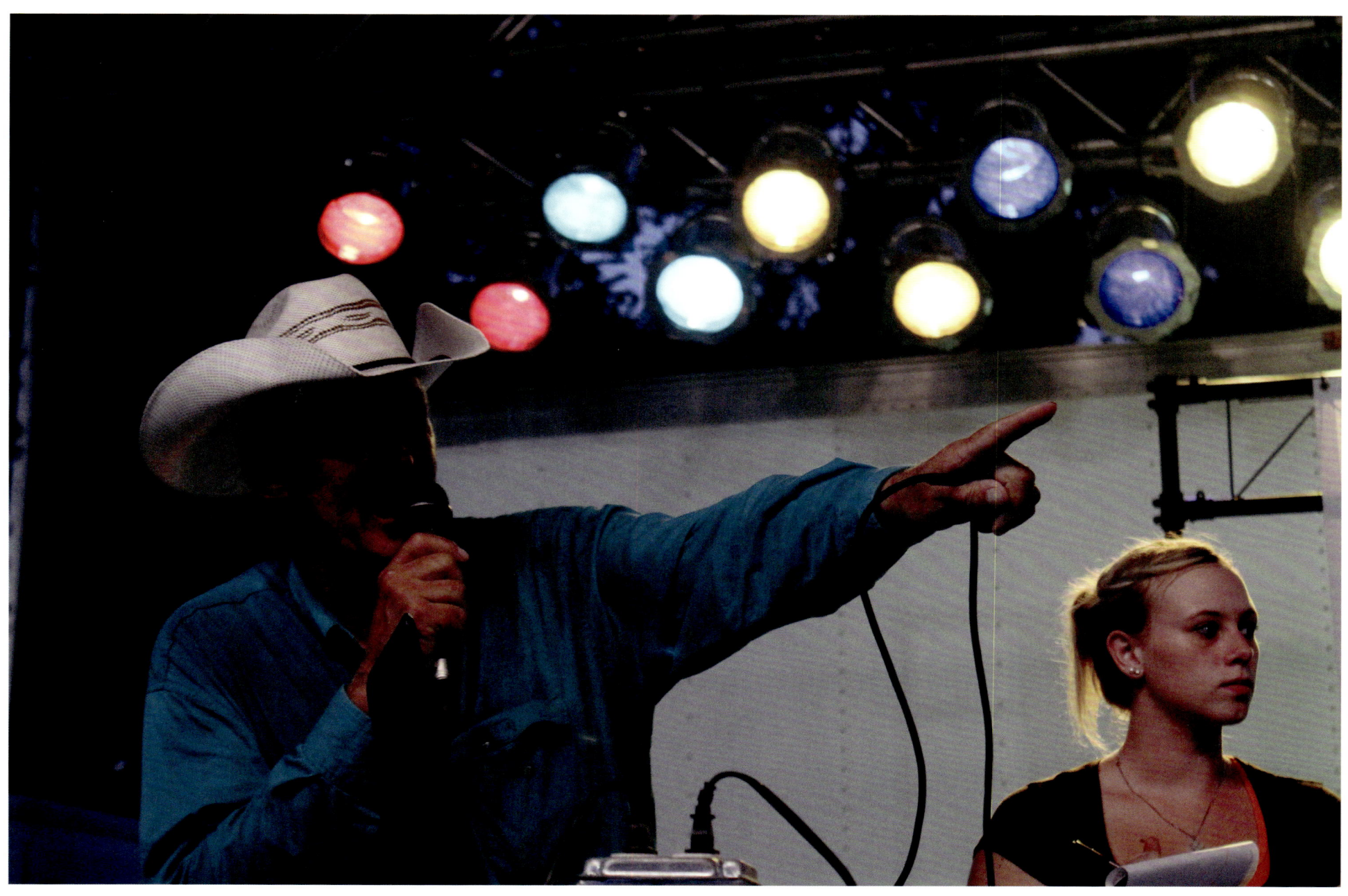

An auctioneer takes a bid on a bull rider during the pre-rodeo "Calcutta." WORMS

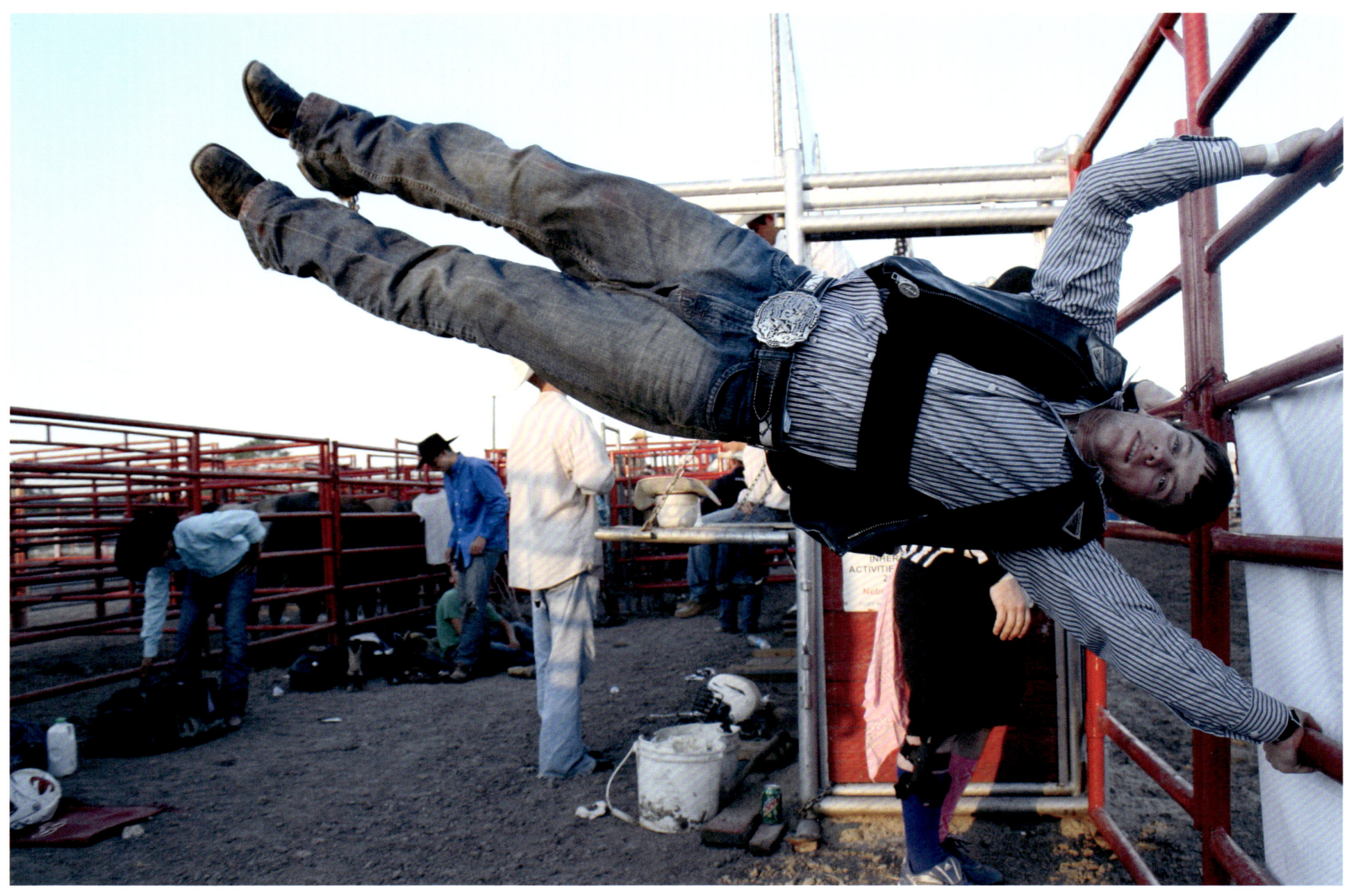

Warming up before his ride, Trevor Reiste is an athletic trainer
and horse jockey when not riding bulls. GENEVA

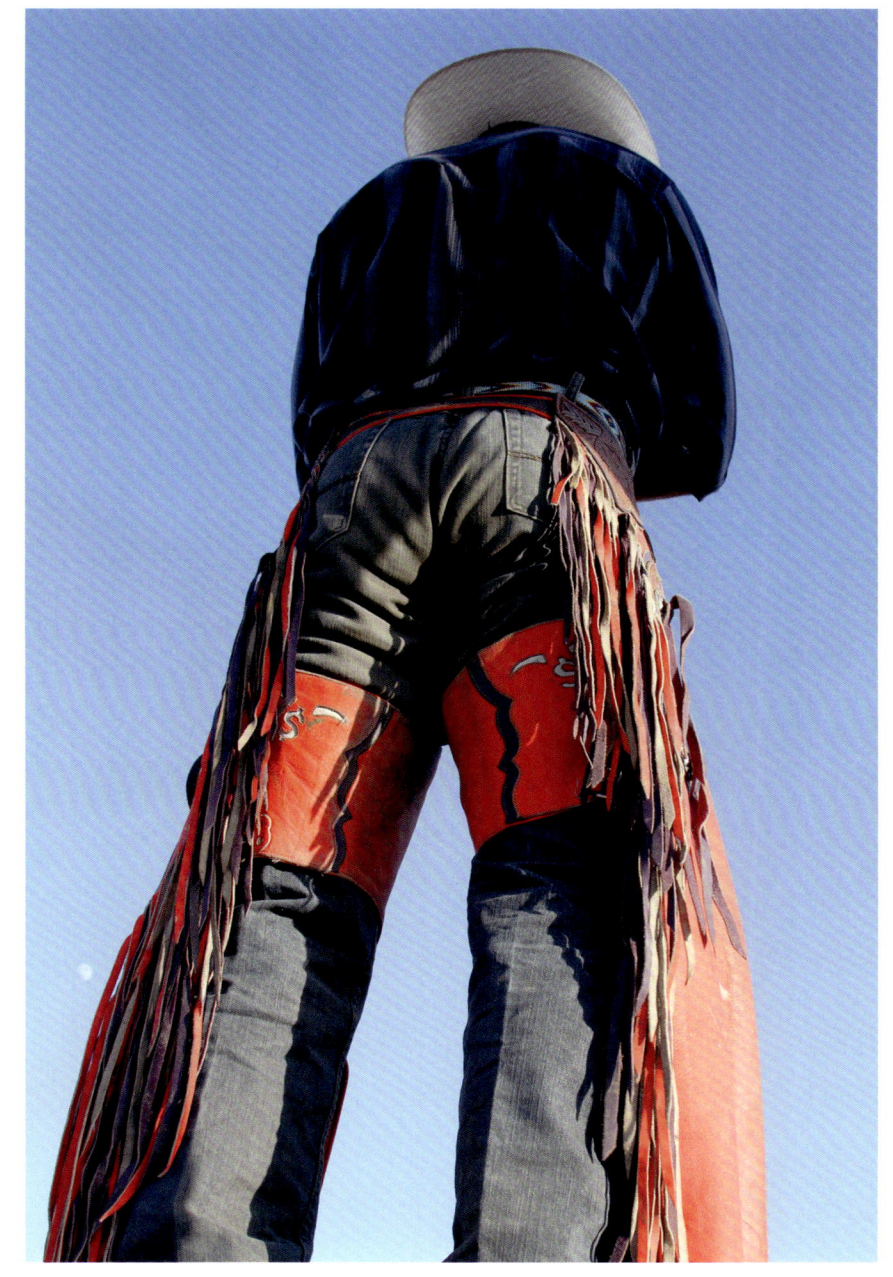

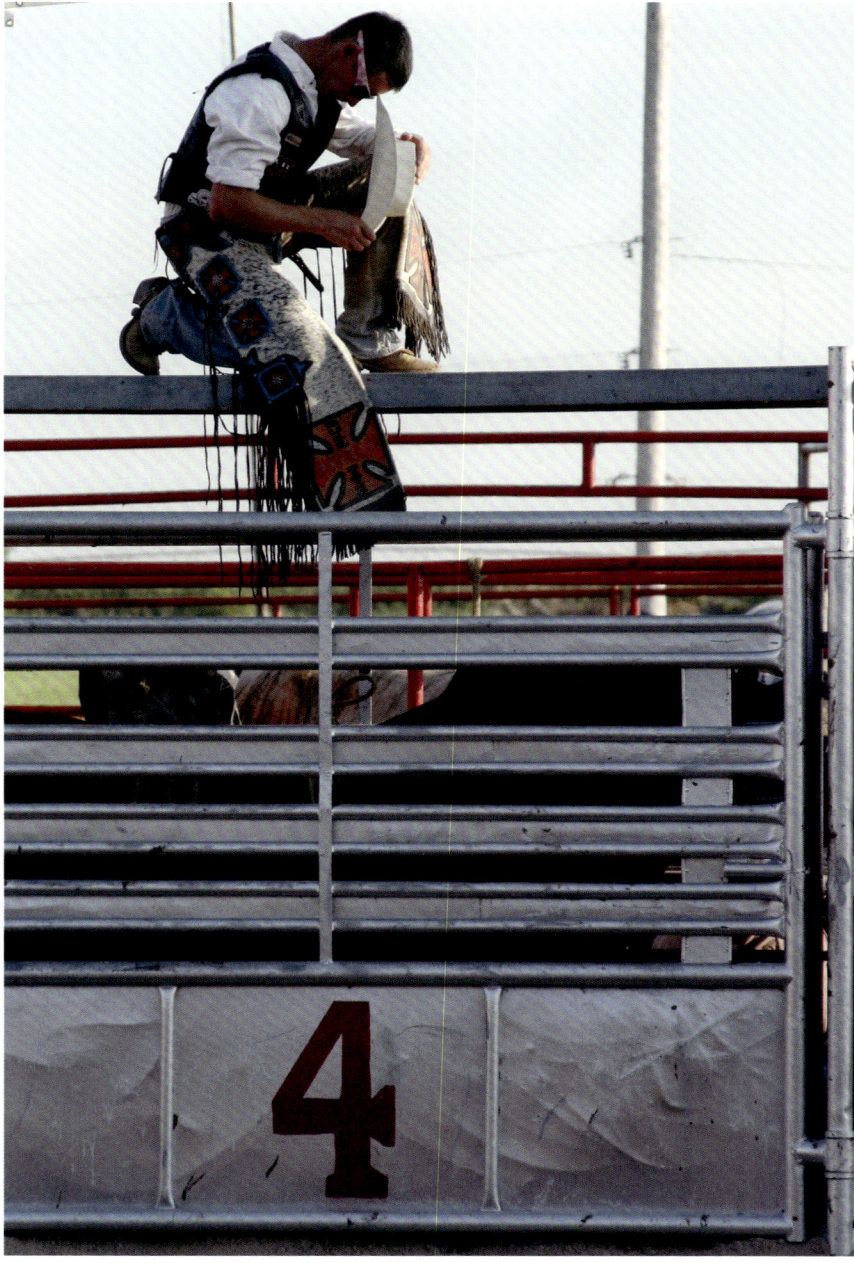

It's a religious group, those who ride, rope, and wrestle. AURORA

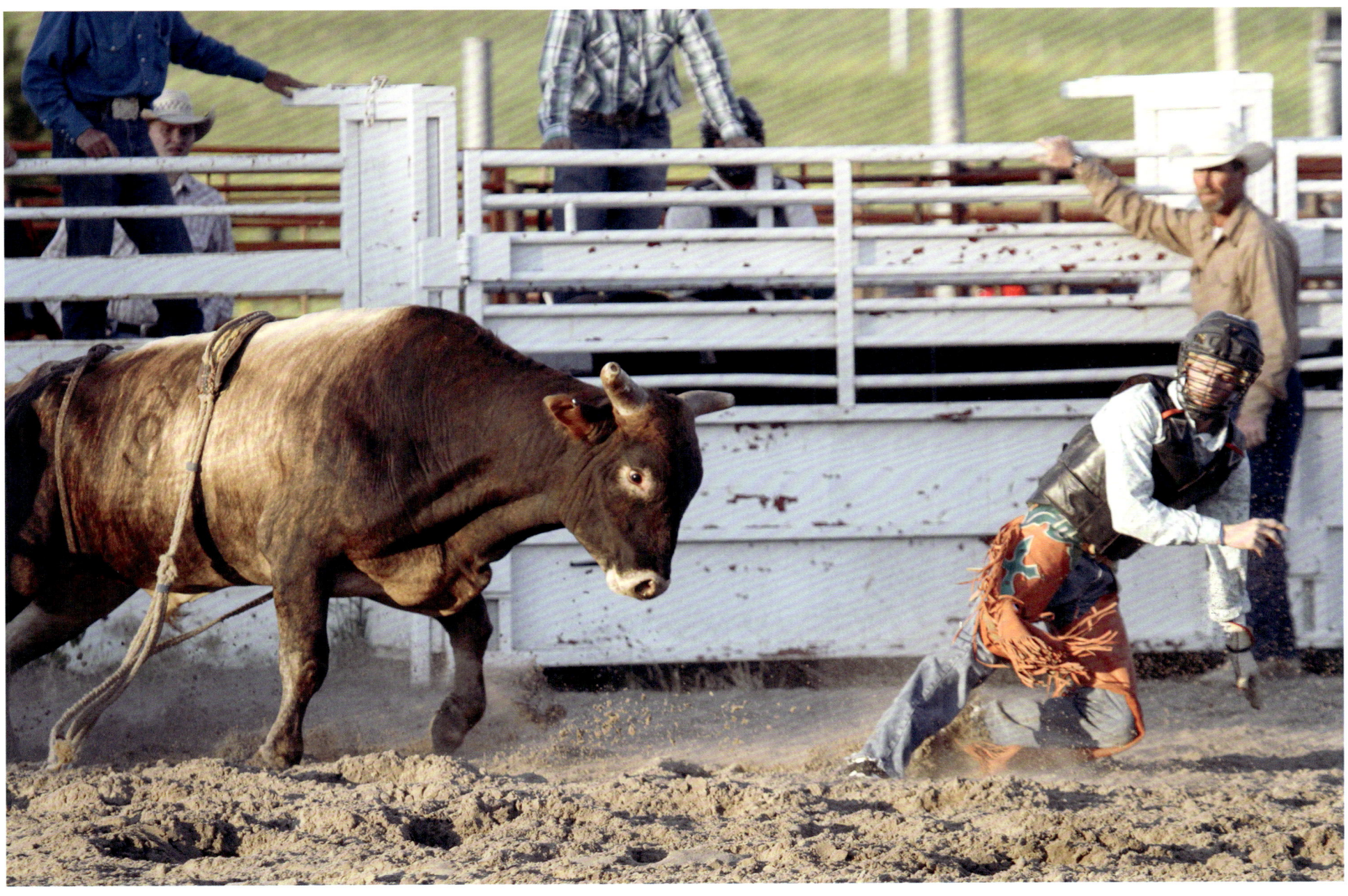

Within several strides, this bull will catch the rider and grind him into the dirt until the shouting, slapping bull fighters save him. THEDFORD

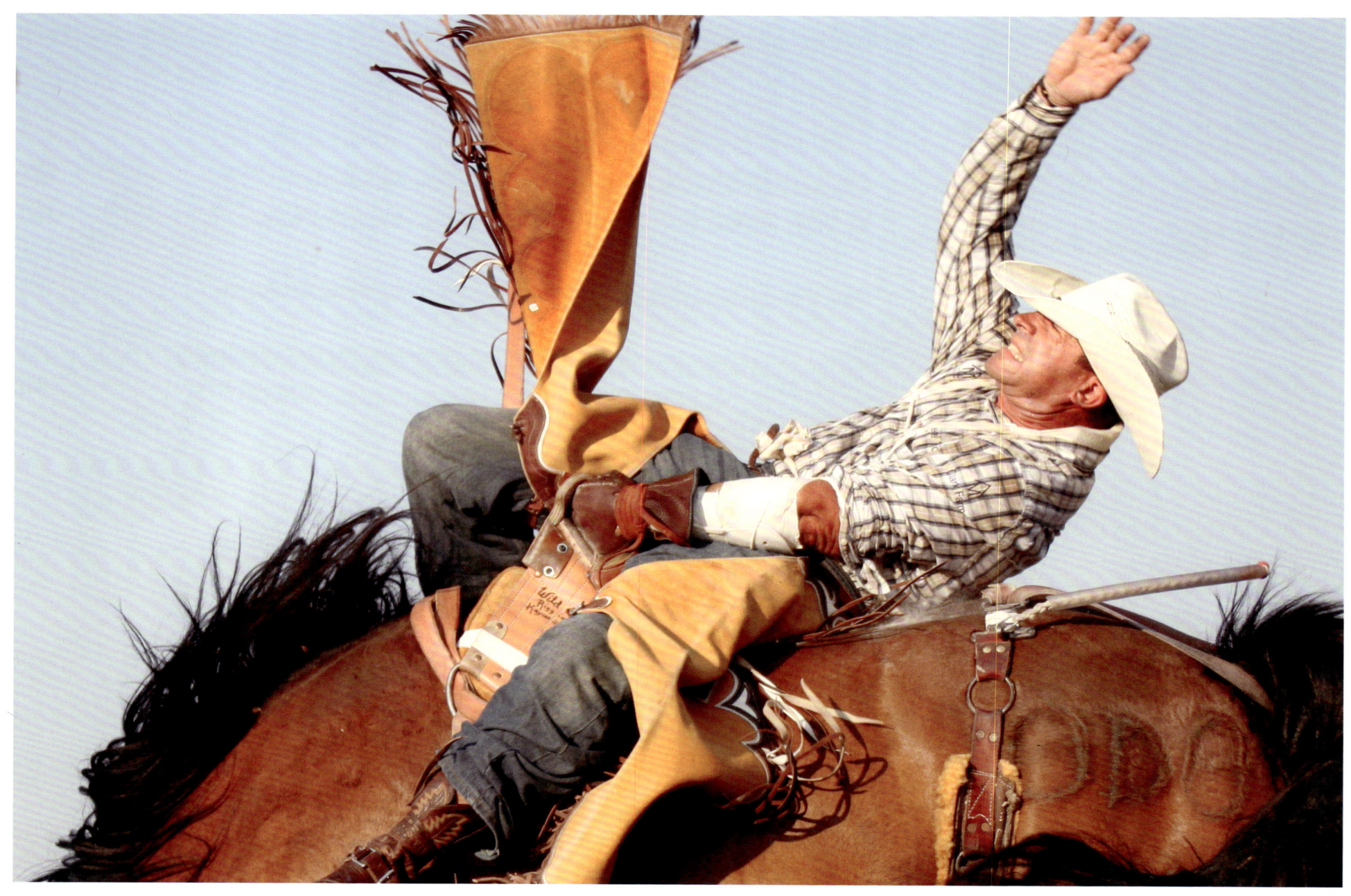

"It's a natural high," say rough-stock riders. Pure adrenaline feeds them all season. BERTRAND

Adrenaline!

"Adrenaline Junkie" is not an official diagnosis, but it is well understood by those in psychiatry. Most of us can remember some frightening thing we did intentionally, such as jumping from a pool's high board or sledding down a steep hill. We sought this feeling as kids and loved it. Some of us still do. Science says this brief exhilaration is all about chemicals: endorphins, dopamine, and norepinephrine—all great stuff in natural doses. Endorphins relieve pain and infuse euphoria, like the drug hydrocodone. Dopamine has several effects on the brain; it's what your brain gets during sex, for instance. It controls the brain's reward and pleasure centers and is sometimes likened to cocaine. Norepinephrine, often associated with our body's fight-or-flight response, makes our brains and bodies work faster and better. Its illicit-drug cousin is amphetamine—speed.

Though adrenaline may drive them, there are also specific human traits in the successful rodeo-competitor formula: high achieving personalities, those type-A people who succeed in anything because they work relentlessly toward long-term goals; toughness, more specifically toughness gained from working with livestock; natural athletic ability; and a bit of obsessive compulsiveness, which is necessary to maintain type-A traits. Toss in the lure of recurring, all-natural shots of addictive neurotransmitters and there you have the outstanding rodeo competitor.

Rough stock riders receive the biggest doses of these chemicals, and though natural doses don't cause harm, the animals that feed the addiction might. Originally I saw little sense in riding bulls or broncs; the risk/reward ratio seemed lopsided. But the more I exposed myself to these events and the closer my camera got to the action, the more I understood. My risk factor was relatively low. If I kept good footing atop metal bars all would be well. But being close to the action, dodging broncs in the arena, climbing around loaded bull chutes, topping my last best photo—it became my addiction. This summer obsession left me wanting by late winter. In spring I went back for my own kind of rush. During the first years without real goals, shooting rodeos simply injected thrill into my life—a bit of joy—and isn't that something we all search for?

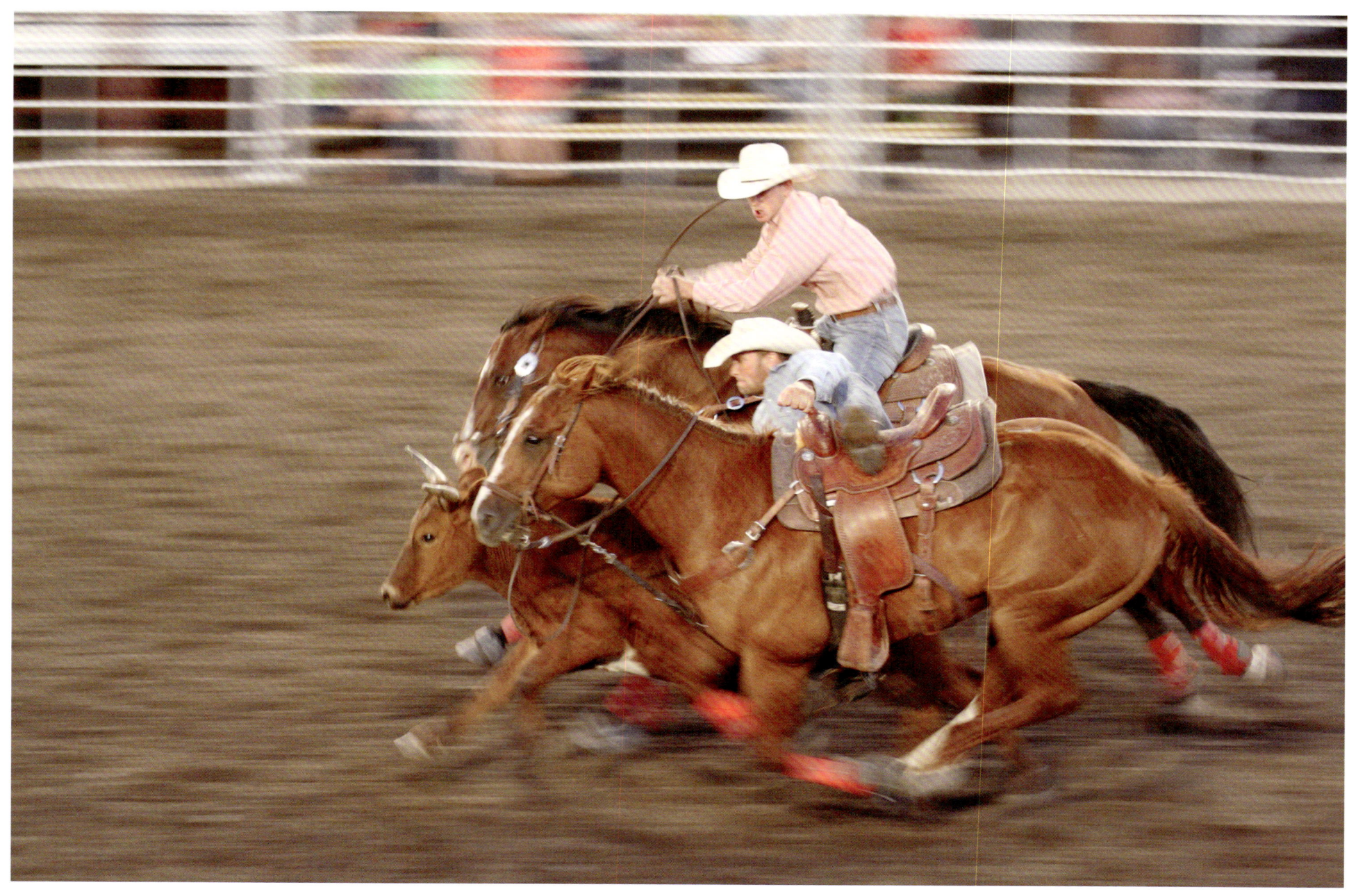

Driven people—type A personalities—find success in rodeo. SIDNEY

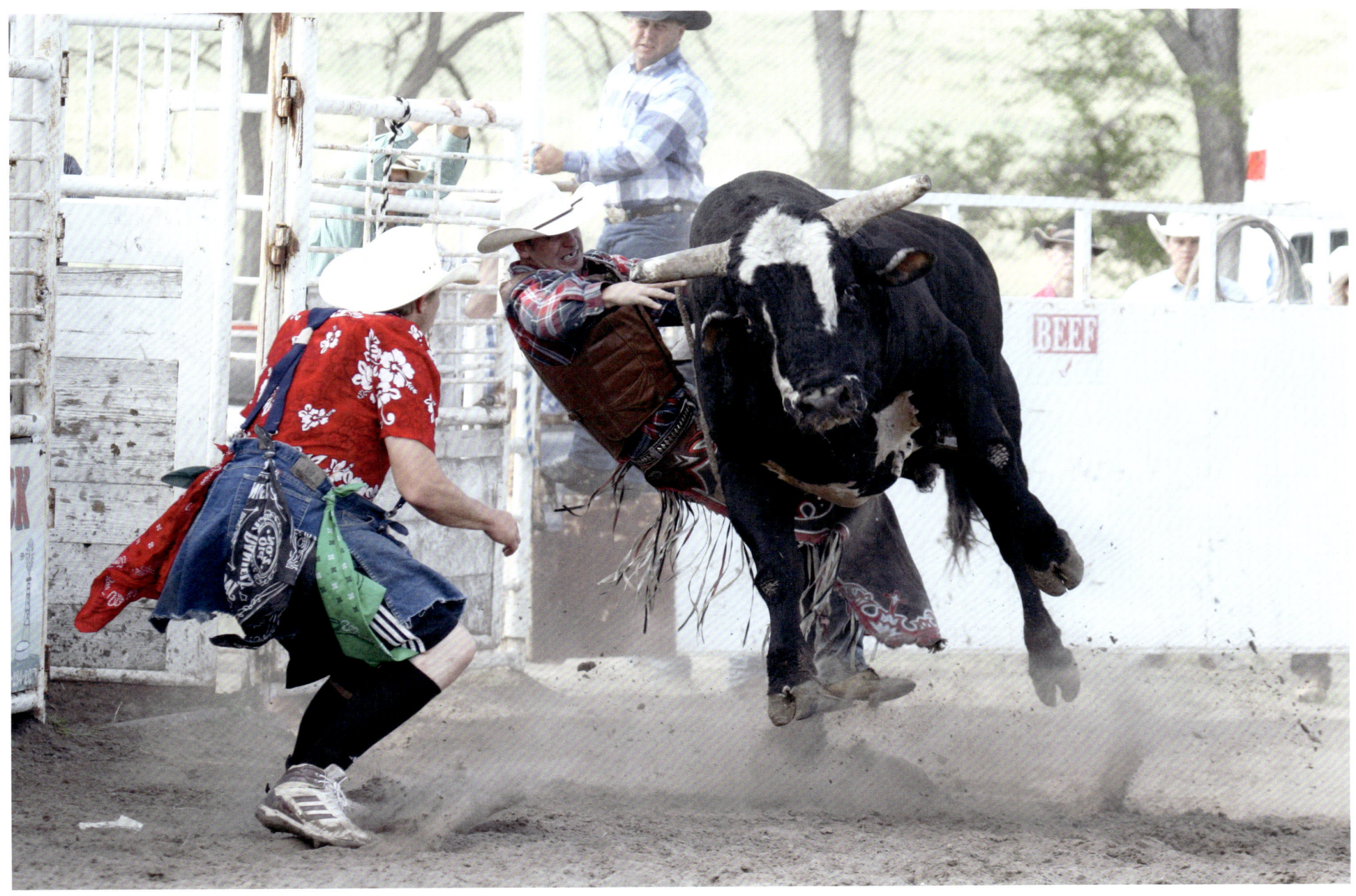

Bull riders get two adrenaline shots: one from the ride itself
and one escaping the ensuing wrath. ARTHUR

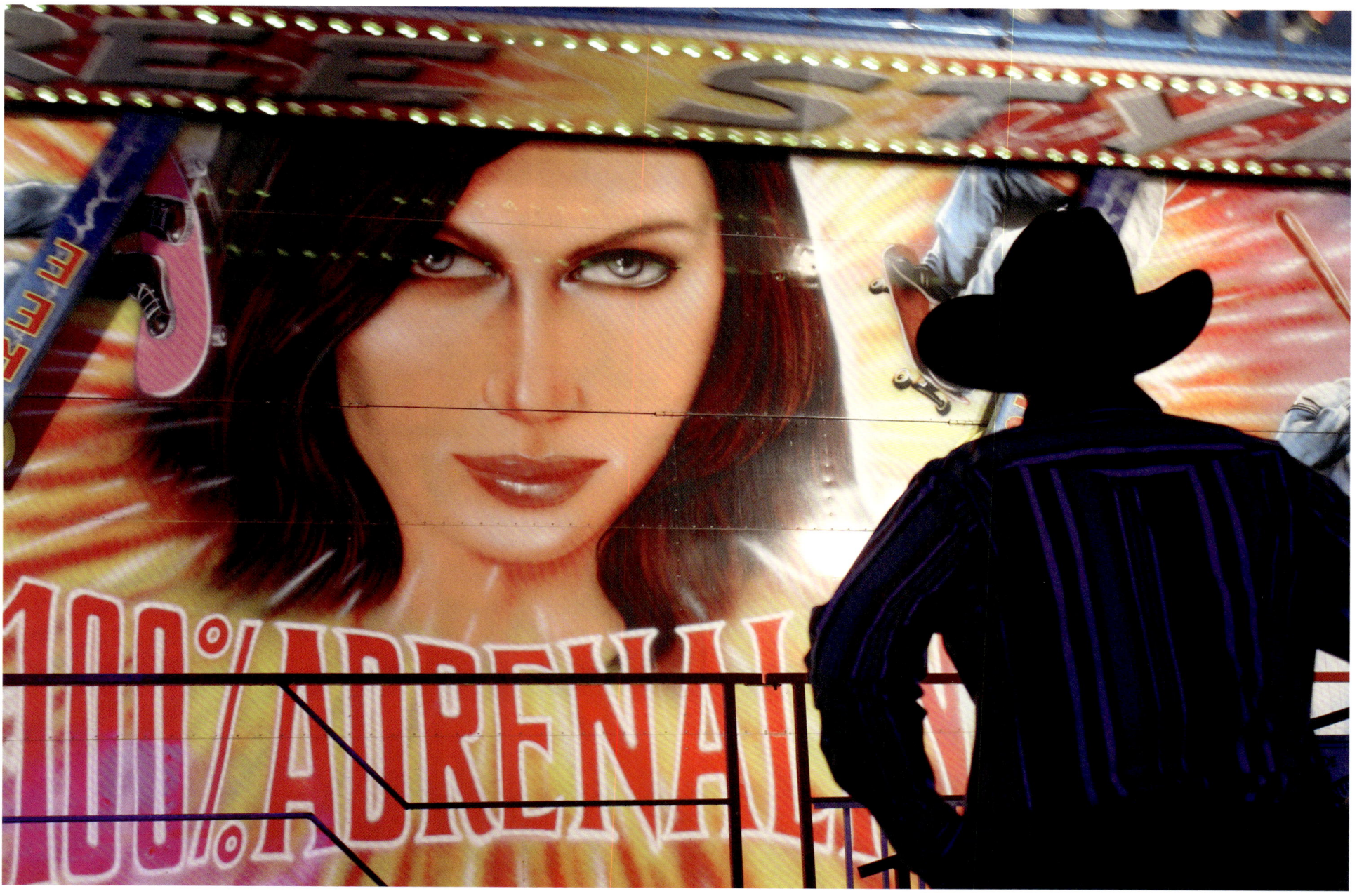

Bull Fighters

Professional bull fighters fill their calendars with towns along the Great Plains circuit ranging from North Dakota to Texas. Not to be confused with rodeo clowns, bull fighters save downed riders from angry bulls. Theirs is the most serious job in rodeo. Riders are in and out of the arena quickly, but bull fighters face every bull. "Those guys are crazy!" says the same bull rider who broke his neck and returned to ride again.

Zach Call from Mullen, Nebraska, is a prototypical bull fighter: agricultural background, former athlete in school, and once a bull rider. An astonishing move saved his own skin one night in Wayne, Nebraska. After the bull threw its rider, Zach made himself a target, which is essentially the job. Some bulls will give up the chase, but this bull resolved to crush Zach and bore down quickly. Zach sprinted toward the fence. It looked certain he would be trapped against the metal bars. Inches from the fence, Zach juked left then dove right, putting his hand on the ground to keep balanced like a running back. The bull followed the fake, hitting the fence and missing Zach by a few inches. A loud clatter reverberated throughout the arena's circumference from the impact of the bull's skull.

A panicked man would have jumped for the fence and been caught. "You never want to go to the fence that tight," Zach says. "You're always setting up a bull so you can step around him." Though one might question their sanity, these men are supremely confident in their ability. They have to be.

As riders cinch up in the chutes, bullfighters read clues. Zach has ways to spot inexperienced riders who often bring trouble. "You can tell if a guy is legit or not by how nervous he is, or maybe his equipment isn't right. No rosin, a junky rope—some guys have a look like they just shouldn't be there." Green riders don't always know what to do when things go wrong and that's a threat to everyone in the arena. Inexperienced bulls pose a different risk—they are most likely the hotheads that will attack. They are the bellowing ruckus kicking at their metal prison, more likely to attempt futile escapes rather than to settle in and endure as the old campaigners do. After the ride, old bulls often seek the way out rather than looking for payback. But nothing is predictable, so bull fighters always prepare for chaos.

When asked if horned bulls make him more nervous than non-horned, Zach replies, "If one type of bull makes you any more nervous than the rest then you shouldn't be in there." That makes sense. Bucking bulls have multiple weapons including horns, hooves, and skulls. At times I've seen all weapons used in one sweeping motion and it is horrifying.

A hung-up rider is another terrible scenario. This happens when the hand, so tightly woven into the bull rope, does not come loose when it should. Men caught this way flop helplessly like a windsock off the bull's side. A conscious man in this predicament is frightening but an unconscious man this way is grave. Bull fighters throw themselves headlong into the bull, trying to loosen the rope with a tug.

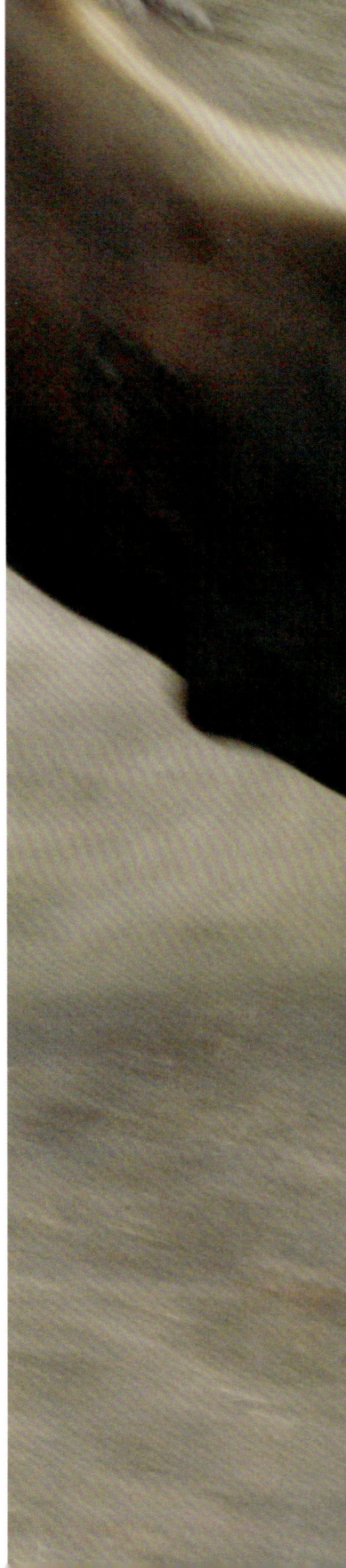

They lurch side-by-side with the stranded man as the bull thrashes. Clowns break character and join the fray. If these attempts fail then others spill into the arena: riders, stock contractors, event organizers, chute bosses . . . they lunge at the bull's neck and head, they ski through dirt latched onto the tail. Like a band of marauding ants, their human mass slowly brings the giant to a near standstill while the rider's hand is freed.

I have witnessed the same heroic phenomenon when men rush in to form a barrier around a grounded unconscious man. Knees bent in action stance, arms raised to look larger; there they stay until the bull is out. Physically this human fence presents no more of an obstacle than a ring of toddlers would to a man, but these men would rather take a hit themselves than allow the bull to grind its hard parts into an unconscious person. It's camaraderie; it's cowboy code.

Even though he is an expert bull manipulator, Dave Jantzi, from Duncan, Oklahoma, has been the downed target at times. "To control a bull you go to the head," he says. "It's like driving a car where the head is the steering wheel. You control where the head goes, you control where the bull goes." Though placing a hand between the bull's eyes guides the attack in the direction desired, one can only keep pace with a charging bull for so long—at some point you need a tactical switch. "At this point," Dave explains, "you're always looking to pull a move to the side to make him slide by, but sometimes you misread it and he catches you."

"It's a helpless feeling," Dave says of being toppled and then mauled in the dirt. "You're still thinking and fighting, but it's fairly hopeless. There's not much you can do but wait for a friend to help." Dave has dozens of bone-healing screws in his body and he's been knocked out several times. "One time I was without memory for seventeen hours. I woke up in a room with my arm in a sling and asked my buddy what happened. He said, 'I'm not telling you again, you've been asking me all night!'" When his predicament finally became clear Dave then argued about what town he was in, certain he was in another place.

Some bull-riding events feature "bullfighting," where bull fighters face riderless Mexican bulls for a long minute, one-on-one in

Mexican bulls are bred only to attack bull fighters in the arena. Smaller than bucking bulls, they are faster and more agile. "Their mind runs a lot quicker than regular bucking bulls," says bull fighter Dave Jantzi. "They're the only type of bull that makes me nervous." OAKLAND

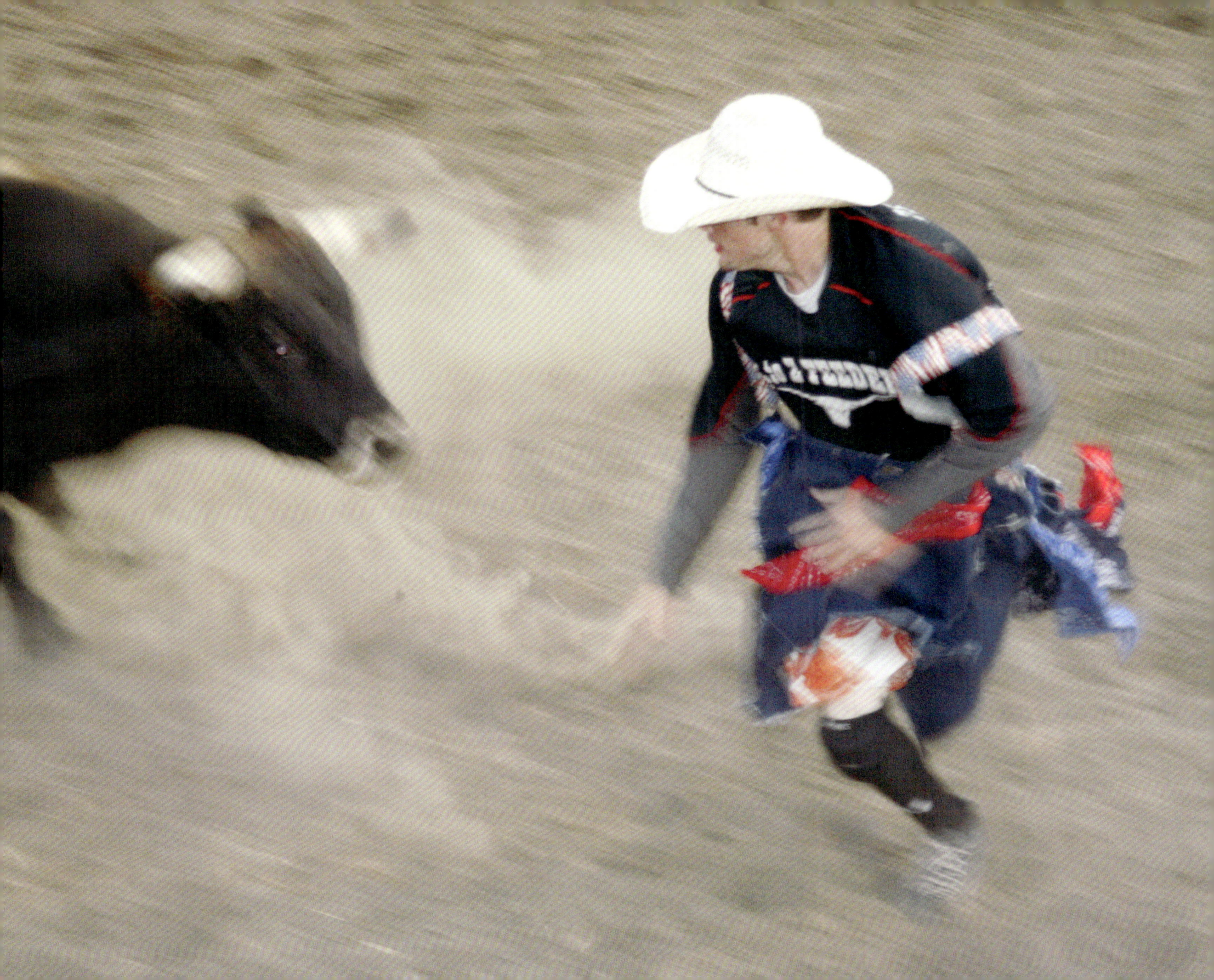

the arena. Smaller, faster, and more aggressive than their American counterparts, these bulls have long, hooked horns and know how to use them. Cleat-shoed challengers wear colorful outfits—one fighter features a bulls-eye on his pants seat, which perfectly defines the competitors' objective. Some bulls, distracted by the crowd, need taunting to attack, but most enter hotheaded and focused. It's a game of chicken, and danger equals points. Judged by daring and moves, fighters juke and dodge to create close calls. They sprint from pursuit, leaving little distance between the bull's head and their rear end. Inches dwindle quickly and men are caught: get thrown high, earn more points. Mexican bulls know where to hook a man for best leverage—just below the rear end on the hamstring. Men fly ten feet high as bulls follow their descent to add consequences. Like a cat with a dead mouse, agile Mexican bulls toss turtled-up men and then pounce to repeat. Competitors vault into the arena—slapping the bull and yelling, they become a new target. It's a brotherhood. Experienced bull fighters craft a grand finale: running straight at the charging bull, they leap as it dips its head to ram. Timed well, their feet skip off the running bull's back and they land safely behind. The crowd cheers; the bull is the chump. Veteran bulls expect this move and a well-timed head heave topples the man midair. The bull spins, knowing who the chump is now. It's breathtaking and I better understand why Roman gladiators drew huge crowds.

Bull fighters liken what they do to drug addiction. Dave calls it a "clean crave," which it is in the sense that it is legal, honorable, and—when rescuing a downed rider— even heroic. But he admits that it is a real addiction. "I crave it so bad. I have dreams all night that I'm doing it."

Travis Petersen is an anomaly in bull fighting—he's a city kid. A bull fighting buddy invited him to give it a try. Once a wrestler and football player, Travis's abilities served him well and he fell in love with saving downed men. Asked what type of bull makes him most uneasy, Travis replied, "Any bull is only is bad as you think he is." OAKLAND

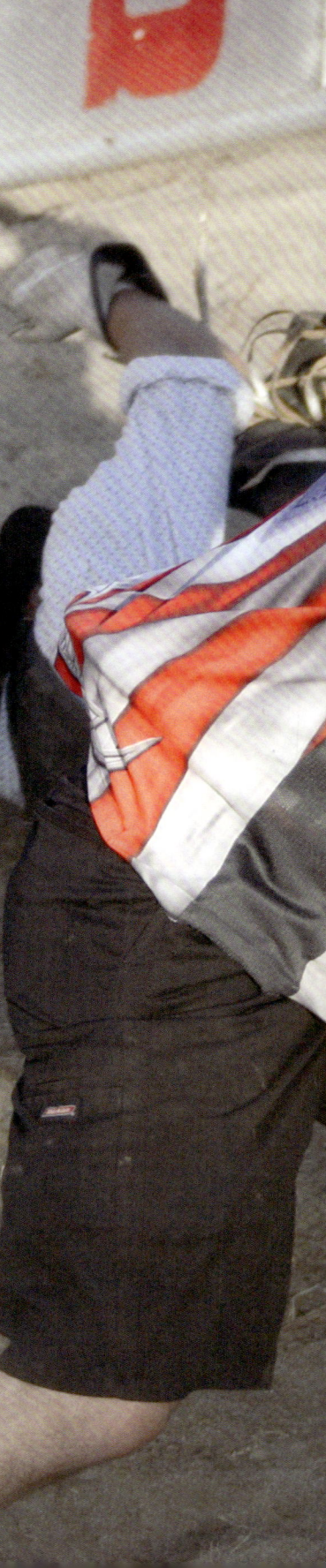

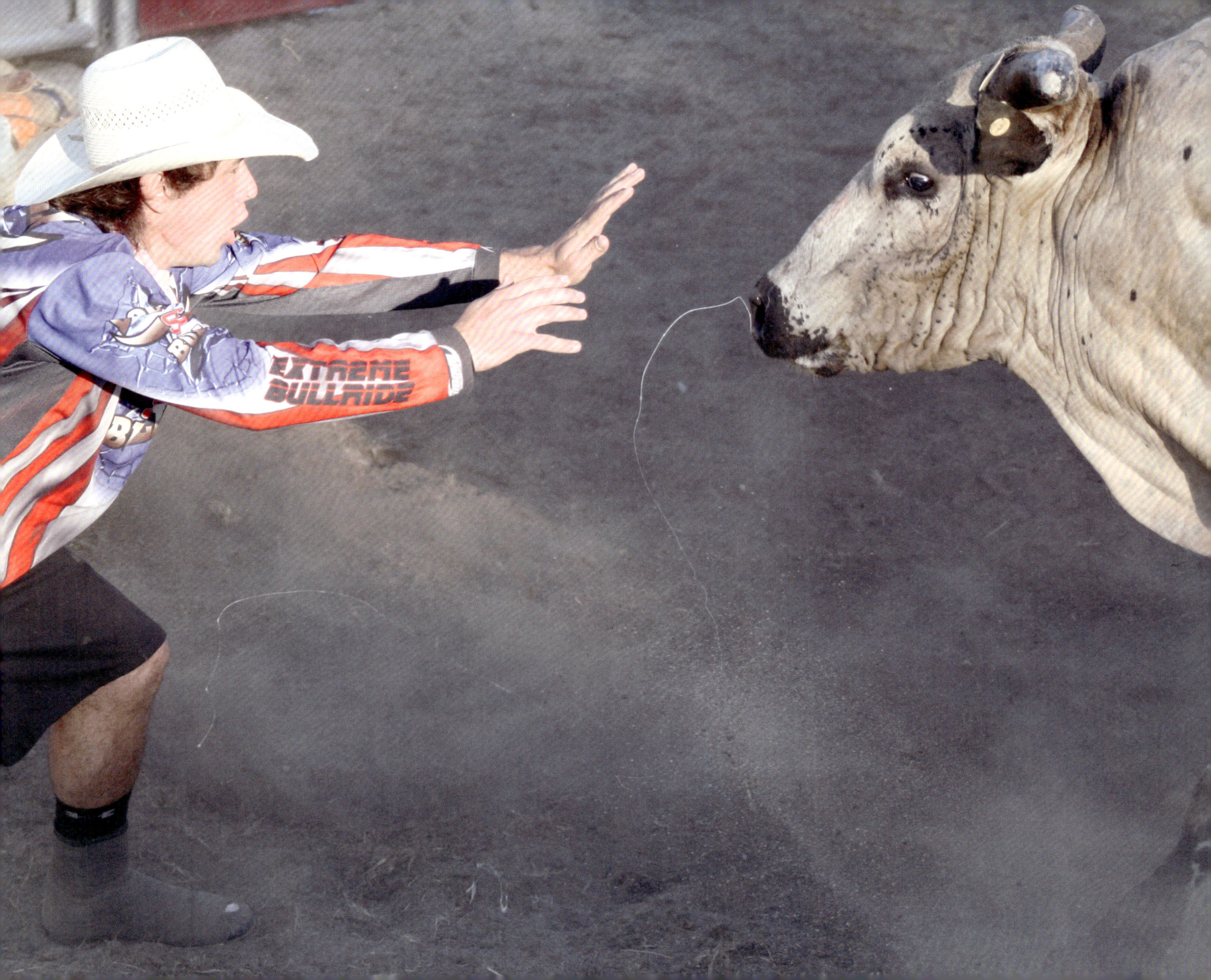

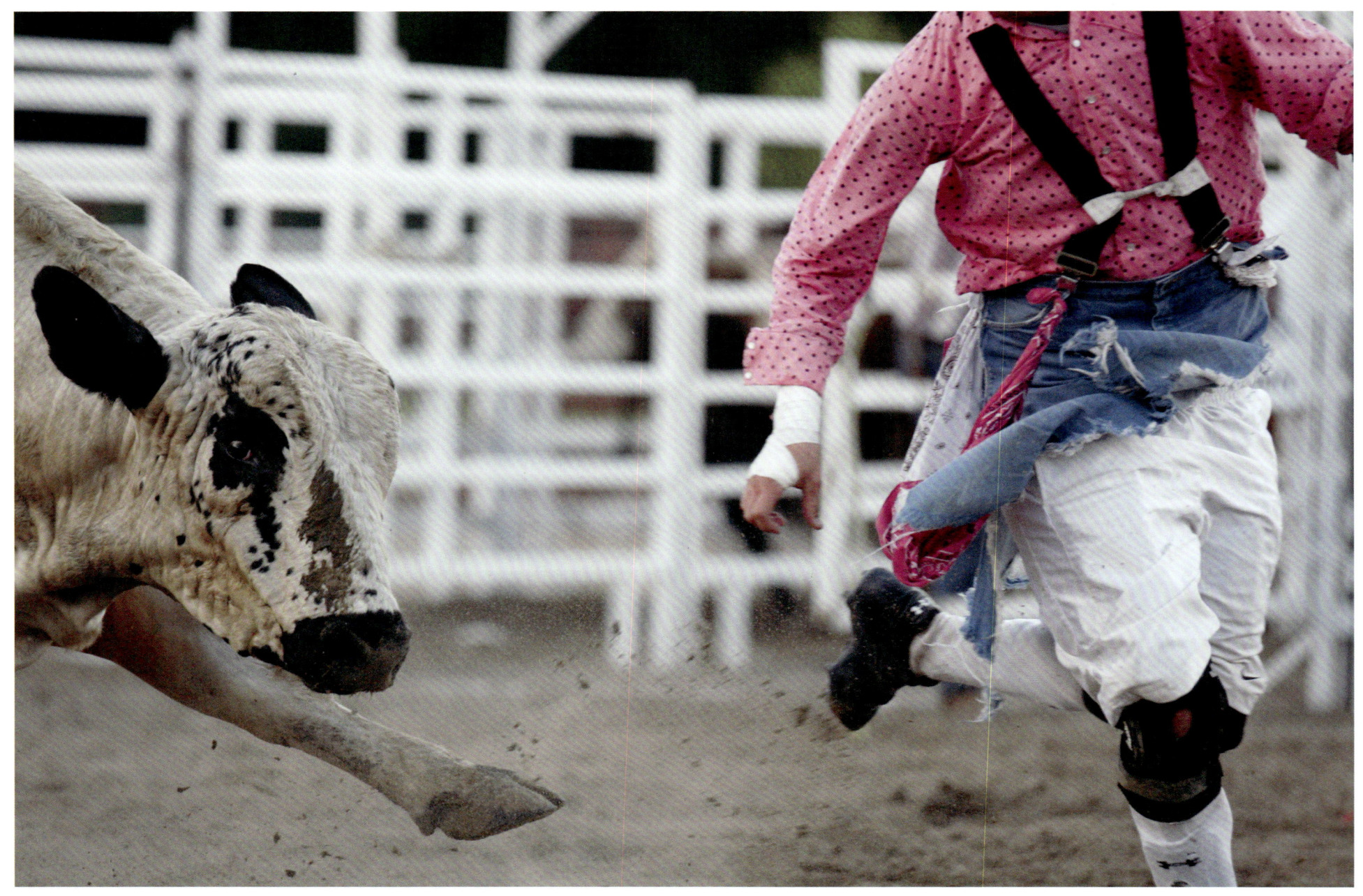

Two steps from being caught, the bull fighter soon jukes left, and then cuts right. An inch is as good as a mile to these men. ORD

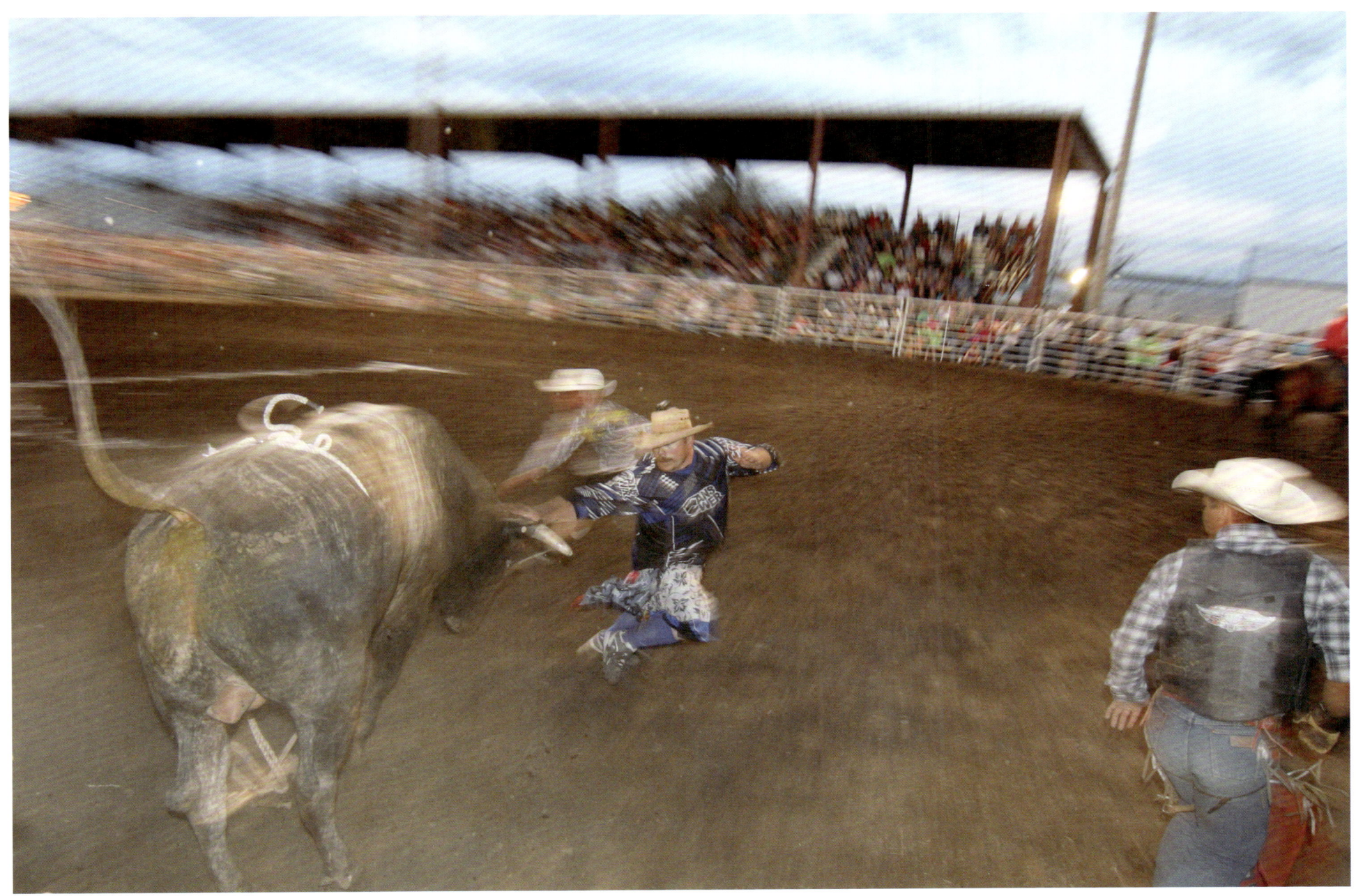

Bull fighter Zach Call, blurred in the back, will rush in to distract the bull as it closes the distance on his partner's back. Bull fighters depend on each other in these close quarters. SIDNEY

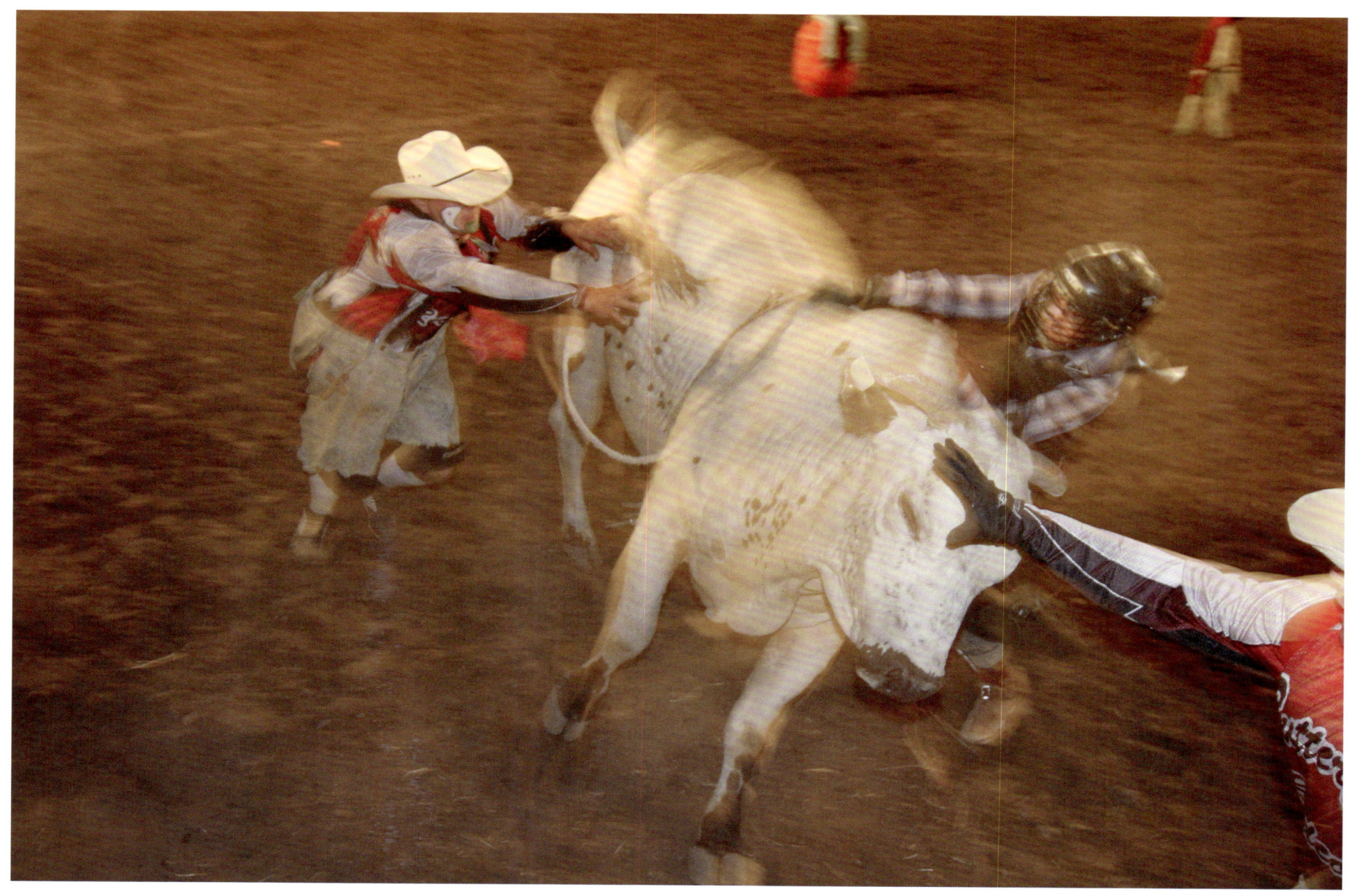

As one bull fighter "steers" the bull with a palm on its forehead, his partner struggles to free the rider's trapped hand. SIDNEY

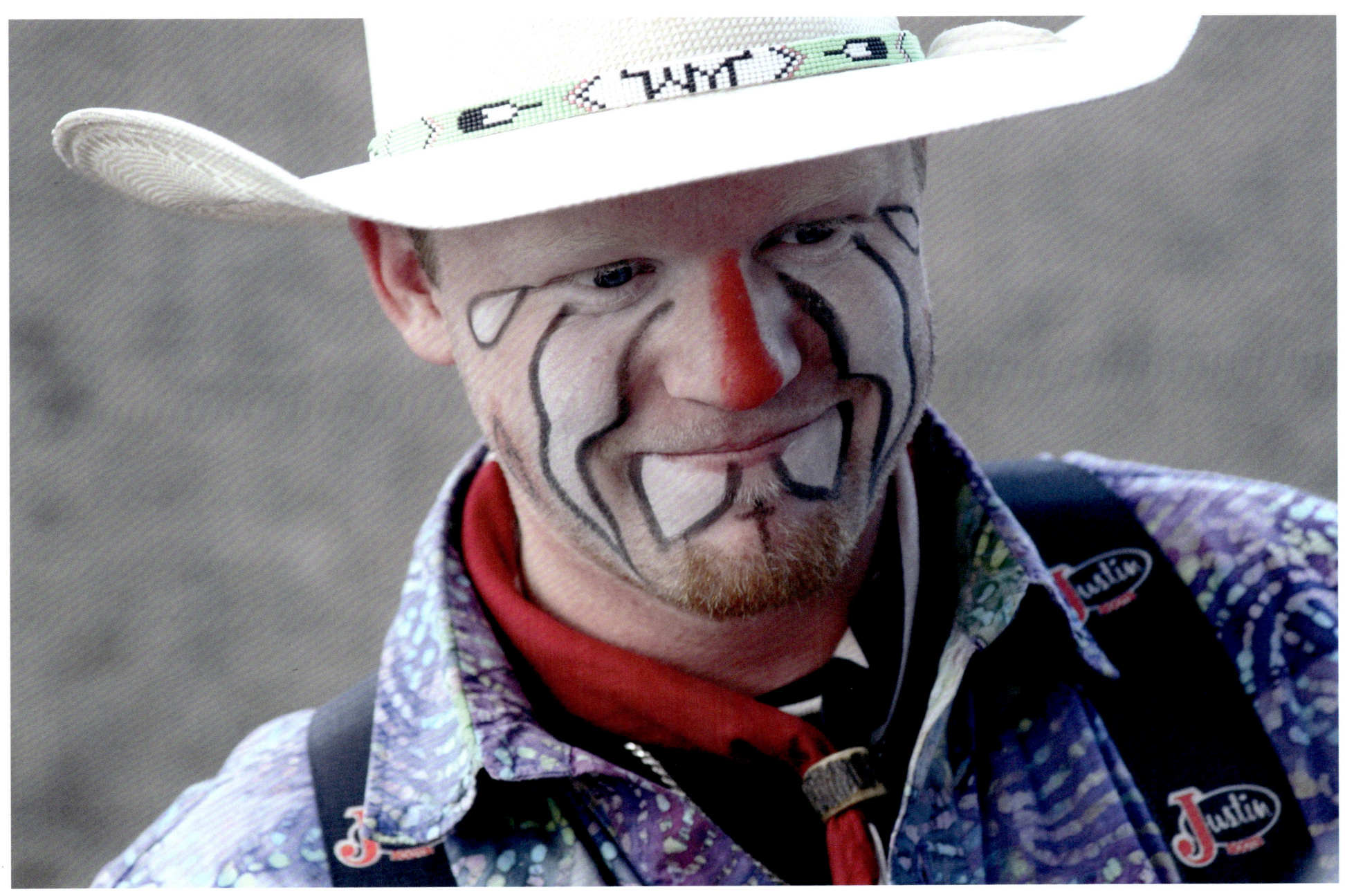

Bull fighter Wacey Muncell. WOLBACH

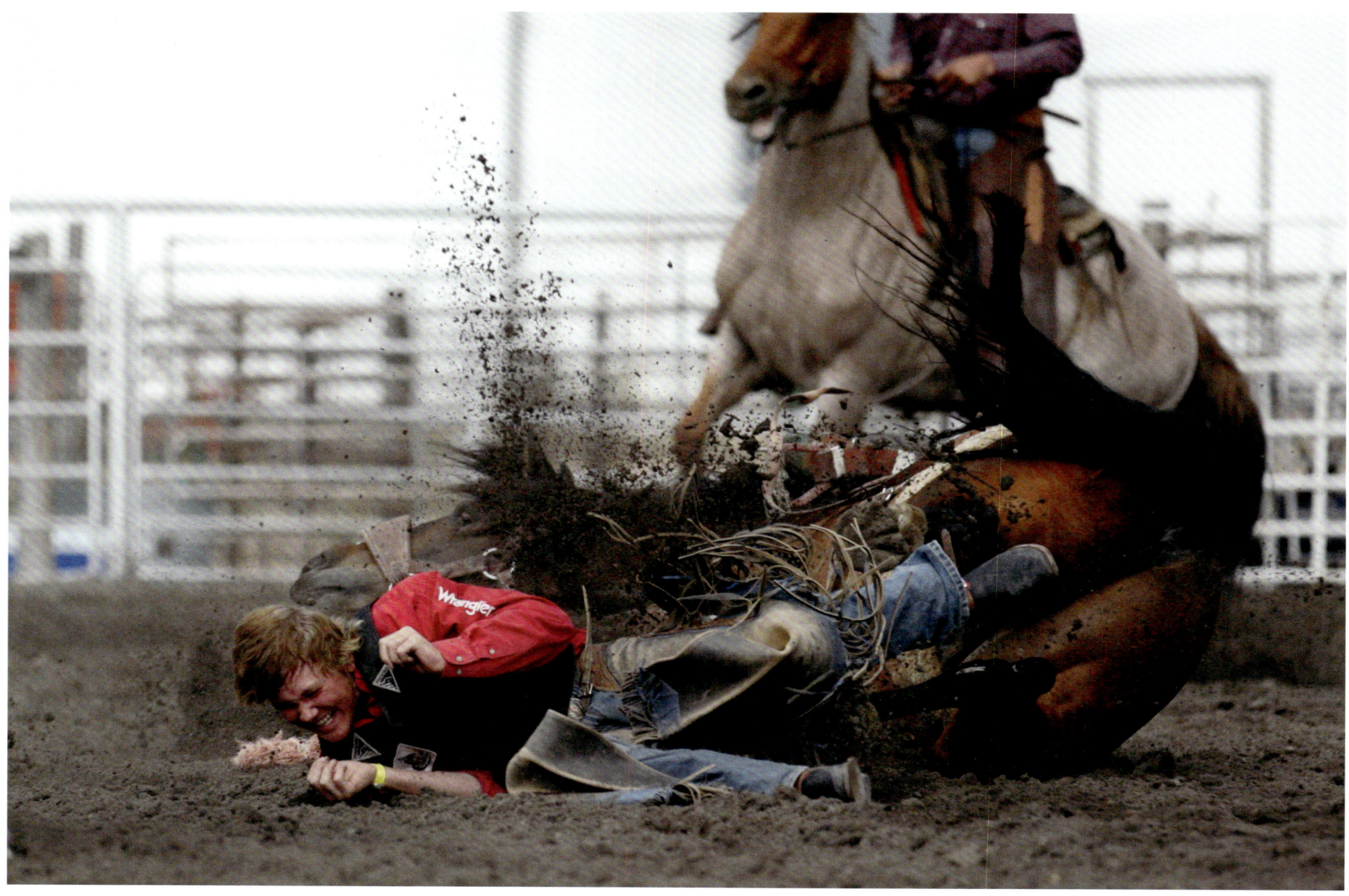

Tristan Eklund goes down hard with his bronc. Young horses might not stick their landing after freaked-out, contorted leaps. SUTHERLAND

Hard Knocks

RODEO AND INJURY

Serious injuries occur every year in Nebraska rodeo, but I don't want to overstate the danger. Though no rodeo is pain free and men frequently walk away with unseen damage, most events are without major injury. A few seem cursed, however, like bull riding at the 2014 Knox County Fair where five men went to the hospital, one requiring reconstructive surgery after catching a bull hoof in the face.

Bull riding is often said to be the most dangerous sport in the world, but considering sports like BASE jumping, cave diving, high-altitude mountain climbing, and a long list of other absurdly hazardous sporting pursuits, it is more accurate to say that bull riding is probably the world's most dangerous *spectator* sport. How does one afford health insurance for regional rodeo? Is there a special clause, a bull rider "rider" tagged onto your annual premium? As one Nebraska competitor admitted with an uncomfortable chuckle, "To be honest, I don't really tell them about it."

Rodeo associations do not typically keep injury statistics. However, Mobile Sports Medicine Systems, Inc., a company providing medical support services to professional rodeo athletes, compiled injury data from 1981 to 2005. Bull and bronc riding comprised 87.6 percent of rodeo injuries in this study, with 50 percent of the total coming from bull riding. In the study's latter years, the head and face replaced the spine and knee as the most likely body part to be injured. This is attributable to more stand-alone bull riding events and to breeding programs producing increasingly athletic, aggressive bulls. By the end of their study, concussions represented 55.8 percent of all injuries.

Focusing mainly on football, a wave of well-funded sports-concussion studies is now underway. No such studies have ever looked into bull riding. According to Dr. Arthur Maerlender, research associate professor and director of clinical research at the Center for Brain Biology and Behavior at the University of Nebraska, "There is a lot to disentangle." So much is simply unknown. "Computer technology exploded the speed at which we can study concussions, but it is still mostly theory and there is no direct evidence yet," Maerlender observes. "We know that getting your head hit is not good for you and the more you do it the worse it is." Second impact syndrome is central to research. "The typical outcome is that a second concussion has a more serious cognitive effect," he says.

According to Dr. Maerlender, regardless of today's hype, scientists don't yet know the facts about long-term concussion damage. "We have known for a long time that people who get hit in the head a lot over their life do suffer, like boxers, but the question is, what's a lot? Accumulating evidence shows that when looking at someone even a year after a concussion there is a difference in their brain physiology, but the problem is that those changes don't necessarily tie to

the concussion. There are all sorts of ways a brain can get messed up." These causes could include chronic psychological stressors, performance enhancing drugs, or even lifestyle or nutritional changes.

Football-focused research shows repeated low-magnitude concussions as most common. Empirical evidence shows that bull riding produces a much greater incidence of single, high-magnitude hits triggering unconsciousness. Long-term consequences of repeated, severe concussions are unknown, but it is known that all forms of concussion are more dangerous to youth. According to Dr. Maerlender, "Damaging the young person's brain interferes with development, causing bigger problems, and it may take longer to recover. If there is a high risk of accumulating head injuries in any sport, then starting earlier is not the best idea." But nothing short of a massive cultural shift will change that. Undeniable scary evidence, if discovered, is the only factor that may alter when kids begin any risky sport.

High school rodeo mandates helmets, but as boys become men many abandon helmets for hats. Thermoplastic foam-lined bull-riding helmets provide some protection but don't compare to stouter football helmets with thicker linings. According to Dr. Maerlender, bull riding helmets with facemasks help spread the force and slow the brain's deceleration a bit but primarily they only shield riders from broken facial bones and skull fractures. That is a great leap in protection from a cowboy hat but the brain still reverberates inside; there is no stopping that. Striking bull hooves, horns, and skulls is like hitting concrete.

During seven years of shooting rodeos I noticed an increase in the number of bull riders wearing helmets around the time nationwide press began speculating about the dangers of repeated concussions in the National Football League. This media scrutiny peaked in 2012. Based on my photographs I estimate that in 2007 roughly 40 percent of Nebraska bull riders wore helmets. This increased to about 60 percent from 2008 through 2012, and was close to 80 percent by 2014.

Safety vests are mandatory, helmets are not. SPRINGFIELD

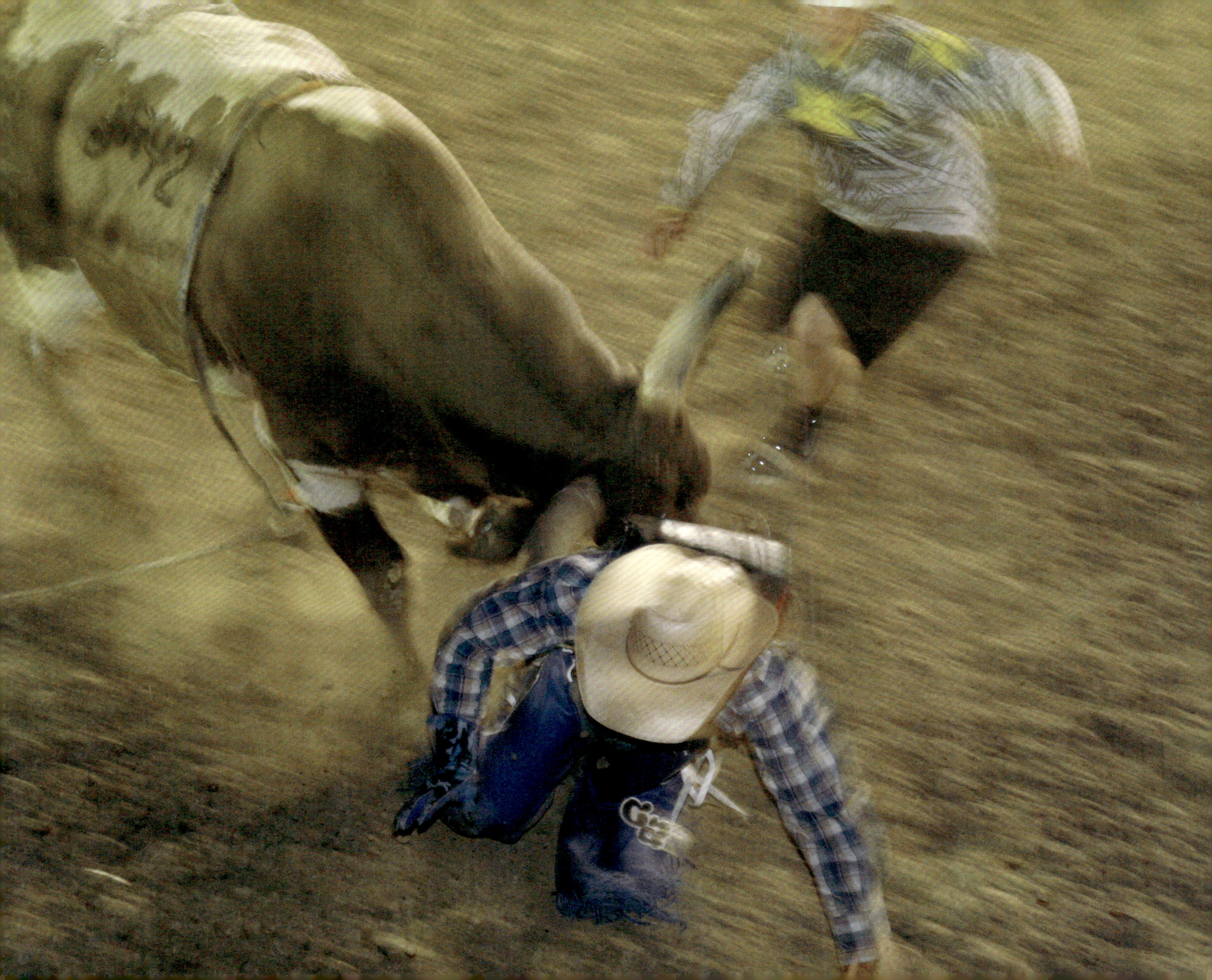

Dr. Maerlender can't imagine any helmetless bull riders in ten years. "I think people will want to wear helmets based on what we learn in our research. If your brain's not working right your performance suffers everywhere, and if you want to have a fulfilled life then you want to protect your brain. The most important question is what are the cultural aspects that drive people to do stupid things? What compels them to ride again after a concussion? Within the culture of different sports, what is it that drives people not to disclose their injury, not to accept the risk? That's one thing we're interested in figuring out. And then how can we come up with ways to educate people to transform their values into something more functional?"

Though football research could affect bull riding practices, bull riding studies are needed. Head injury statistics in pro rodeo are incomplete and it is impossible to gauge concussions within regional rodeo. Most injuries go unchecked. I have seen a bull fighter knocked unconscious by a charging bull and return to the arena fifteen minutes later. "If the first concussion caused subdural bleeding then the second one could kill you," Maerlender says. Here lies the chasm between being tough and being informed. This cultural mentality also ties to ranching in general. Cowboys and cowgirls are tough—not overtly, not with bravado nor even consciously so—it is an inherent, quiet resilience. To succeed in ranching you must love the grueling challenge of working land and livestock. This is how these competitors were brought up, how their fathers and mothers were raised, and how they will likely raise their own.

Youthful temperament also clouds the line between toughness and recklessness. Just as young soldiers don't always consider their mortality, young bull riders don't always reflect on what a second concussion might do to them, or a fifth, or another broken neck.

Statistically, bareback riding is second only to bull riding in rodeo injuries. BRIDGEPORT

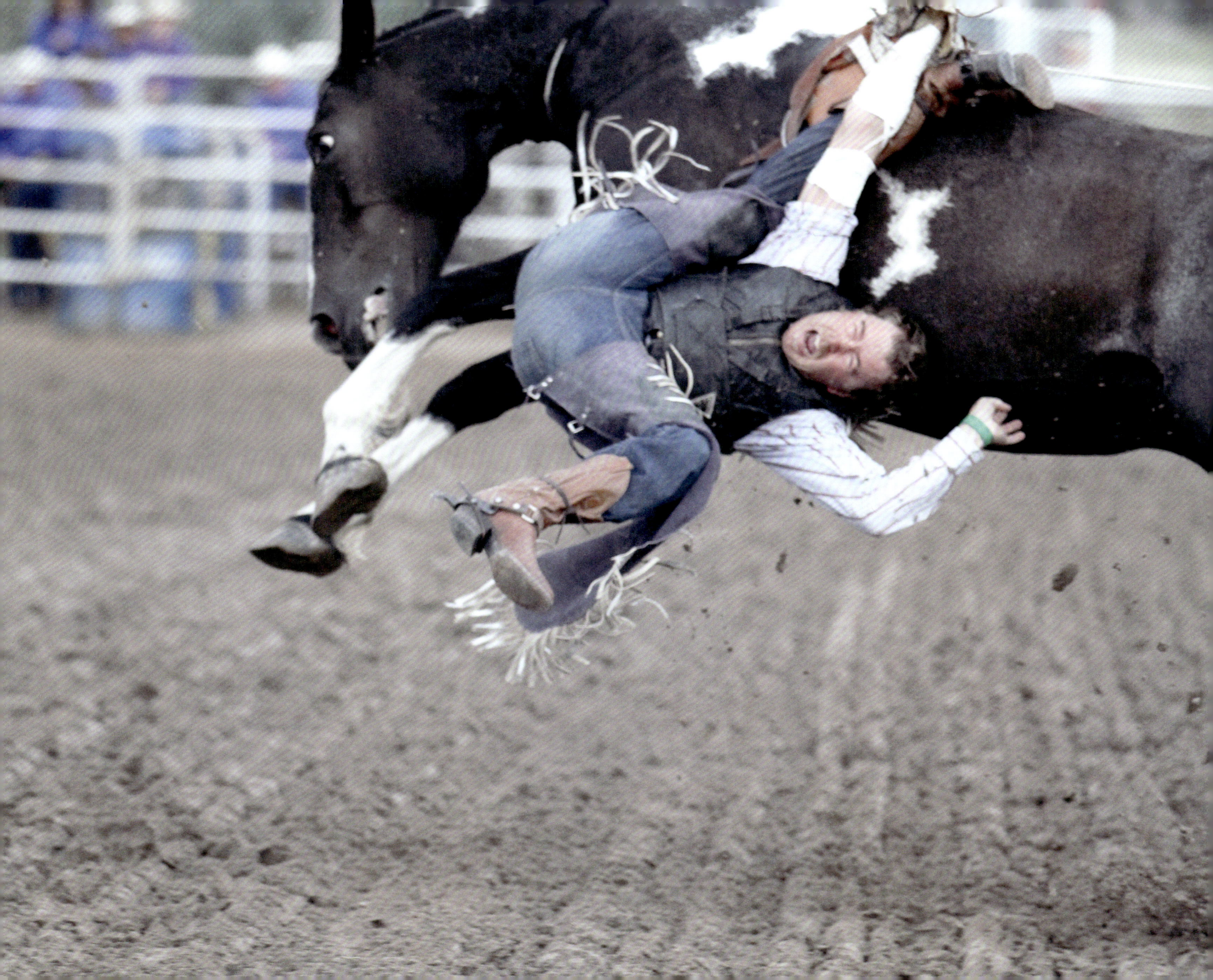

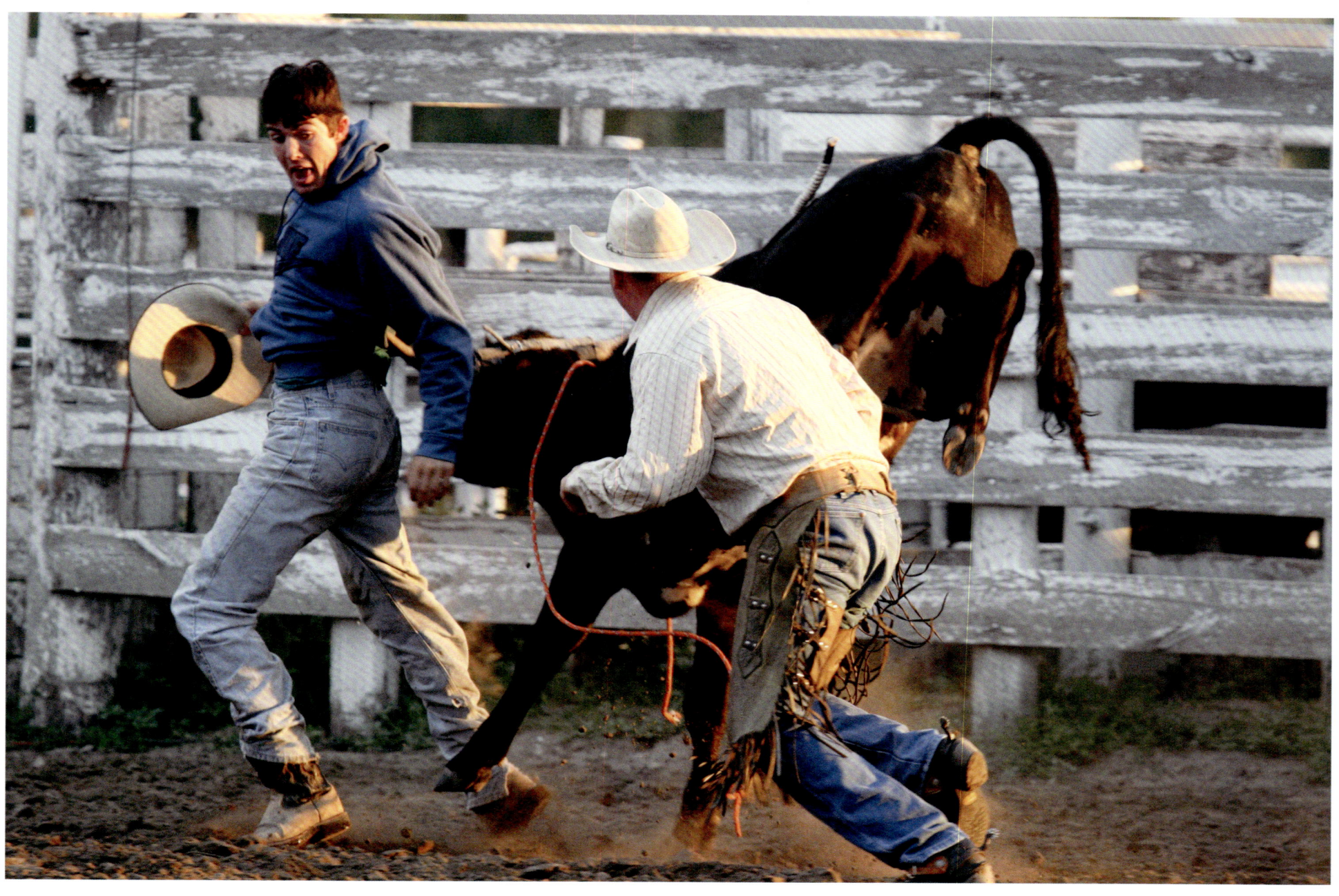

Nothing in rodeo is predictable. Steers are normally docile. FORT ROBINSON

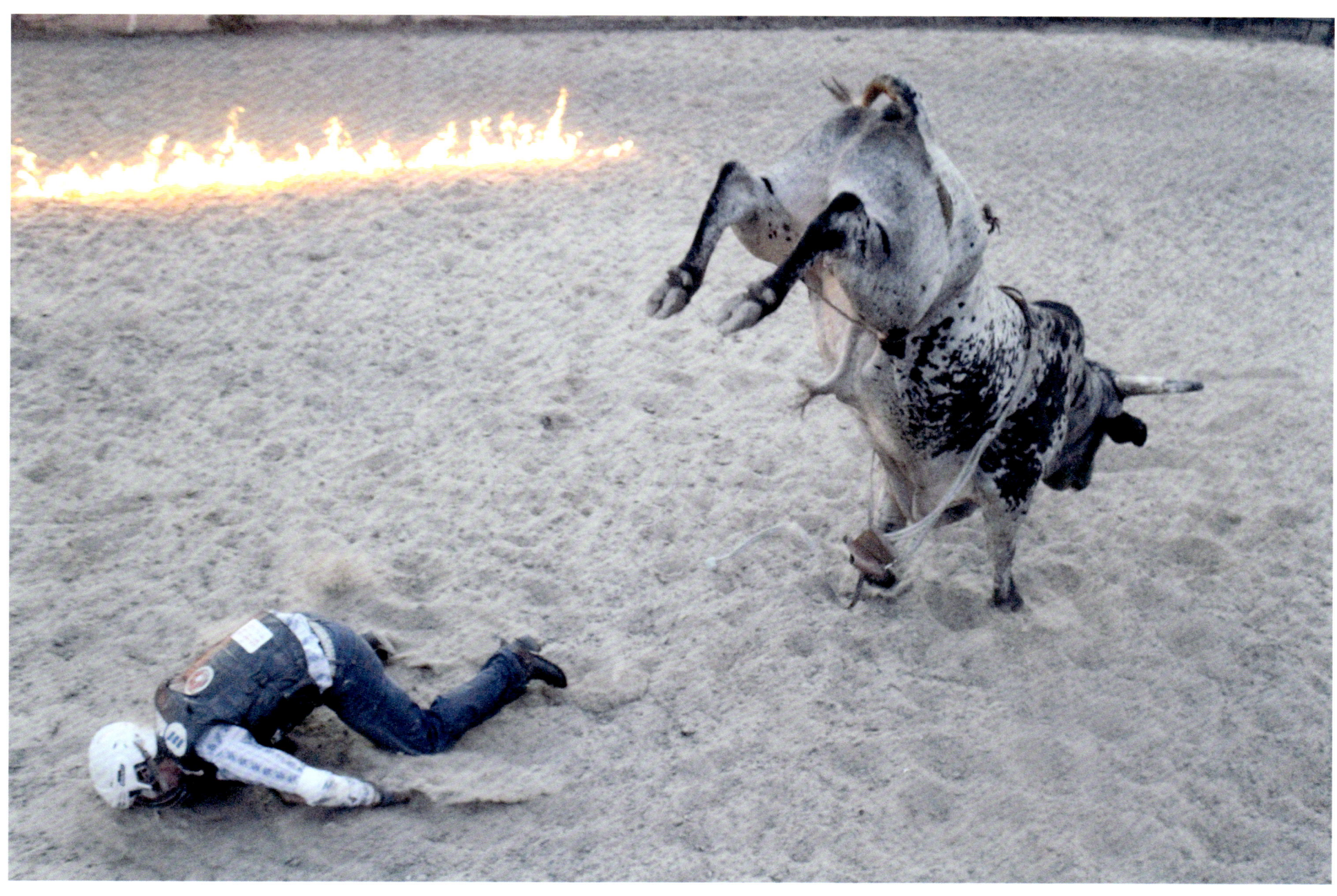

You don't need a reason to set dirt on fire in the Extreme Bull Riding Tour. GENEVA

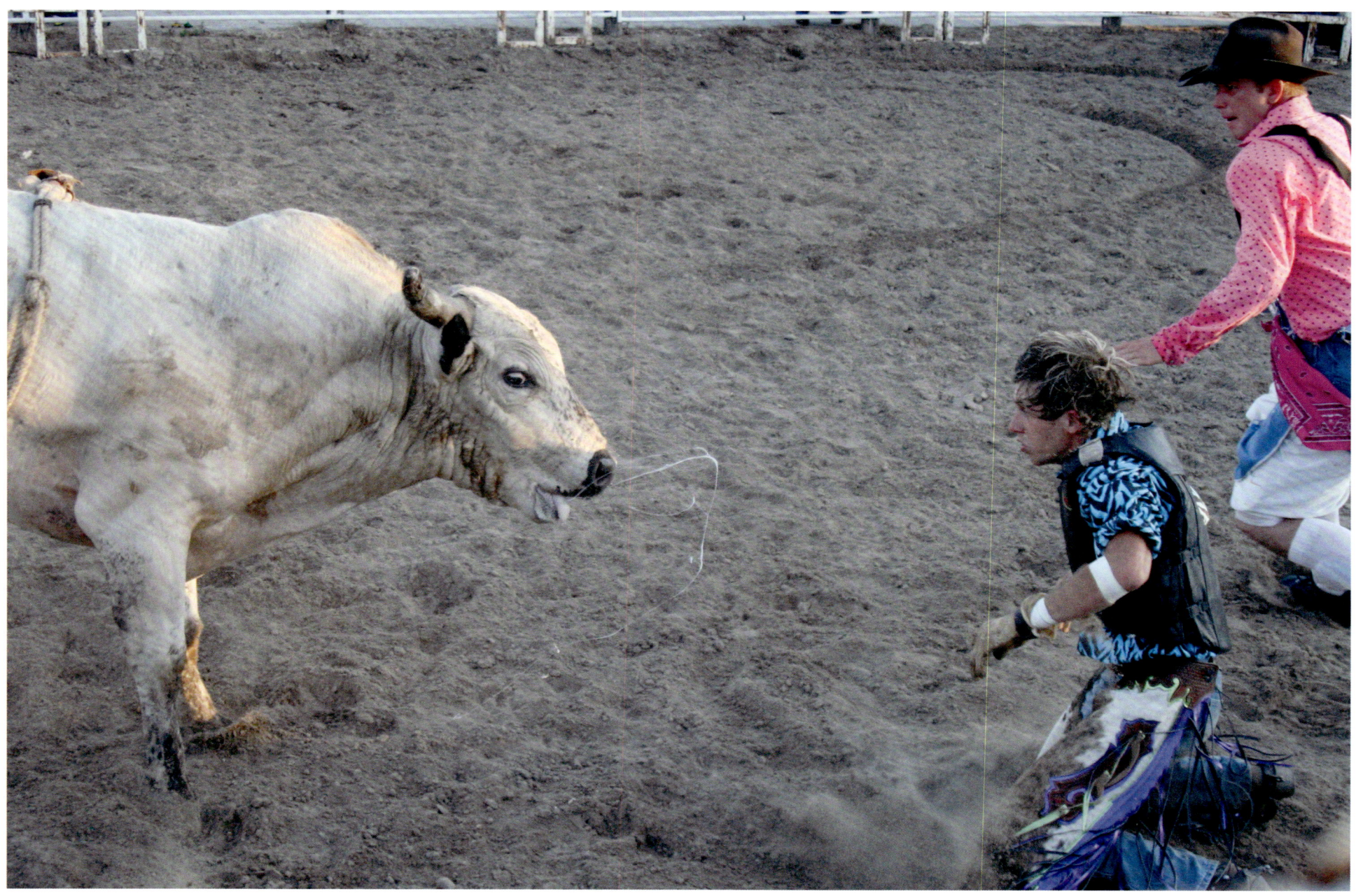

If not for the bull fighters, this rider is doomed. He escapes unharmed. ORD

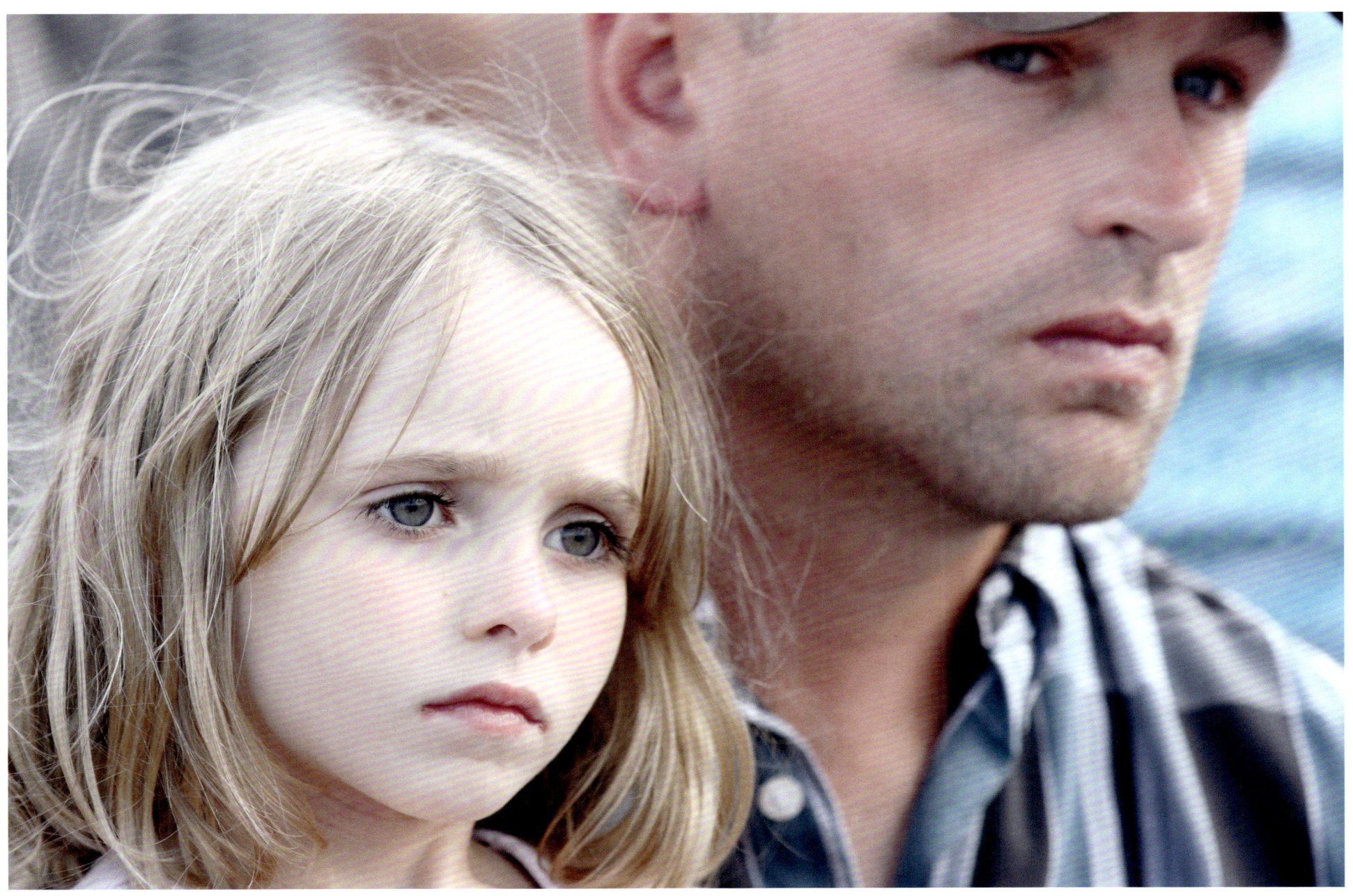

Father and daughter watch as paramedics attend to a bull rider. ORD

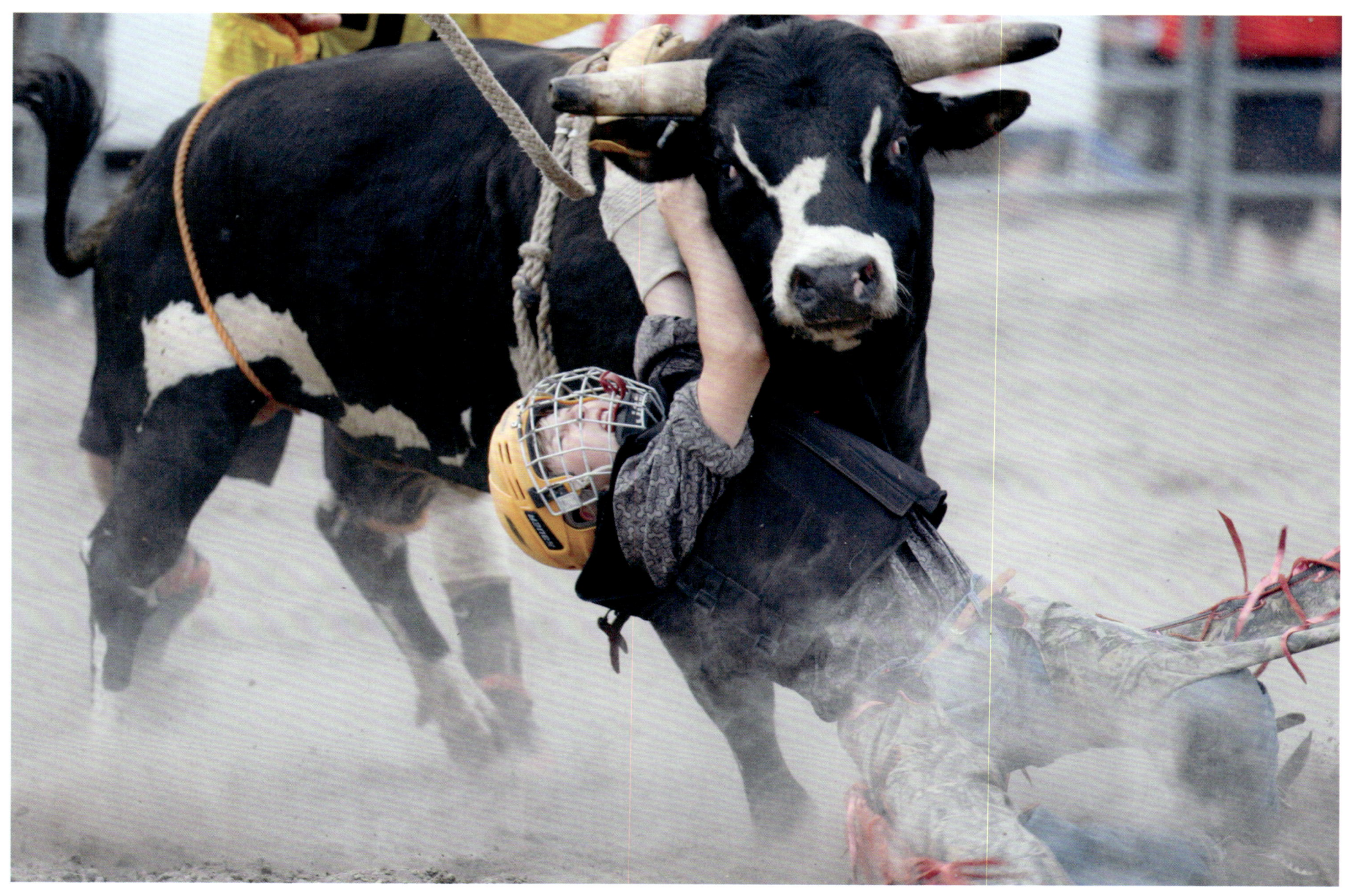

Twelve years old and hung up on his bull rope, this youngster will endure
many seconds of hell until freed by bull fighters. KEARNEY

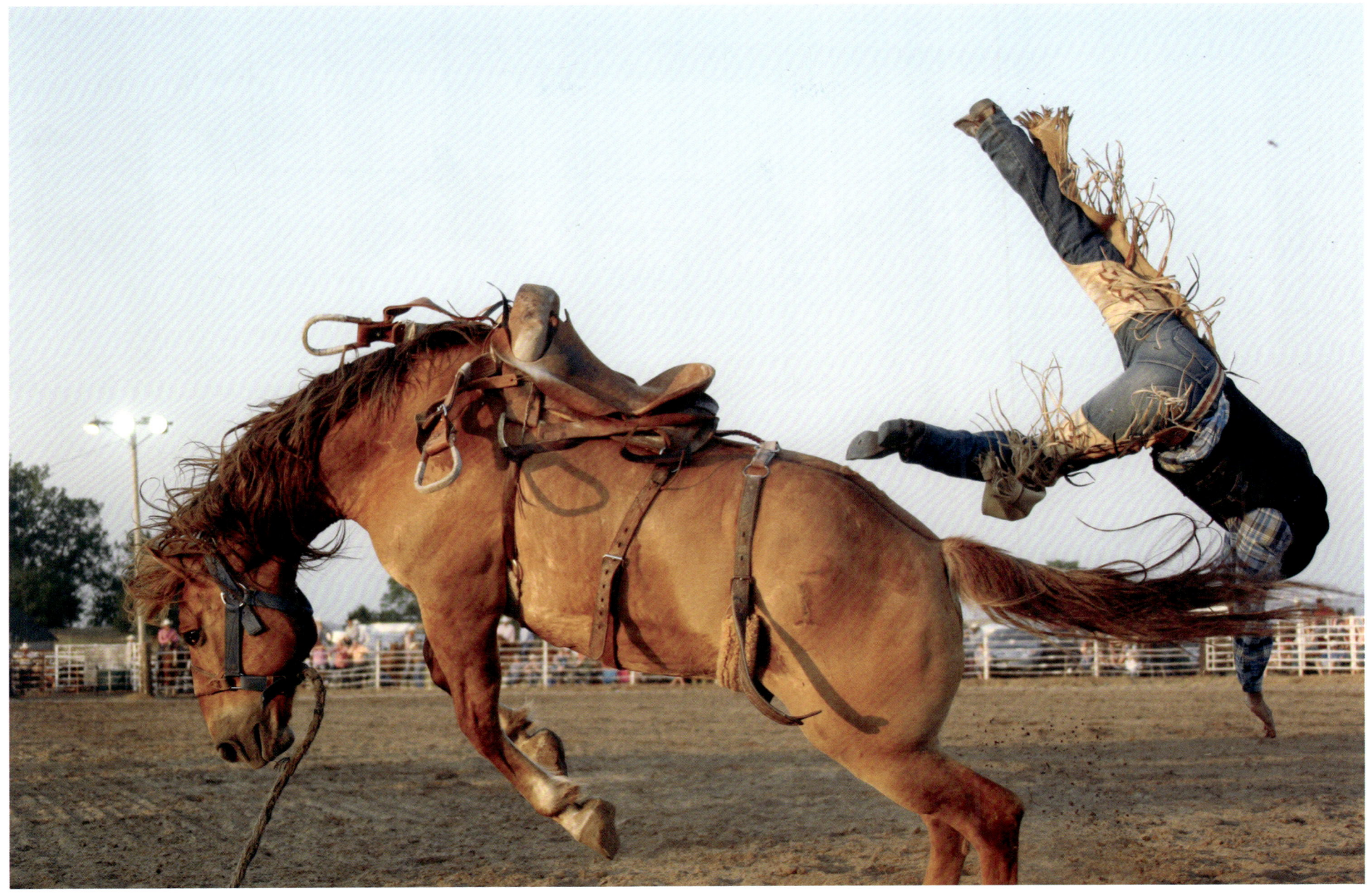

BERTRAND

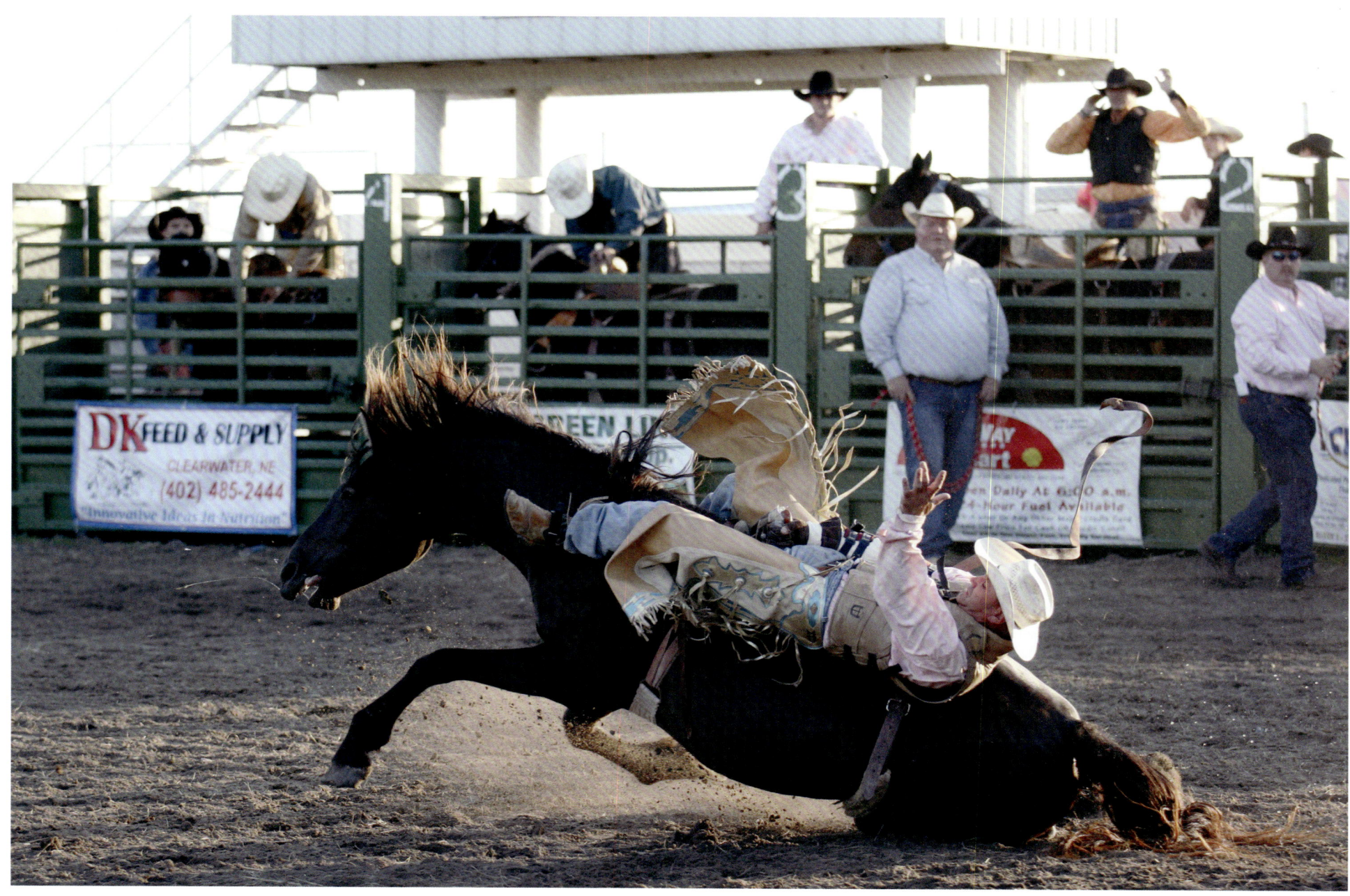

Many broncs have gone down beneath forty-six-year-old champion Corey Evans. In this ride, both horse and rider recover and the bucking resumes. CLEARWATER

Animal Welfare

Using animals to compete is a touchy subject, and becoming more so as American society moves toward a more urban mindset. I understand each side's rationale. Being a full-blown animal lover, cruelty to animals makes me furious. But I am also the grandson of a Wyoming cattle rancher, and I have spent a good portion of my life at what is now my mother's bison ranch. Being a city dweller with some ranching background I'll try to balance the perspectives.

Animal advocacy groups serve a crucial role in helping direct the advancement of civility toward animals. At various degrees in different societies, humans have a long path to travel before becoming truly civilized toward animals and toward each other. The future will judge what is right or wrong with all societies' practices, including rodeo.

For decades, rodeo rules and methods have evolved toward safer, more humane use of animals. Everyone involved benefits from higher safety standards and safer events. Humans eventually move this way; it's just a matter of discovering new ways to tweak things in that direction.

Most animal advocacy groups have a valid and accurate focus regarding domestic animals of all sorts, and some of what they say about rodeo is correct, but much is not. Collectively these groups speak of cruel methods used to induce wild bucking in rough stock events, such as burrs placed under flank straps or of animals enraged by electric devices. After standing near the chutes at eighty-two competitive events I confidently attest that those claims are false. Every stock contractor does have an electric zapper in his back pocket, though these are only used as a last resort to move a stubborn bull through the chutes after all manner of rump slapping has failed. I may see one bull zapped at every third event on average, but this is to uncork the bottleneck, never to rile.

Flank strap use is also widely misunderstood by advocacy groups and by the general public. The commonly accepted myth is that flank straps cinch around a bucking animal's scrotum. A distant view without good knowledge of animal anatomy might lead to this conclusion, but straps actually attach just ahead of the animal's hips. Bull scrotums swing untouched. Broncs have no functional scrotums, being either geldings or mares, and their sheep's-wool strap is secured in the same spot as are bulls' ropes. The strap is pulled tight as the bronc leaves the chute, but the apparatus will not tighten beyond a preset point.

True, horses and bulls don't like things wrapped around their hindquarters, and people are indeed being unkind by imposing this added stress, but it is all mental. Soft and affixed only tight enough to stay put, straps and ropes are not designed to constrict or to inflict pain. Strapless rough stock will buck with a man on their back, but flank straps bring more consistent upwards and outwards kicking, thus a more challenging ride. I have heard announcers explain that broncs and bulls are "tickled" by straps and ropes, but that is an understatement. They hate it. What animal wouldn't? If you have ever chased down the family pet to free them from something they've gotten caught up on, like a cat through a plastic grocery bag handle, then you understand the phenomenon.

Spurring draws advocacy groups' attention as well. Blunt and on rollers, spurs help the rider keep balanced and bring style points if used correctly. Spurs don't scratch horses' skin, which is five times as thick as human skin. Bull skin is seven times thicker than ours. Though they are certainly aggravated by spurs, I have never seen a spur mark on an animal after a ride.

A few stock contractors and bronc riders told me they believe broncs enjoy bucking. As a prize fighter thrills in putting down an opponent, the claim is that broncs thrive on the challenge of dismounting the rider. After observing hundreds of rides, I'm sure they do not. Broncs know their job when a man mounts them, but they dislike everything about the arena regardless of what precautions men take to improve their safety, and that will never change. If they enjoyed their work they wouldn't act like broncs. The consolation is that they likely don't fret about their jobs the other 99.99 percent of their lives.

With specific graphic accounts documented on their websites, animal advocacy groups speak of tragic individual occurrences, which are described accurately. Terrible incidents do happen. I have seen them and they are heartbreaking. They are also relatively rare. Statistics back that up and there is no contrary data. Studies carried out by the Pro Rodeo Cowboys Association (PRCA) show consistently low rates of injury per "animal exposure," which is, for instance, a calf in calf roping or a bronc in bronc riding. A 2000 study showed this injury rate to be .00052, or 38 animal injuries out of 71,743 exposures. The PRCA's 1997 study revealed a rate of .00047 and the American Professional Rodeo Association showed similar results in 1994 at .00072.

The PRCA also surveyed onsite independent rodeo veterinarians about livestock welfare in 2009. Of 75,472 animal exposures in that survey there were 28 injuries at the rate of .00037. These studies do not mention animal deaths, but it is likely that some of these injuries were fatal.

One should consider all sporting events involving animals when judging animal injuries or deaths in rodeo. For instance, according to the Equine Injury Database, horse racing in the U.S. generates a verified *death rate* of .0019. That is a death rate three times the rodeo *injury rate*.

My regional observations align with the national studies. Of the 62 competitive rodeos and 20 bull riding events I photographed in Nebraska, in sanctioned events I saw three animals injured out of roughly 5,400 exposures. That is a rate of .00055. Subtract all stand-alone bull riding events, because bulls are least likely to be injured, and my observed injury rate is still in line with national studies at .00065. Competitor injuries are certainly many times higher.

Most advocacy groups focus on calves being roped and steers being wrestled. At times it does look traumatic when a rope flips a running calf, and being roped and tied certainly is not a good moment for them. On very rare occasions things go wrong and animals can be injured or even killed, but after watching over 2,000 men's roping and wrestling events I have never witnessed harm to the targeted animal. I have often watched for aftereffects in pens where calves and steers are placed after their ordeal, and their transition from being roughly handled to casually munching hay is quick. I have never noticed signs of trauma. It is important to remember that cattle skin is tough. It's leather. Their neck muscles are thick, and though it is true that these animals endure several seconds of distress at various levels, we should not imagine their bodies being affected in the way our vulnerable bipedal frames would be under the same circumstances.

Though the numbers speak well on an objective level, the numbers seem distant when an animal goes down. In seven years of photographing sanctioned events I saw three animal injuries and each was lethal. A team-roping horse broke its leg in a collision with a steer, and though able to limp into a trailer, it was likely put down later.

Seldom does a barrel racing horse go down, but mud or sandy ground increases that risk. Women tell me that it is like slow motion when they fall, and that their only concern is for their horse. Here both rider and horse will arise unhurt. STAPLETON

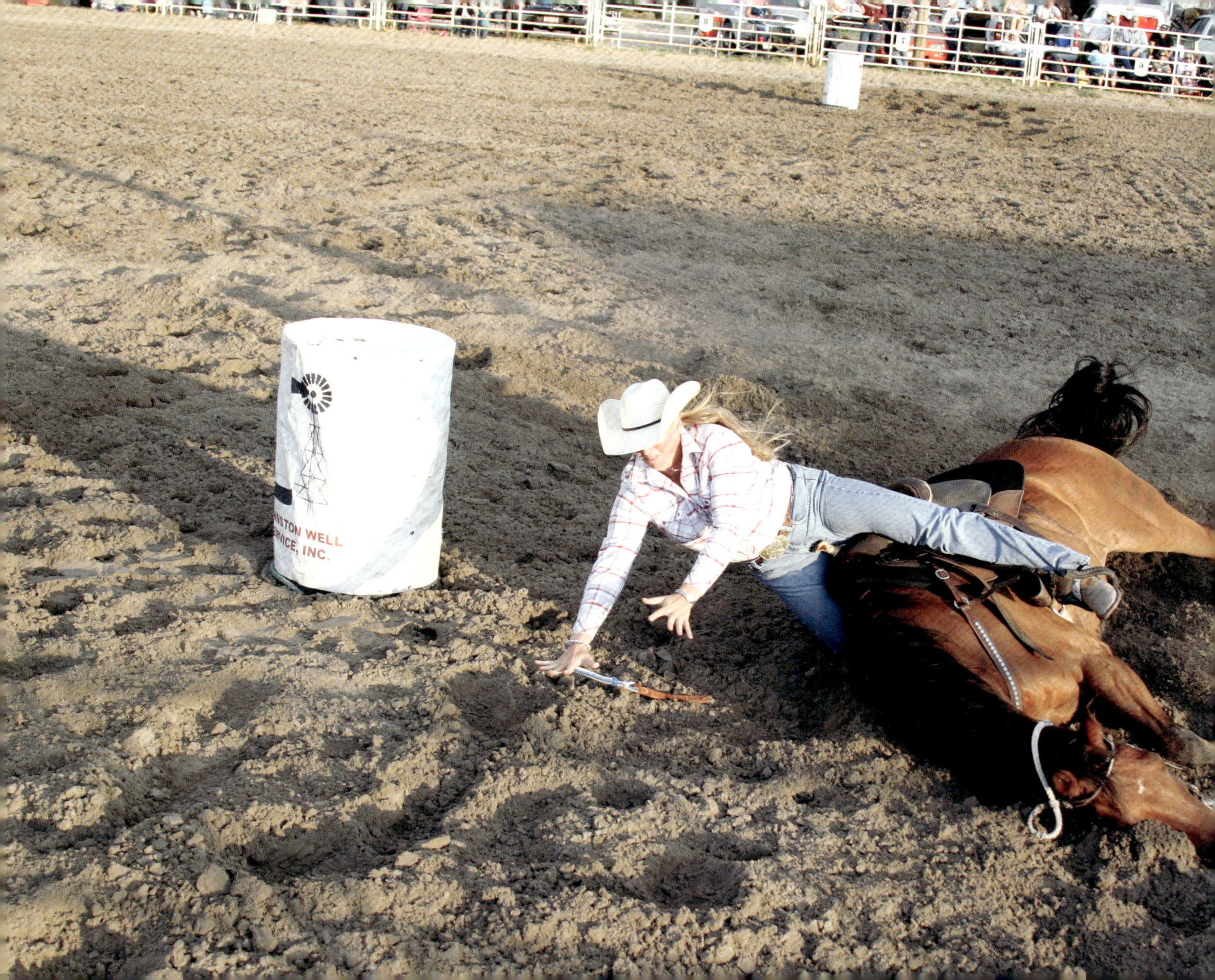

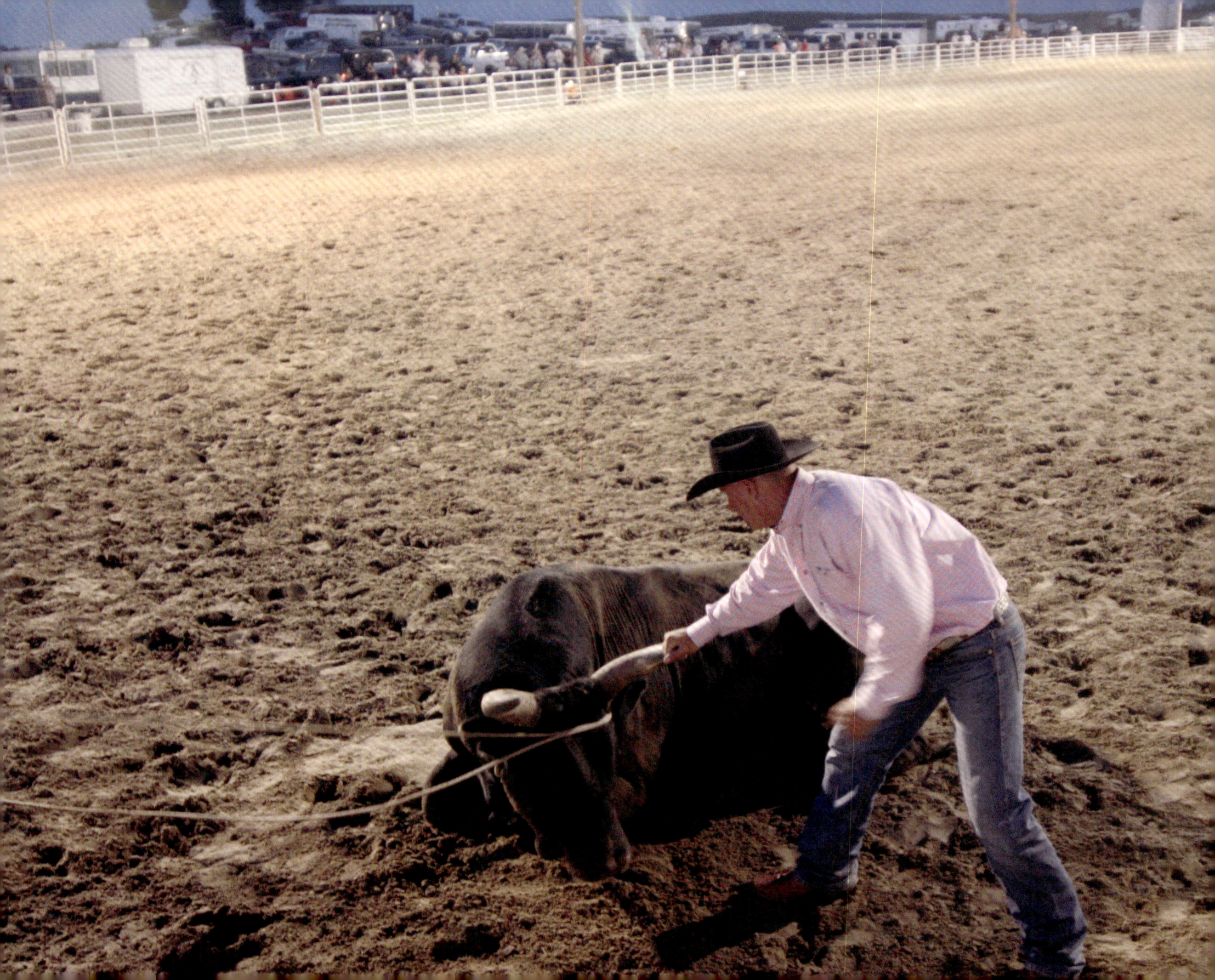

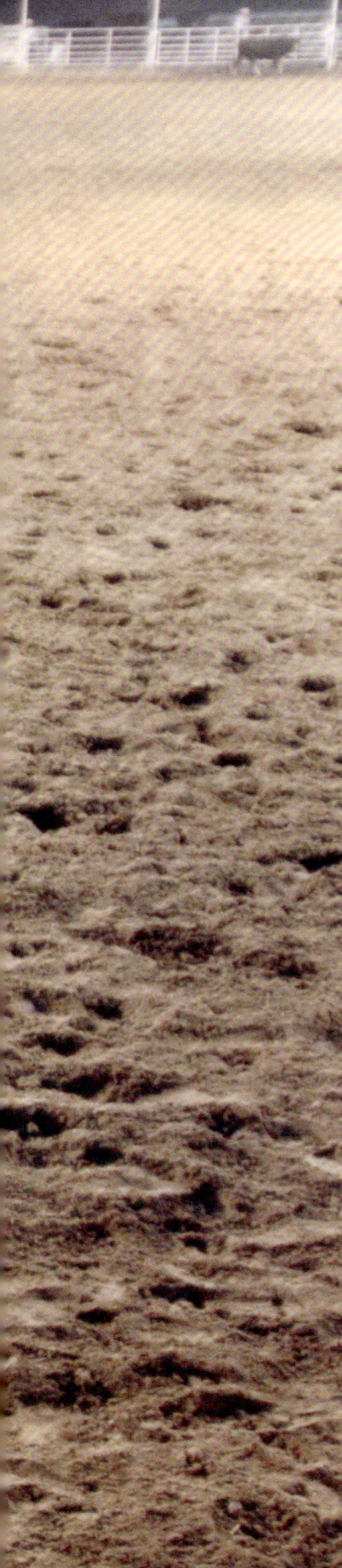

And I saw two broncs go down. One suffered an apparent heart attack immediately out of the chute and the other broke its vertebrae while bucking. Both were later euthanized. Appalling though these were, no currently known preventative measure would have made a difference.

Animal welfare is a central component in today's rodeo associations and policies are in place to improve safety. Other regulations will follow and animal injuries will become even rarer as technology and methods progress. Though rodeo has come a long way in protecting stock, animals will always face brief moments of hazard in the arena.

When considering what role livestock have in our society it is important to keep things in perspective. On a worldwide scale of animal suffering at human hands, how high does rodeo really rate? The human race is deeply immersed in the practice of using animals for work, food, and sport.

Refusing to exit the arena, this exhausted bull drops after several minutes of fighting pickup horses' pull. As this cowboy shoves a horn to get it to rise, the bull shows he has something left in the tank by lurching up to give the man a bloody forehead. STAPLETON

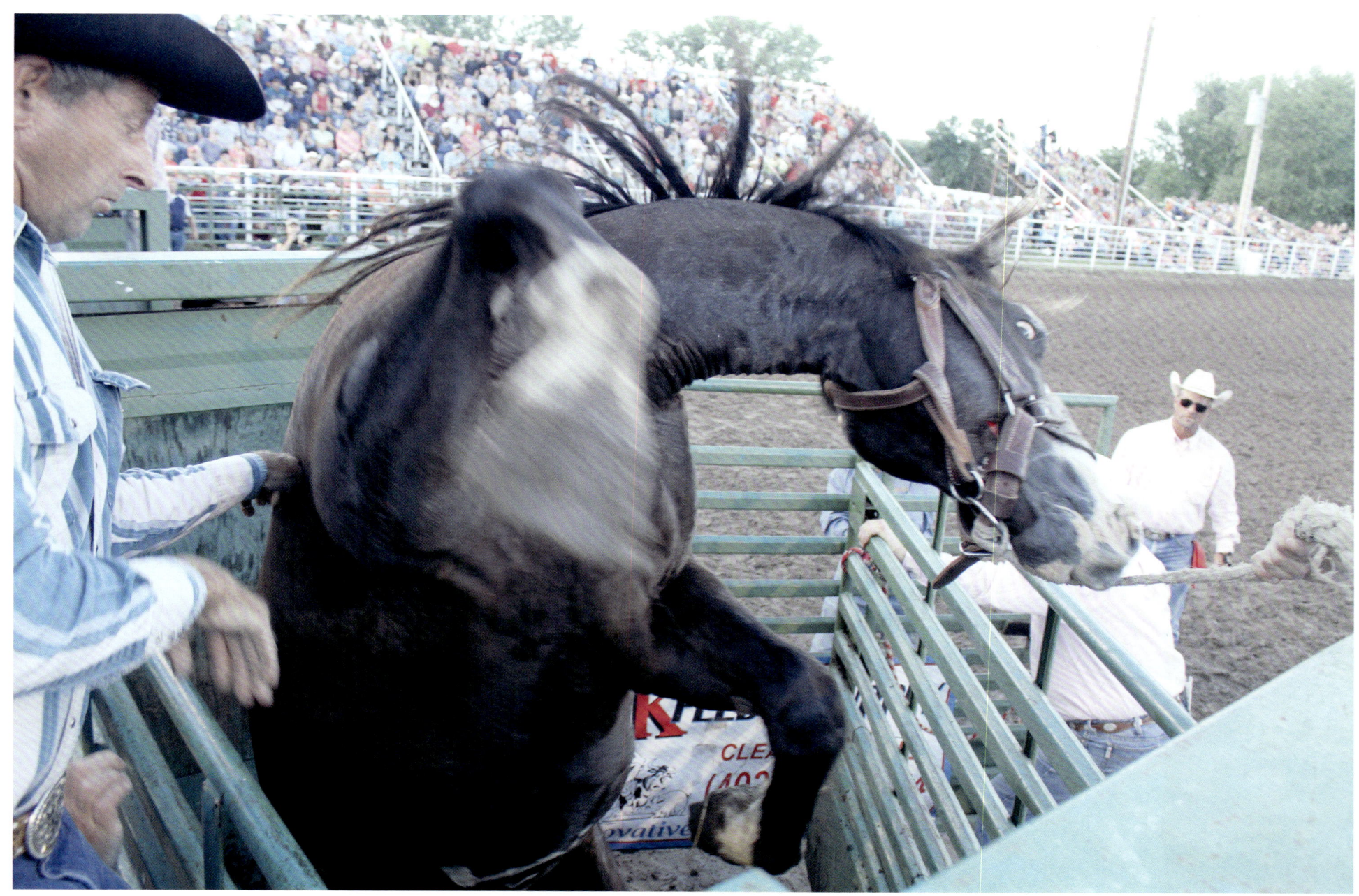

Younger, less experienced broncs are more likely to go ballistic in the chutes. CLEARWATER

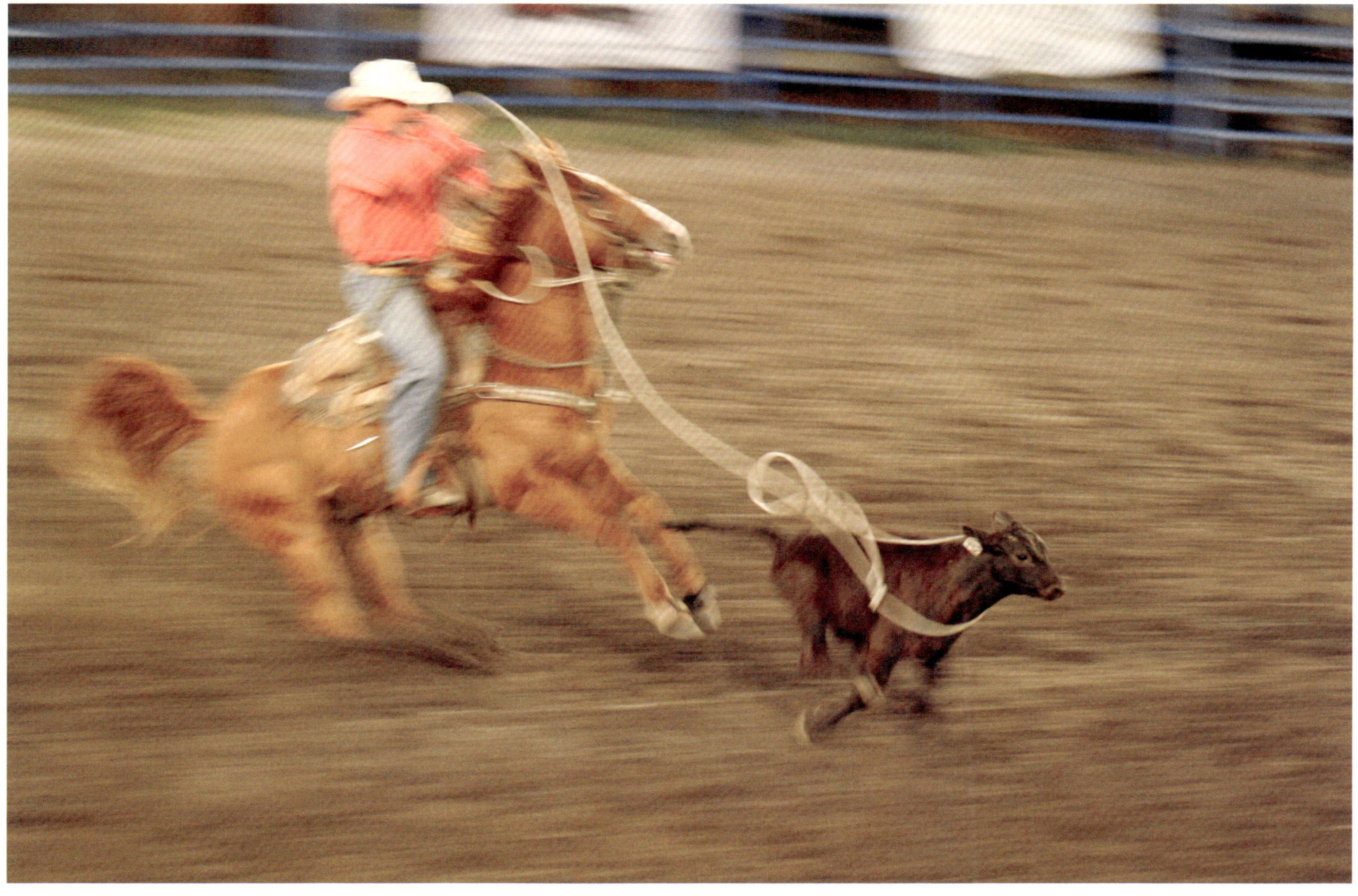

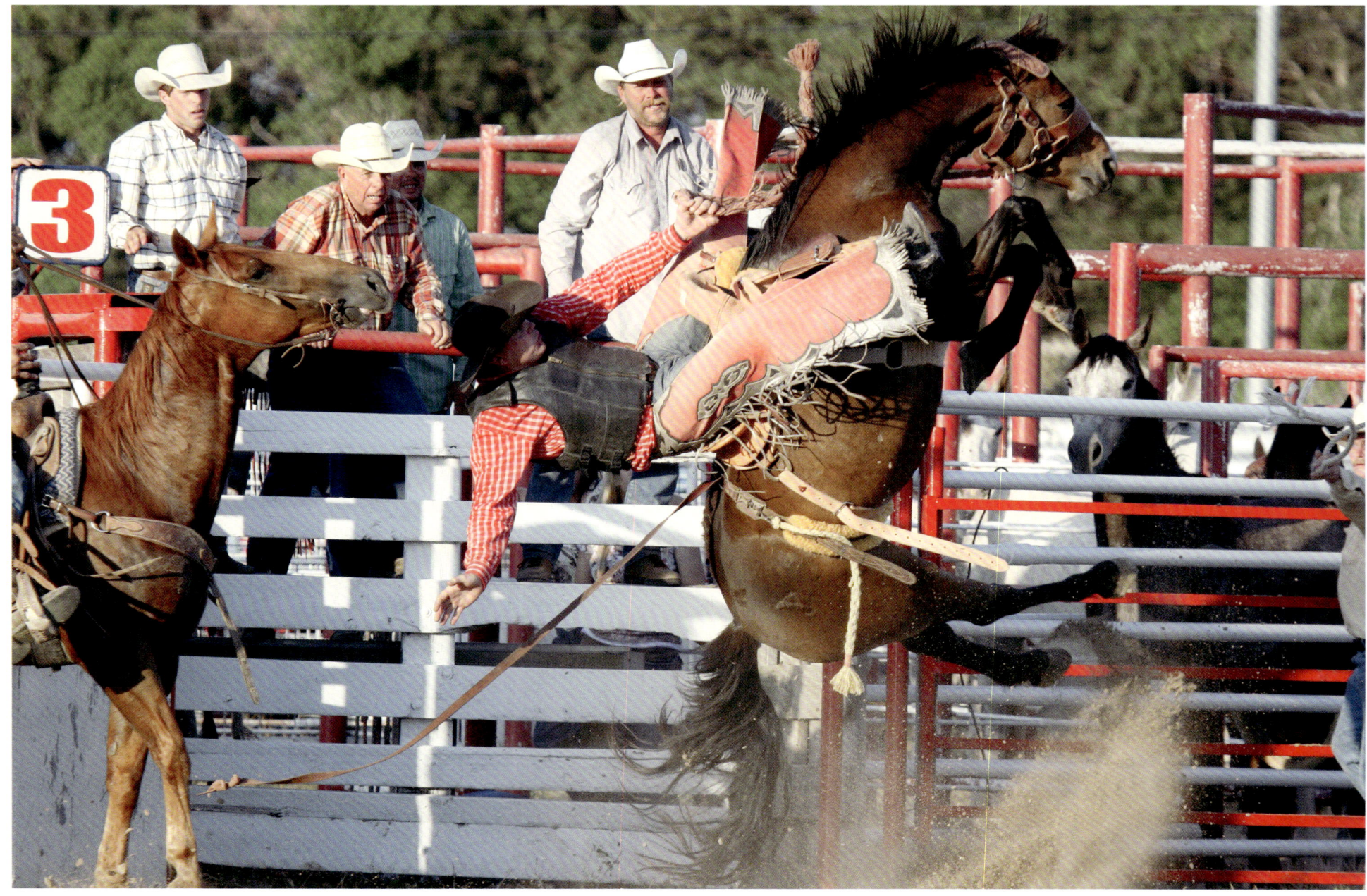

It's uncommon, but broncs do die. Leaping toward an impossible touchdown, this bronc is having a heart attack and will land unconscious. GOTHENBURG

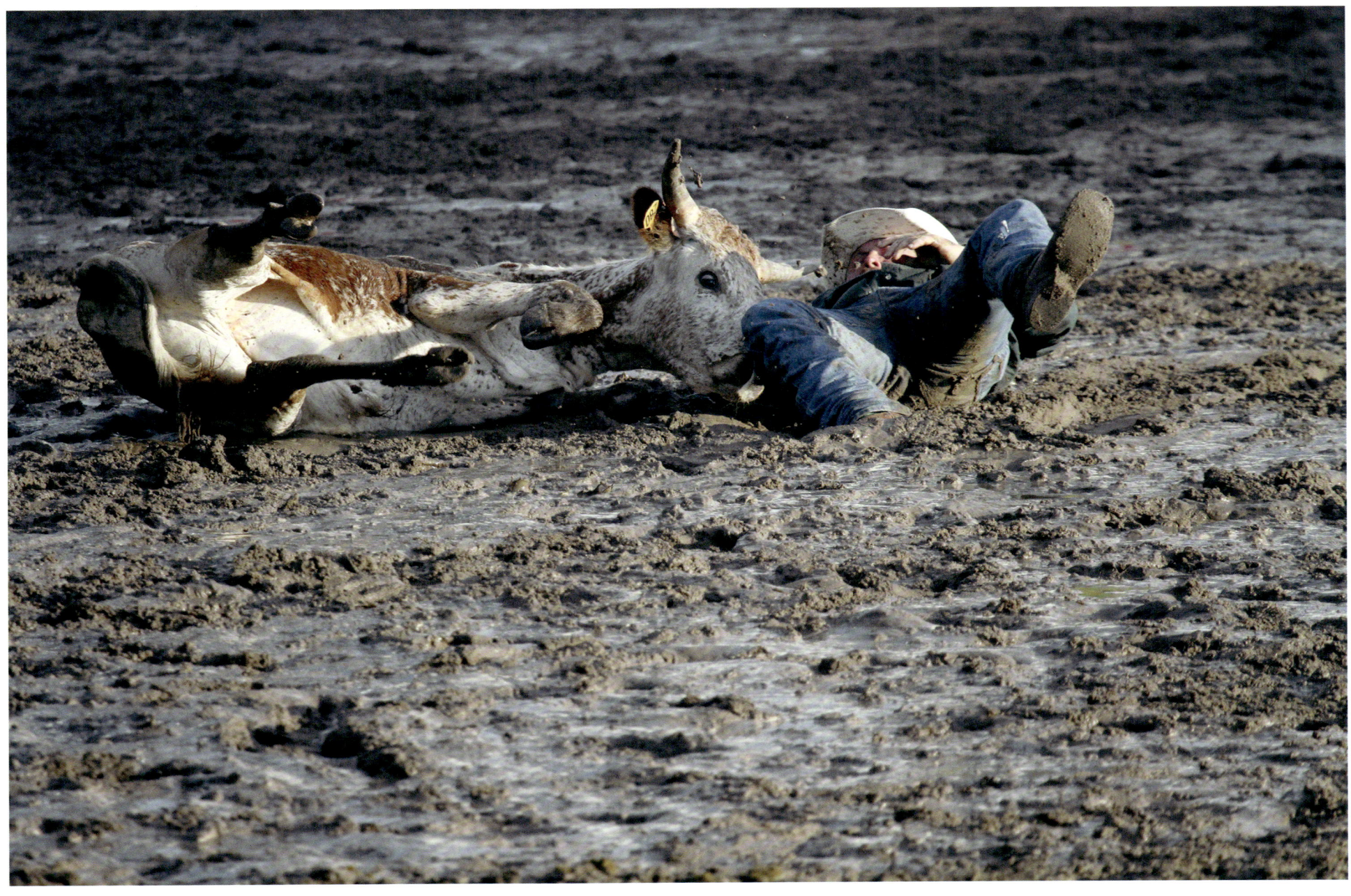

Wrestler and steer recover from the run. VALENTINE

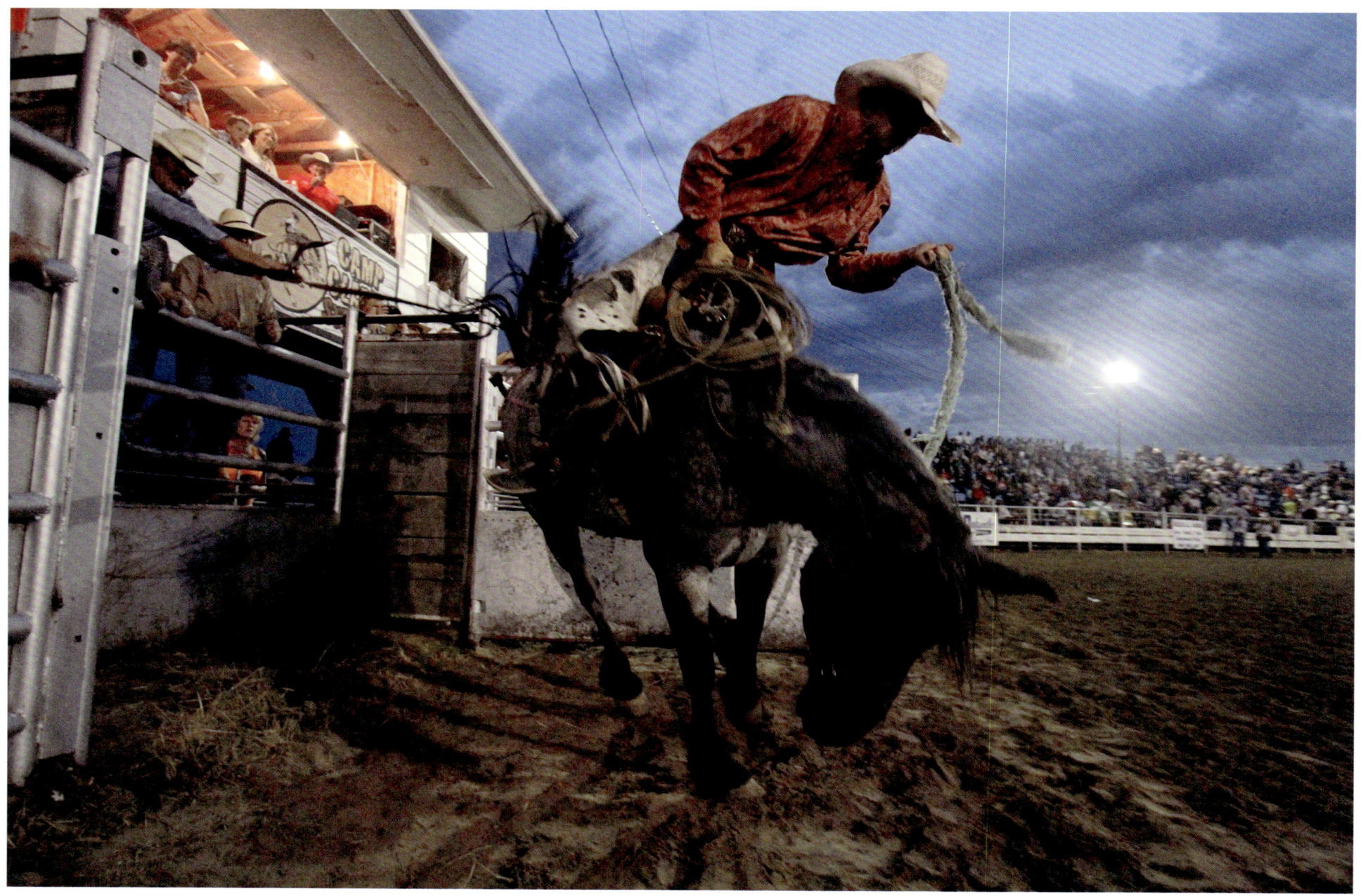

Ranch-bronc rider Andy Sherfey competes against his father at this event. In a side-bet, he who does the worst buys the other a new saddle. Andy hung on a second less. BRIDGEPORT

Weird Wild West

UNSANCTIONED EVENTS

Throw a standard saddle on a bronc, set a local cowboy on its back, and there you have ranch bronc riding. Though not sanctioned as an official Nebraska rodeo event, many ranch-bronc riders belong to a national association dedicated to that sport alone. Some, like Andy Sherfey of Lisco, compete several times per year in their region. Most are just beginners. Andy started riding broncs two years ago as an offshoot of his horse training profession. "I bet my dad who could stay on the longest at the Bridgeport rodeo," he chuckles. "The winner got a new saddle from the loser. Dad [age forty-nine] won at seven and a half seconds."

Style matters in ranch bronc riding. The rules are about the same, though cheers and points are gained by waving your hat in the air, or better yet, smacking the bronc's butt with it. Most don't; they are too busy surviving. Outrageous chaps or just jeans, baseball cap or sombrero, and even wilder outfits might help your score—anything goes. Anyone may enter and occasionally novices take a shot. Beginners are thrown instantly. Andy says, "You don't realize a horse has that much power until it's bucking under you. If you can get in time with the bucking then that neutralizes it." But beginners won't neutralize any bronc. Even Spiderman wouldn't make the buzzer—though that may not stop him from trying again. According to Andy, "When they get on that first bronc and get their head planted in the dirt, their first response is wow! Then that will either seed their adrenaline so

they want to do it again, or they'll be done with it right there. The adrenaline is unbelievable either way."

Unsanctioned rodeo events also include wild horse races, wild cow races, and the bizarrely-yet-accurately titled wild-cow milking contests. These competitions are popular with crowds and about 20 percent of Nebraska rodeos hold them. I admit being amused at first, but that was from a naïve outlook. The more I photographed these absurd events the better I understood the stresses the animals endure. Contestants are not part of the competitive rodeo crowd, and though several regional wild-horse-racing teams travel the circuit competing in matching shirts, most are local entrants looking for limelight. Many of the men are unfit and susceptible to injury; some are older guys.

Before one wild horse race, a middle-aged participant's wife scolded him as he walked away from paying his entry fee, hissing, "You get hurt and our entire business shuts down!" Likely hearing the truth, he ignored her. Most of these blue-collar men need functioning limbs to earn paychecks. This husband escaped injury but his team lost. Locals almost never win. It's the guys in matching shirts who walk away with loot.

Seeing men injured in wild horse races is upsetting, but they entered this madness willingly. Horses have no choice. Herded into chutes and haltered, their ropes are handed through metal bars to three-man teams. All gates then open at once, creating instant chaos. The goal is to restrain your thrashing horse, saddle it, and then ride it across the arena. Animals chosen for wild horse races are broncs that have not been bucking well lately—many of them are older horses. Their next stage in life will likely be the sale barn.

Animals experience enormous stress from the menacing nature of three zealous men bearing down upon them, plus a ridiculously long five-minute event time. This is twenty times longer than what any sanctioned-event animal endures in the arena. Broncs rear and pull, desperately struggling to escape. One man, the "Anchor," holds the rope while a second, the "Mugger," attempts immobilizing the horse via headlock. Then the "Rider" works to strap on the saddle. It's the same scene in wild cow contests yet weirder: they're saddling a cow! Cows unused to human hands are desperate to be free and just like the horses do, they suffer five minutes of hell. Men are tossed like ragdolls and some animals fall in the struggle.

I watched a horse die at my feet in this event one exceptionally hot Nebraska night. Fallen, tangled in rope, and held to the ground by men, its heart stopped from some combination of exhaustion, anxiety, heat prostration, or difficulty breathing in a lying position. I will never forget that sickening moment. A similar scenario unfolded at another venue where a horse went down exhausted. It might have died there if not for a contestant pinching its ear to bring it back to its senses and to its feet. But this did not end its agony. The men continued controlling it until mercifully it escaped and joined the herd of fugitives being pursued round the arena.

Wild horse and cow races are dangerous spectacles and I believe they need improved oversight or outright elimination. Based on conversations I've had, the competitive rodeo community would not argue with that statement.

Less experienced ranch-bronc riders sometimes suffer quick, ferocious dismounts. STAPLETON

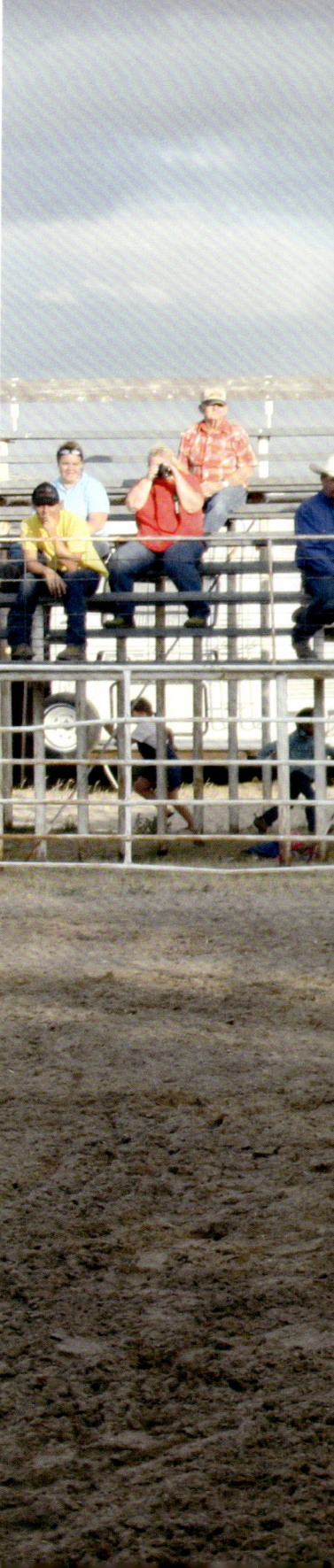

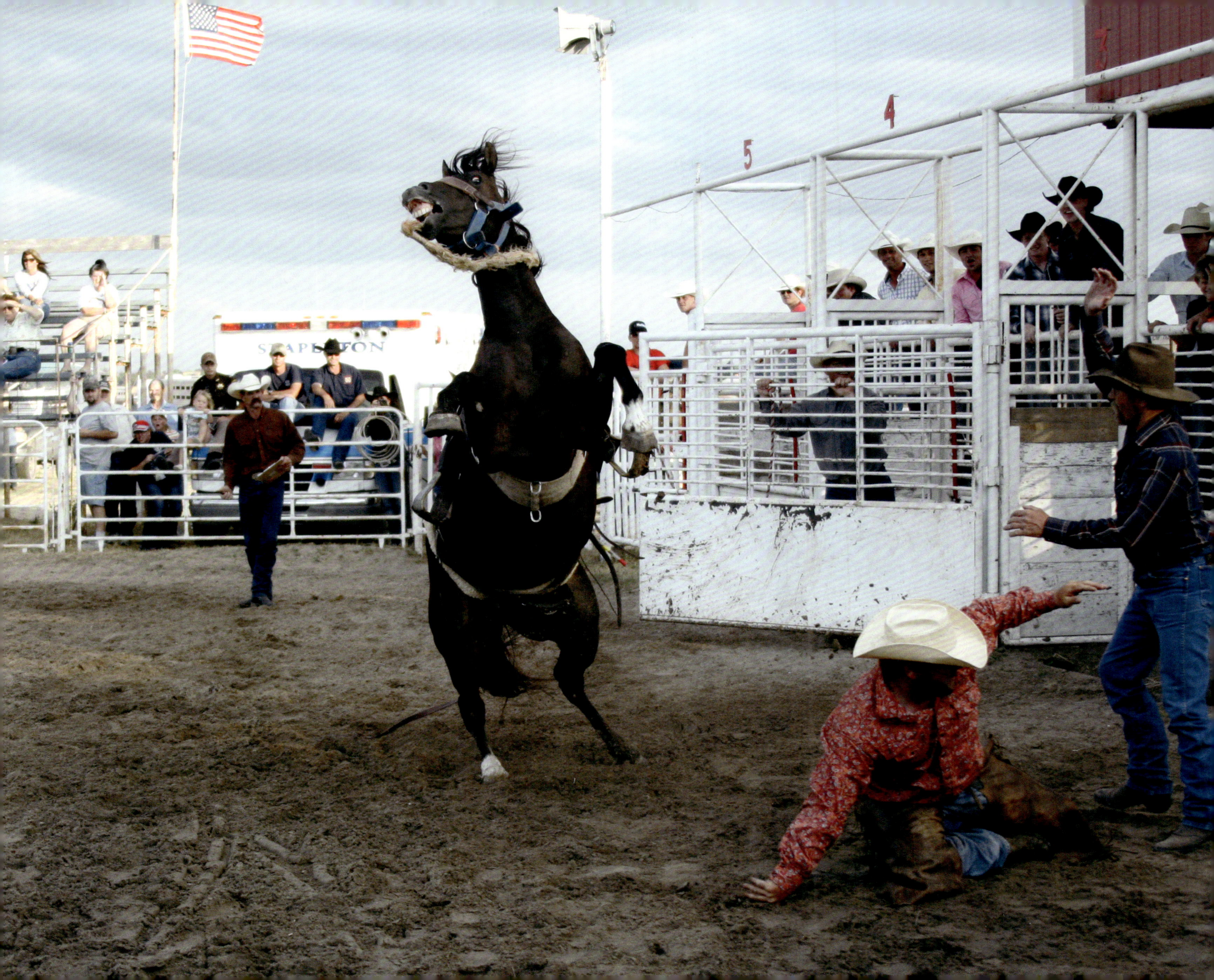

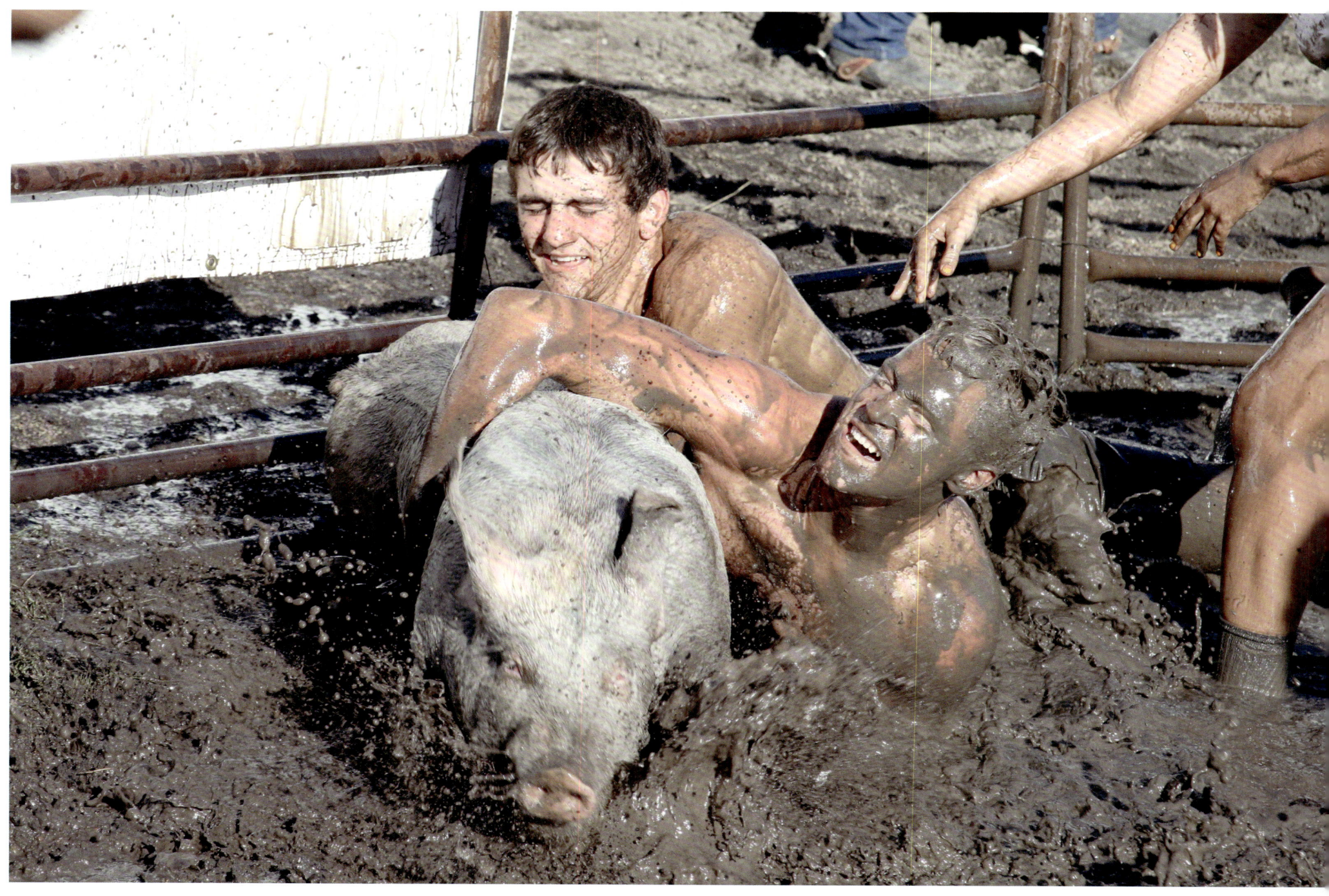

(*opposite*) Before one rodeo, teenage teams wrestle pigs, competing to tie ribbons around tails in the best time. After a few hellish minutes, this exhausted pig still fights to escape and I fight the urge to jump in and free it from its assailants. BRIDGEPORT

(*right*) Ranch-bronc riding brings flare. The chaps alone may help his score. BRIDGEPORT

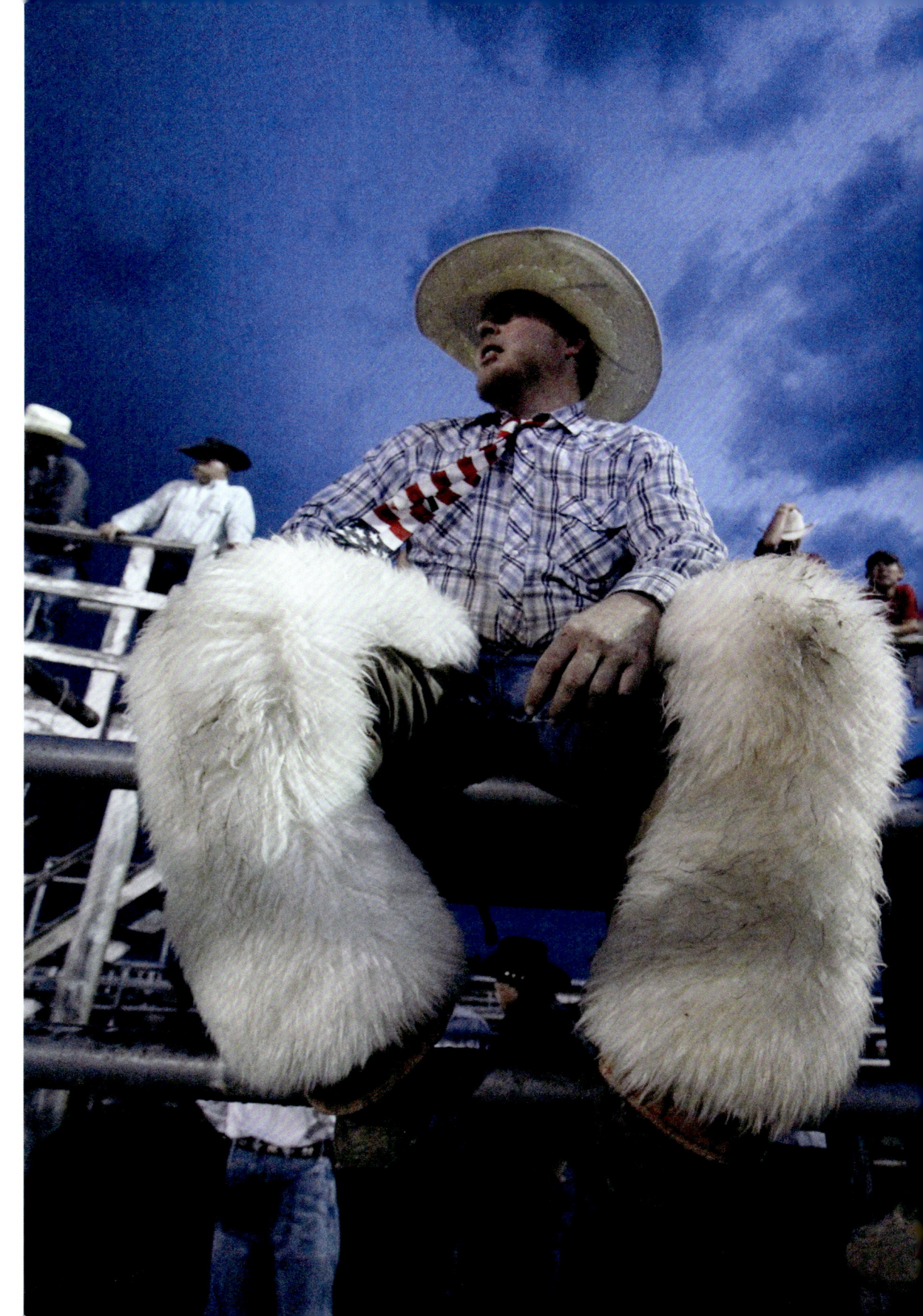

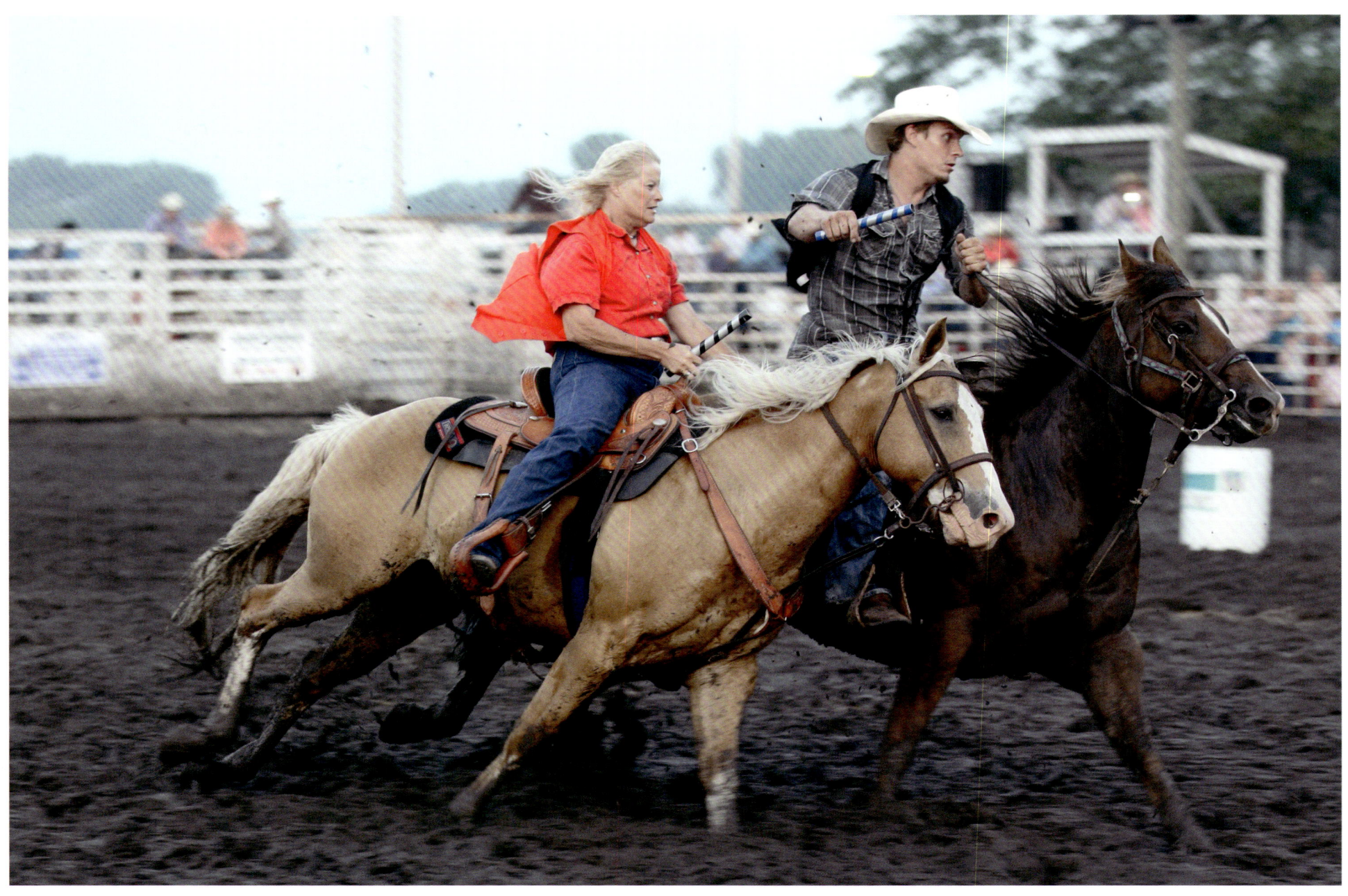

Midway through the rodeo, local riding clubs compete in a high-speed relay race. HARTINGTON

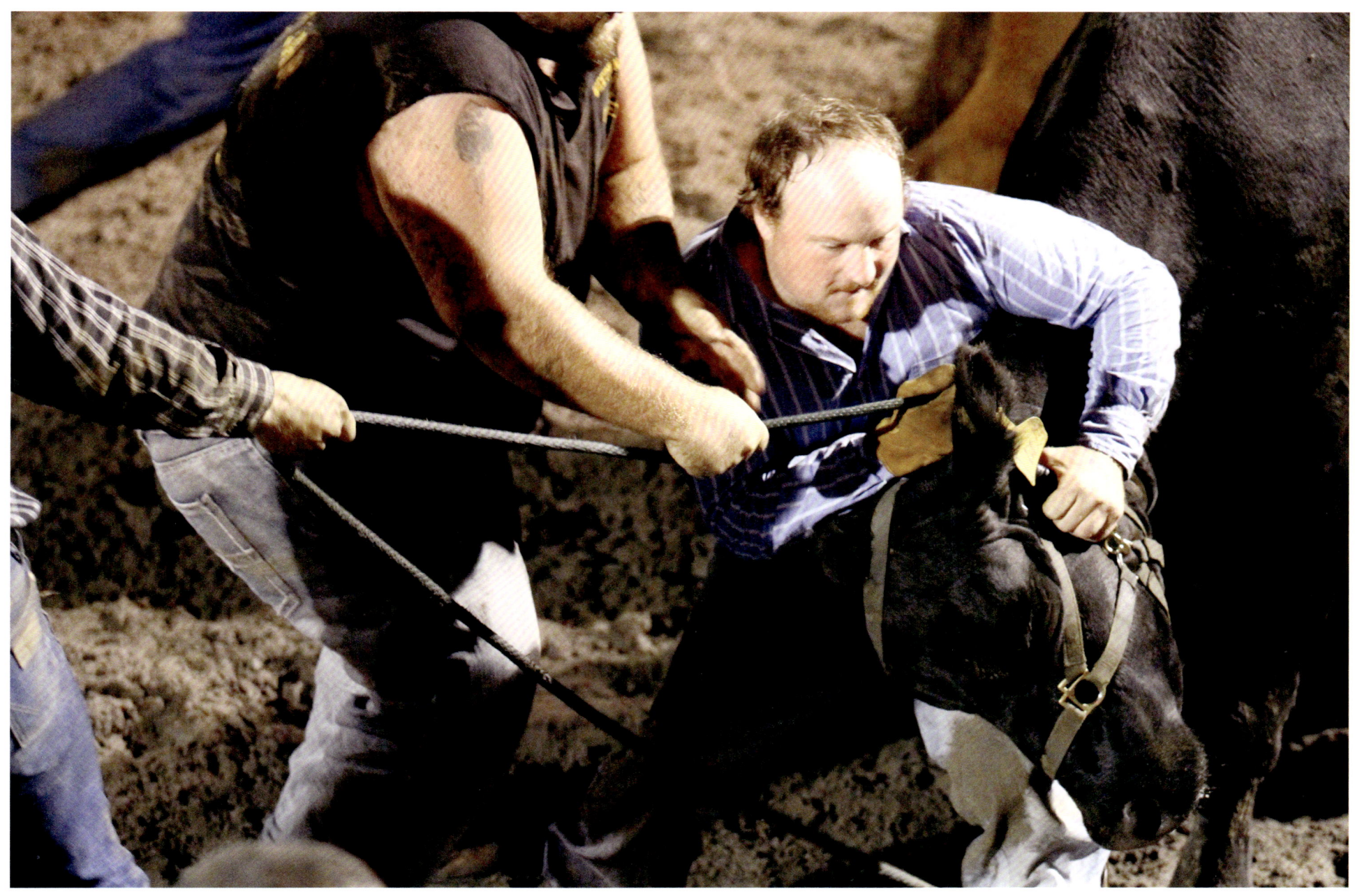

Locals looking for limelight struggle for control during a wild-cow race. CLEARWATER

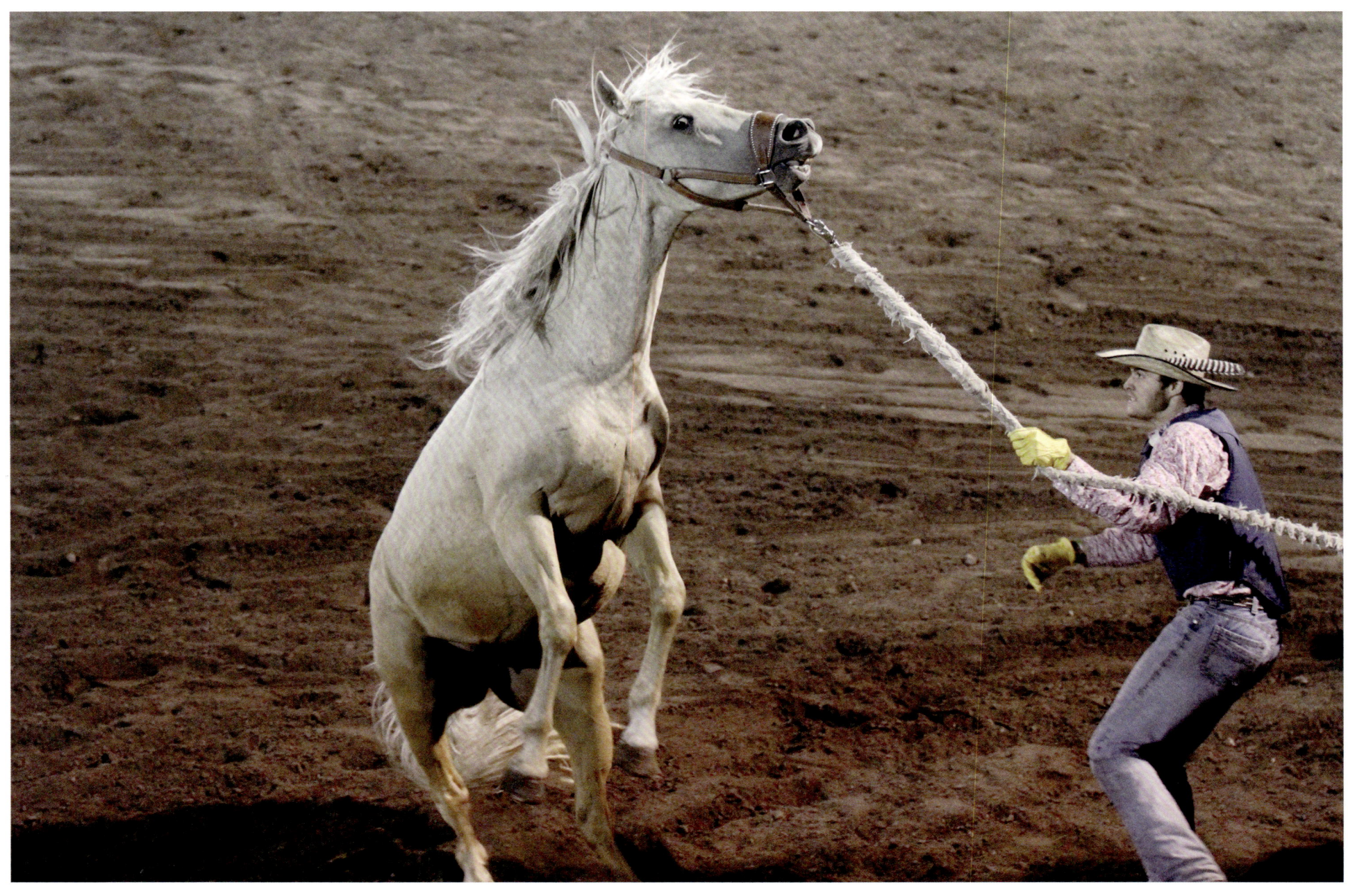

Broncs desperately use all their might to escape
a wild-horse race. SUTHERLAND

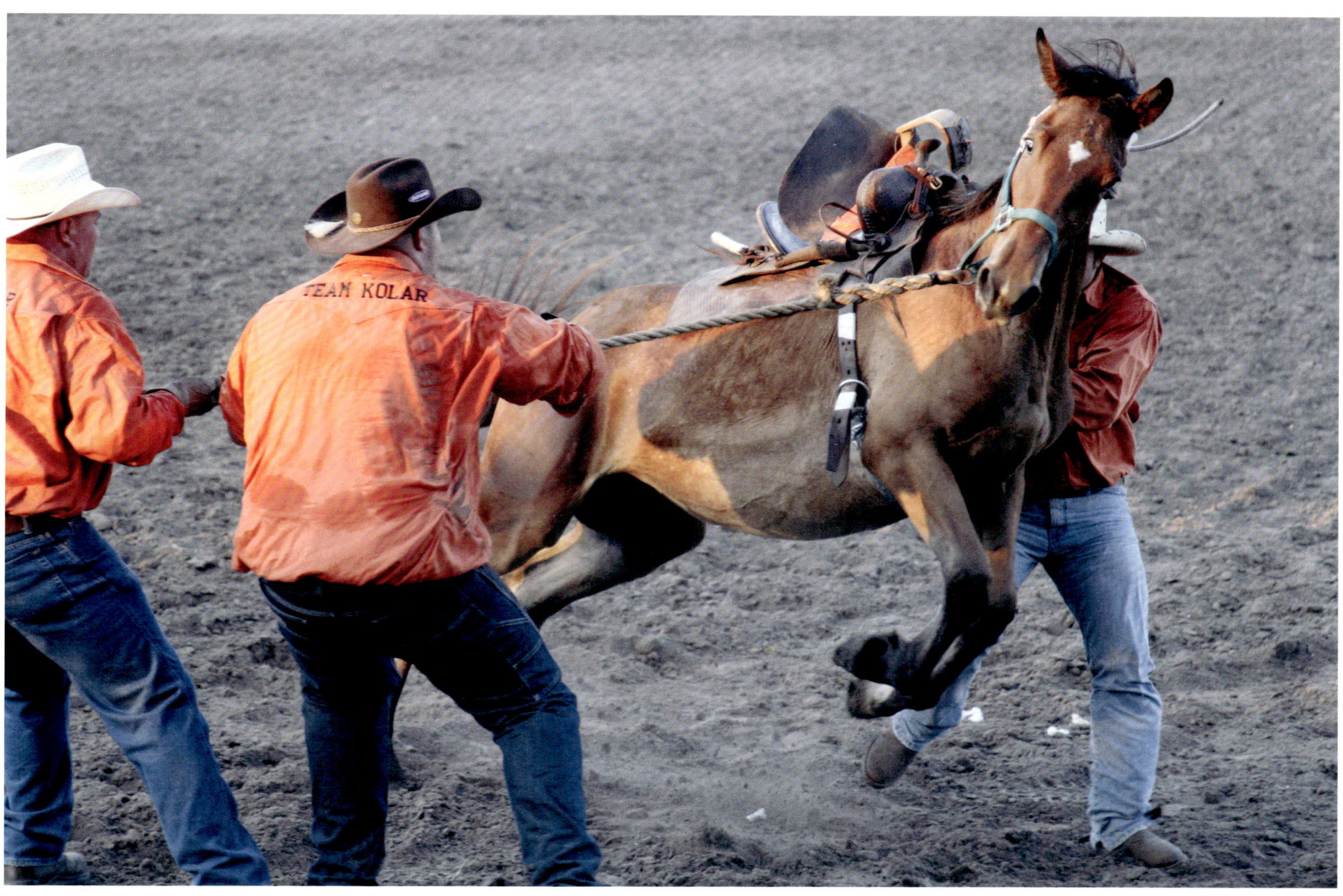

A bronc's power is about equal to three large men on a rope.
This struggle can last up to five minutes. WOLBACH

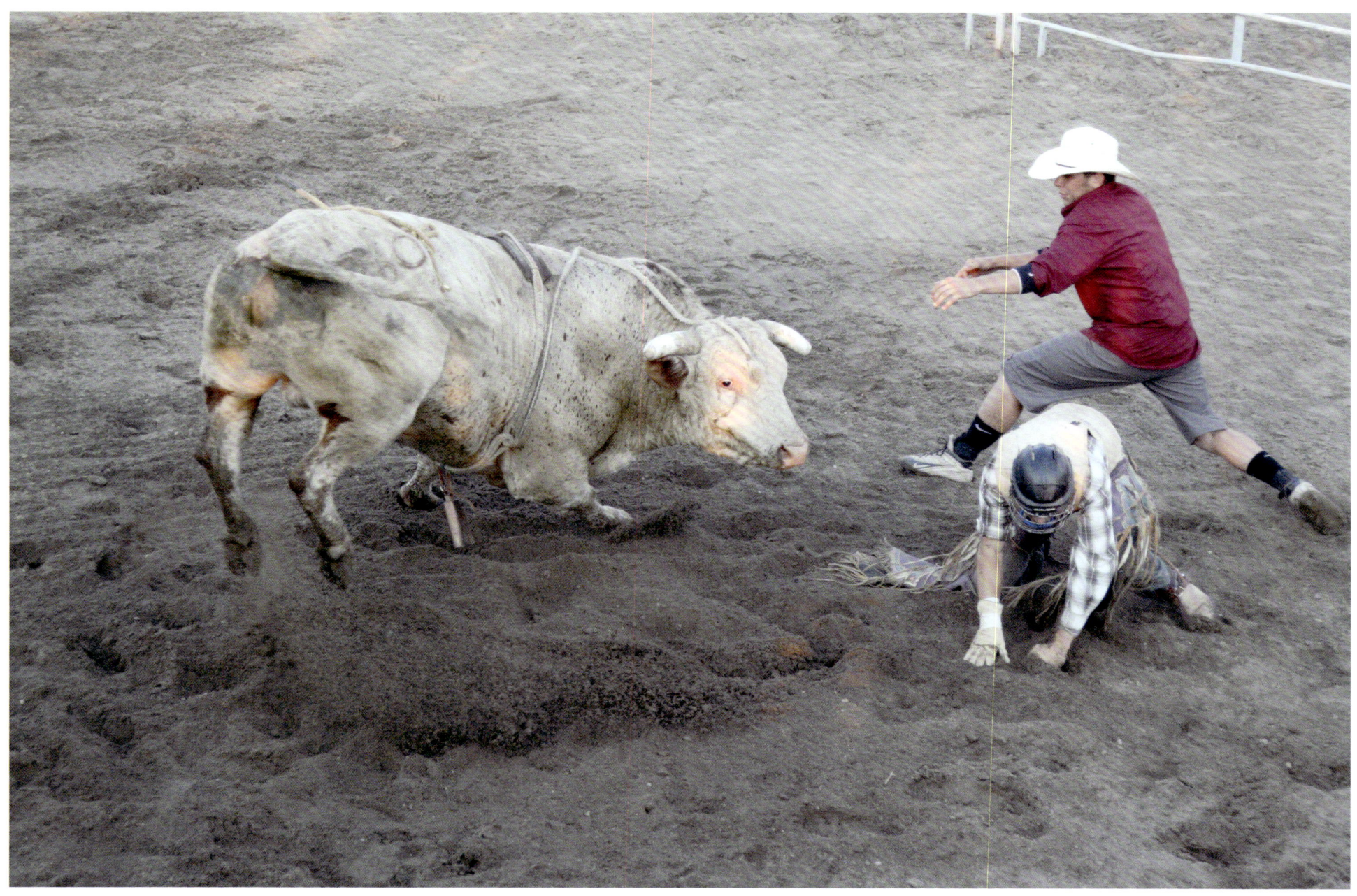

A Coleman bull bears down. This bull will veer away, sparing the
rider to pursue the aggressive bullfighters. BLOOMFIELD

Making Monsters

BULL CONTRACTORS

Nebraska has a handful of bull contractors, but to meet the state's demand many come from across the borders of Iowa, Kansas, Wyoming, and South Dakota. Just a rifle shot from Nebraska across the Missouri River near Springfield, South Dakota, Jack Coleman raises bucking bulls. In 2010, my son and I visited Jack, his wife Kathy and their son Shawn. At that time they bred fourteen cows a year to their best bulls—and these bucker's mothers are not your ordinary cows. Horned and muscular, their offspring are not well-mannered. Visiting again in 2015, I found twice as many "bucking cows," as Jack calls them; the bucking bull industry is thriving.

On that crisp October day in 2010, Jack and Shawn toured me and my son, Colton, around their property in a crew-cab truck with rear seats piled full of bull ropes and a long, empty stock trailer bouncing along behind us. Stopping at their main corral, Shawn and I enter on foot to approach the wary bull herd. Their diversity is notable: spotted, splotched, brindled, tall, short, lean, hulking, horned, hornless, and even banana-horned. "Look out for that gray one," Shawn warns over his shoulder as he approaches a tall, black, hornless bull. Standing only ten feet from the black bull, he nods its way and announces, "He's the dominant one in the herd now, but he's also the friendliest." Here in their home corral their tolerant behavior belies their purpose. My son sits on the fence wide-eyed as I stand among these creatures he has only known before as threatening monsters. I watch out for the gray bull.

Coleman bulls nap before event time, but moods change when contestants appear. Lying bulls rise as cowboys rub ropes with sticky rosin; their agitation is palpable. Every herd holds a bully that smashes into fences trying to hurt riders on the opposite side, pushing other bulls aside, huffing and angry at the world. Like Jekyll and Hyde, one sleepy-eyed bull lets me touch its forehead. Ten minutes later it bends thick metal fence bars apart like Superman.

Shawn allows the bulls out of the corral and into the pasture as Jack shows up with a tractor-load of feed, but the bulls scatter to the hills rather than to remain near strangers. Dust flies from dry Russian thistle as the dominant bull finds another black bull to spar with. Skull to skull they push until the friendly leader reasserts his rule.

The Colemans frequently buy bulls for bucking and breeding. "Sometimes it's cheaper to buy a four-year-old bucking bull rather than feed and raise one the four years it takes to make a bucker," Jack says. Their long-distance record shipped from Hawaii with an airfare alone of $2,000. Regardless of price, the bulls must perform. "If they don't buck, or if they break out of the pastures enough, then they become hamburger," which is the fate of most cattle they raise. Jack calls toward the retreating bulls with a resounding "C'BOSSS!" but outsiders are not welcome in their pasture and they stay away.

In a dimly-lit barn toward evening, Jack and Shawn force medicine down the throats of two pneumonia-stricken calves. Shawn uses just one hand; his riding arm hangs in a sling from a rodeo injury. "That'll make you feel better buddy," Jack says gently as the last calf is dosed.

As the sun sets Shawn and I bump through grassy pastures in an old four-door sedan also loaded with bull ropes. Looking over the Missouri River I ask if he spent much time playing there as a kid. "No, never did," he said with a hint of loss. "Everything was about the ranch. Things weren't so good back in those days. Dad started this place from nothin', and that's a tough living."

Living on the ranch now gives Shawn a competitive advantage. A repeating regional champion, in the off season he often phones buddies to come practice. Asked how long the practices last, he replies, "Oh, we each ride three or four times or until someone gets hurt."

"You're stayin' for supper, aren't ya?" Jack asks as my son and I thank him for their time. I politely decline but Jack confidently states, "I'm sure Kathy'll be expecting you." And she was; that's rural hospitality. These are wide open spaces where people count on one another, and to be there at supper time meant sharing supper. Later, enjoying dessert, the phone rings. A neighbor alerts Jack that one of his bulls was walking down the rural highway. Jack and Shawn give goodbyes as they grab hats and jackets to set off in the dark. I hope this bull is not a repeat offender.

Four and a half years later I find that Shawn had married and moved 100 miles north. And there is a new Coleman from this union named Kadillac Jack. When Grandpa Jack told me the name, he added, "I'm not kiddin'!" But I knew he wasn't; by now there is no cowboy name that could surprise me.

To prepare a new bull to do this at a rodeo, the breeder will load young bulls into his own bucking chutes, strap a remote-release dummy weight on their back and swing the gate. First timers might carry a thirty-pound weight just a couple seconds to get used to having something on their back—which they loathe! As a bull's confidence grows, so does the dummy time—up to the standard eight seconds. Some don't buck well and won't make the cut. Others go ballistic and the bull breeder smiles. KEARNEY

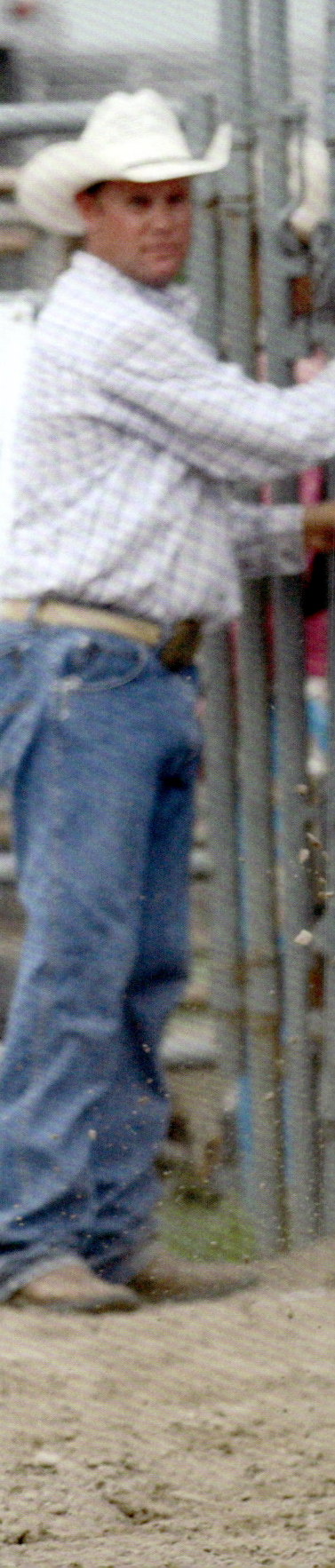

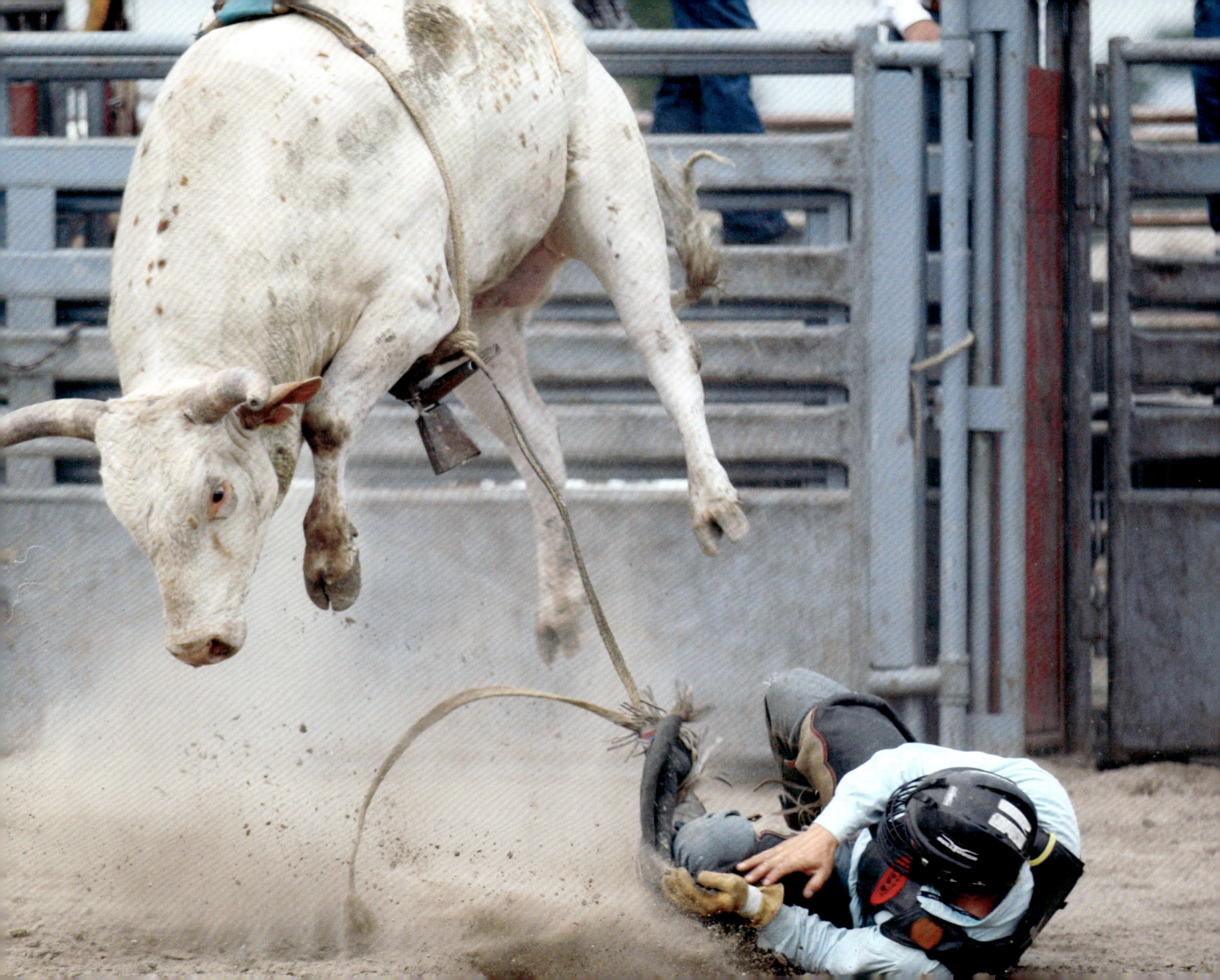

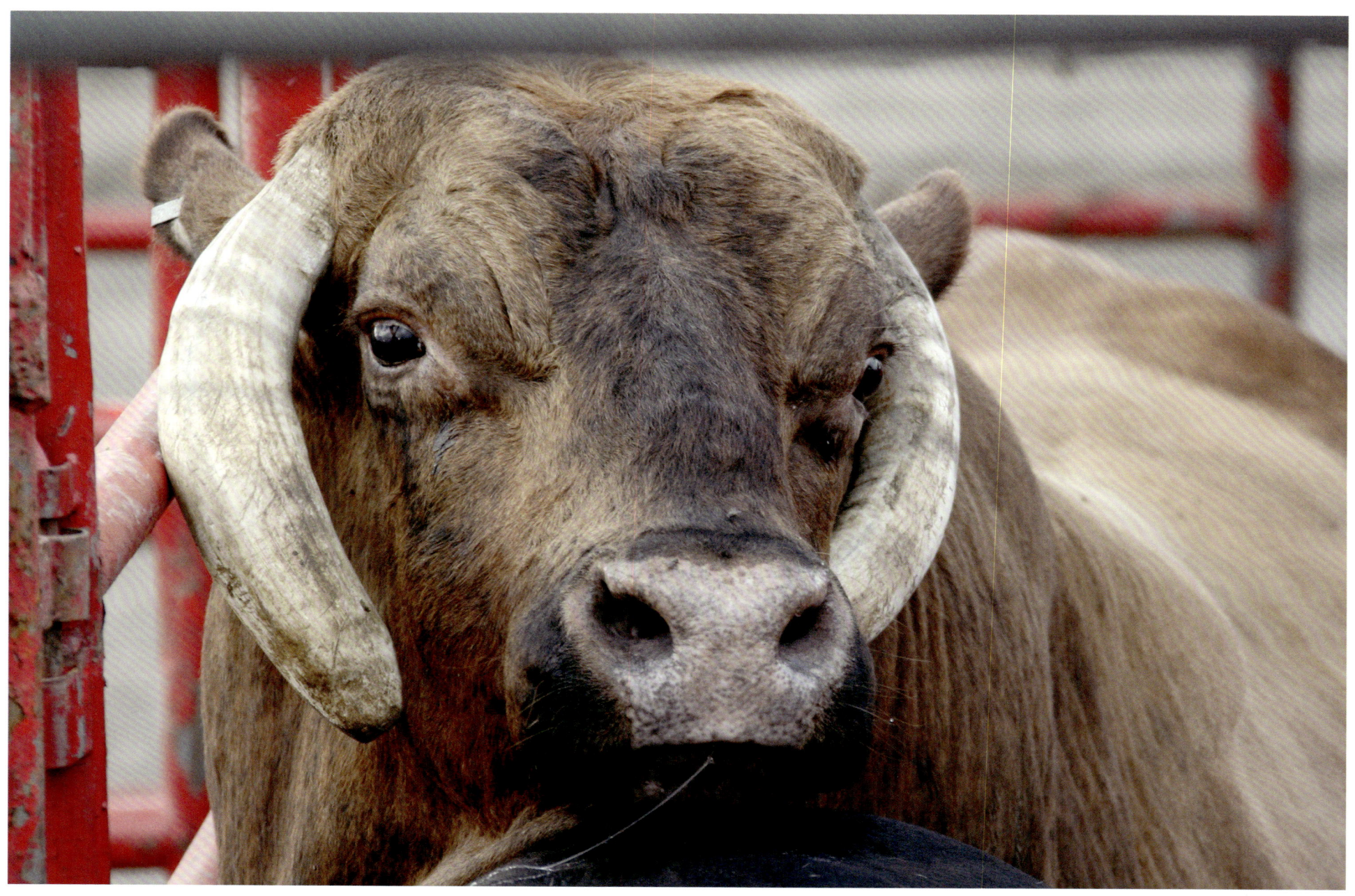

A "banana horned" bull waits his turn in the chutes. GENEVA

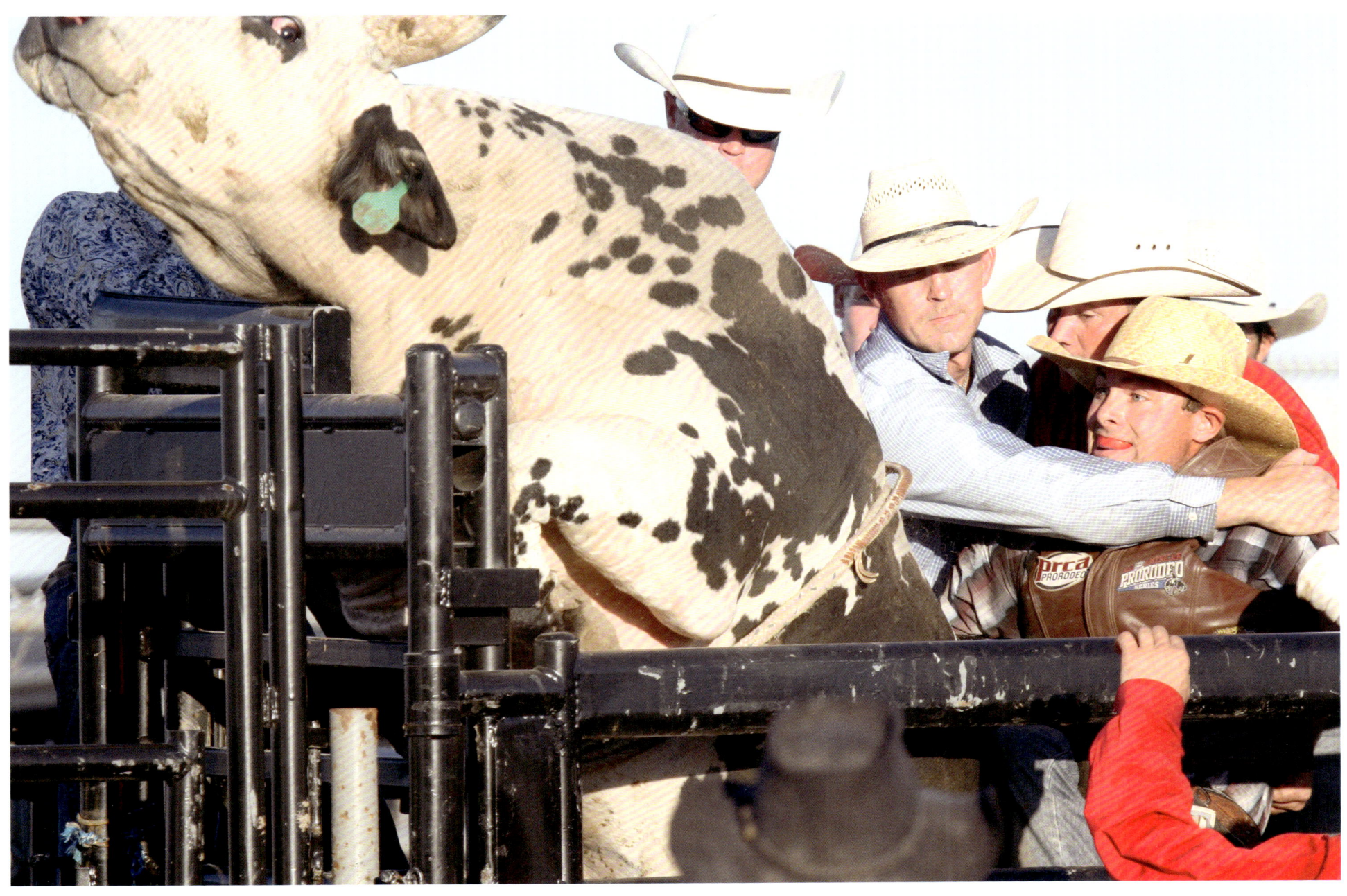

Bred for craziness, a Coleman bull launches prematurely in the chute. KEARNEY

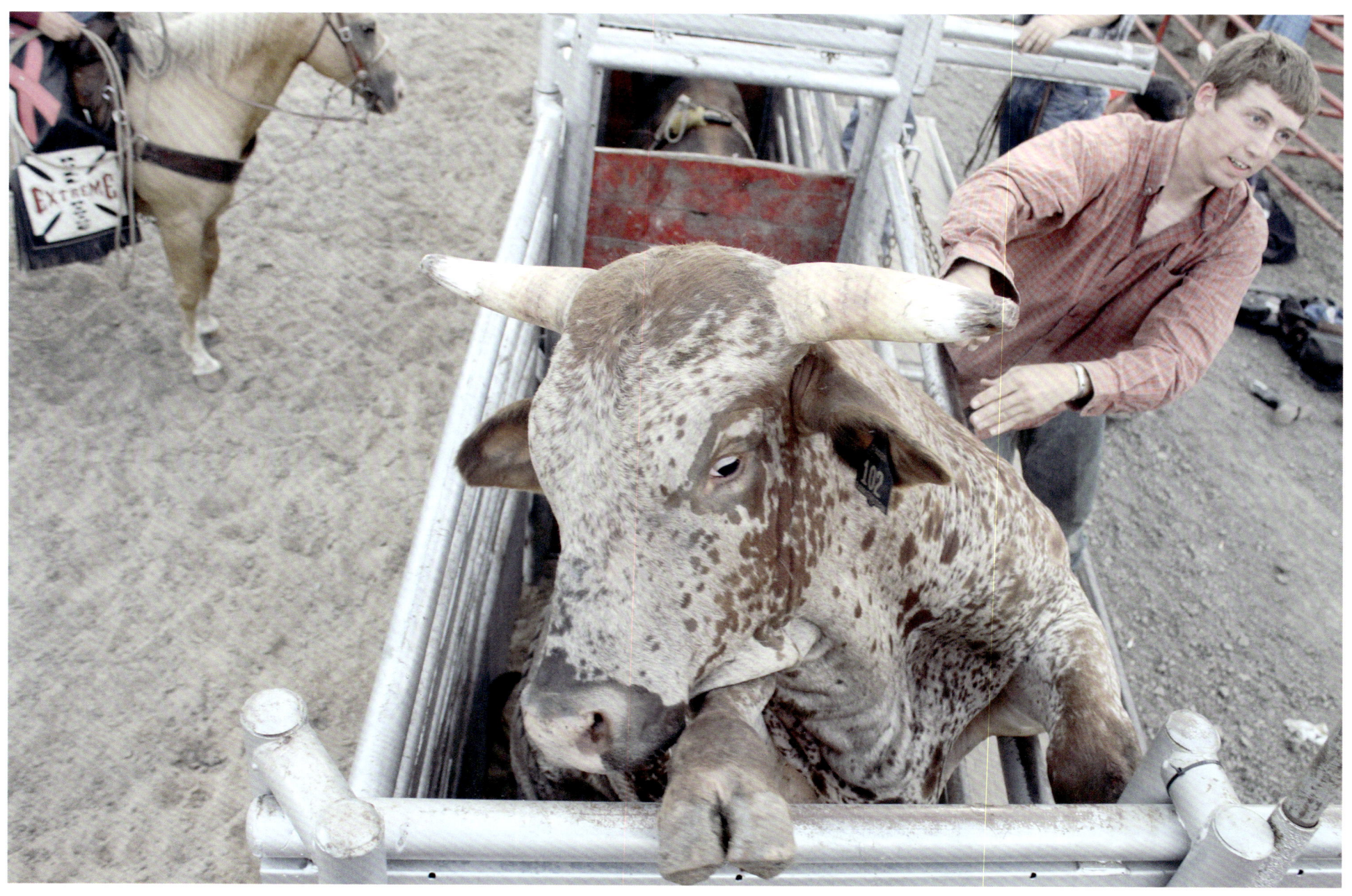

"Age has a lot to do with how a bull acts in the chute," says bull fighter Dave Jantzi.
"A three-year-old is more scared; a seven-year-old knows it's game time." GENEVA

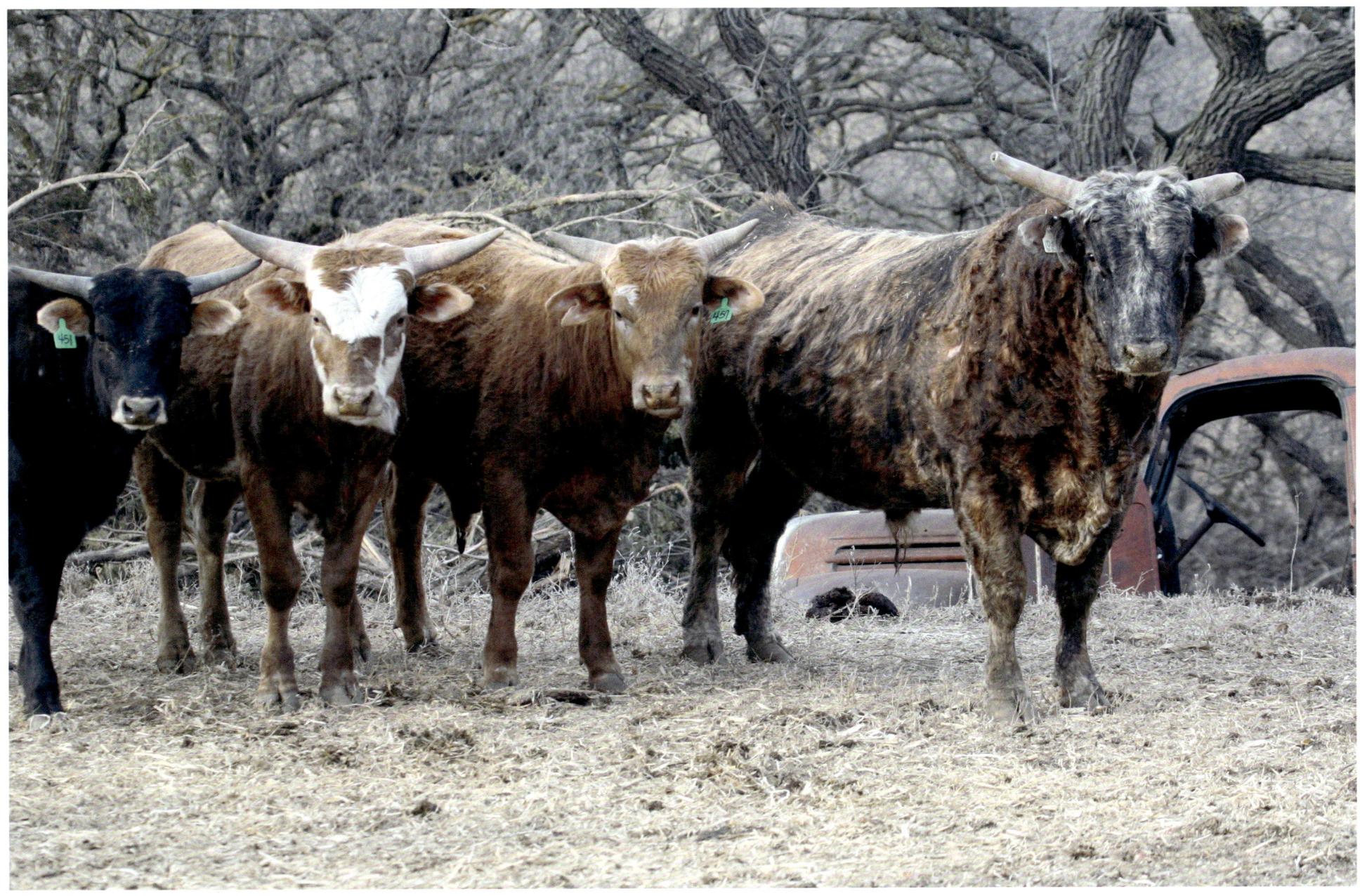

Yearling bulls yet to prove their bucking ability stand next to veteran super-bucker Toytiger. One bull at a time leads the bucking herd's hierarchy, and he must take on any challenger at any time. One fight led to a stronger bull pushing the challenger off a 200-foot embankment, killing it instantly. COLEMAN RANCH, NEAR SPRINGFIELD, SD

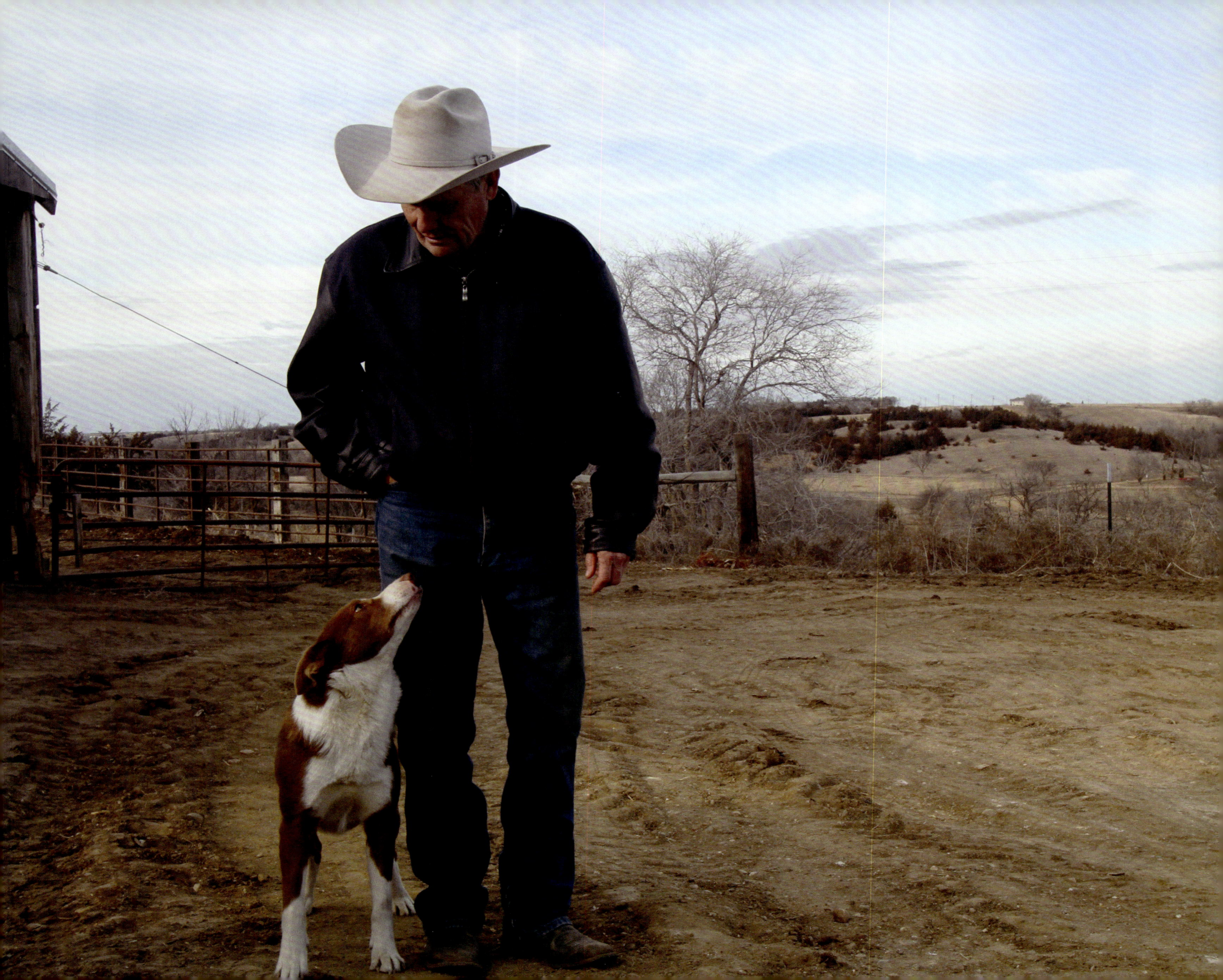

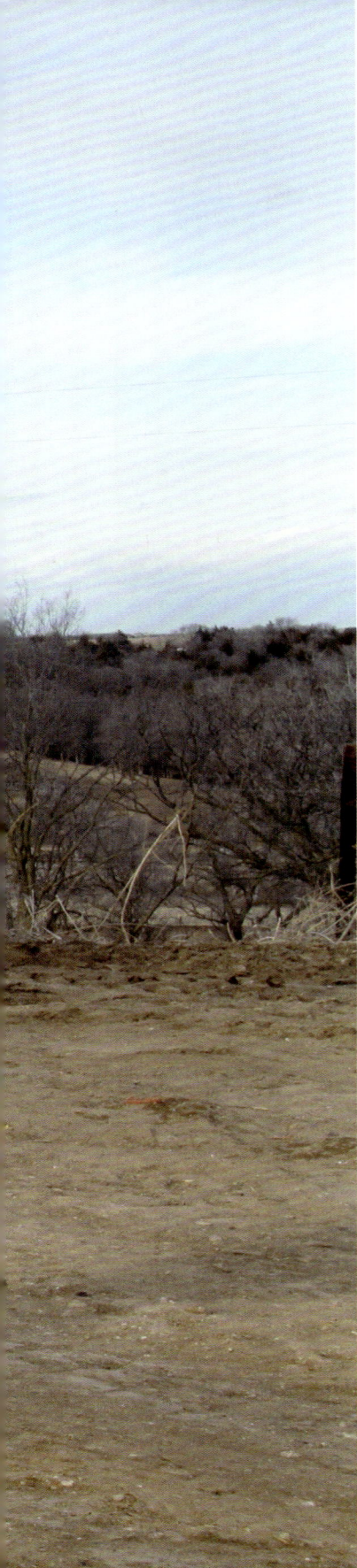

Bull breeder Jack Coleman and his Australian Cattle Dog, Howdy.
Says Jack, "Howdy likes to work, or get in the way . . . depending."
COLEMAN RANCH, NEAR SPRINGFIELD, SD

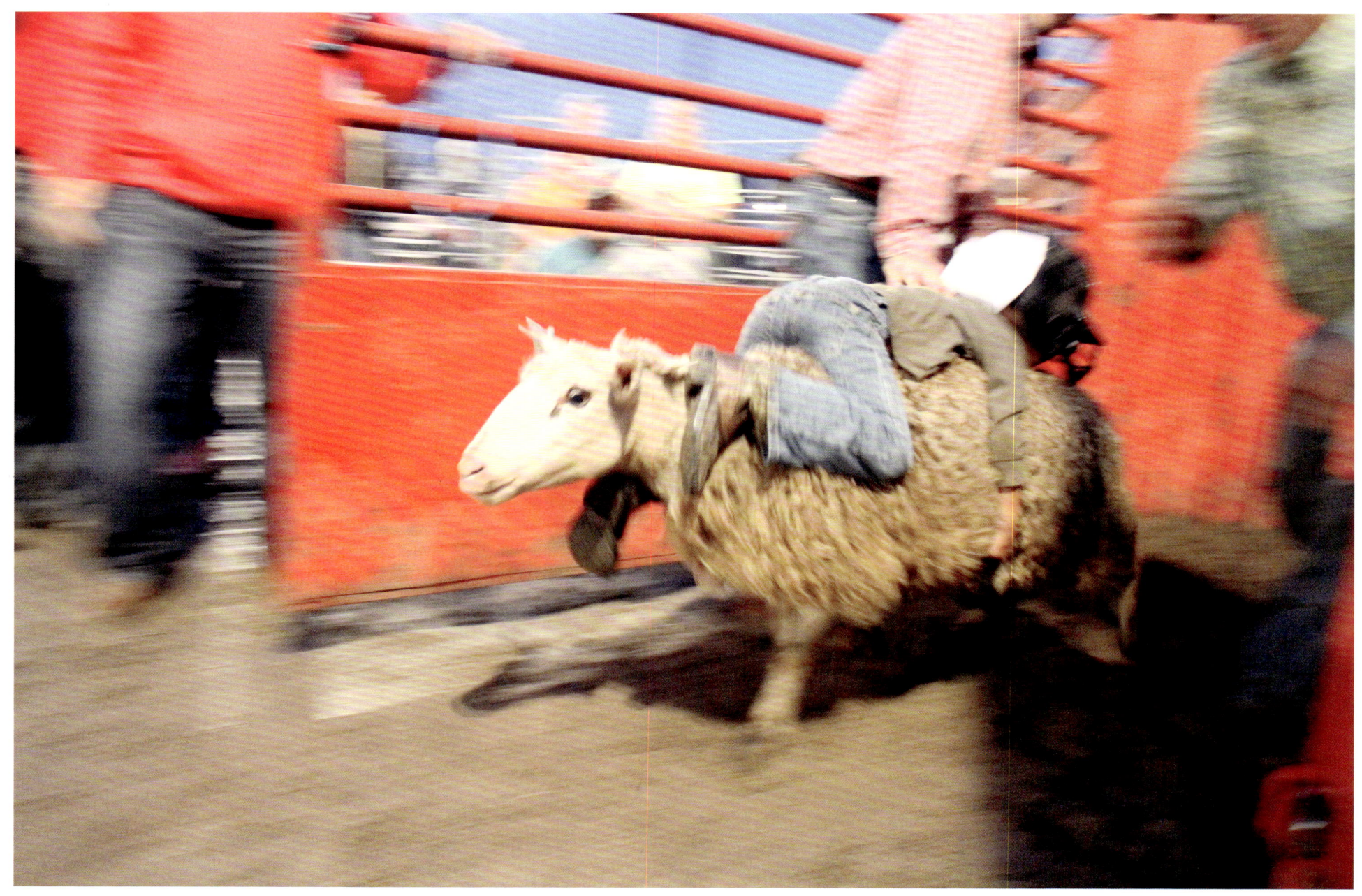

A mutton bustin' veteran rides backwards for style; these kids
are on horseback long before bicycles. BLOOMFIELD

Get on Young and Ride 'em Hard

KIDS' EVENTS

Mutton bustin' translated is sheep riding. Many future adult competitors first ride the wool. Not all, but many Nebraska rodeos "buck" sheep for kids. There is no minimum age limit; if you can grab two fistfuls of wool and hang on, then you qualify. Afterwards, all participants receive a dollar or two for their bravery, but it's a year's worth of bragging rights they want. It is easy to spot veterans here just as it is in adult rough stock events. Excited and happy, those are the vets. Nervous and straight-faced, those are the rookies. But every kid is wary; many will end up nose first in the dirt and these sheep are fast.

Youngsters watch those riding before them intently, processing risk vs. reward in their little heads. Occasionally parents withdraw crying kids from the line. Other parents tactfully push kids over the hump of fear, but some parents are unforgiving, warning "Don't you cry!" as their teary-eyed young ones watch others wreck. Some are plunked onto sheep kicking and screaming. Others, like one boy wearing spurs and full-blown riding gear at the Valentine rodeo, coolly size up their mount as they approach. Chin barely clearing the sheep's back, he is a bull fighter's son and is frightened by no sheep. He will ride until gravity takes him.

Bull fighters serve a new role here. Sheep are one-million times safer than bulls but require twice the sprinting. Kids mount prone on a sheep's back, feet clamping sheep belly and fingers grabbing wool shoulders. Rocketing sheep will not slow until child-free. Humanely,

very small children and terrified criers are yanked off at once as the sheep darts away. Though they don't enter the arena, they've still been onboard long enough to say they rode a sheep. Next year they will really ride. Older kids try for best distance. Bull fighters sprint behind for safety and serve post-crash, helping the boy or girl out of the dirt with a compassionate hug if need be. Tough landings bring tears. Some kids stick like ticks and must be chased down and grabbed as their sheep nears the arena's edge. Serious contenders may finish nearly upside down as their will gives way to their balance. Grinning announcers interview dirt-caked sheep riders between rides while the rodeo queen hands them their cash. At the Clearwater rodeo one successful little fellow proudly tells the amused crowd, "I've been ridin' sheep all the way down to Texas."

Calf Scrambles might interrupt adult events as well. Pure bedlam, calves sporting ribbons tied to their tails enter the arena against a long row of kids. Children in boots and sneakers set off through the arena toward the huddling calves. Capturing a ribbon brings a prize, but calves don't tolerate dozens of sprinting kids so the chase is on. Winning is about persistence, positioning and luck. Experienced kids hug the fences; calves gravitate there, always looking for a way out.

Older kids, serious about the sport, compete in junior rodeos scattered across Nebraska. Perfect preambles to high school rodeo, junior competitions lead to performing in the big show one day. Featured events include chute doggin', in which a steer is held in place just long enough for a kid to put its horns in a wrestling grip, then it is let loose to be wrestled down. Little ones with ropes lasso stationary dummy steer heads for prizes, and kids zigzag on horseback between tall poles in the timed pole-bending race. Goat tying is hilarious. Kids charge on horseback toward a bleating goat tethered to a stake, flinging themselves off the saddle to tie a ribbon onto the goat's tail. Goats are uncooperative 100 percent of the time.

Watching a speeding kid on horseback can be nerve-racking to anyone who doesn't understand how much experience the young riders bring. With pintsized loads on man-sized mounts, when boots kick haunches these horses can rip. Smallest legs barely clear the saddle, but these kids have ridden solo since their city counterparts began riding tricycles. Hordes of cowkids socialize on horseback while waiting their turn at the Harrison rodeo. Sitting backwards or on rump bones behind the saddle, they goof off with friends. A girl stretches prone along her horse's long muscular neck with arms and legs drooping alongside. Twenty times their partner's weight, tolerant horses are used to shenanigans and stand patiently.

Riding calves and steers hone future bull-riding skills, but there is another possible progression toward riding with the big boys— miniature bulls. Selective breeding works both ways. Full grown but little, miniature bulls stand waist high to an adult and weigh 700-900 pounds, but they buck like their bigger cousins.

Nerves run high among young bull riders, or perhaps it's just that they haven't yet learned to hide it. It takes man-sized nerve to get on the backs of these mini livewires. Youth bull riding might seem physically and emotionally excessive for kids ten to fourteen years old, and considering new concussion science it might be so. But these

Warming up with the adults before the rodeo, the joy of riding begins early and will last a lifetime for ranch boys like the Morava twins. FORT ROBINSON

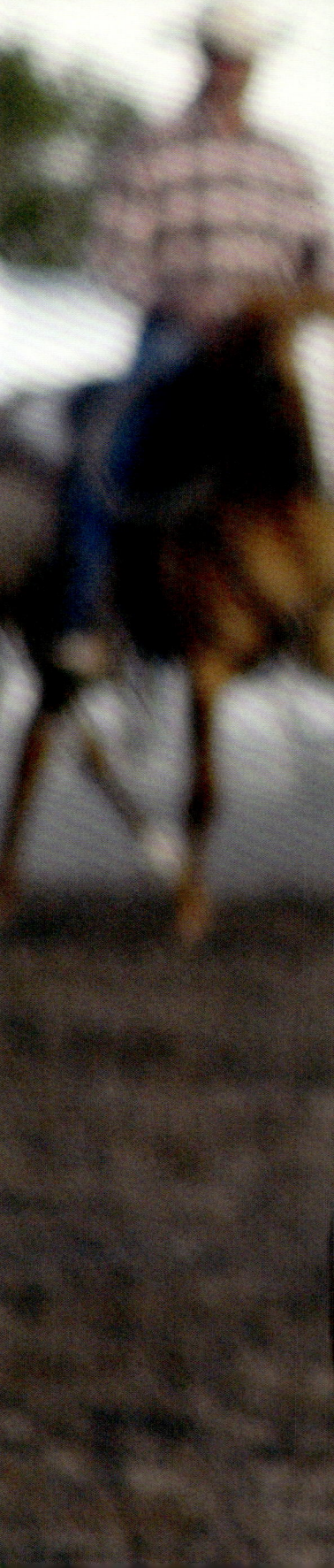

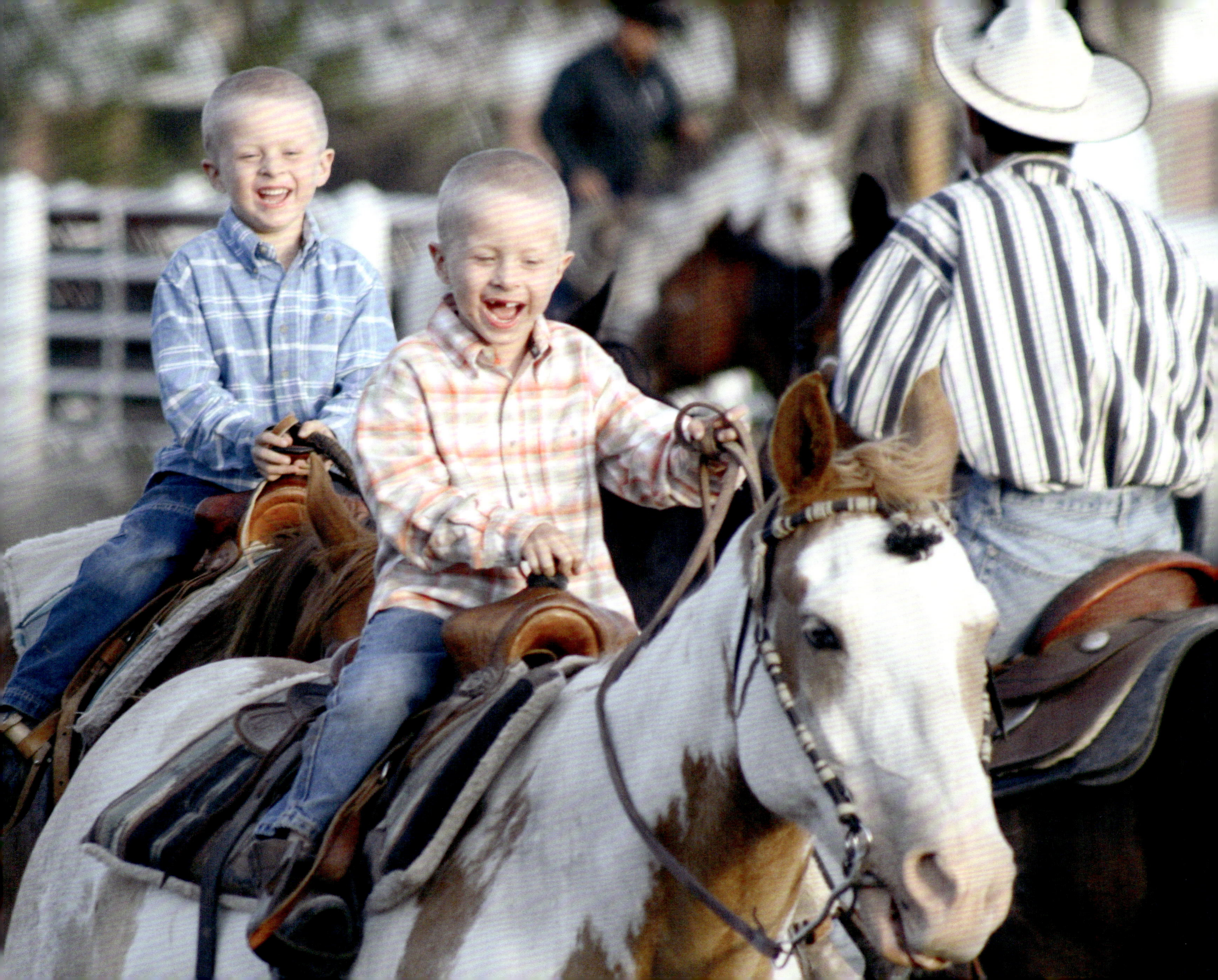

boys have ridden any creature large enough to mount throughout their lives, probably including the family dog.

Son of bull contractor Shad Smith, eight-year-old Cade Smith rides bulls. It sounds unreasonable at that age, but not when you see his tiny mutant bull. Stumpy and bug-eyed, as if bred with a Chinese Pug, its path is predictable and bull fighters follow closely until the eight-second horn when Cade dismounts to throw his hat Frisbee-like toward the cheering crowd. Living a bucking-bull life, Cade will be a champion one day.

The older boys are in for serious bucking, and though mini bulls tend to be a bit less aggressive once the rider is thrown, they are as determined as any bull to rid themselves of the rider. Wrecks can be bad. Young boys often compete on regular-sized bulls—older animals that have lost a step or two. Sending twelve-year-olds out on the backs of enormous bulls seems crazy, but bull riding is their soccer. They are hardened by a lifetime immersed in this culture and these traits will serve them well throughout their lives.

A boy is hung up on his bull. In the chutes before this event, an adult straddled his bull and asked for a "spot," someone to hold his vest in case the bull acted up. A small twelve-year-old rider realized he was the only one that heard the request, so he moved in and grabbed on. An adult soon stepped in, saying, "I like that, little man, but I don't think you got enough lead in your ass." PIERCE

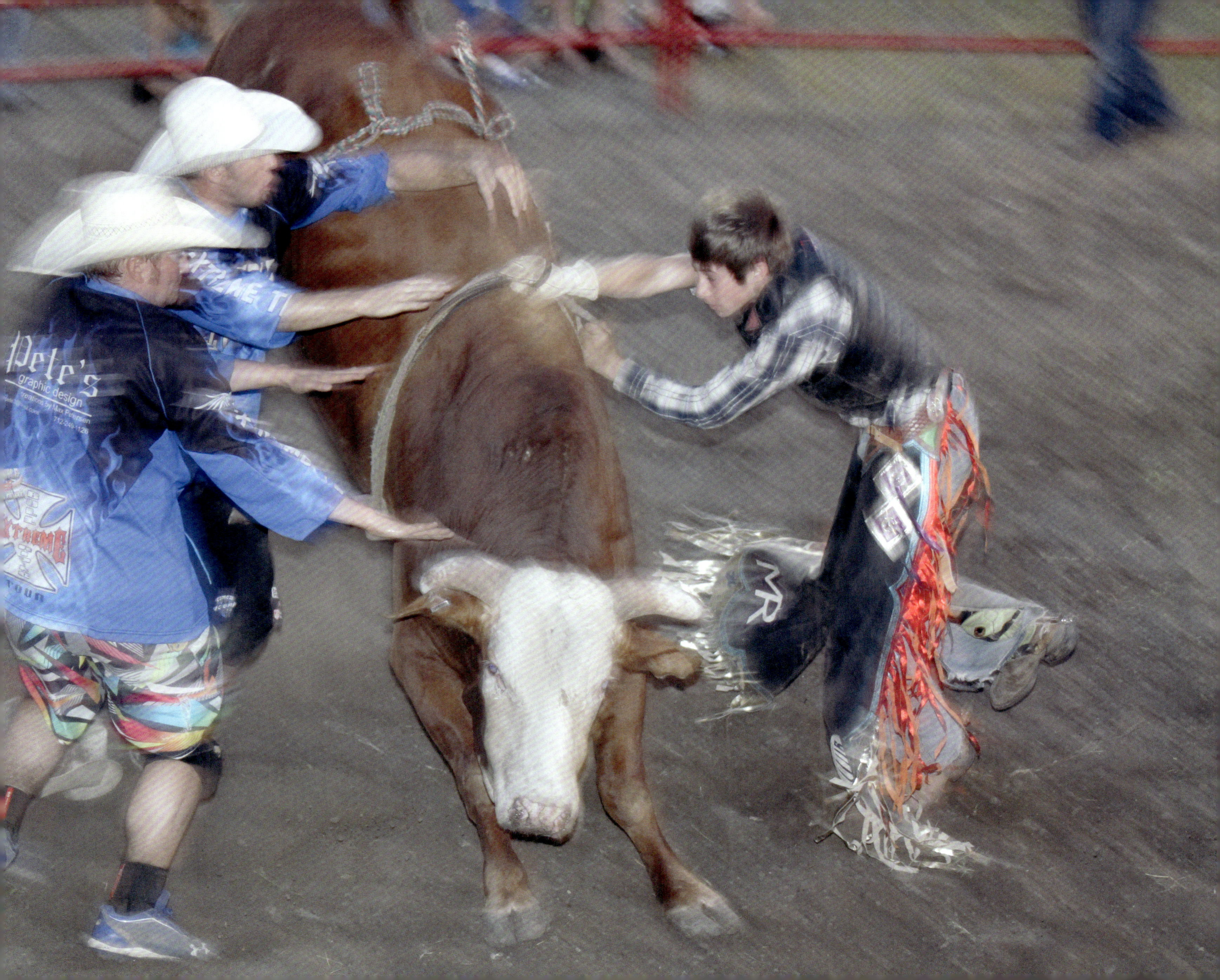

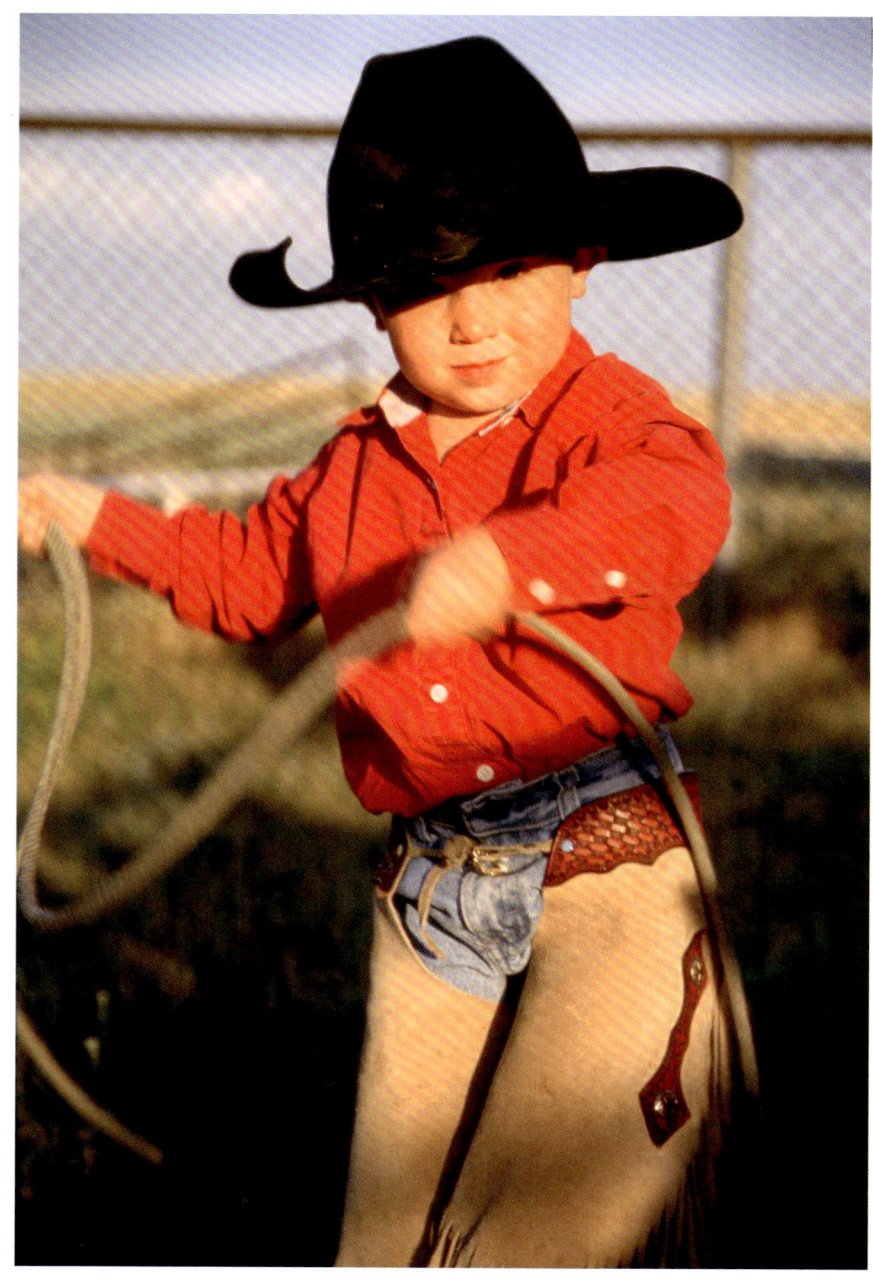

The Sioux County Kids' Rodeo in 2006, my first rodeo shoot and the event that compelled me learn more about Nebraska's rodeo culture. HARRISON

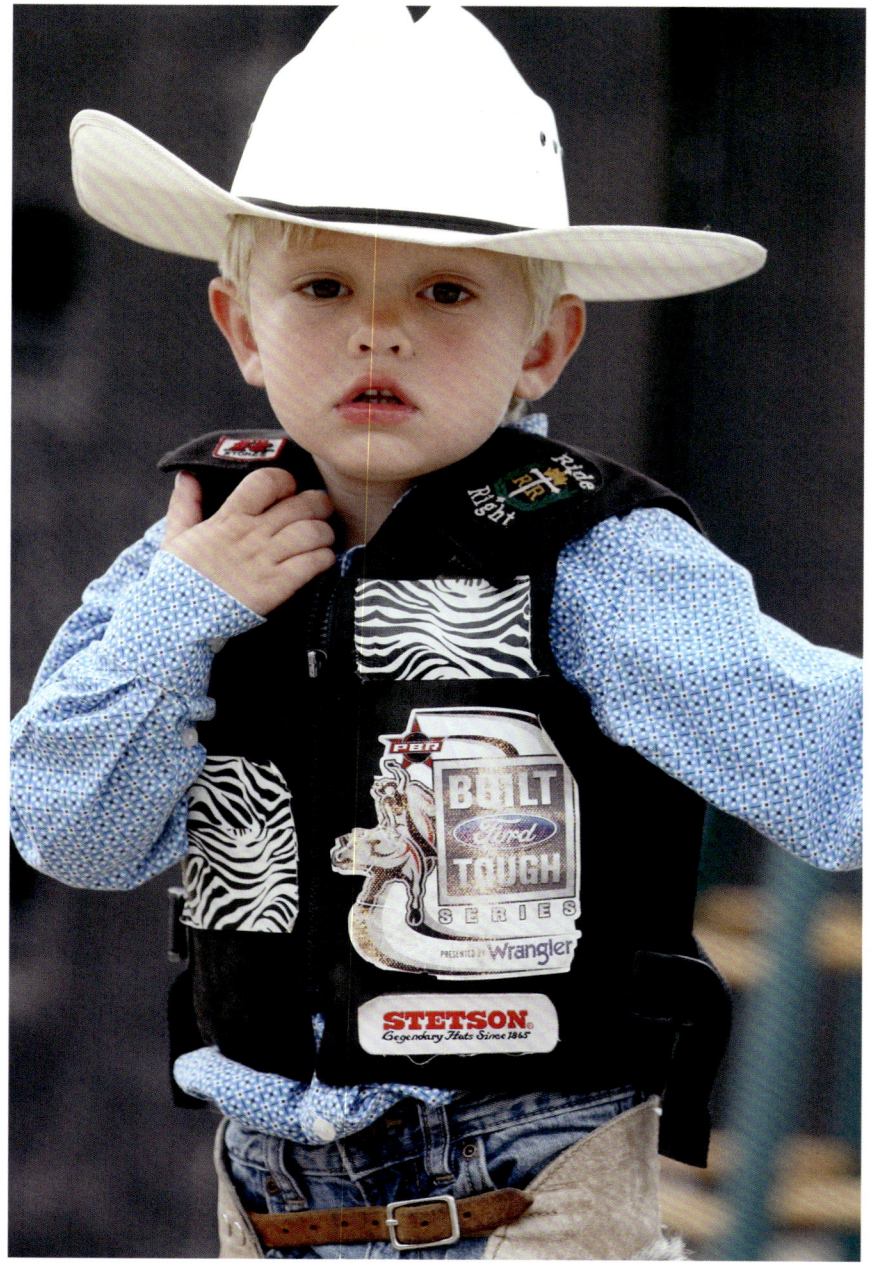

Serious about sheep, this boy waits his turn to ride. He is the next generation of Nebraska's rough-stock rider. KEARNEY

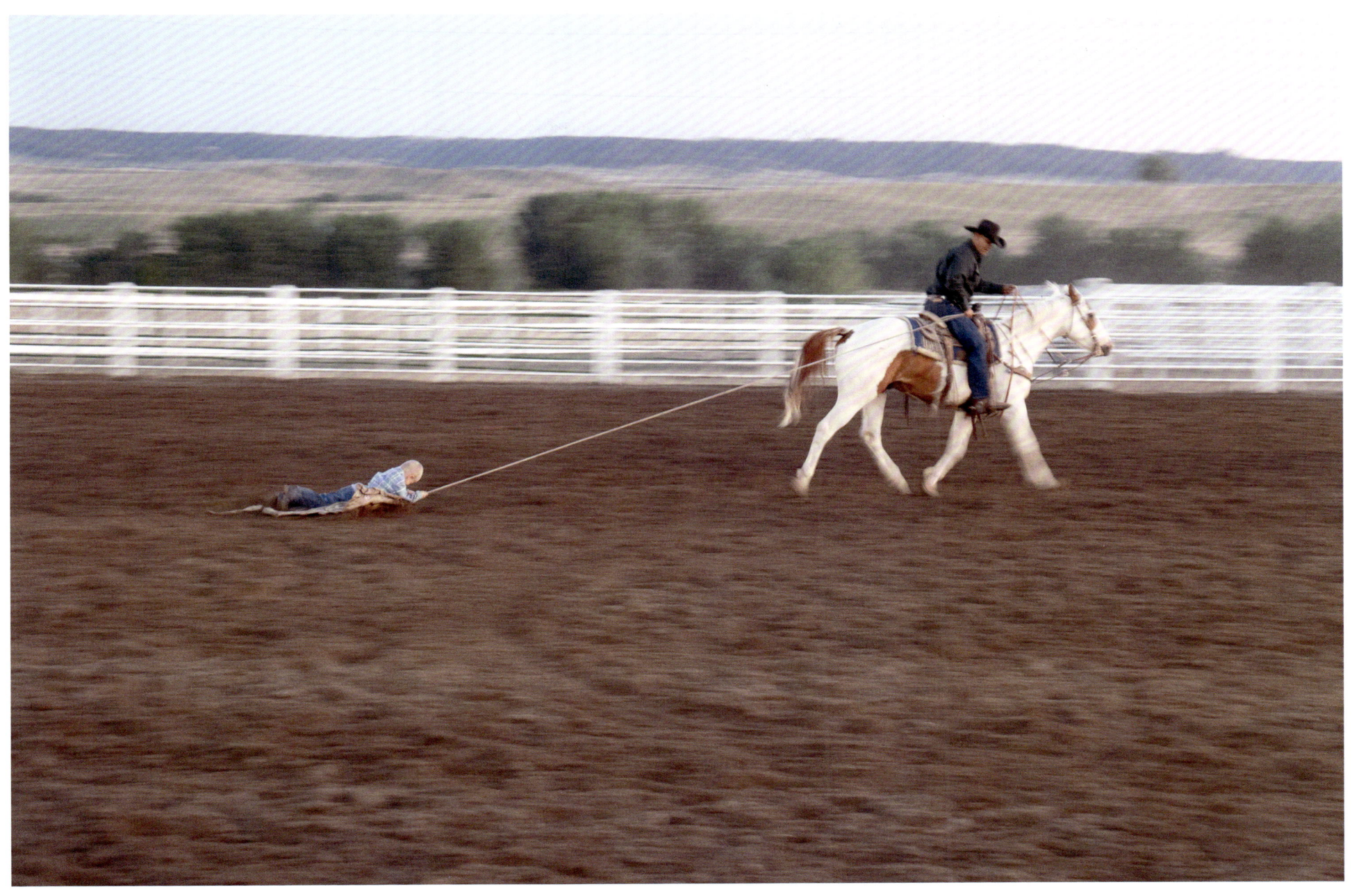

After this rodeo, brave kids from the audience line up to be dragged on a bison hide; most would rather watch. FORT ROBINSON

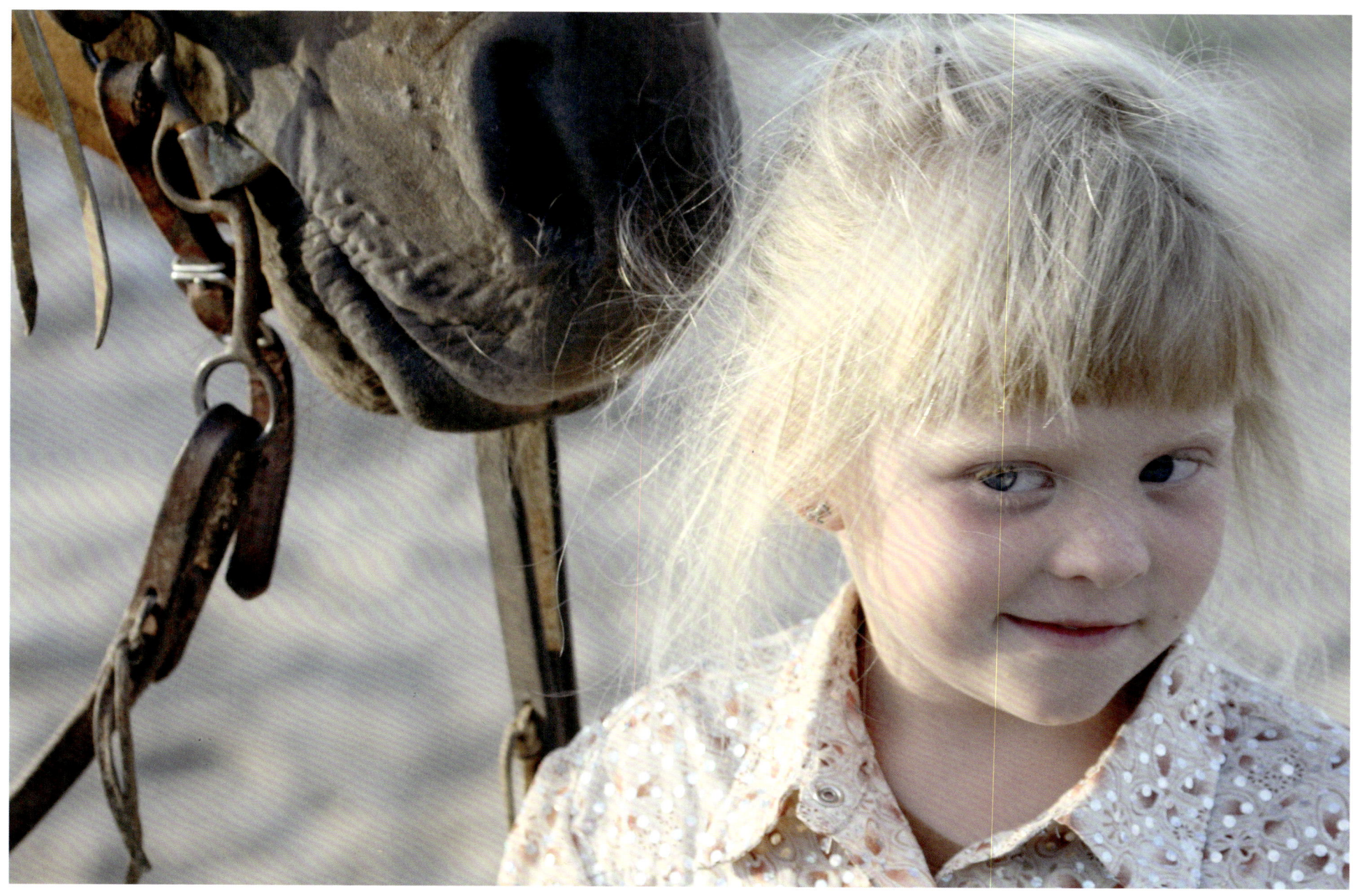

Nudging playfully, a horse waits with partner before their
turn at the pole-bending competition. HARRISON

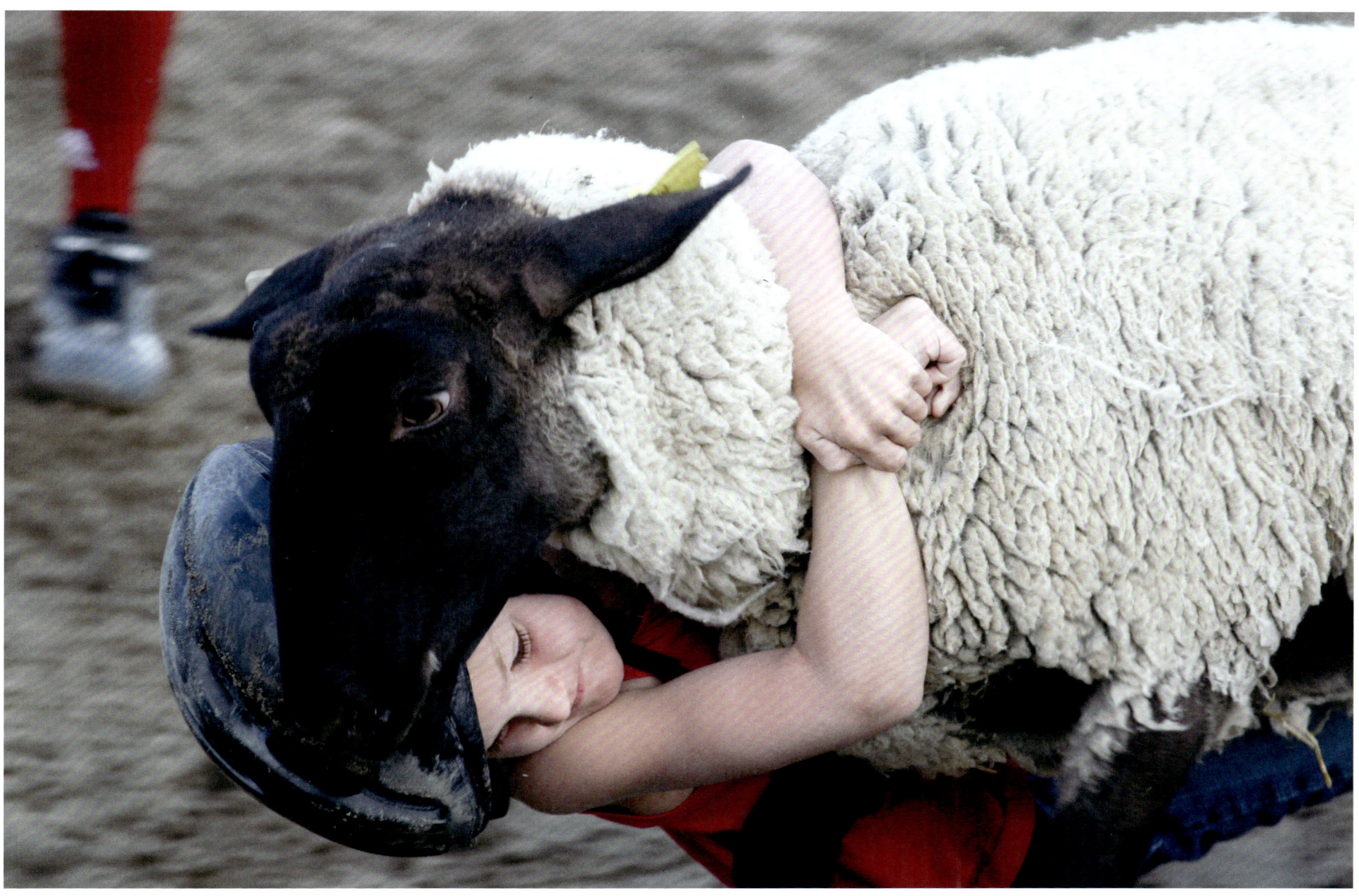

BLOOMFIELD

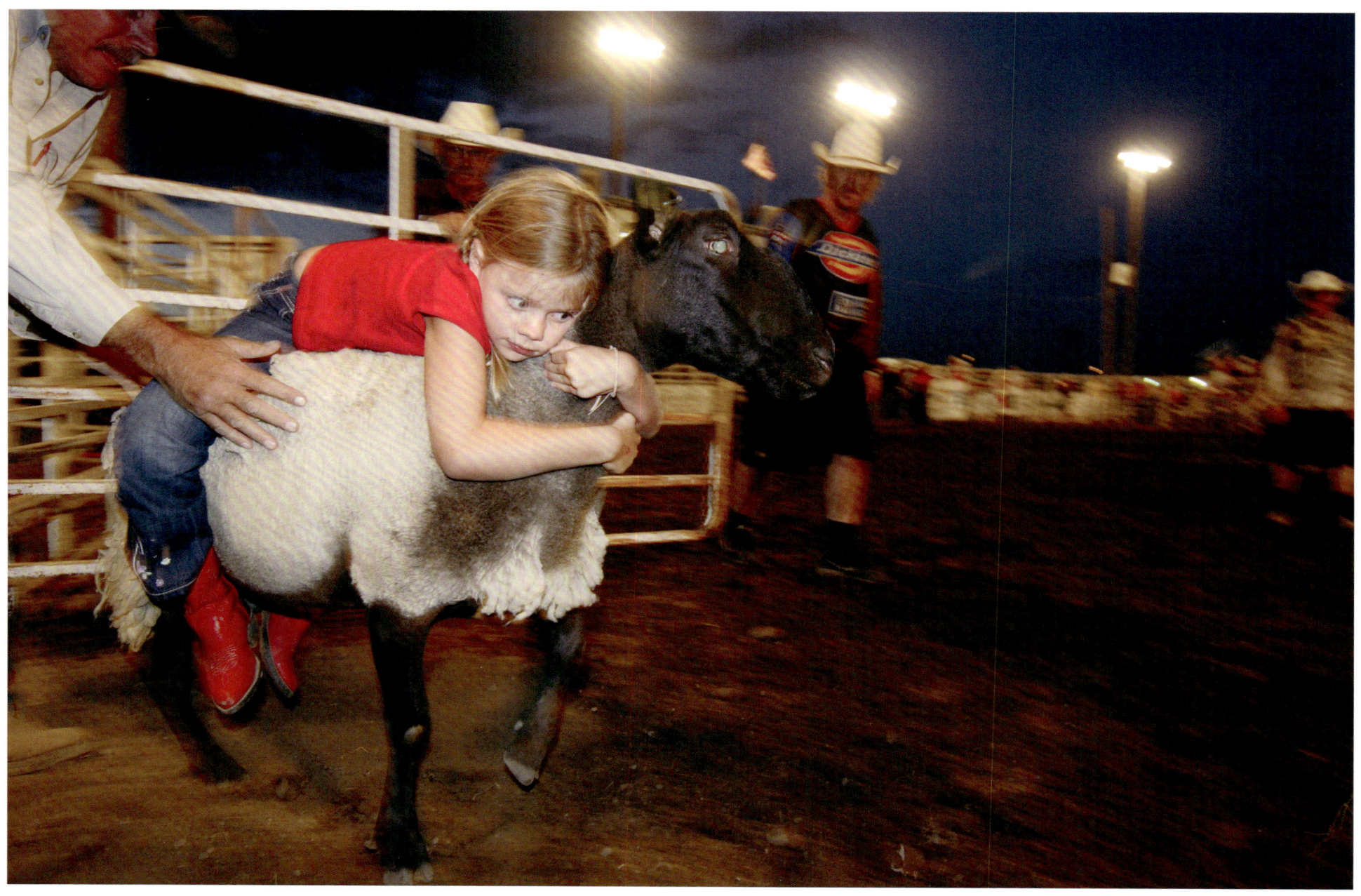

A first-timer will never forget this proud moment. SIDNEY

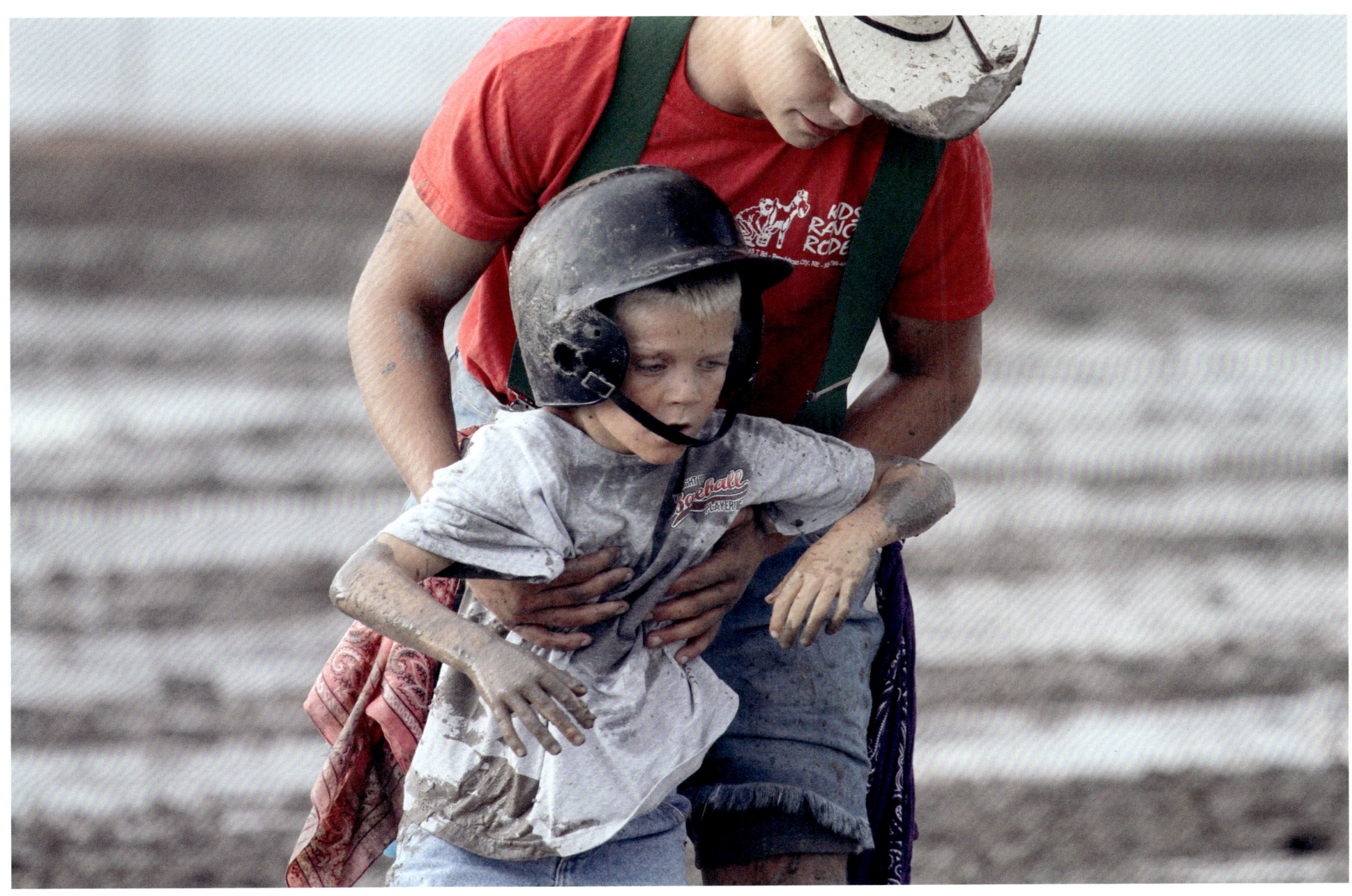

Recovering from a backwards somersault off a sprinting sheep, this rider will joke and laugh about his wreck once the shock wears off. VALENTINE

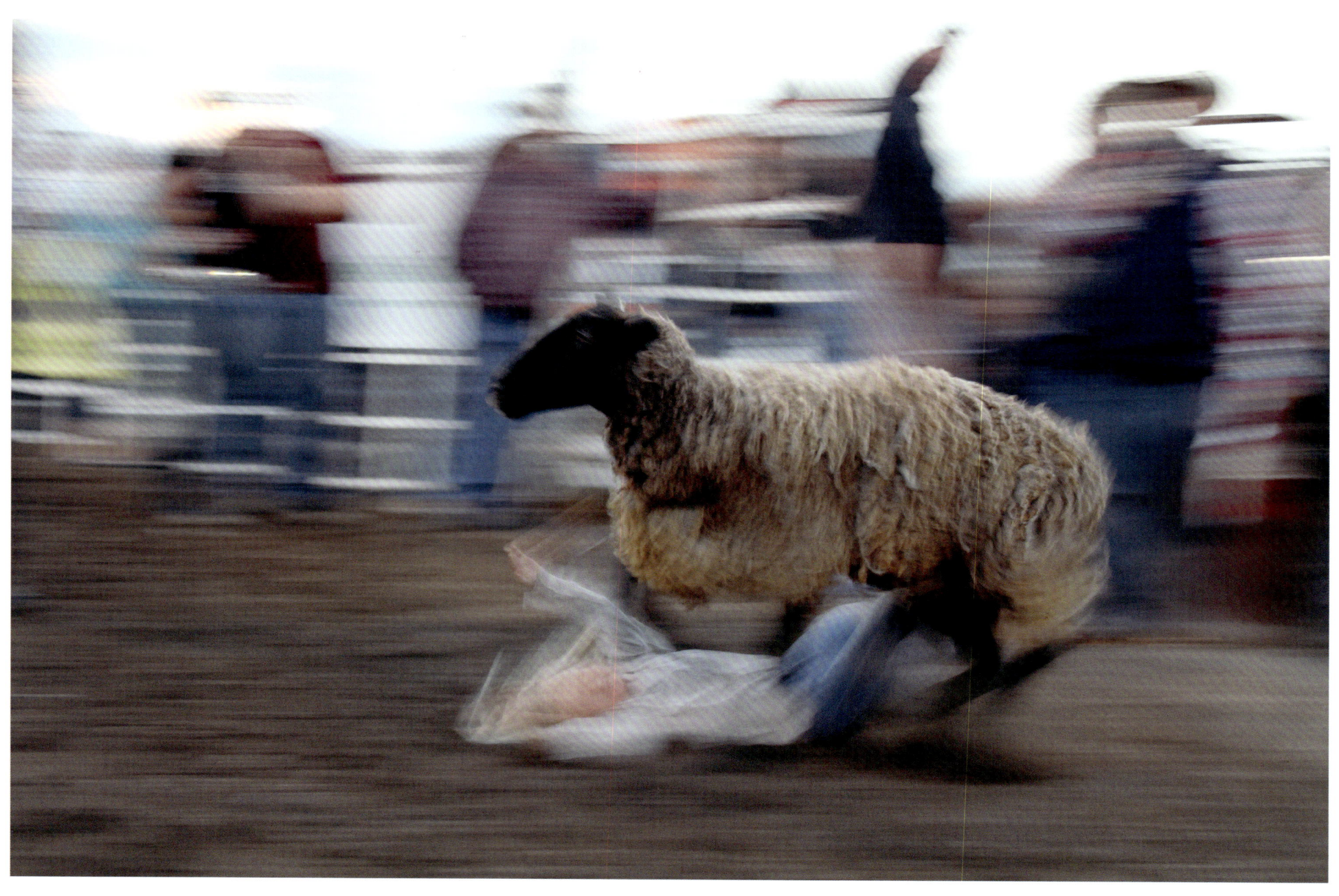

Hard landings bring tears. Mutton bustin' is country tough. SIDNEY

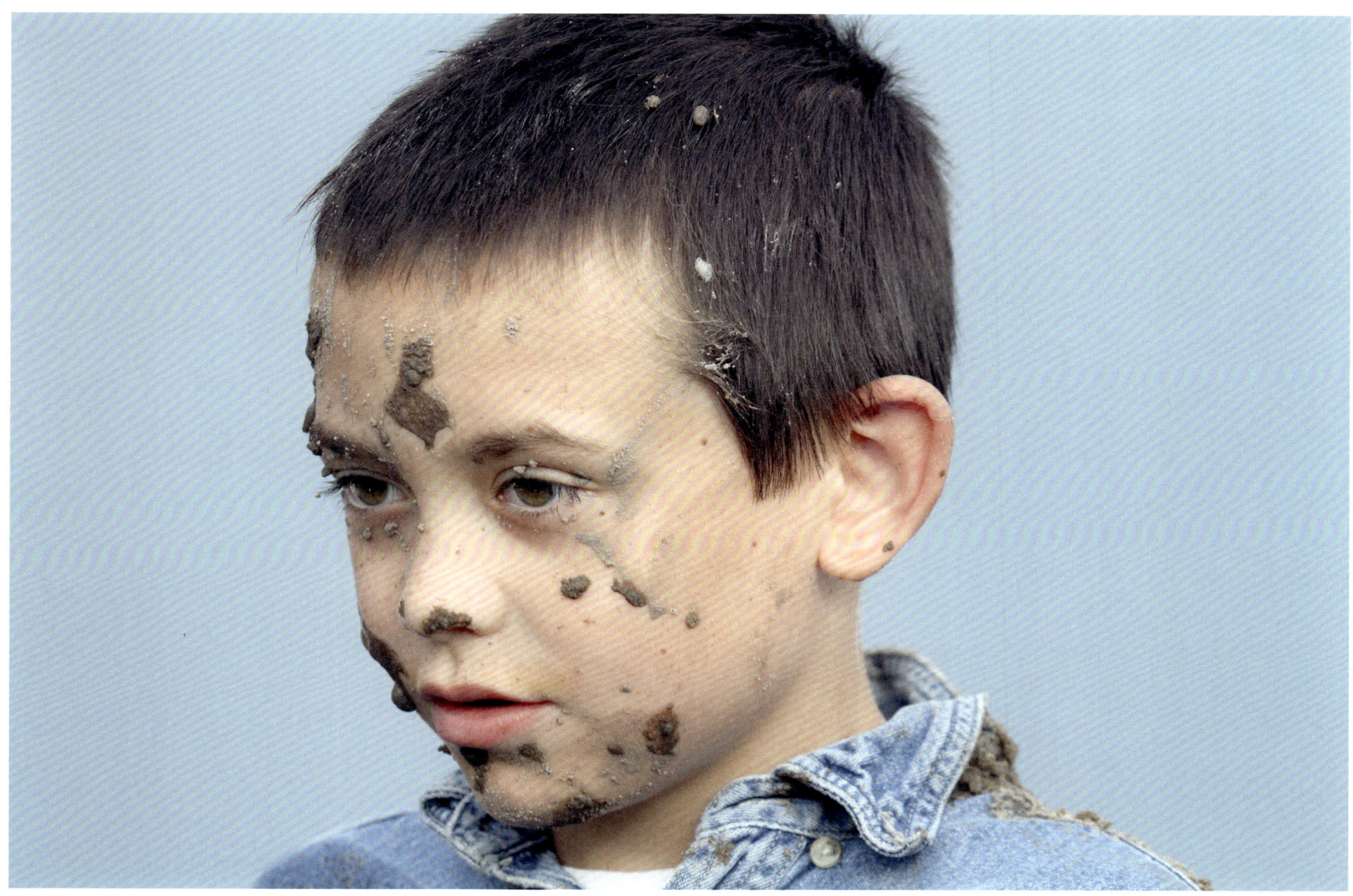

This mutton buster wears his mud like a medal for the rodeo's duration. VALENTINE

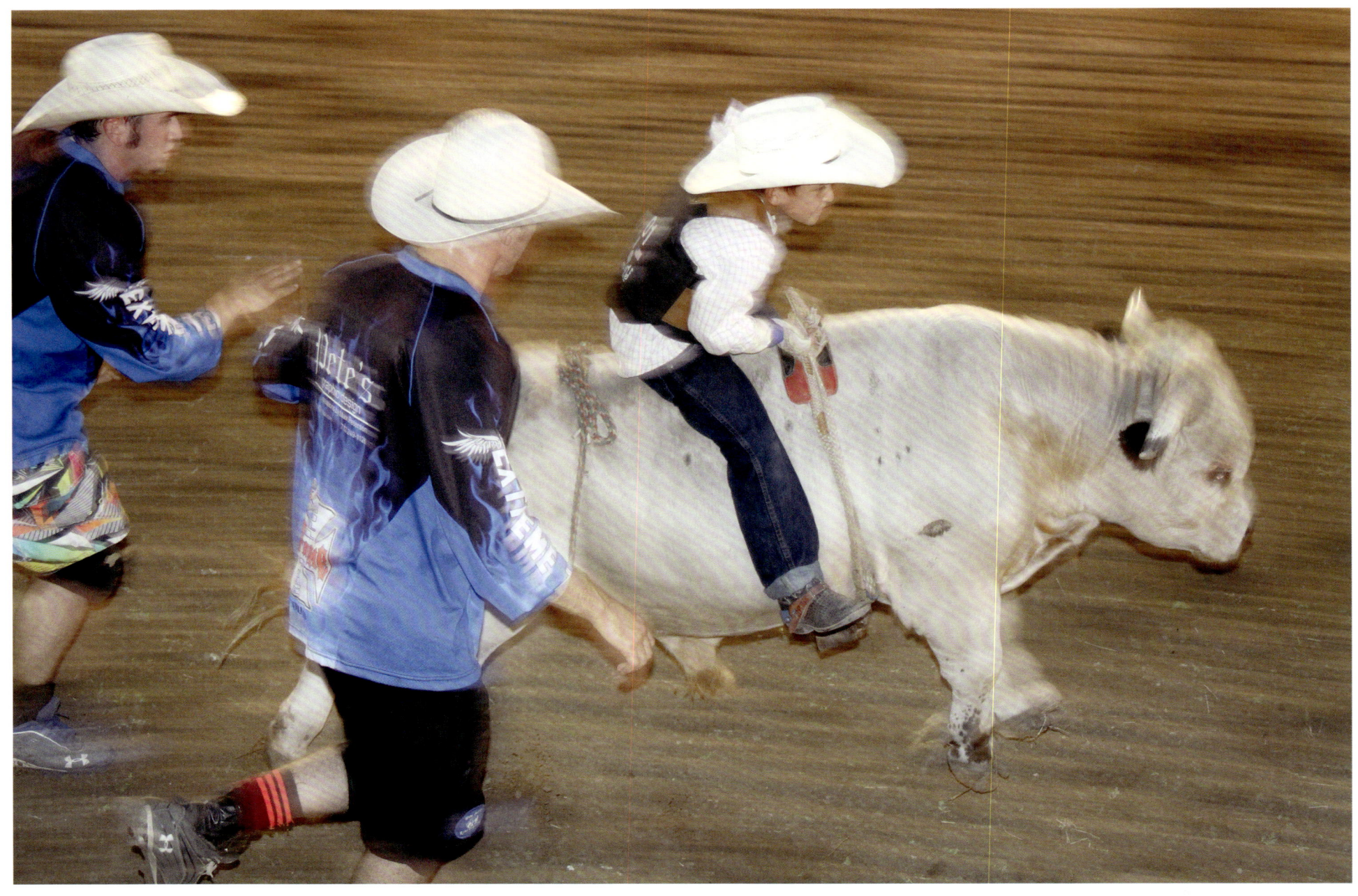

Son of bull contractor Shad Smith, eight-year-old Cade Smith
rides an extra-tiny mutant mini-bull. PIERCE

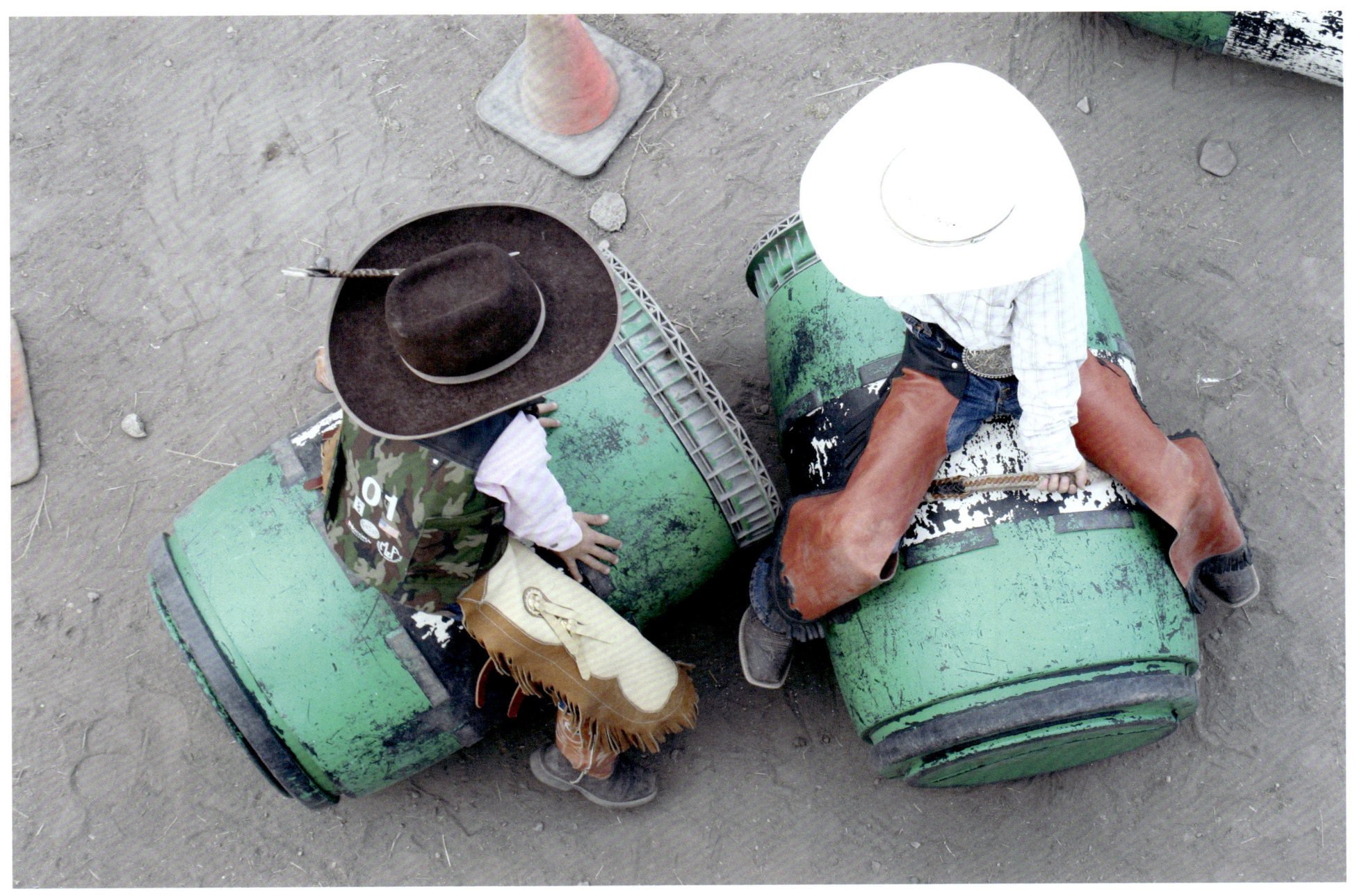

Barrels serve as mock bulls for future bull riders hanging out behind the chutes. SIDNEY

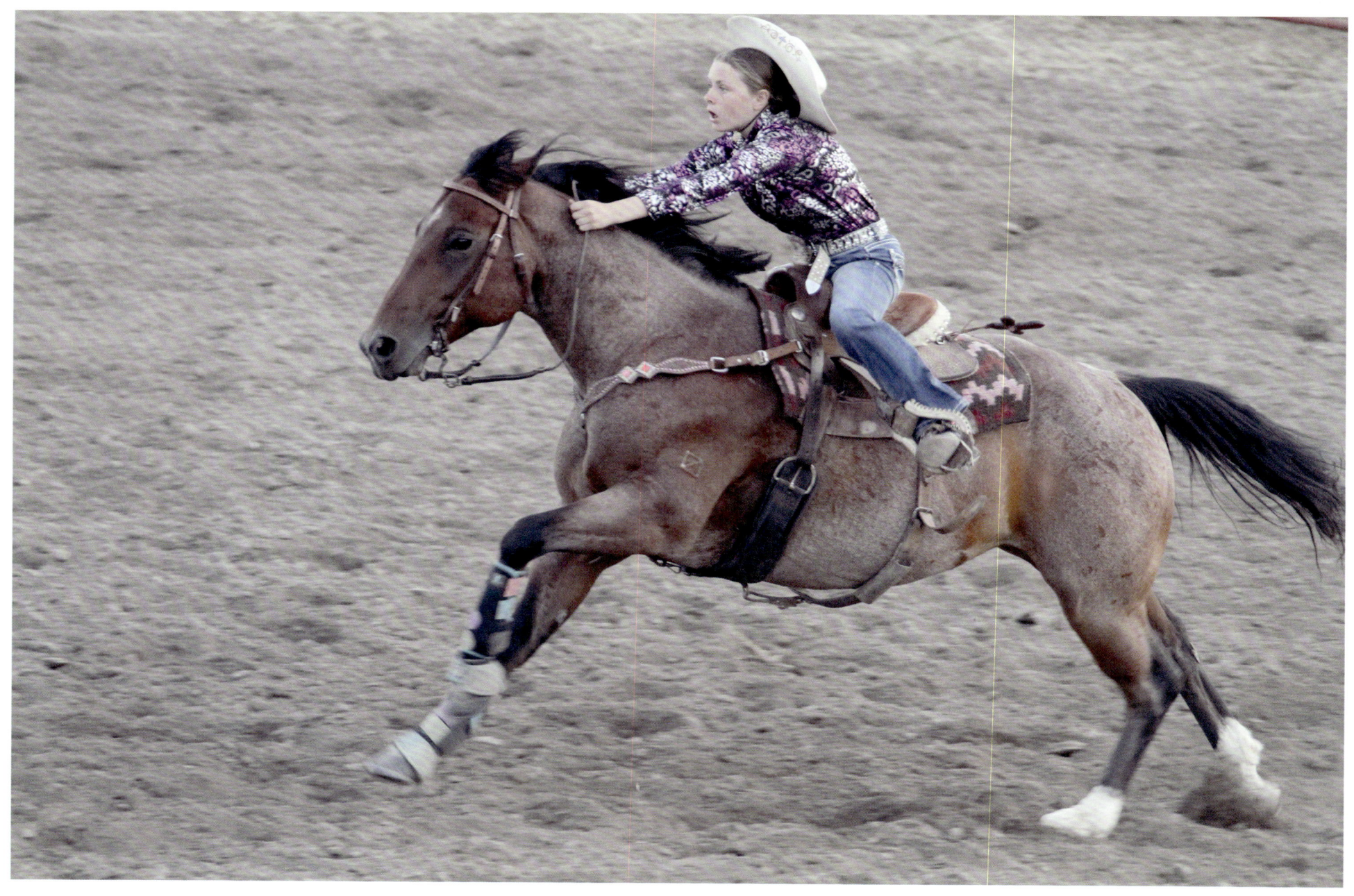

A junior barrel racer rips it and wins. TRENTON

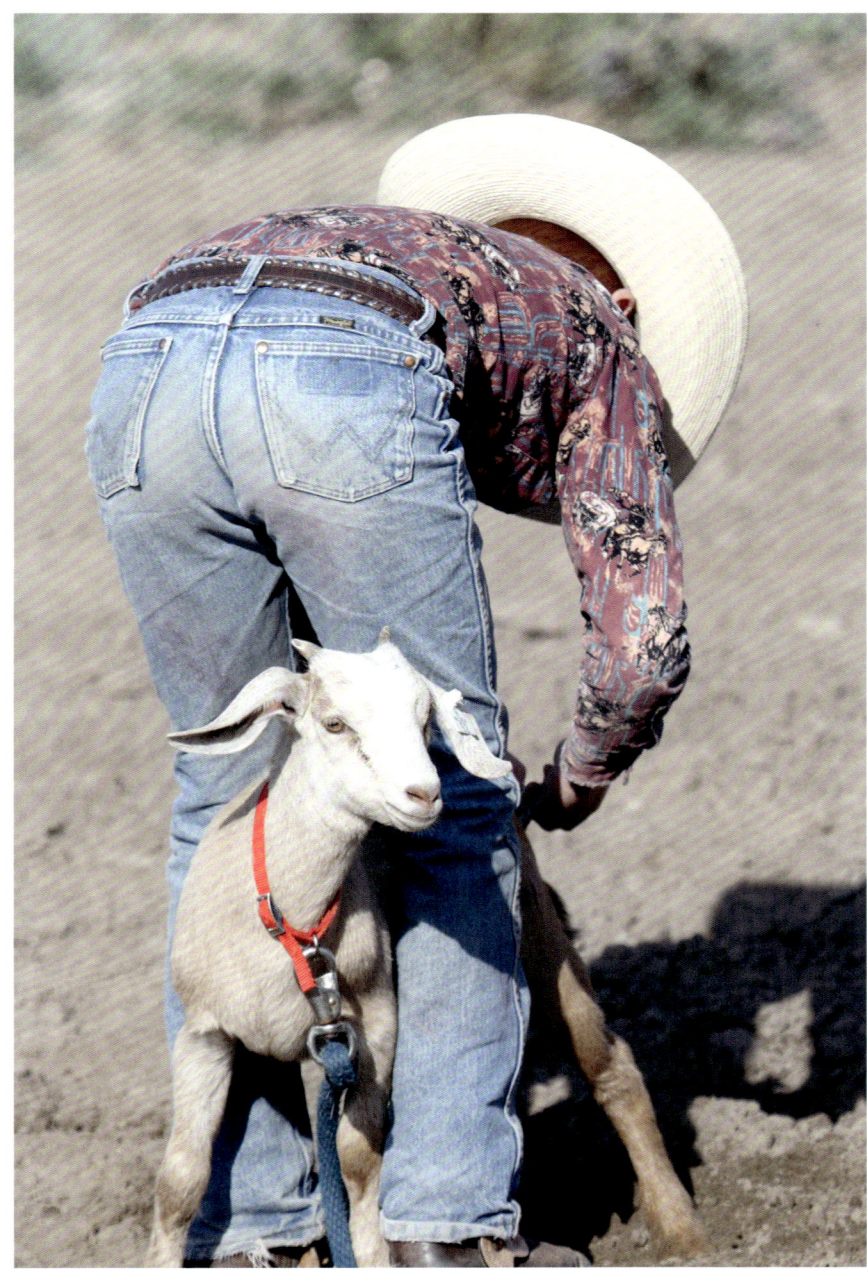

Race up on horseback, dismount, grab the goat and tie a ribbon on its tail; this is goat-tying. HARRISON

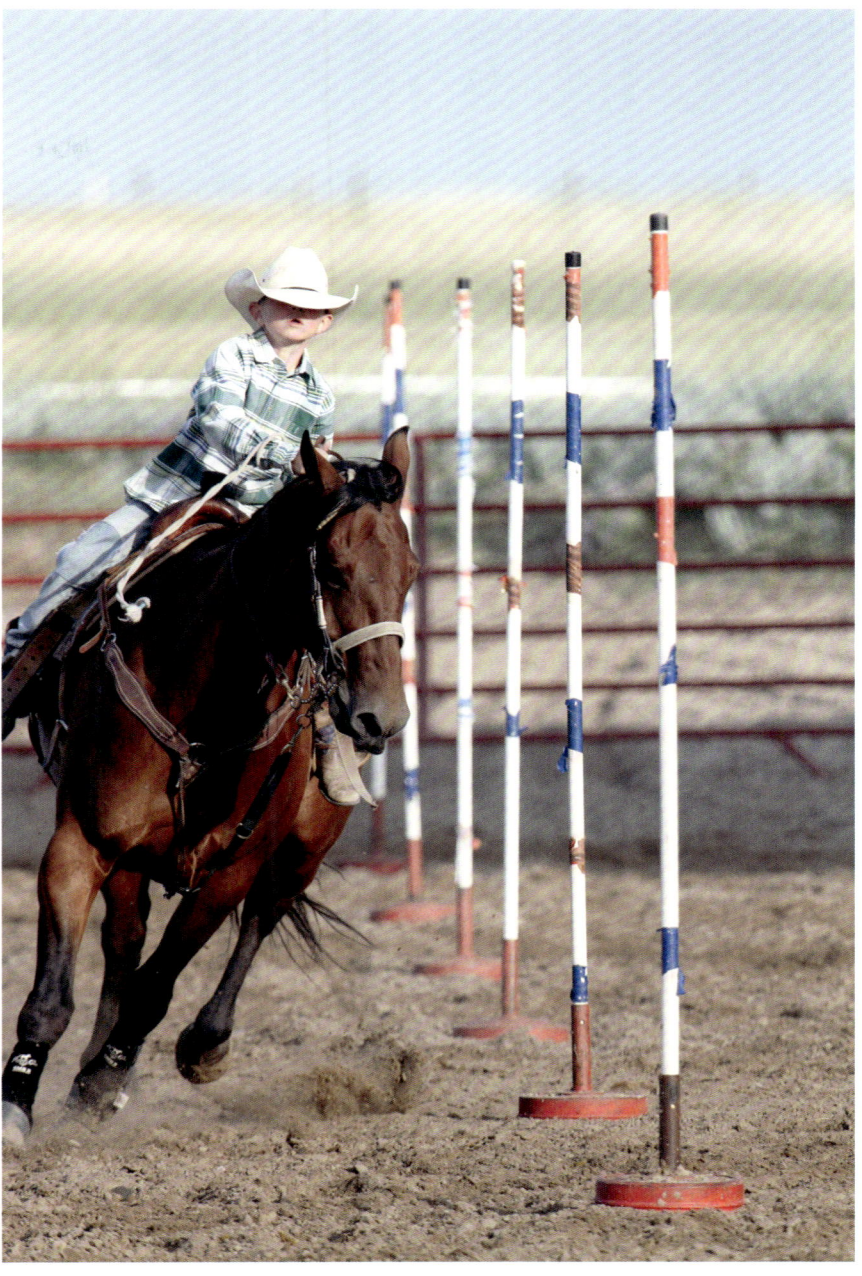

"Pole bending" at speeds that would make a soccer mom cringe, this boy and his horse show experience. HARRISON

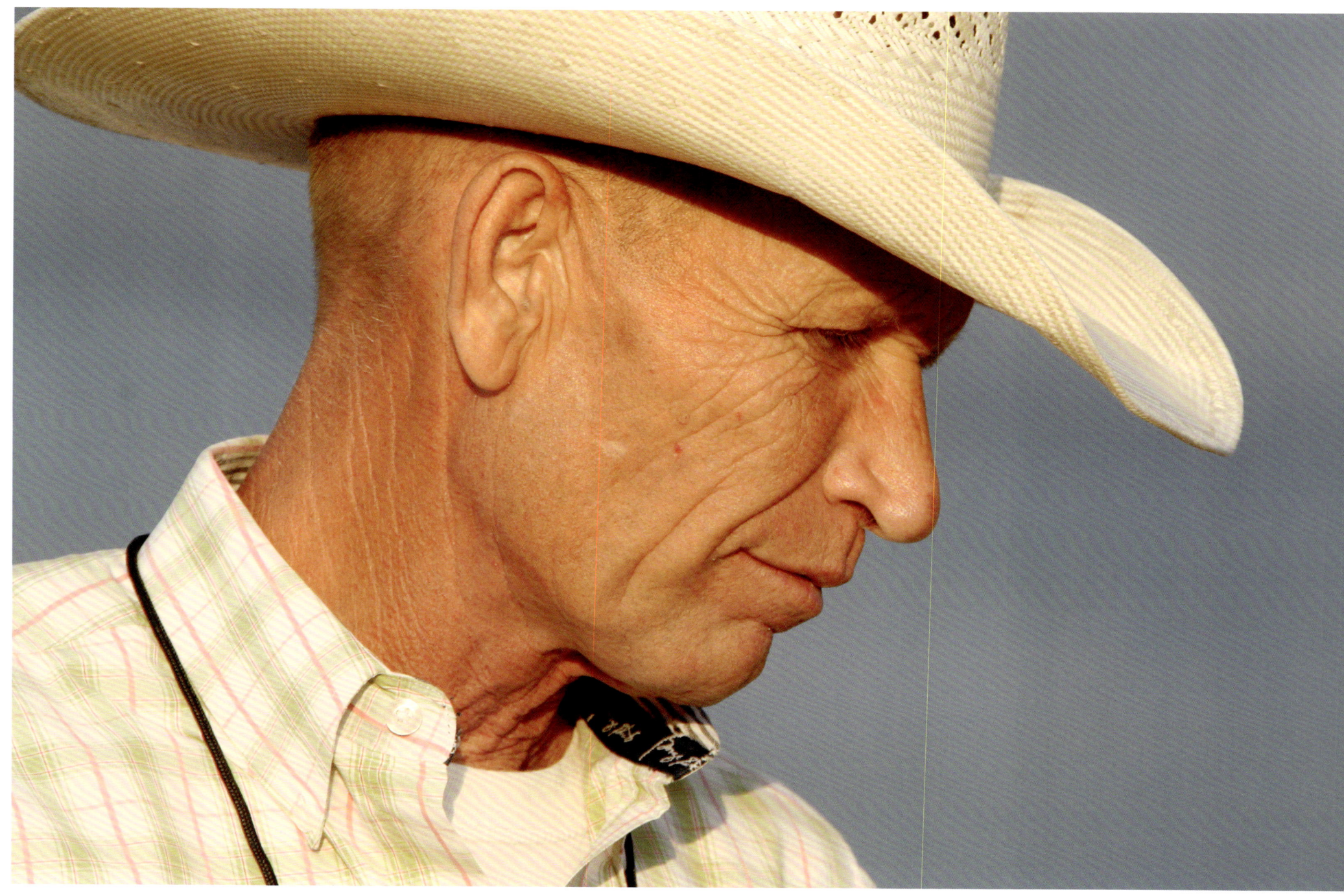

Age and Experience

SENIORS

Rodeos provide a forty-five-and-up category for tie-down ropers, but in any other event the oldsters must compete against the young and spry. Men over forty are rare in bronc riding and nearly nonexistent in bull riding, but men do continue steer wrestling and roping well past that mark. Many compete in both the over-forty category and in the general competition against the younger guys. There is a precarious balance between greater experience and older age in this sport and each must decide when that line is crossed. Older fellows still competing have my utmost respect. At an age where most gentlemen are thankful to get in and out of the recliner without difficulty, here we see seniors jumping off horses to throw and tie calves. It is inspiring to those of us who realize what limitations the body imposes as one grows older.

Appearing occasionally in Nebraska venues is the National Senior Pro Rodeo Association. With an age minimum of forty, it is not limited to roping events; they ride rough stock including bulls. Speaking to older bull riders, I am not surprised to learn that what drives them is the same thing the younger riders talk about: the adrenaline high and the need to succeed. But getting on a bull at this age is not the same as it is for a twenty-year-old man. Body parts rip and break easier and mend slower. All cowboys put up with pain, but older cowboys do more. It is part of growing older, but riding broncs or bulls must amplify the physics of aging and the levels of hurting. I would like to see M.R.I.s of their spines. After thirty years of rough riding they have

North Platte banker Terry Correll rode bareback for fourteen years in the Professional Rodeo Cowboys Association. At age fifty-seven he now competes on cutting and roping horses. Here, Terry serves as Judge for Stapleton's Beauty and the Beast rodeo. STAPLETON

to be a mess. Any ride could be their last so they relish every event. Competing at their age, these guys aren't only tough, they are lucky.

Chuck Schroeder, 63, grew up near Palisade. Roping and rodeo defined him until his early thirties when career trumped competition. As Chuck aged he noticed a growing competitive void in his life. Friends encouraged him to get back into the game. "Who are you really?" asked one. "You spend a lot of time in a coat and tie, but the truth is you're a cowboy! You need to get back in the dirt, talk dirty, and stop denying that shadow side." Then a phenomenal young mare named Jinx entered the picture in Chuck's late fifties and that was the tipping point. Still a Lincoln executive, he's now nationally one of the best heelers in his division.

"It all begins with the horse," Chuck says. "It's about people discovering their relationship with a horse first and only then looking for the opportunity to take that to another stage. Every team roper I know worries just as much about their horsemanship as they do how to swing a rope." But even the best young horse does no better than the person guiding it. At age fifty-nine Chuck collided with reality. "I thought I'd jump in, compete, and have those old skills back, but that didn't happen. I wasn't competitive, my body was sore." The solution: practice, more than he ever imagined. "I'm in the ropin' pen 100 times a year, constantly making adjustments. It's work."

As the header turns the steer 180 degrees, the heeler deals with intense sideways torque following that maneuver's whip end. Hips, quads, and inner thighs grip the saddle, and the hand that throws the rope must be strong. "I had to work hard to get all that strength back," Chuck says. "It took a long time, but when you set a goal that big you find all kinds of old things coming from the heart you thought had been lost after youth."

I ask how much longer he might compete, what level of pain might make him quit? Chuck shakes his head, saying, "It won't be about pain. Not being competitive any more—that's what will stop me." Chuck is addicted to the camaraderie of other horse people, age be damned. "It's a fraternity. We love the dirt, we love the smell. It's a quest of the soul that you either respond to or spend a lot of time regretting you didn't."

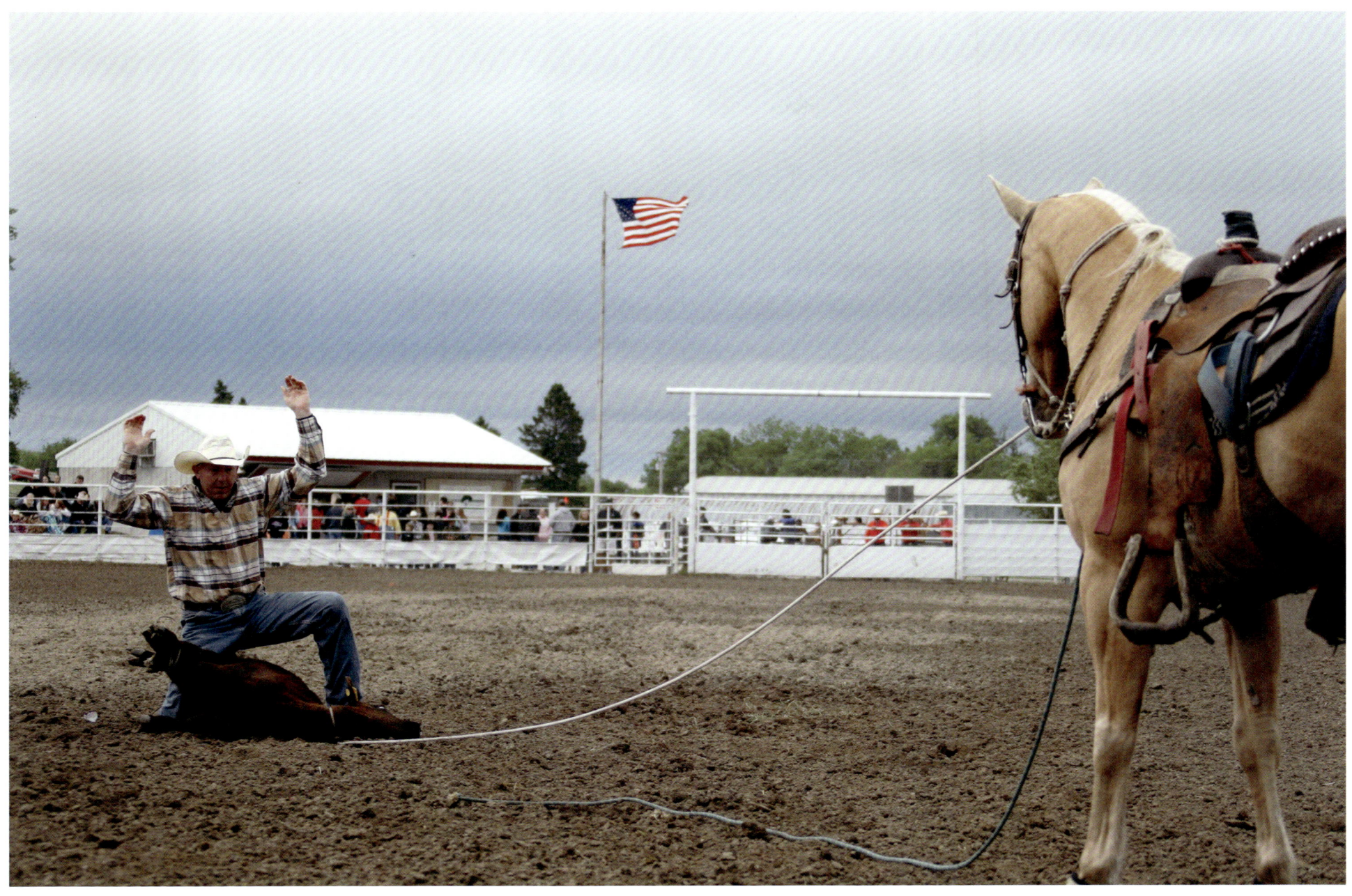

"Pain has nothing to do with when to retire," say senior competitors. It's about how long they can stay competitive, pain be damned. TEKAMAH

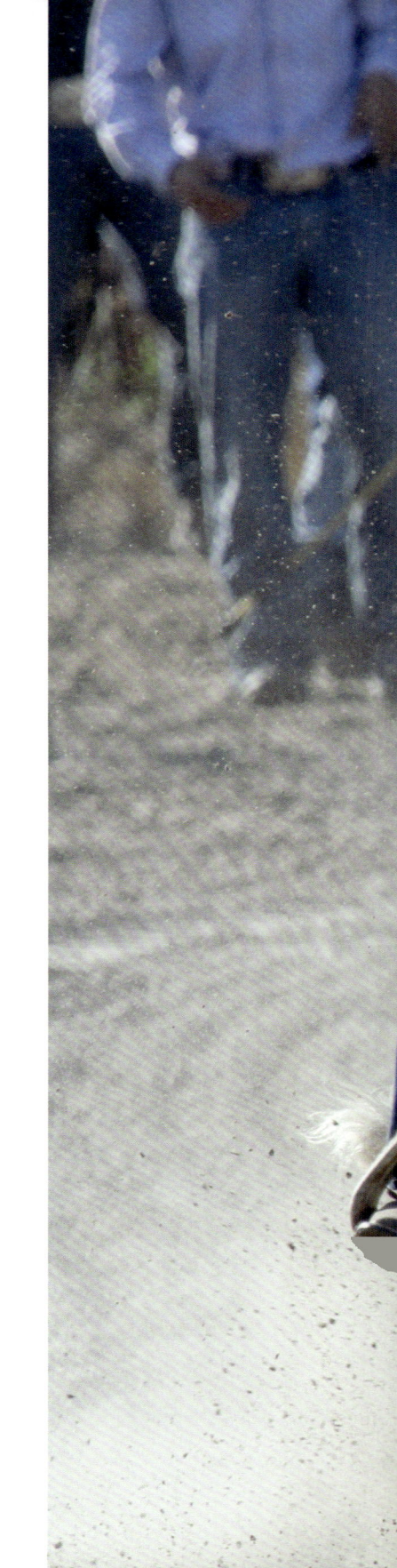

At an age where most are content getting in and out of their recliner without too much trouble, some men wrestle steers. THEDFORD

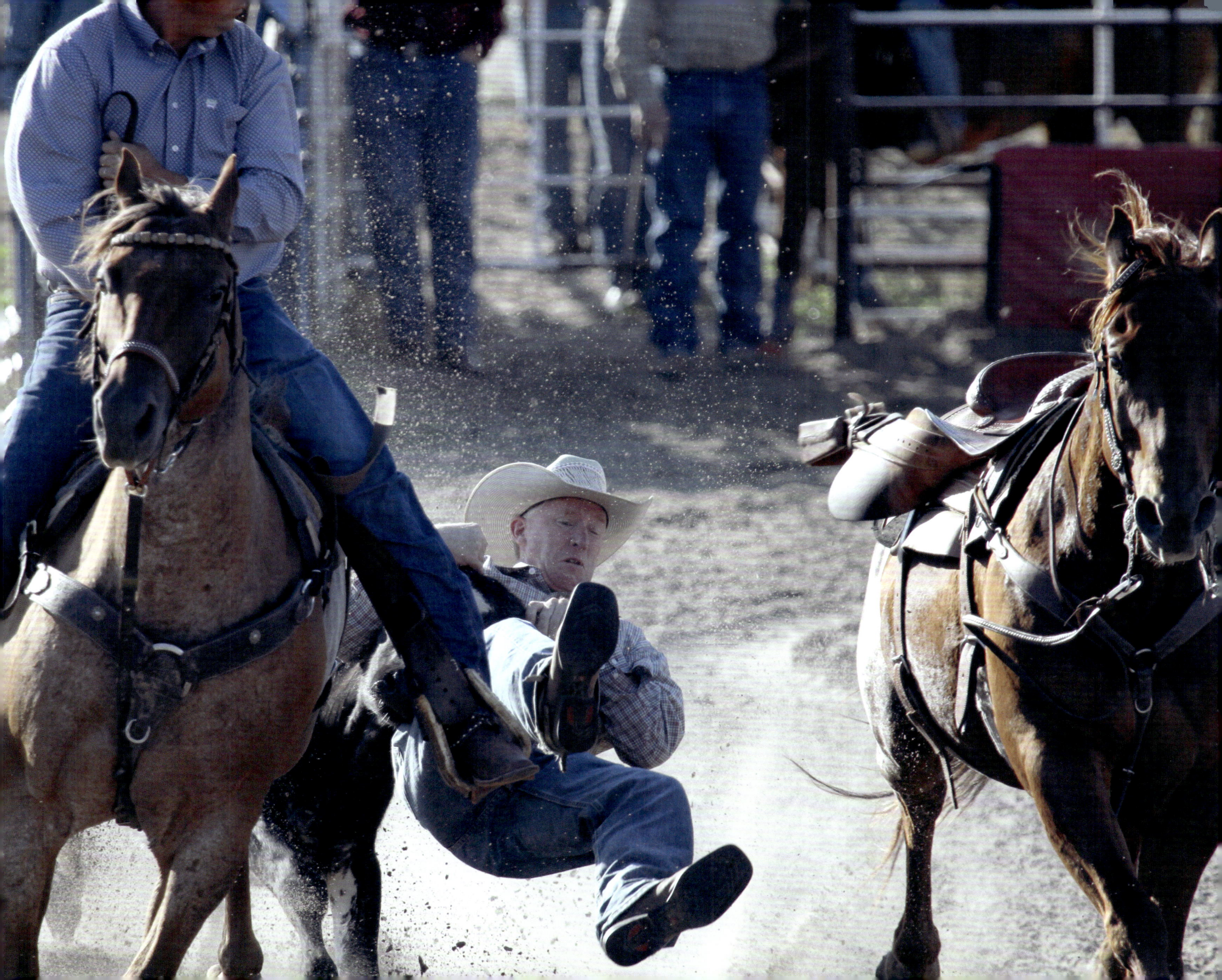

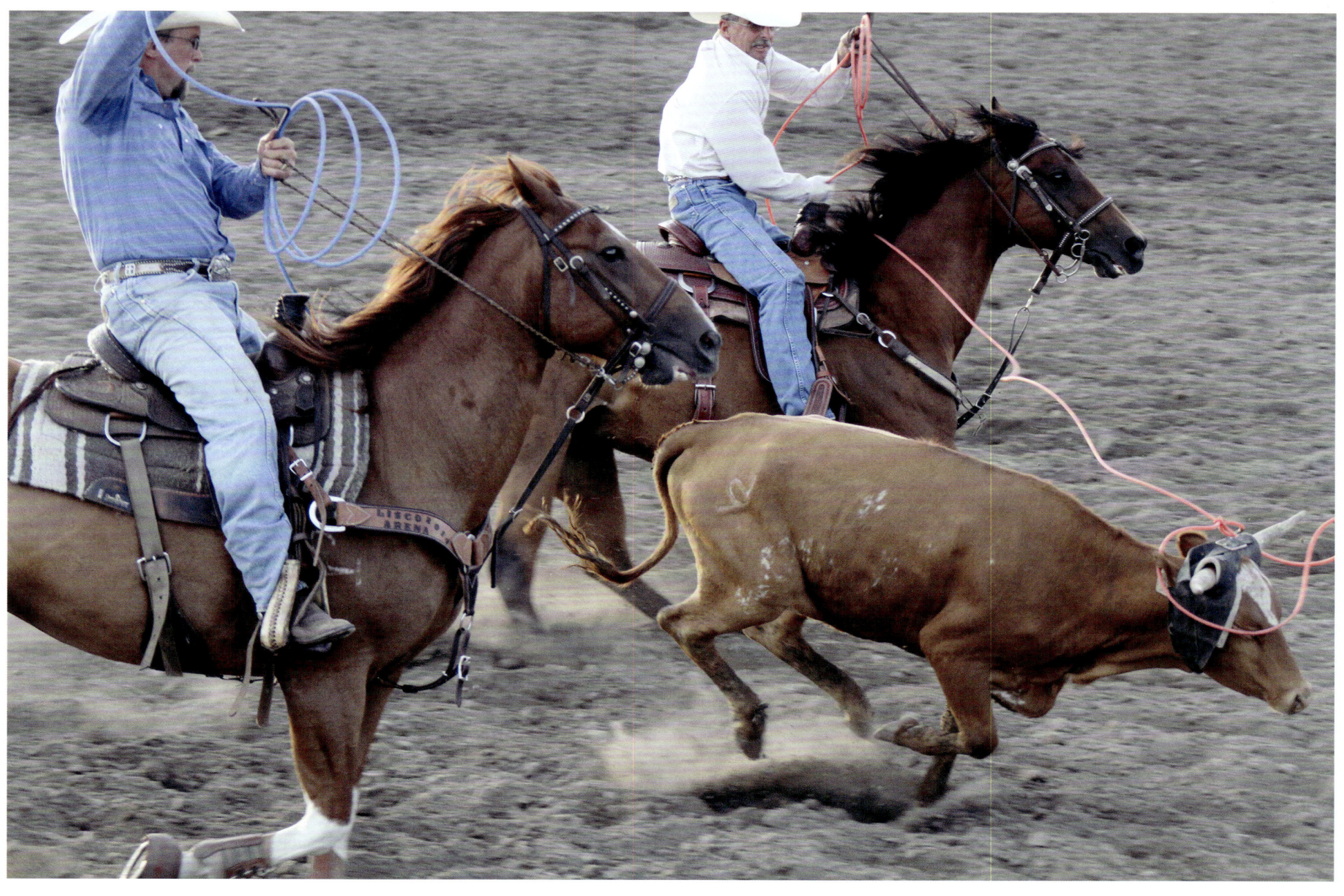

"I'll be ropin' 'til I can't rope no more," says one ex-champ. TRENTON

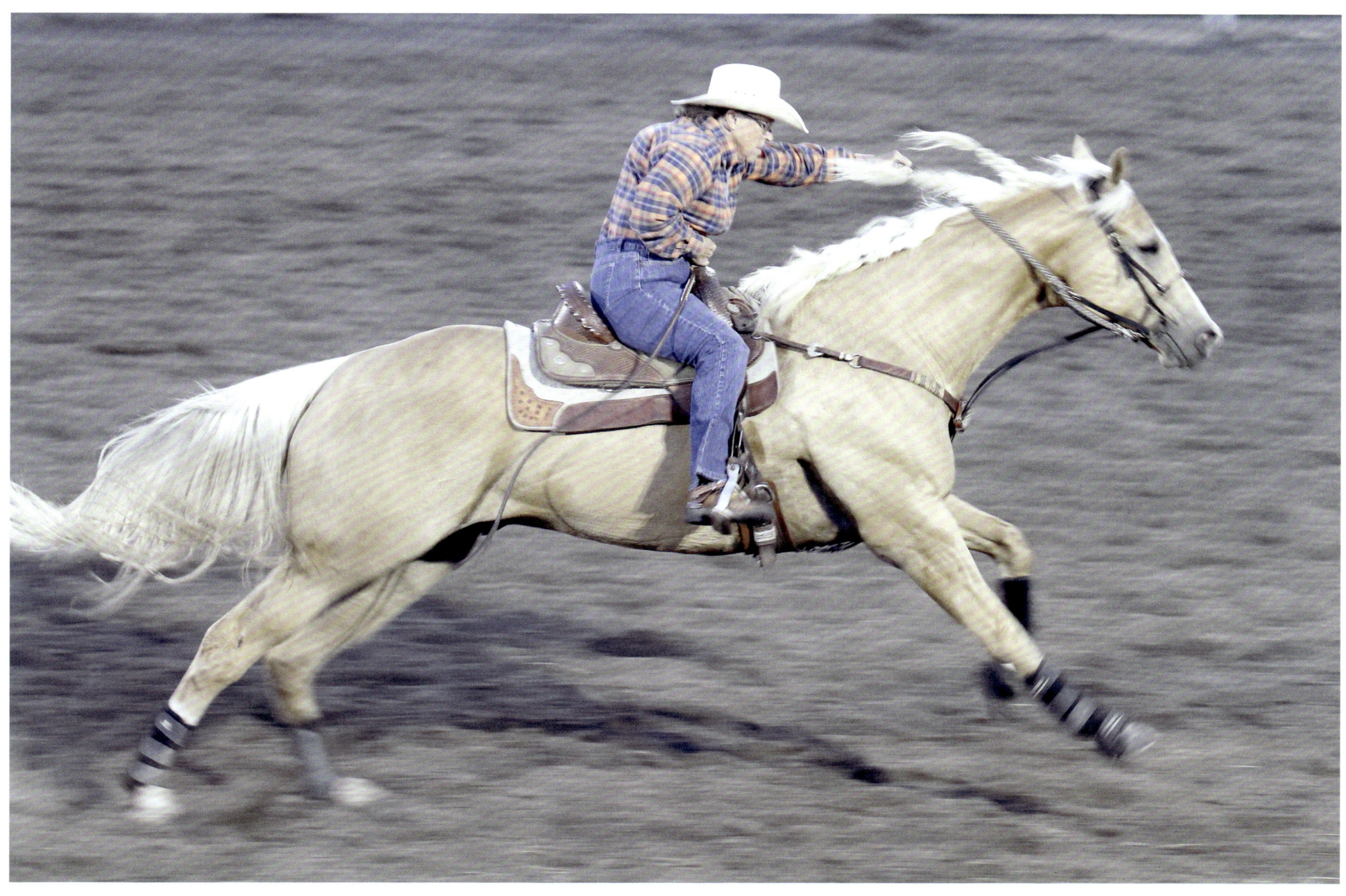

A young-at-heart rider barrel racing on her spry horse. FREMONT

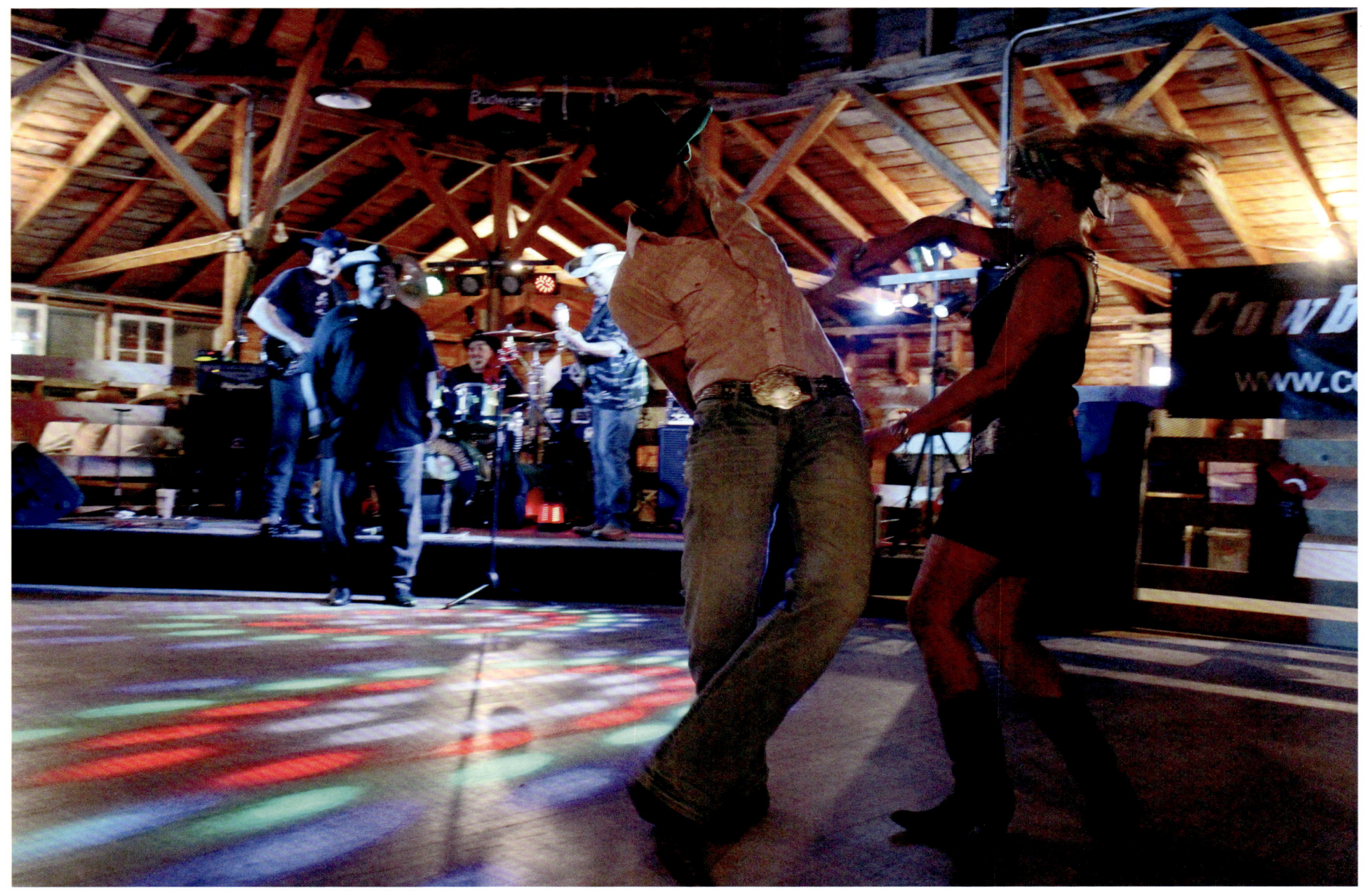

After the rodeo these dancers create an invisible force field; others
allow them extra space for their practiced moves. NORDEN

Small Towns and Summer Nights

A sash-draped rodeo queen on horseback races the American flag around the arena as the rodeo begins. The announcer talks of patriotism, freedom, and our troops. Heads bow for a lengthy prayer tailored with a rodeo theme. Hats and hands cover hearts while a local sings the National Anthem, and then the show begins. It smells of popcorn and hotdogs in the stands and of dung and urine behind the chutes. Relaxed socialization ensues on one side of the fence, nervous bursts of commotion on the other.

Nebraska's summer evenings can be oppressively hot and humid; heat indexes in the nineties are common. The worst I endured was a hazy 114 degrees in Walthill. Audience and livestock limit their motion in these conditions. Sweaty people glisten, fanning faces with programs; livestock are statuesque except for fly-flipping tails. Porta-potties become hellish torture chambers.

Rain doesn't stop a rodeo and rarely does lightning. Only once, in Callaway, did I see a rodeo break while a storm passed through. People knew it was coming; dark bulbous clouds advanced, shedding long flashes of cloud-to-ground lightning. I showed the announcer its path on my phone's radar screen and he let the crowd know it was headed their way, but the show went on. Five minutes later, all at once the temperature plunged, the winds tripled, and dirt plastered squinting faces. The audience scrambled toward parked cars, heads downturned against Mother Nature as horizontal rain caught them midway there. Stolid livestock turned rumps to the storm, closed their eyes and waited. Hail pounded parked cars as people within wiped grit from their faces.

The rodeo resumed under light rain as the storm rolled east. Some cowboys donned rain slickers and others rode soaked. Those that returned to the stands exchanged wide-eyed looks when nearer lightning bolts struck the prairie sounding like the devil's whip. Cowboys and cowgirls in the arena largely ignored it. I've seen this disregard of lightning many times at rodeos. In conditions that would send soccer moms sprinting for cover, rodeo folks don't flinch. These people work outdoors and they haven't been struck yet.

Inside the only guaranteed dry spot and overlooking every rodeo from the "crow's nest," is the rodeo announcer. Cowboy drawls come with the trade, but a few become more Texan when the microphone is on. Their job is to keep the crowd informed, to keep the show moving, and to entertain. Good ones are soothing and spontaneous.

Gregg McGreer, from Big Springs, Nebraska, is a natural. Being the butt of clown jokes, he knows when to take it on the chin and when to jab back with equally animated humor. In a way everyone can understand, Gregg gives the rodeo's play-by-play. Traveling the region with him for thirty years, his wife Susan serves as musical technician and all-around assistant. Keeping the crowd engaged, Susan has a vast digital array of music and a song to enhance each moment. Country music sets the tone as people fill the stands, but a well-managed combination of rock and pop accompanies riders in most events, the hardest rock saved for bull riding. Announcing is teamwork and the McGreers set the benchmark in this profession.

Gregg rode bareback in his younger days. "Every now and then I look down there and think how great it would be to jump on that horse one more time," he says. During a lifetime involved in rodeo, Gregg has watched everything evolve: timed-event horses, rough stock, equipment, competitors, and the music. "If just twenty years ago someone told me we'd be playing rock music at rodeos I'd have thought they were out of their mind!" he laughs. "That changed when PBR (Pro Bull Riding) got their foothold." PBR exploded in popularity in the early 2000s with their brand of hi-octane action and matching music. "Not that long ago it was an organ player accompanying each event or maybe a local band," he says.

Bareback riggin's were no more than loose ropes in McGreer's riding days, while now riders use solid, individually stylized handles. Rough stock has kept pace with equipment technology. "In my day they were riding Brahman bulls!" Gregg says. With their distinctive shoulder hump, Brahmans are smaller and wirier than todays' monstrous bucking bulls. "Brahmans had a lot of jump in them, but none compare to what we have now. Genetics built stock today that is every bit the athlete as the cowboy that's getting down on them," Gregg says. "Decades ago bucking animals were pulled from normal stock and cowboys relied on raw talent. Now it's genes, technology and learning. High school rodeo changed everything. A champion instructor in a classroom teaches youngsters more in a week than they could learn going up and down the road all year. We've refined the sport, but it still takes a lot of heart and mind and that's what I admire about rodeo."

Both funnyman and athlete, the rodeo clown is the announcer's show partner. Also known as the "barrel man" during bull riding, they keep a safe distance during rides and disappear into a reinforced barrel when targeted by the bull. They are also the first to intervene if bull fighters meet with trouble. Those with a quick, twisted sense of humor do well. Not all have the knack and that aptitude can't simply be obtained; you're either weird or you're not. Ordinary personalities behind face paint can produce awkward show-time banter. Irreverence, a few props, and a quick wit—that is the formula. Political humor is guaranteed. A huge majority of Nebraska rodeo goers are Republicans and Obama slams prevailed during my rodeo tours, always with cheers. Some clowns went too far, forgetting that a silent minority of Democrats might be insulted. In seven years of Obama jokes, only one Nebraska venue brought boos alongside ovations—Springfield—set between Nebraska's largest cities, Lincoln and Omaha.

The last bull ride normally signals a rodeo's end, but the night's entertainment doesn't always stop there. Local taverns fill quickly. Old timers share stories of their glory days as townsfolk prolong the night drinking American-brewed beer with friends and neighbors. Rodeo competitors are not present; they are miles down the road, rolling home or toward the next venue.

Dances sometimes follow, and no rodeo dance is bigger than that of the tiny unincorporated town of Norden. Legendary in these remote regions of northern Nebraska, Norden's population will swell by 300 times come nightfall—same factor as Woodstock. The population is only three, but the math still works. Since 1931, folks within a broad rural radius have gathered every other summer night at the Norden Dance Hall, and rodeo night brings the most. High wheat-colored crossbeams frame a sprawling dance floor smoothed by decades of sliding boot soles.

August evening air slowly cools the hall through open windows, but it's hot. Sweaty dancers don't care; they smile and swing to the live band. I gauge the span of relationships by measuring smiles shared. Some young couples throw down impressive swinging moves and are given wide berths as if creating their own kinetic force field. Choreography is the general rule; you can't merely bust a random move at country dances, so that mercifully leaves me out. It's loud. I limit my nearness to the twangy band like one would to a cracked nuclear reactor, for fear of permanent damage.

Almost imperceptibly, all couples move counterclockwise around the floor, spinning like planetary systems within a greater revolving galaxy. And as the center of a galaxy does, this place pulls. Regionally it's the event of the year yet it remains generally unknown to most Nebraskans.

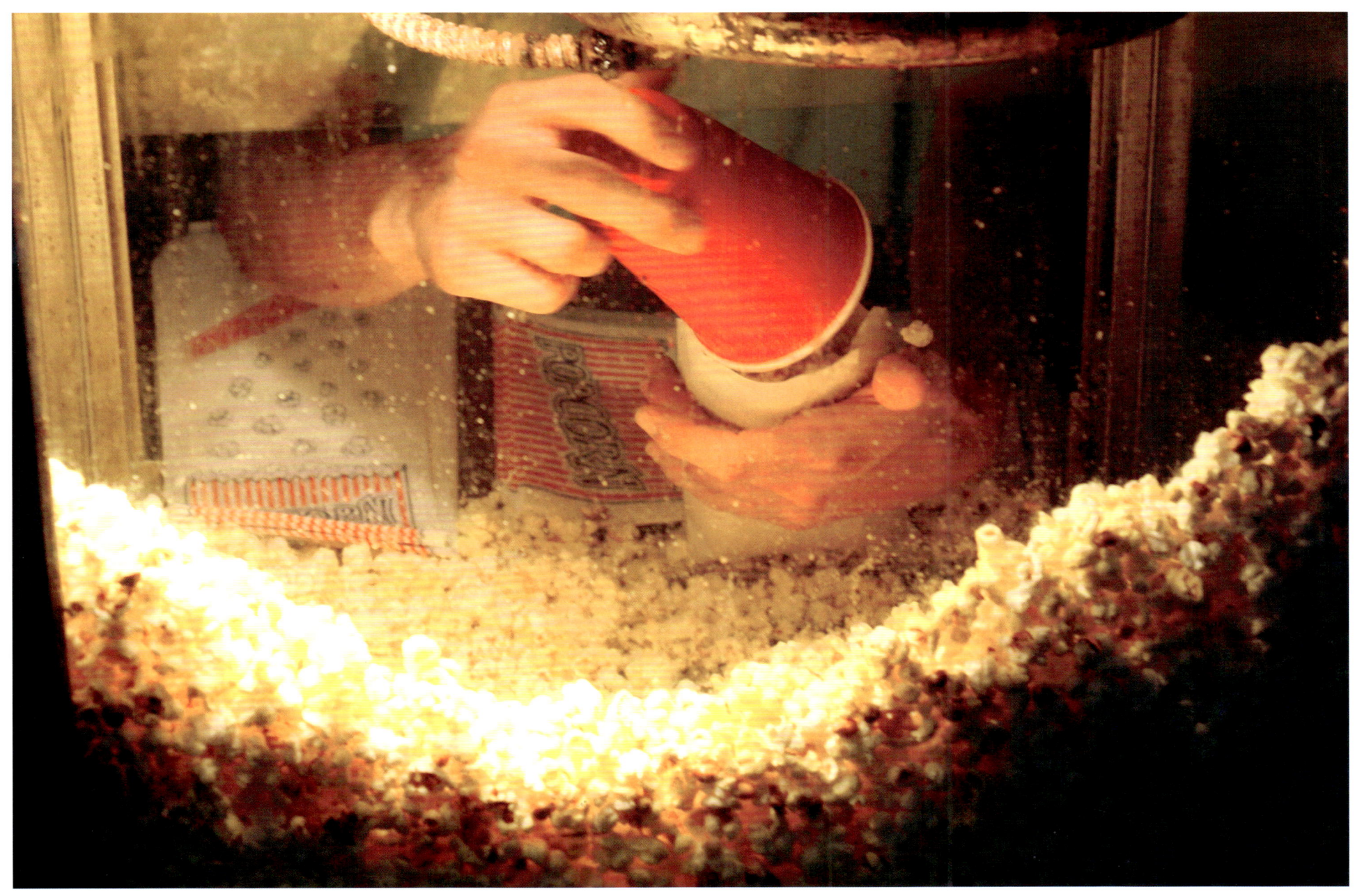

The smell of popcorn fills the rodeo bleachers. Behind the
chutes the smell is altogether different. ARLINGTON

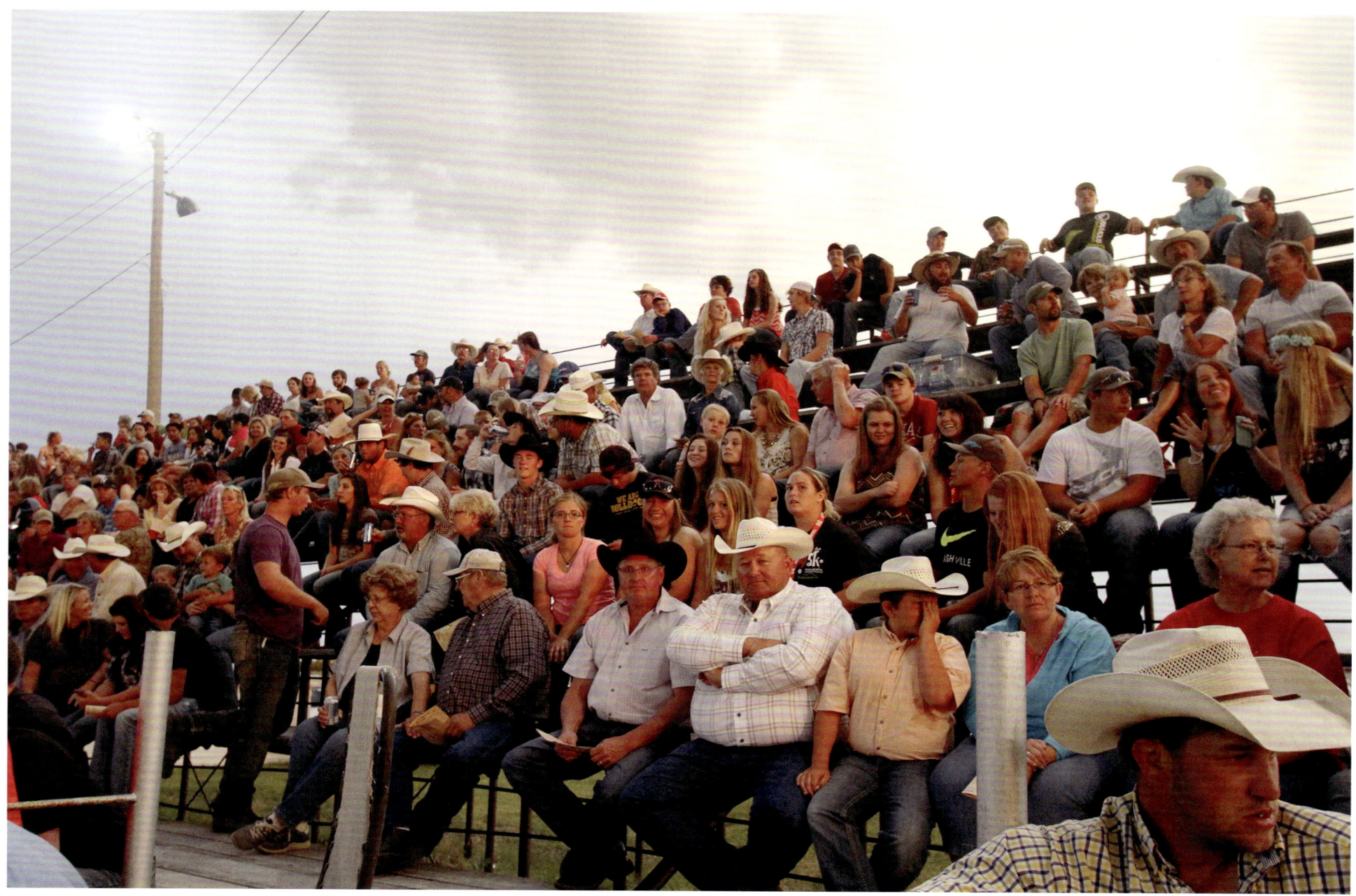

BRIDGEPORT

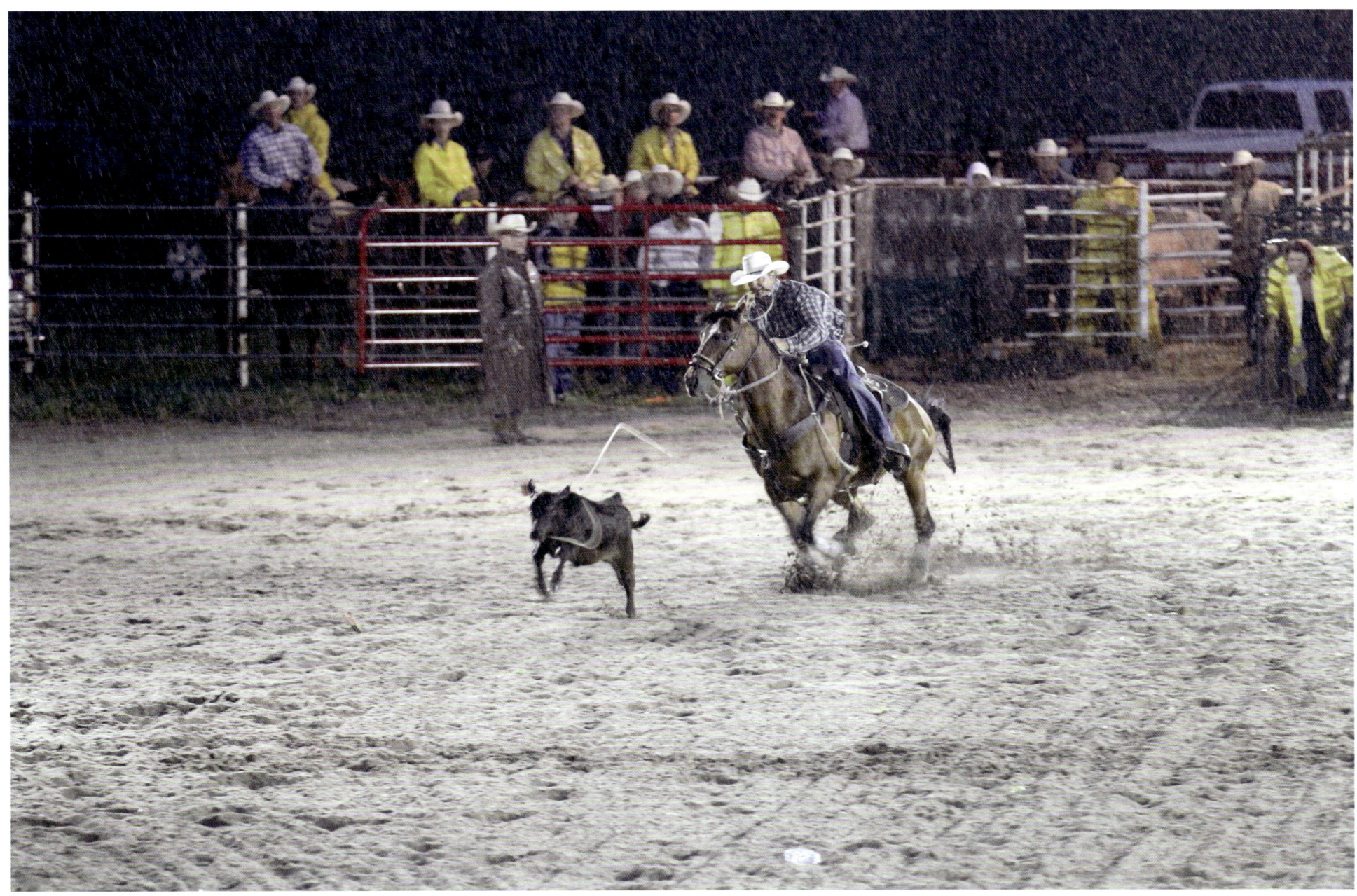

The audience may head home, but rain does not stop rodeo competition.
When you work the land, getting wet is just part of life. CALLAWAY

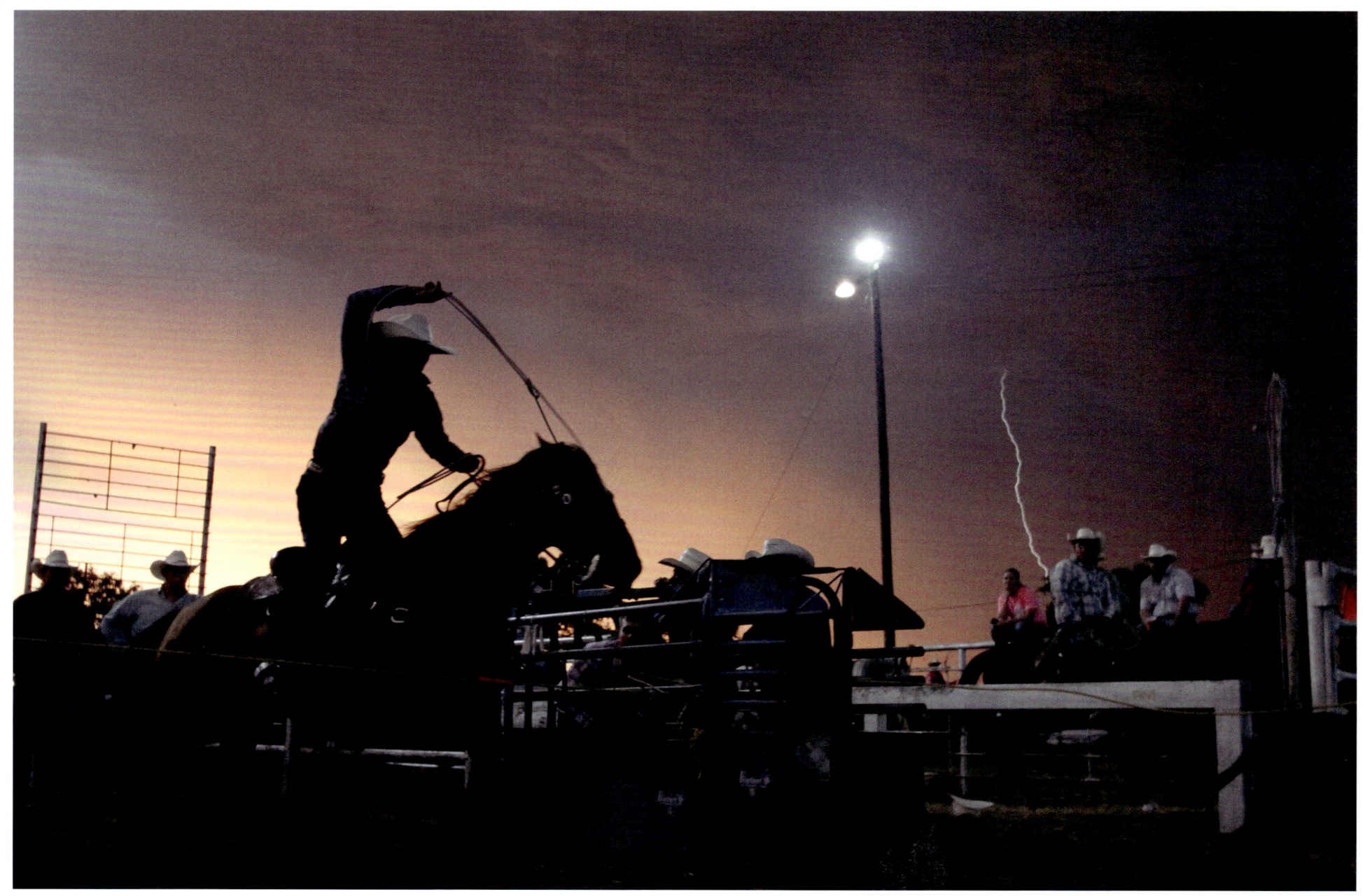

There is a curious disregard for lightning in rodeo culture. Few competitors bat an eye; crowds in high metal bleachers exchange nervous laughs, but they stay. BRIDGEPORT

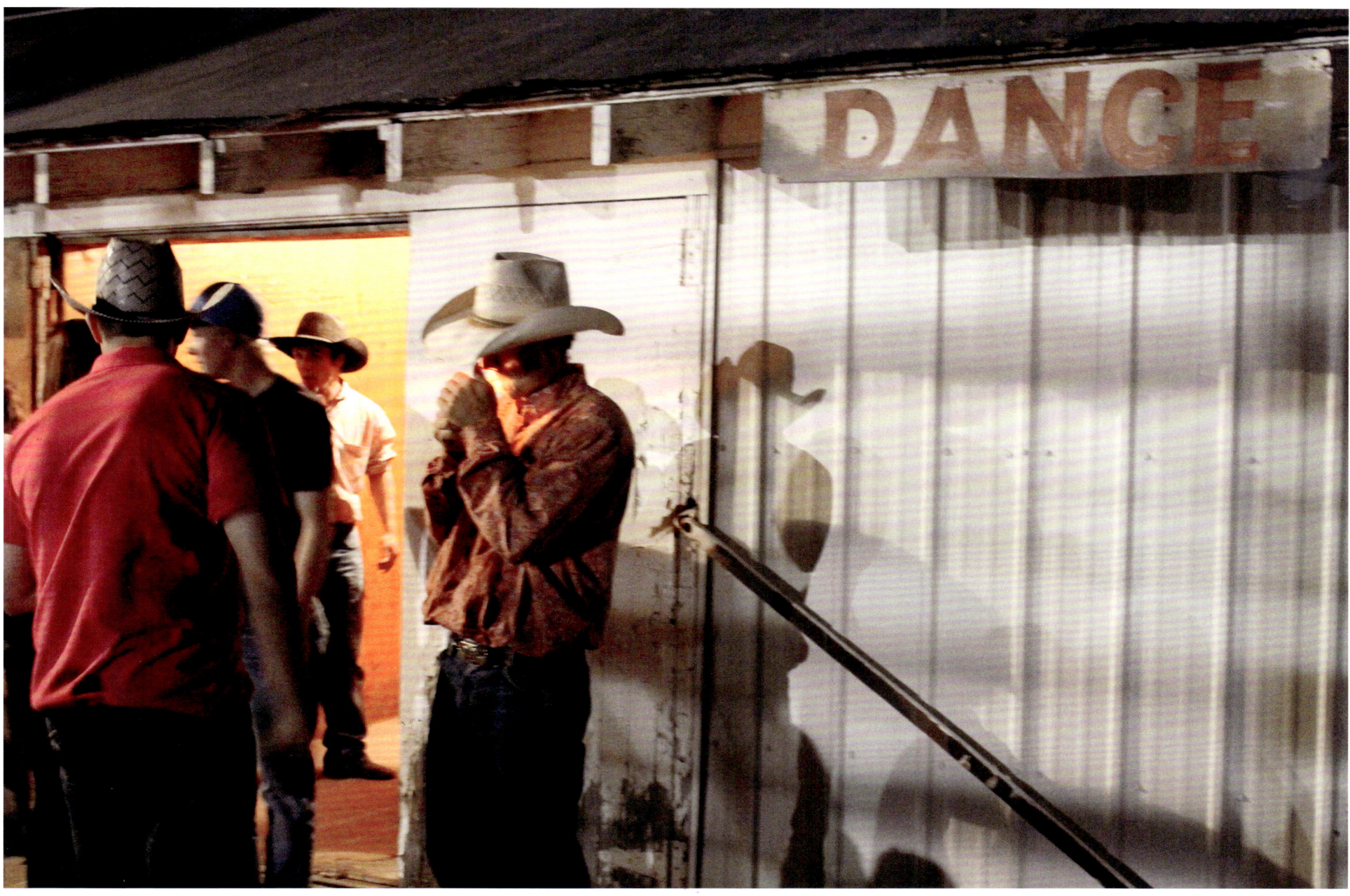

BRIDGEPORT

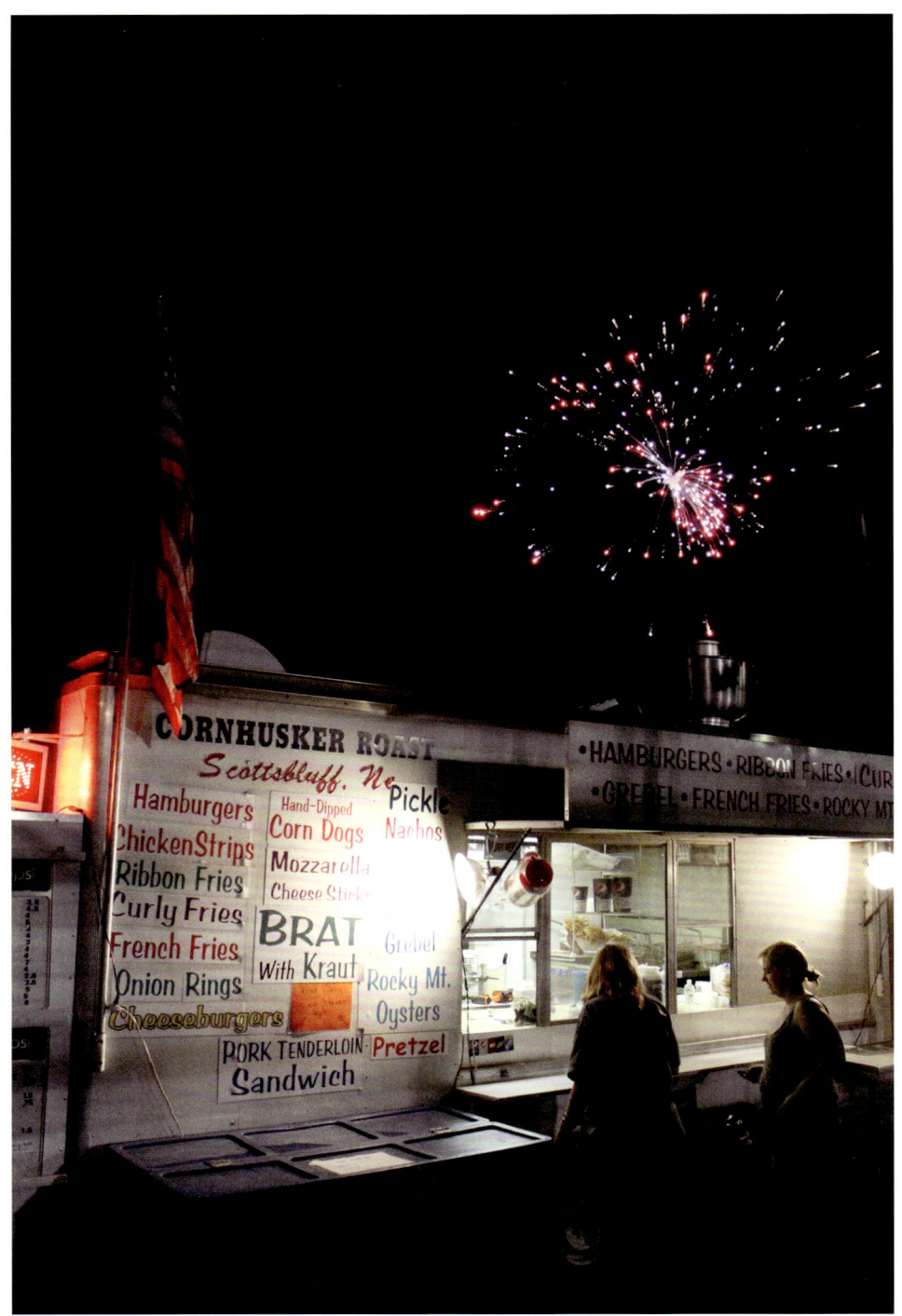

July 4th week is "Cowboy Christmas" when many events are scheduled in the western half of Nebraska. Some riders will hurry to make two rodeos in one day. BRIDGEPORT

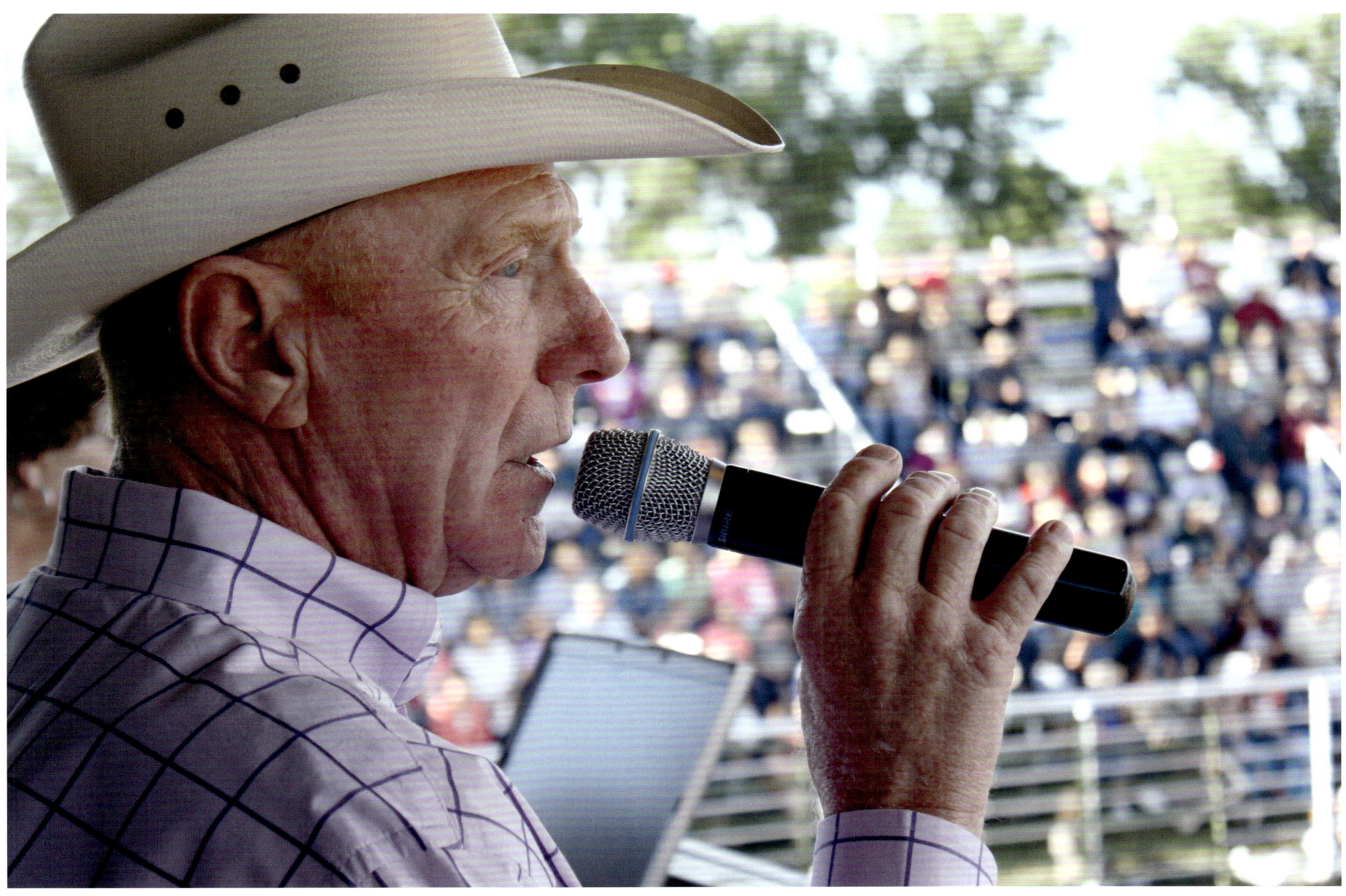

Traveling the region for thirty years, rodeo announcer Gregg McGreer of Big Springs is one of the country's best. CLEARWATER

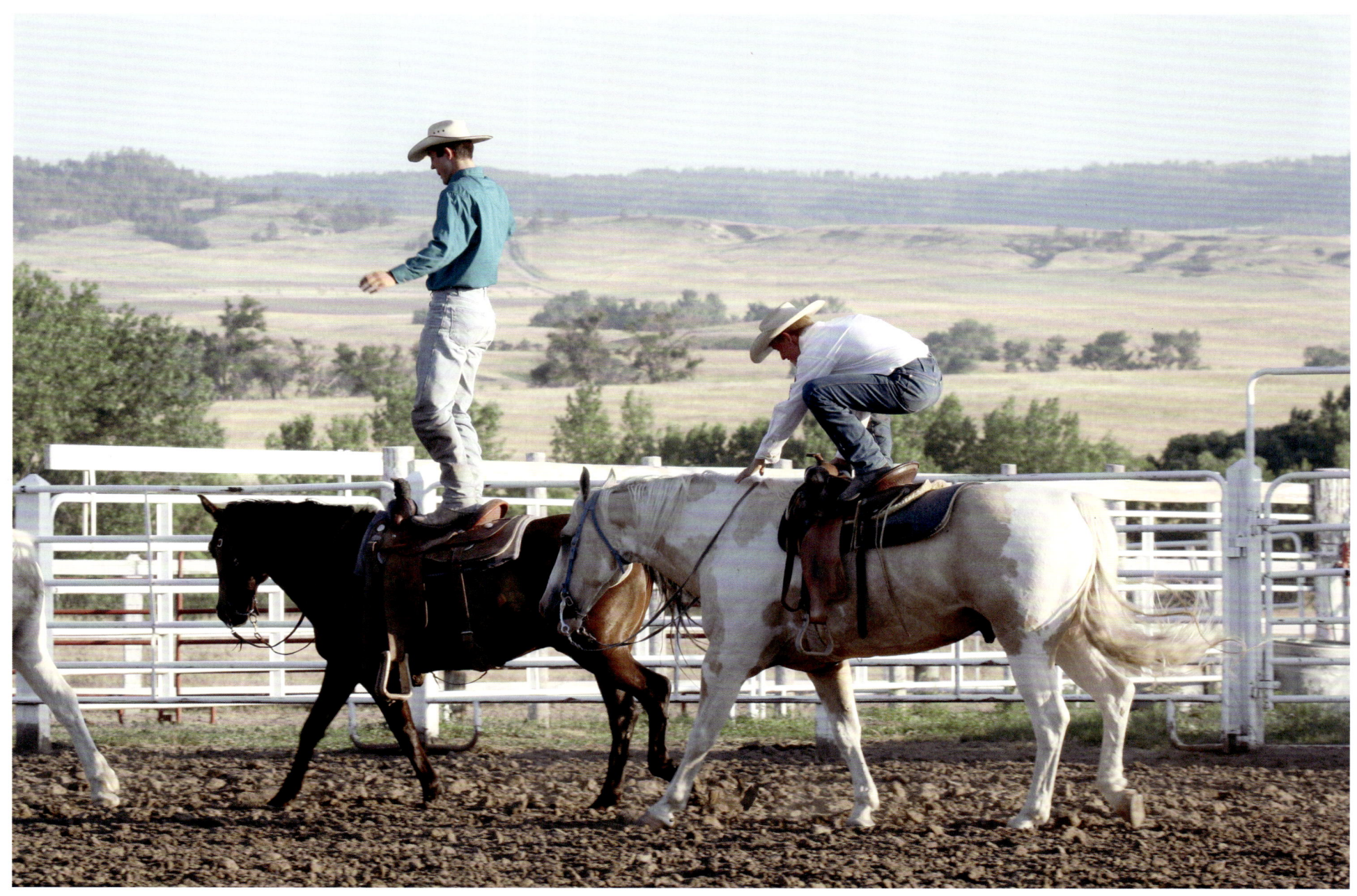

Young men show off skills on tolerant horses during warmup. FORT ROBINSON

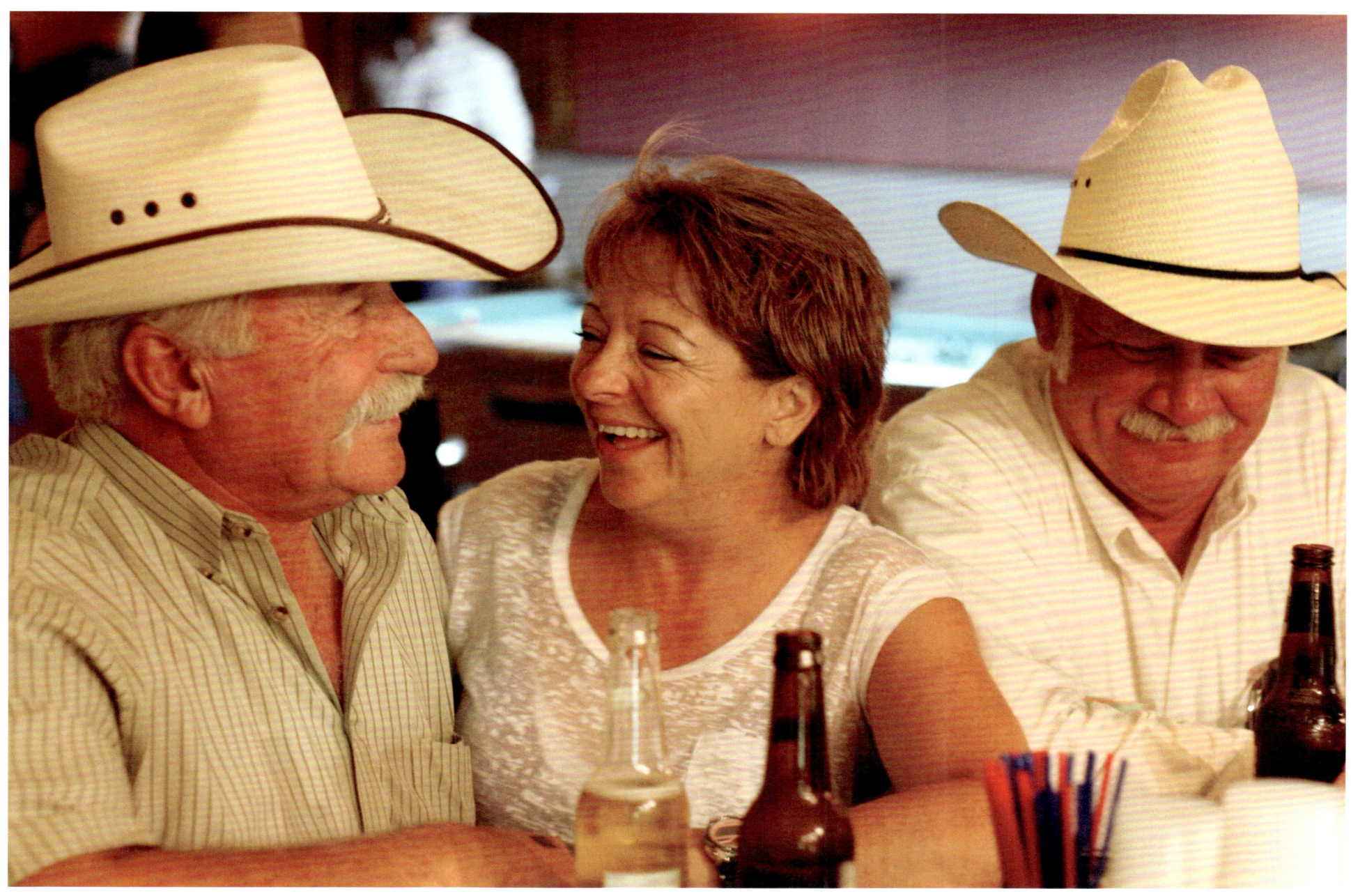

Drinking American beer and sharing rodeo-day stories at the local bar after the event. GORDON

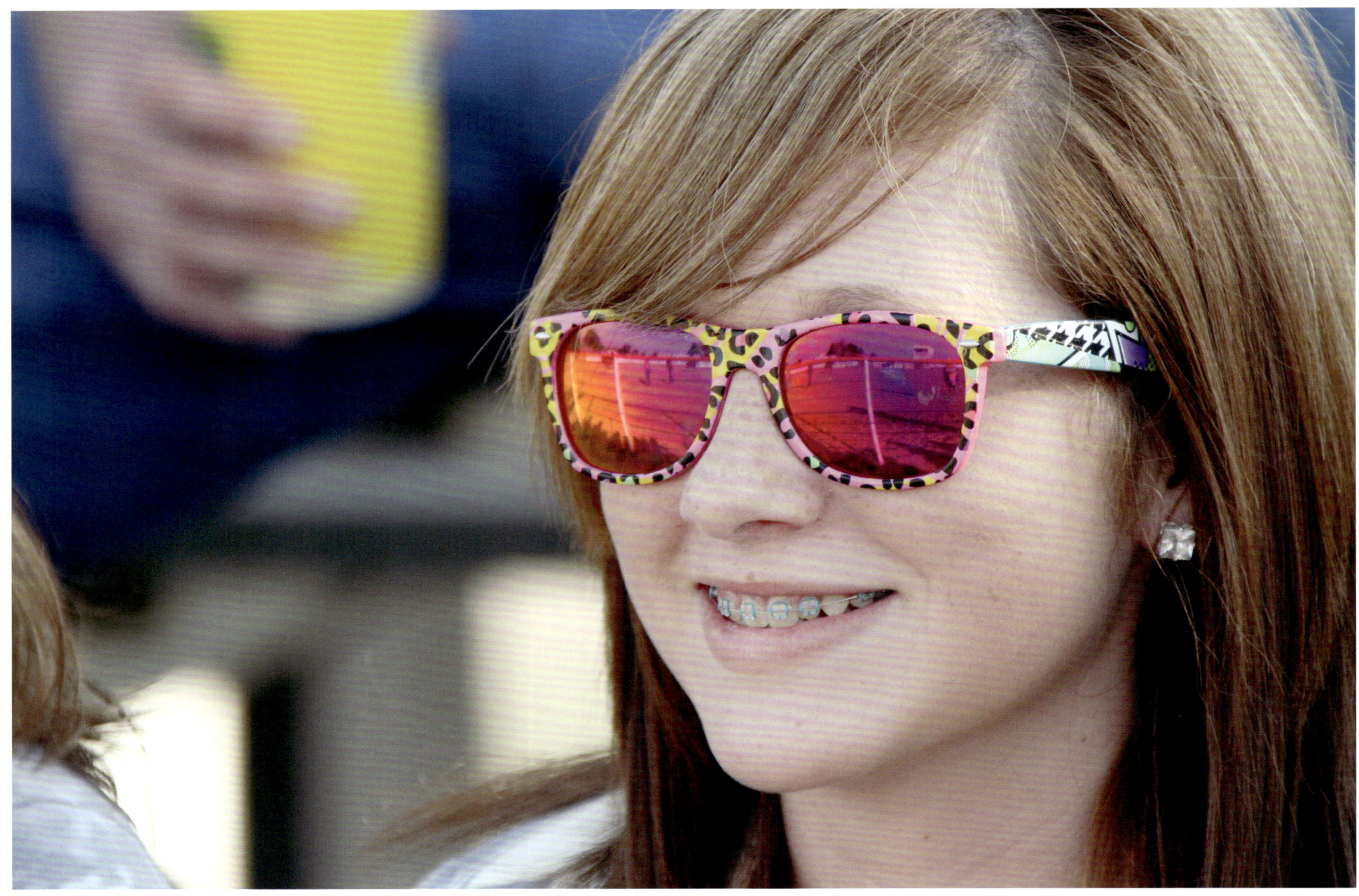

Rodeos are only about social time for some. It's a small town's event of the year. GOTHENBURG

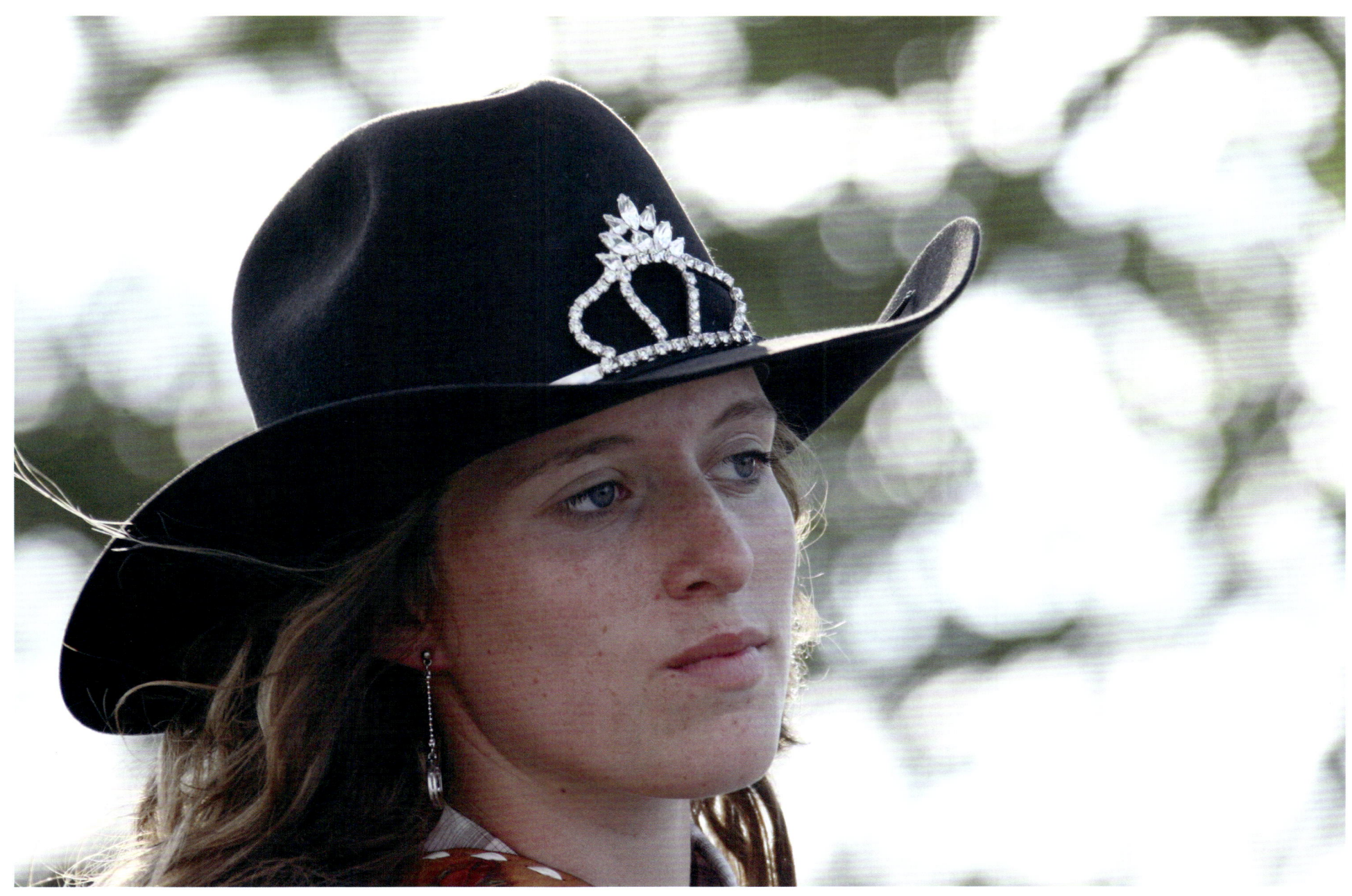

A rodeo queen takes a quiet moment before displaying
the American flag at a gallop. STAPLETON

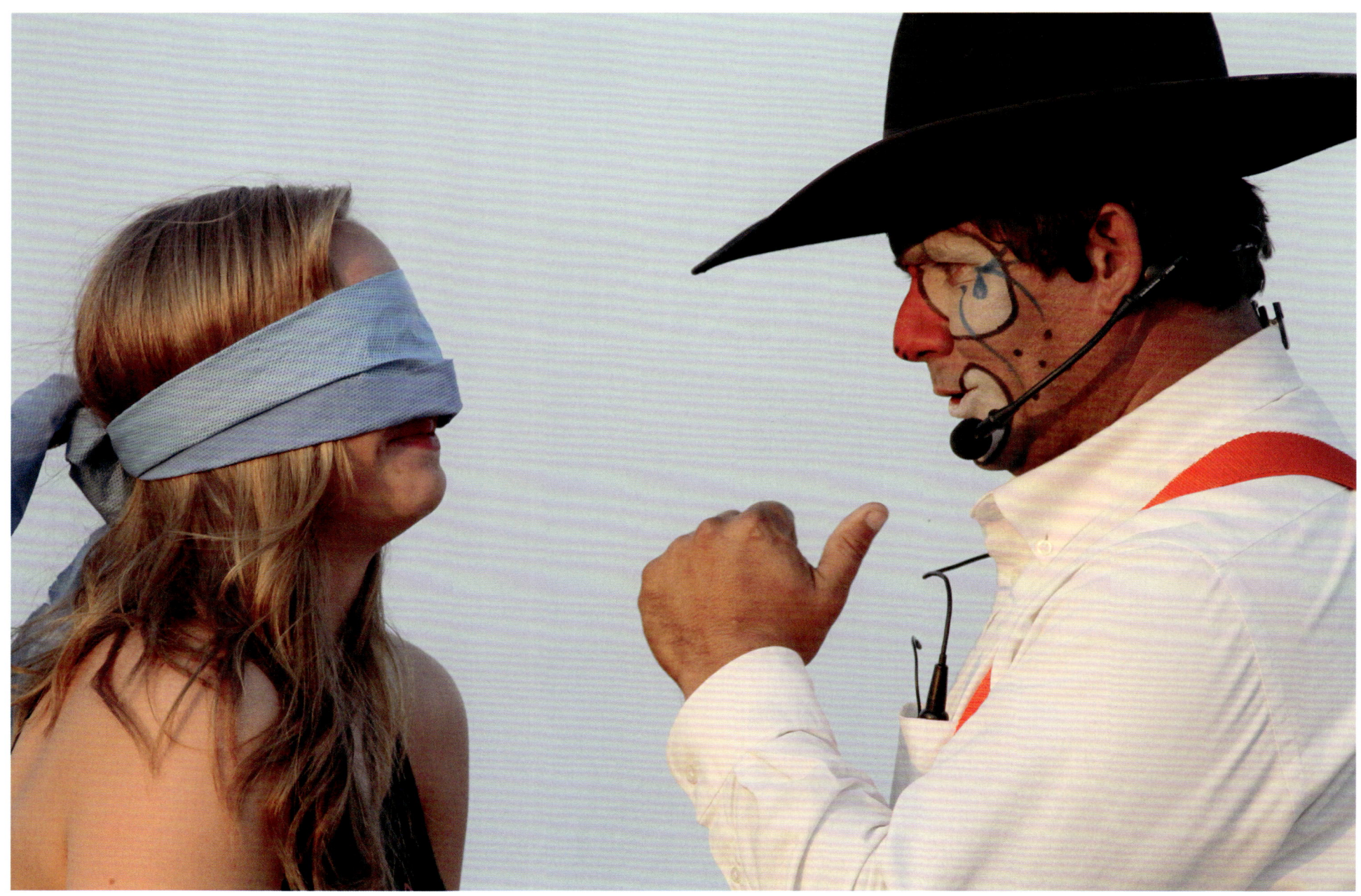

Standing mid-arena, a clown pokes fun at an embarrassed volunteer. Thinking she is in a dance-off with two friends, when the blindfold comes off she sees she was solo all along. SUTHERLAND

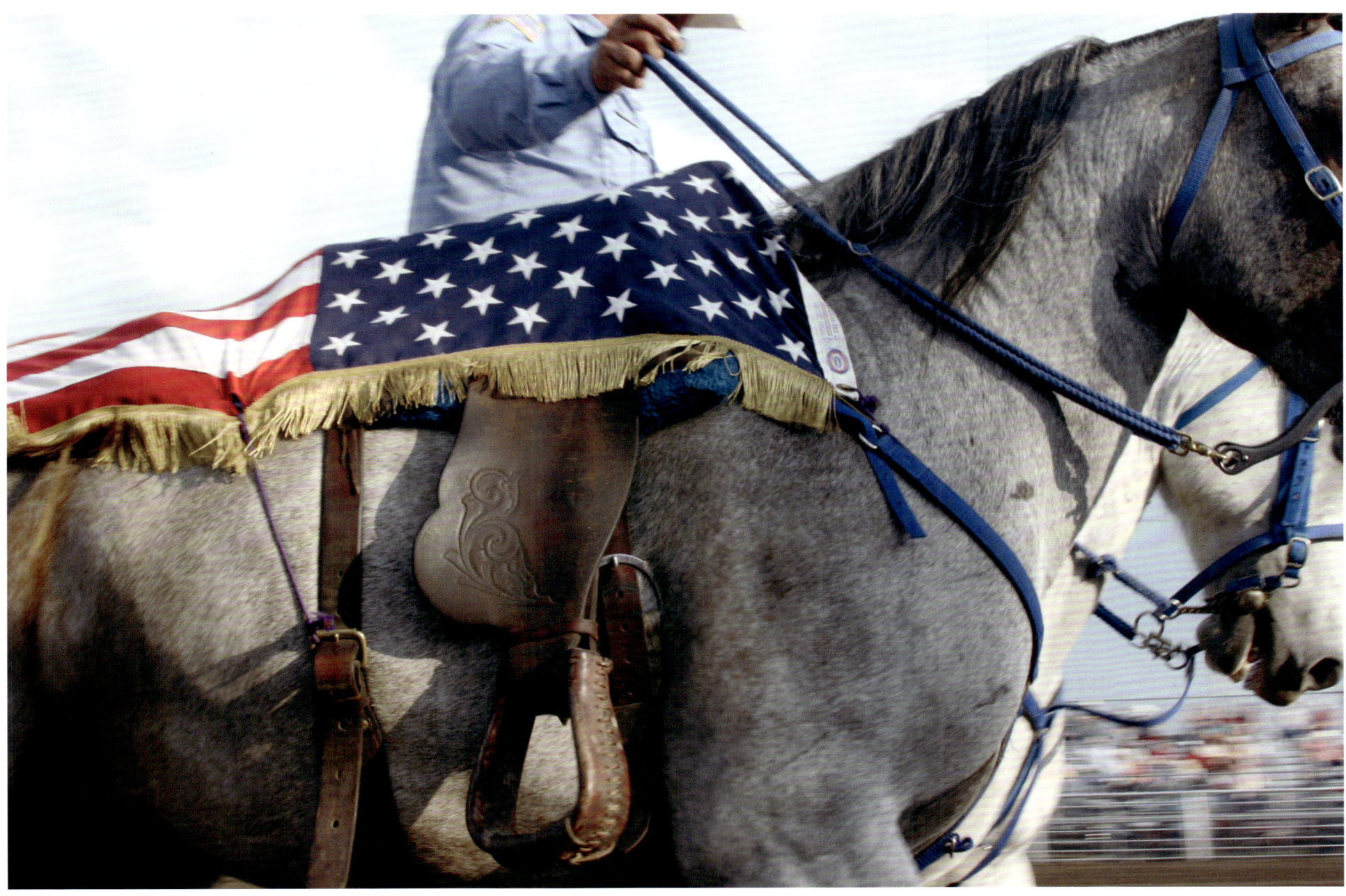

A flag-draped horse rounds the area honoring a deceased rodeo organizer as the announcer speaks his praises. SUTHERLAND

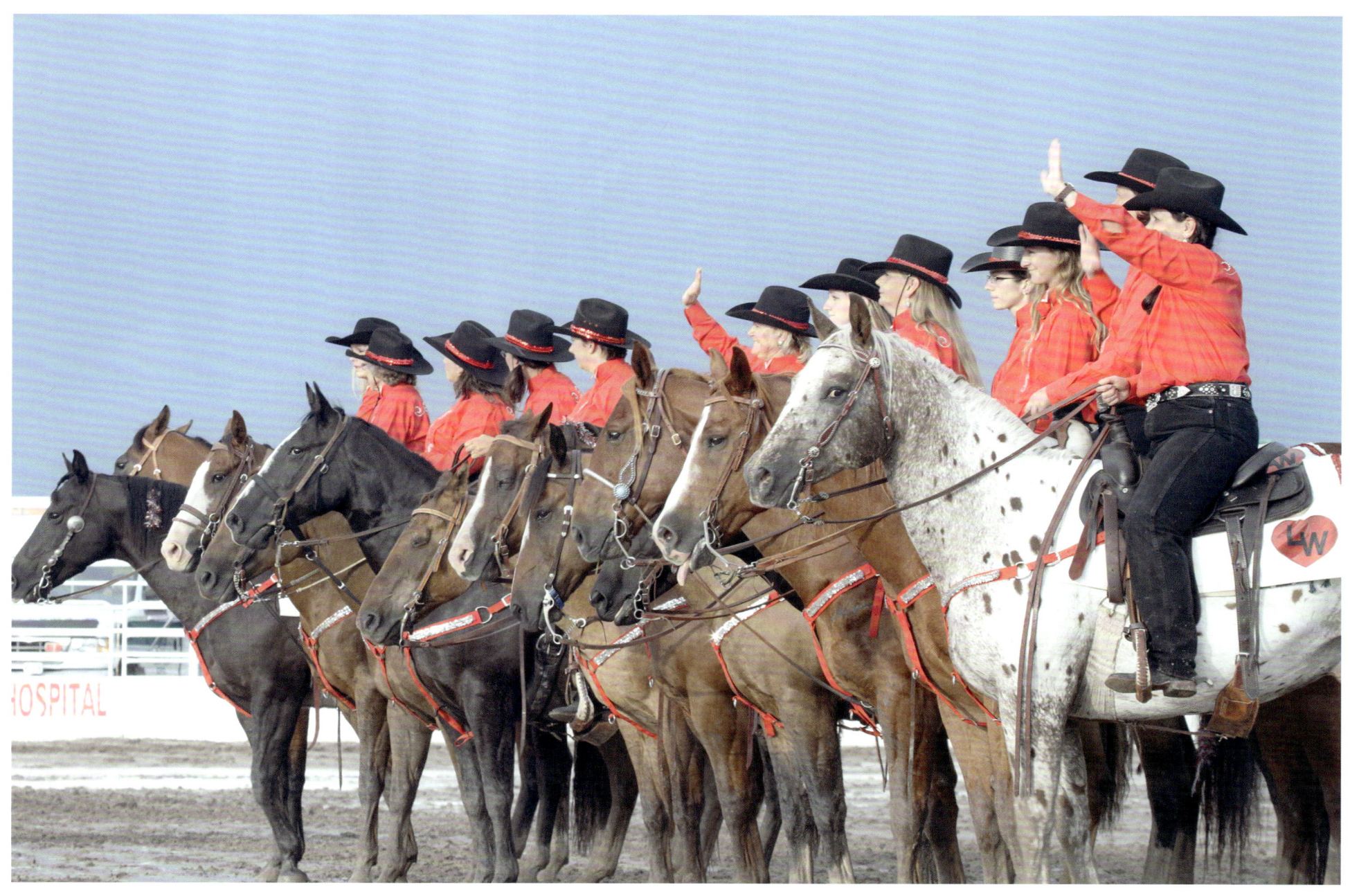

The local Ladies Saddle Club thanks the crowd after their
crisscrossing performance. VALENTINE

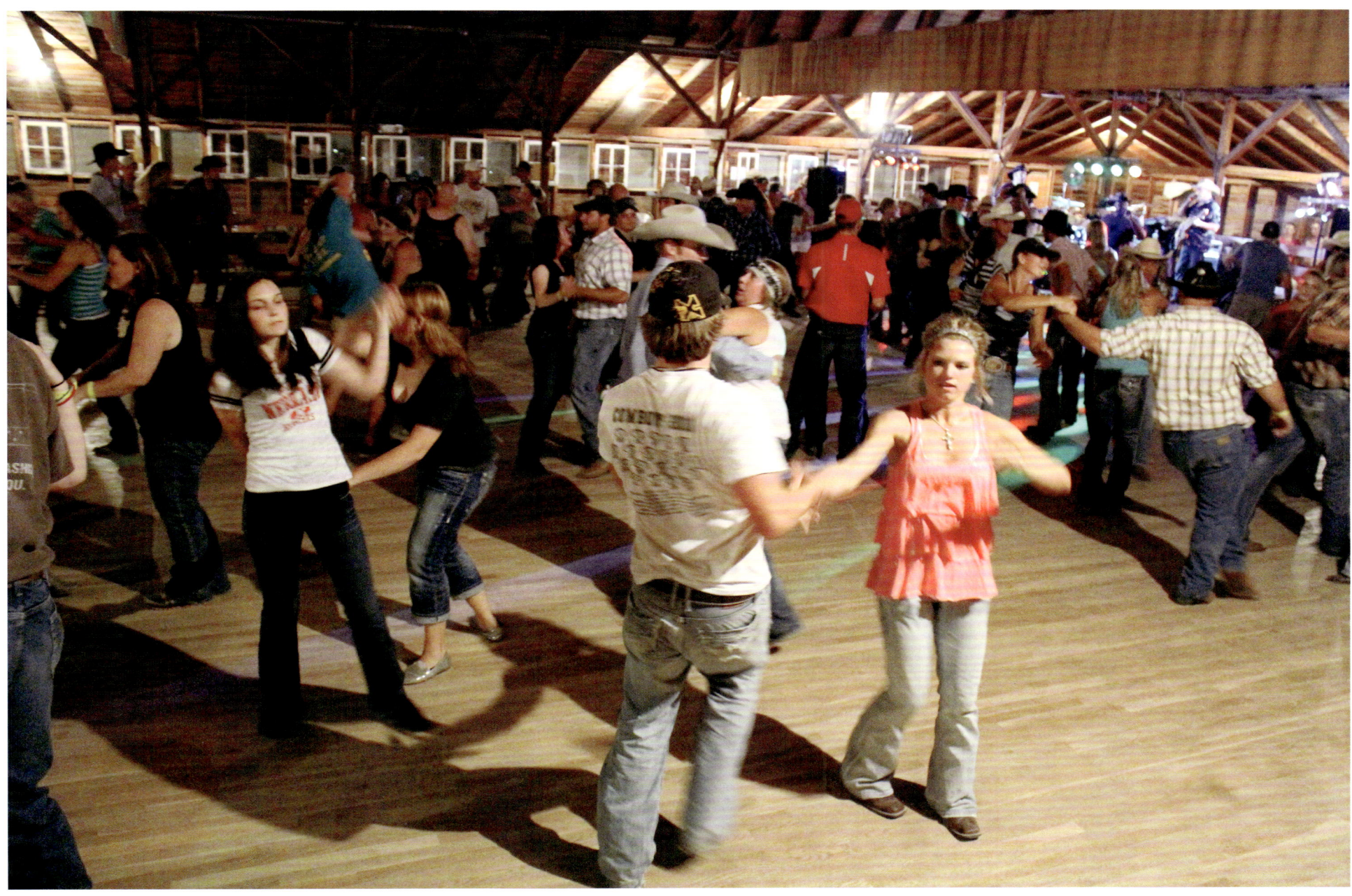

You won't find competitors dancing after the rodeo; they are rolling
down dark highways toward home or to the next event. NORDEN

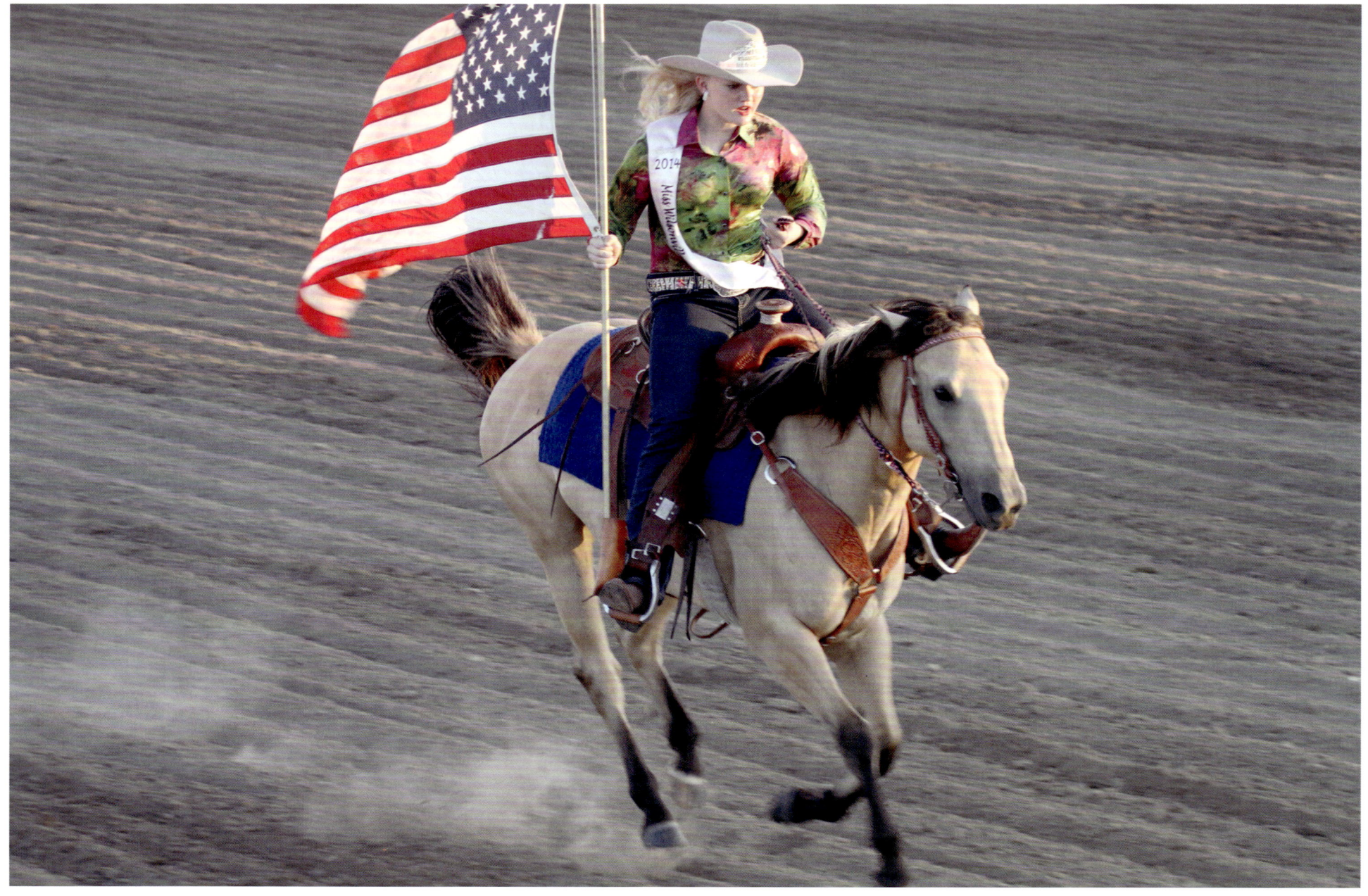

BENKELMAN

Rodeo's Future

A bit of sorrow followed my last rodeo shoot. I will miss the thrill of dodging broncs, the banter between rough stock riders, the lonely rural highways, and even the mom-and-pop motels. My journey into Nebraska's rodeo subculture was inspirational and rejuvenating. I feel lucky to have chanced down this path.

Rodeo has become a solid niche in American sports. Facing factors such as an unstoppable rural-to-urban population shift, modern entertainment's ever-expanding choices, and the toughening scrutiny of animal rights groups, it will undergo many long-term changes. Rodeo started as a simple showcase for a cowboy's skills, but it has become something more dazzling and it will continue pushing that way. Though there are fewer working ranches, lessening the actual need for authentic horse and livestock skills, the rodeo culture endures. Enthusiastic competitors and their followers drive the sport and will perpetuate its skills into the distant future. It is impossible to project what it will be like in a hundred years, but I believe its future is entrenched. As men become more proficient, rough stock will become nastier, speed horses will move faster, and records will break. Training harder and smarter, in fifty years, competitors' skills will transcend what we can now imagine.

Skyrocketing winnings in the Pro Rodeo Association, regional roping jackpots, and the rapidly growing bull riding scene will lead the way. It has become big business, with worldwide popularity spawned by regional rodeo competitors like those who ride in Nebraska. Safety for riders and animals will improve as techniques and technology advance. Vital to rodeo's growth, entertainment will modernize into a slicker, more colorful spectacle. As announcer Gregg McGreer put it, "A lot of facets will shine up in the future." Gregg also believes rodeo culture will remain strong. "I look down behind the bucking chutes and see all the guys down on one knee and I know we're all together—that what we stand for in America is still there. Rodeo is a bond that won't break."

Winters distant from now, cowboys and cowgirls will crave warmer months and yearn to travel lonely rural roads. When summer comes, crowds will gather for their town's biggest event. Kids will scramble around grandstands and hotdogs will sell. Bulls and broncs will bellow and buck, ropes will whirl and hooves will pound. Eyes will go wide witnessing close calls in the arena, gasps will ascend as grimacing cowboys fall, and clowns will bring laughter with absurdity. As it has for generations, the dirt will fly. This is Nebraska rodeo and within it, we see our heritage.

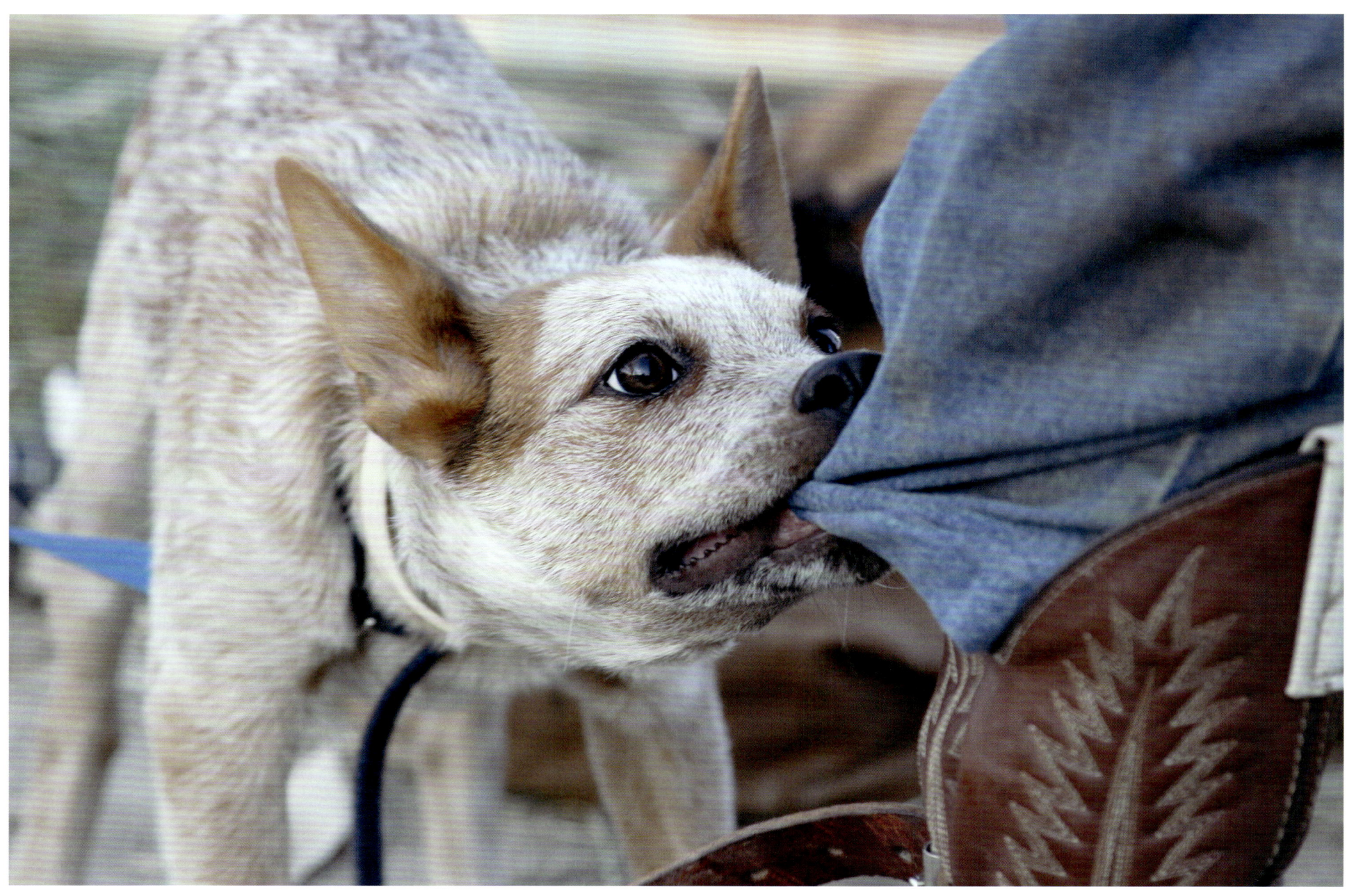

A forty-five-year-old bull rider plays with his pup before
riding at the Senior Pro Rodeo. CRAWFORD

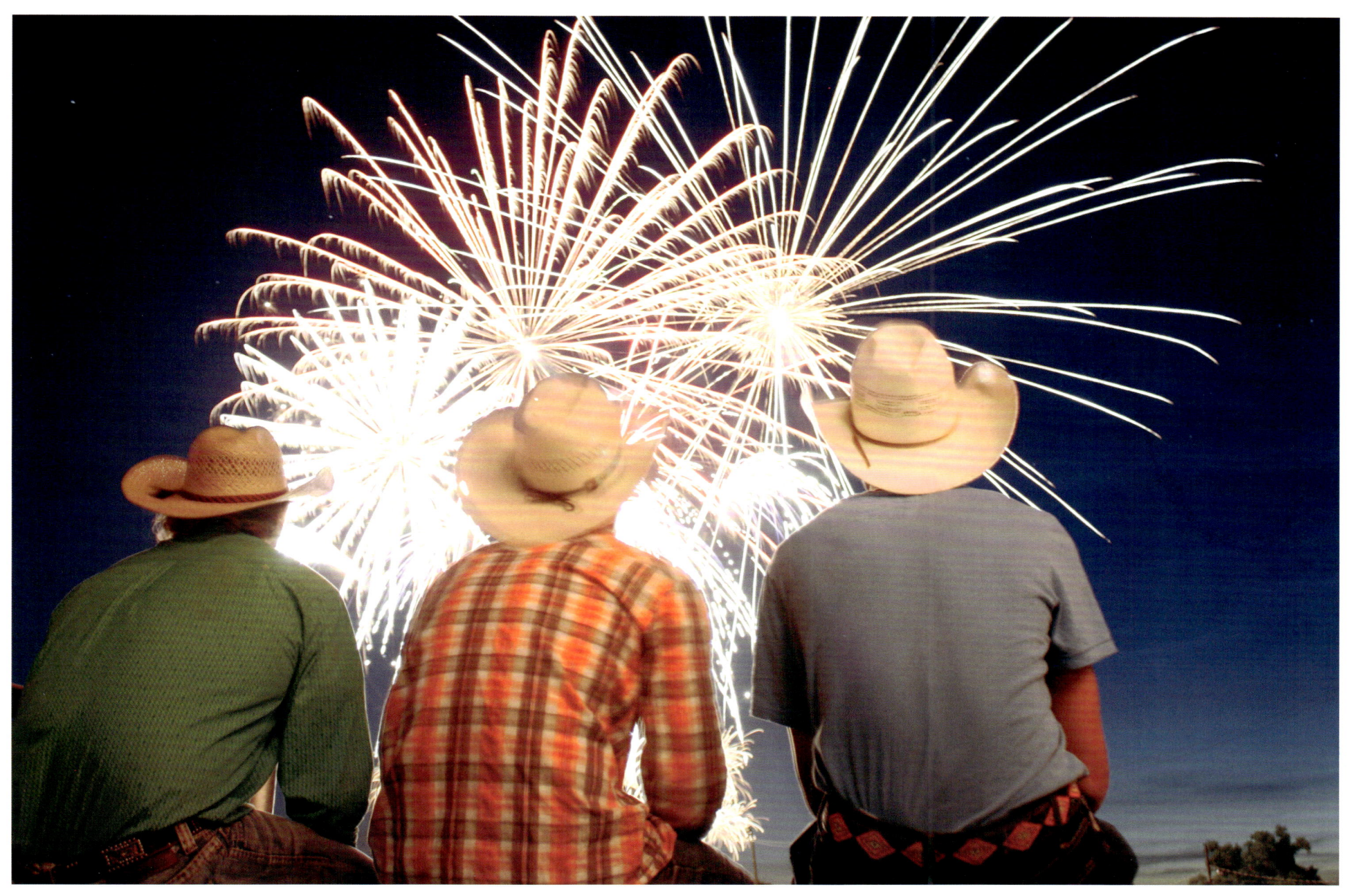

Bronc riders on bucking chutes watch the July 4th show. BRIDGEPORT

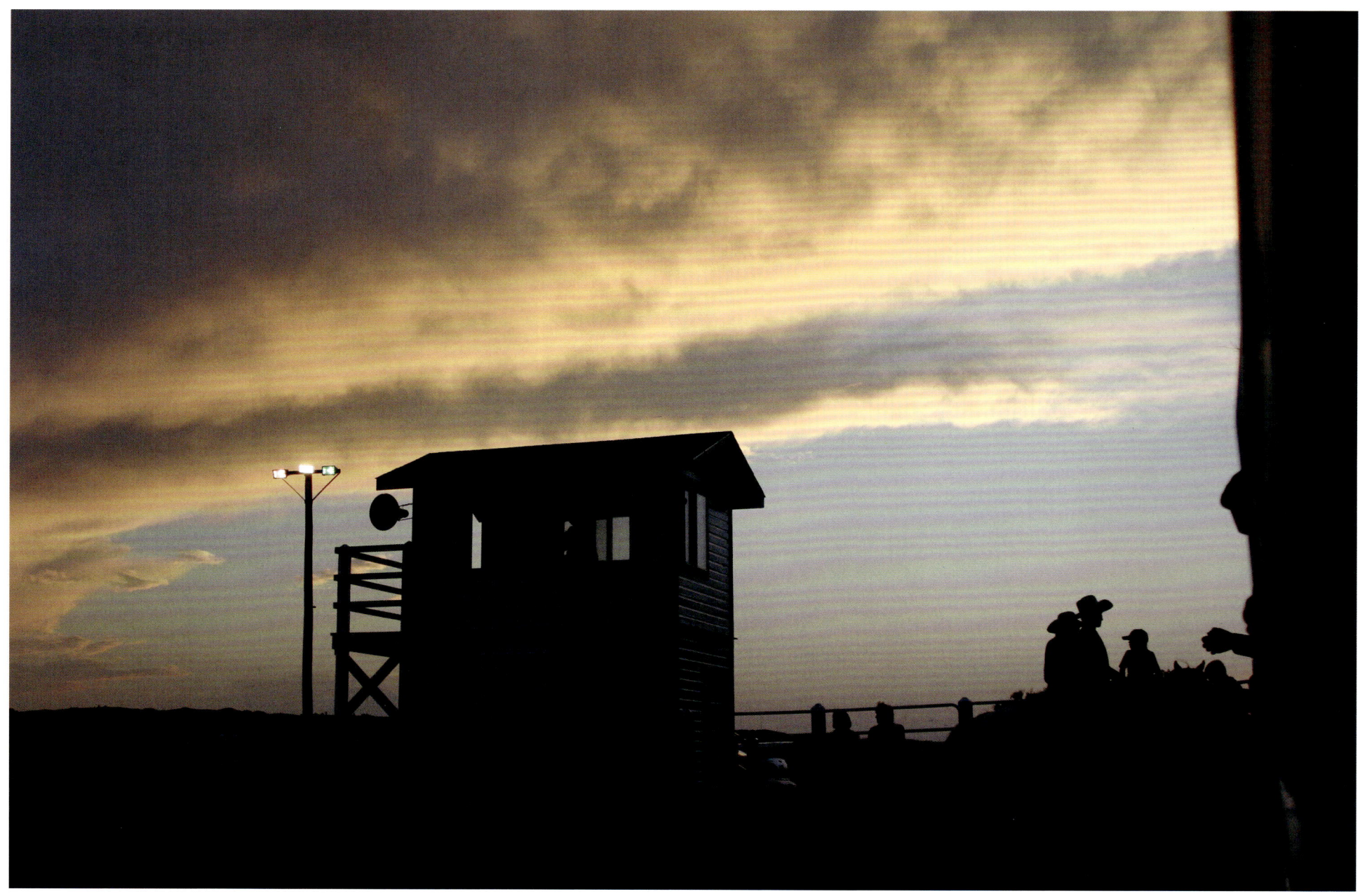

FORT ROBINSON

ACKNOWLEDGEMENTS

I would like to thank the following people for their assistance with this project:

PEG GERKE, my English-major mom, for her patient help,

JOEL SARTORE, *National Geographic* photographer, for pushing me,

KENNY and ANGIE KRAMER of Gypsy Joe Rodeo Co.,

JACK COLEMAN of Territorial Professional Bull Riding,

TODD CRASE and SHAD SMITH of the Double S Bull Company, LLC—Extreme Bull Riding Tour,

MARK and KELLY WARD of L4 Livestock, LLC,

The many local Nebraska rodeo organizers for their kind cooperation,

DAVID BRISTOW, editor, Nebraska State Historical Society,

And state and rural law enforcement agencies, for warnings instead of tickets!